The Effective High School Principal

by

Gene E. Megiveron, Ed.D.

An ETC Publication

Library of Congress Cataloging-in-Publication Data

Megiveron, Gene E., 1931—
 The effective high school principal/ by Gene E.
Megiveron. p. cm. — (Effective school
administration series; no. 4) Includes bibliographical
references and index.
 ISBN 0-88280-096-5
 1. High schools—United States—Administration.
 2. High school principals—United States. 3. School
supervision—United States. 4. School personnel
management—United States. I. Title. II. Series
 LB2822.2.M44 1992   CIP
 373.12'012'0973—dc20   91-14490

Effective School Administration Series—Number Four

Published by ETC Publications
           700 East Vereda Sur
           Palm Springs, CA 92262

Printed in the United States of America.

ABOUT THE BOOK

In the more than one-hundred graduate classes I have taught over more than a quarter of a century in five states, the constant ending theme has been, "...now that we are comfortable with what we have to do and how to do it, how do we learn *when to do it?*" The book responds to this dilemma.

I kept my desk-top appointment books and task calendars for the ten years that I was a high school principal. The comments that I made on them formed the basis for developing the lists in Part II around which the book is prepared. Throughout the book, information is provided in a fashion to assist the principal as the year pro-gresses.

The book is written so that the harried principal of a high school today (and tomorrow) can go beyond being effective and become efficient. Many practical, day-to-day skills and tools are explained. The book will provide information to use as a definitive guide throughout the school year. Whether a principal is new or experienced, s/he can use this reference and know when to start, develop, and culminate mandatory tasks.

The book is divided into two major parts. Part I contains sound advice to give to any current principal to launch significant activities. It will be helpful to any serious student of educational administration to grasp the breadth of the tasks performed by successful principals in structuring the office of the high school. Part II, the heart of the book, lists over 1,800 yearly tasks to be completed during the months of July through June. Part I is culminated by the listing of selected references from which the reader may obtain further information on the topics or tasks listed. The book is for the practitioner with little time to read volumes in order to find a tool for immediate use.

Part I embodies the first of two purposes of the book. *The first purpose is to provide assistance to the busy principal so that s/he can learn the requisite skills before the school year actually starts.* Chapter One, "Getting Prepared," contains three major units. These units are: General Planning, Self Management in the Office, and Structuring One's Own Niche. Within these three units are twenty-nine subunits. Chapter Two, "Structuring the Office Routine," consists of four major units. The four units are: Establishing A Managerial Aura, Paperwork and People Aids, Preparation of Significant Statements, and Substructures for Sound Support. These have been subdivided into thirty-one subunits.

Part II launches the second purpose of the book. *It is to assist the principal in not only what to do but WHEN to do it as well.* Chapter 3, "Work in the Summer Months," consists of a list of tasks for July and August plus orientation. Chapter 4, "Work in the Fall Months," details tasks that must be done in September, October, and November. Chapter 5, "Work in the Winter Months," continues the task lists for December, January, February, and March. Chapter 6, "Work in the Spring Months," has task lists for April, May, and June. Just as Chapter 3 was concluded by a subunit on orientation, Chapter 6 is brought to a closure with a special subunit called End of Year Preparation. The four chapters consist of fourteen units. There are summary grids prepared to package the tasks from the lists by month.

Each unit from Chapters Three to Six discusses the workload of the principal. Each set of task lists is shown in the prioritized order of instruction, students, staff, school/community relations, and business/building management. Over 1,800 tasks have been identified for completion throughout the year.

I have had the privilege of being selected to participate in three national study groups. With this national exposure and twenty-eight years working in educational administration, I have utilized my experience, training, and research (as well as that of my colleagues) to benefit those who are pursuing careers in principalships at the secondary level. The material is field-tested through my own experi-

prises which form the high school program. However, s/he must do much more than direct the operation through others. The work of the principal must be in *administration to assist the staff in the accomplishment of the district's goals*, through *leadership to assist the staff in the completion of its own goals* and to *supervise by assisting others to improve their skills*. These four roles are constantly being merged and employed in the overall operation of the high school. To perform this balancing act is an art.

It is the thesis of this book that to be both effective and efficient the high school principal must:

1. Become a skilled manager of the office, personnel, instruction, and programs.

2. Learn tools used in the fields of business, industry, military, and commerce.

3. Teach others to become more effective and efficient by practicing proper leadership irrespective of the role the staff member is in at the time.

4. Practice the best possible skills in the adminstration of the school.

THE EFFECTIVE HIGH SCHOOL PRINCIPAL is a book which can be used in the university classroom for both education and management classes. It is a reference which belongs on every principal's desk as a guide to the complex operation s/he heads. Superintendents and other Chief Executive Officers can use the information contained in this volume by reorienting minimally the material.

The book's two parts are each developed independently but are intertwined in their application. The material is ready to be used just as it is presented. There is no need for translation from industry or business applications. That has already been done.

Abbeville, Louisiana   Gene E. Megiveron

ACKNOWLEDGMENTS

The work could not have been done without the assistance of the hundreds of graduate students who challenged, researched on their own, and adapted the material to use and critique. It has been this discourse that provided the stimulation for developing this material.

The significant others who have influenced this material are my three great, young adult children: Michael William, Kevin Gene, and my daughter, Lorene Kaye. Each attended the public schools (K - 16) of Michigan and brought home many samples of administrivia and challenged their validity. Answering their questions was tough. Some soul-searching had to be done. I found principals who did not utilize their time effectively because they did not have the requisite organizational skills nor did they possess a manual that covered the organizational skills necessary for their job. Therefore, the advice in this book stems from my children's questions in many cases.

Six excellent school administrators and friends of mine in education kept the concept of this book alive. My first superintendent, Mr. Howard E. Parr, inspired me to begin writing in this field. Mr. Thomas E. Prenkert has applied the material in the area of business management and community relations. Mr. Thomas O. Mc Cormick assisted in the refinement of skills necessary for a high school principal. Dr. Jerry J. Herman inspired me to write this instead of another series of articles. Dr. John A. Beleutz, my successor as superintendent, whetted my interest in the application of this material to the instructional program. Mr. Terry G. Semones is mentioned often in the text. Terry remains a supporter of the material and its use. Each of these men supported me by their constant application of the ideas and concepts to make them operational. To each, I am forever dedicated.

I would be remiss not to mention Mrs. Patricia Dartez, the lady who did the final edit of the material. She is an English teacher and a graduate student in administration. Mrs. Dartez has given me a great deal of support for the culmination of the work. Her constant pressure to pull the material into a cohesive package was needed and appreciated. The countless hours of assistance can never be fully compensated.

My darling wife, Barbara, stood by me through my entire twenty-eight year career as a public school administrator. She was an inspiration by constantly asking, "Why don't you publish a book with those great ideas?" Her gentle, but firm pressure for me to search for the truth in what I was doing was a great help. The influence of this lovely lady will forever be respected and appreciated. I miss very much her cogent and sage advice as this book is completed.

- PERMISSIONS BY PUBLISHERS -

(85) T. Frank Hardesty and W. Wayne Scott for the work in *Action Tools for Increasing Individual Productivity*, author's copyright, Volume 1, pp. 107-113, all rights reserved.

(131) *The Time Trap: Managing Your Way Out.* by R. Alec Mackenzie, page 27 copyright 1972 AMACOM, a division of American Management Association, New York. All rights reserved.

(132) Harvard Educational Review - for the work by Dr. R. Alec Mackenzie

(134) James G. March, the author, permission granted for use in this book, all rights reserved.

(137) McGraw-Hill Book Company - for the work by Maynard, H. B., editor-in-chief. *Handbook of Business Administration*. NY: McGraw-Hill, copyright 1970. Reprinted by permission of McGraw-Hill Book Company, New York, New York. All rights reserved.

(170) Midwest Administration Center - for the work by Dr. Getzels in "Administration as a Social Process," Chapter 7

PART I

PREPARING THE OFFICE
AND
ONESELF

So much to do and so little time to do it

PART I INTRODUCTION
- PREPARING THE OFFICE AND ONESELF -

Chapter 1. Getting Prepared
Chapter 2. Structuring The Office Routine

Part I is about the economic use of time through the implementation of quality organizational and management skills. The result is effective and efficient management as the principal prepares for a year of excellence.

The paradox facing principals in the high schools is one of the proper use of time and timing. On the one hand, if the principal moves cautiously and makes every attempt to determine the single best route to take in his/her decision-making, the program will become so immersed in detail that staff and students will not bother to ask the questions they ought to be asking. If, however, the principal moves with what appears to be near reckless abandon, s/he will again be ignored by the students and staff, for people are not basically risk takers. There is a great deal to do in the high school. Decisions need to be made. Sometimes these decisions must be made rapidly. At other times a great deal of concentration and checking of details will be necessary. Which is the principal's pattern to be? If s/he moves too cautiously, the program suffers. If s/he moves too rapid-ly, the program sufffers. The effective principal must be a risk-taker who is cautious in his/her relationships with people. The balancing act is a joy to watch and even more satisfying to accomplish. A way out of this trap may well be to respond to concerns of the staff and students with this caveat, "At this point in time and with the information available to me, the answer is . . . " This is not a means of avoidance. It is a means of telling the staff and students that as things change, the decision might well change also.

The seven units in these two chapters will make the office a center of effectiveness and efficiency. The principal can then do what s/he was hired to do -- be an instructional leader.

To do instructional work, the principal must have time away from the office and the pressure of paper work. The work in the office must be under control by a competent SECRETary who will also enjoy learning the new skills and tools presented here.

The following list of terms will become a part of the working vocabulary of the efficient manager by the end of Part I.

SPECIFIC TERMS USED IN PART I

Accountability	The sum of responsibility and authority.
Accountability Formula	Developed by Donald Stewart, it determines the Boredom Factor, Instructional Effectiveness, and Instructional Efficiency of what has been taught by using the results of pre/post testing.
Action Bucket	One of the Scintillating Six folders which contain items that need to be acted upon during the day.
Administration	Art of assisting others to accomplish institutional goals.
Assistant To	A person with a specific assignment who may NOT become trained to be elevated to a more responsible position.
Authority	The provided "rights" to carry out measured responsibilities. Can be delegated to a subordinate.
Brainstorming	The skill to get the best and most creative thinking from a group in a short length of time.

Bucket	A term used in the book denoting a heavy index folder.
Building Policy	A procedure or practice given administrative support for subordinate action to follow for clarity of performance in delegated authority - not responsibility.
Bylaws	Rules governing the organization and operation of the administrative team in a building.
Case Study	A conference of all adults with whom a specific student has contact during any given semester of school.
Centralization	The placing of all authority and decision-making into the hands of the appointed few in an organization.
Contact Report	A summarization of the contact between persons whether it be completed by phone, conference, or other means.
Critical Action Paper	A paper designed to report those elements in need of further work, dates, and suggested resultant action.
Daily Log	A prepared form on which items of necessity are listed for that particular day.
Decentralization	The act of dispersing responsibility for particular and specific functions to a subordinate.
Delegation	The art of assigning tasks to be completed to the lowest effective level operative that can do it.

Effective	Doing right things.
Effecient	Doing things right.
Entrance/Exit Questionnaires	A questionnaire designed to request information from one who is entering or leaving a school to improve the program for all the students enrolled.
Exceptional	A student who by all commonly accepted measures varies from the norm to preclude "regular" participation in the learning processes.
FARMER	An acronym used for the Scintillating Six: File, Action, Route, Meetings, Expedite, and Review.
Five M's of Management	R. Alec Mackenzie's: Men, Money, Machines, Minutes, and Material.
Five Roles of Principals	Students, Staff, Instruction, Community Relations, and Business/ Building Management.
Five Roles of Schools	Selection, Placement, Instruction, Custodialship, and Socialization.
Four Keys to Delegating	What are your (1) Objectives, (2) Opportunities, (3) Resources, (4) Strategies?
Functional Box - T. O.	A Table of Organization drawn in a manner whereby the roles are shown in lieu of the names of the person occupying the box or position.
Goal Setting MEGRID	A 15 cell grid showing the relationships of the 5 M's of management to the present and future objectives applied to the best route to take.

Instruction	The process of providing multiple and diverse opportunities for the development of students on the physical, intellectual, emotional, and social levels which result in measurable improvement and growth.
Job Description	Statements, when grouped, become the definition of a person's position and against which evaluation of performance is based.
Leadership	The art and skills of assisting a group in the accomplishment of its goals.
Line Box, T.O.	Tables of Organization drawn to show the innerworkings and relationships of persons and titles in an organization.
Management	The art and skill of getting things done by and through others.
Management By exception	Skill in developing a management style which will then dictate that not every item being completed or developed need to be brought to the attention of the boss.
Managing the Boss	The art of protecting oneself against unfair criticism from the superordinate. In the vernacular = C. Y. A.
Monitoring	Collection of data from testing/surveys/ audits while remaining alert to programs under one's supervision.
Motivation	Skill in assisting others to accept responsibility not only for planned and assigned work but to accomplish tasks at the highest level of proficiency.

Objective's Parts	Givens, Expectations, Proficiency, and Time Line.
Observation	The systematic collection of data to verify intended results of classroom instruction on prescribed objectives in a pre-specified length of time.
Personal Time Clock	That (often) unrecognized cycle of the human when s/he is most and/or least productive at work or play.
Planning	A managerial function: predetermining a course of action.
Policy	The "laws" adopted by the Board of Education.
Rationale	Explanations of the purpose behind a recommendation.
Regular	Classrooms built for "typical" instructional programs in the language arts, social sciences, etc. Rooms can be used for any non-lab section of students.
Rules (Regs)	Detail statements for directions to put policy into practice with consistency.
Responsibility	The work assigned to complete a given task or set of tasks in the organization. <u>Cannot be delegated.</u>
Scaler T.O.	A representation whereby those reporting to another are shown on a line and fit into the scheme horizontally.
School	An institution controlled by adults for learners where all people can come

to learn skills and receive training while they gain knowledge to develop physically, intellectually, emotionally, and socially and perfect this development with a dedicated staff utilizing explicit, implicit, and null curricula based on the needs of the learner and the community for current and future life applications.

Scintillating Six

A paper management package utilizing the elements of the acronym FARMER.

Simon's Participation Hypothesis

A hypothesis which holds "that significant changes in human behavior can be brought about rapidly when persons who are expected to change participate in determining the change and how it shall be made."

S.O.P.P.A.D.A

Stands for Subject, Objective, Present Situation, Proposal, Advantage, Disadvantage, Action - for developing a memo.

Special Classrooms

Classrooms built for specific units of instruction but can be used for many audiences with limited success because of their acoustics or other restrictions. Example: Choral.

Standard Operting Procedure

The elucidation of recurring items for clarity for continuing operation of a school or district.

Standard Practice Bulletin

A format to follow to proceduralize continuity of an operation in a school or school district.

Supervision	The art of assisting others to improve upon their skills.
T. O.	Initialism for Table of Organization.
Task Card	A special form on which to record specific work to be completed by an administrator as designed by Thomas E. Prenkert. Referred to as the "TEPCARD" in this book.
Tickler Files	Buckets which contain the work of the day or month.
Time Line	Clock or calendar elements included in an objective statement in evaluation and in instruction.
Unique Classrooms	Classrooms built for a specific reason and not amenable to uses other than that for which it was built.
Upbucking	The giving to the superordinate by the subordinate, the subordinate's task.
Urgency	That task which takes precedence over the important too many times in the superordinate's day if the subordinate is not helped to assess the difference.
Wheel Organization Chart	A table of organization set in concentric circles in which each "layer" reports to the one it rests upon. A channel is arranged for immediate contact with anyone in the organization without necessarily going through all levels.

-- CHAPTER ONE INTRODUCTION --
Getting Prepared

Unit titles in this chapter are the following:

General Planning
Self Management in the Office
Structuring One's Own Niche

These three units are built around the philosophy that the three main elements in working within the schools is self, people, and paperwork. If the principal is to become a manager then s/he has to learn or at the least sharpen the skills already practiced.

The chapter is designed to be of assistance to both the neophyte or the experienced administrator. For the neophyte, planning and structuring will encompass much of the first efforts necessary to become successful in a leadership position in schools. For the experienced administrator, the chapter will assist him/her to alter some practices already in place in the style s/he has accepted. The material will allow the principal to get out from behind the desk and do what needs to be done in instruction and **with students.**

The units are put in place in an order for assumption of duties. If the principal follows the book to learn what needs to be done and how to do it from unit one on planning through unit three on structuring his/her own niche, s/he will more likely be successful. The experiences emanating from this book can be enjoyable.

- UNIT ONE INTRODUCTION -
General Planning

Topics to be covered in this unit are:

Planning   Planning Each Day
Goal Setting   Force Field Analysis

11

Initial Job Analysis   Five Year Planning
Brainstorming   Problem Census

Unit One is specifically for planning. The topic deals with the term MANAGEMENT to review the basics to promote strong leadership, administration, and supervision. In a taxonomy, the terms look like this:

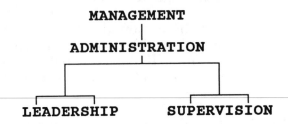

MANAGEMENT

ADMINISTRATION

LEADERSHIP   **SUPERVISION**

Thus, in order for the principal to understand the focus of this entire book, the term MANAGEMENT is explained early. It is synonymous with the term principalship. The principal must get things done by and through others, which is the definition of management. There are fourteen essential quotes about planning in the introductory information about General Planning, the first subunit. Each quote needs to be remembered *and become routine* as the principal works day-to-day in the high school.

Planning traps, tips, barriers, some of Murphy's Laws, some essentials, questions, and some of the tools for one's use as an effective manager (principal) are highlighted. The unit on planning is concluded with statements for the principal to consider when deciding about what a high school is to the students.

An Initial Job Analysis is reviewed for the principal's application. The five basic elements of the job are prioritized and listed here for communication:

Instruction   (The principal must be
Students   ((accountable in each of
Staff   ((the five tasks areas
Community Relations   ((as listed. The tasks
Business/Building Mgt.   (are listed in Part II.

12

When one has the most significant job in the district, s/he must be able to plan each day. That is the prelude for the week, then the month, the semester, and the year. Each day is valuable, and one wasted is never reclaimed. The ADOPT SELF MANAGEMENT ROUTINE emphasizes what must be accomplished on a daily basis. A separate discussion is held on the Daily Log, which can be the salvation of the harried principal.

Setting a workable and sensible five-year plan in motion is a primary concern. The plan is a cyclic tool which begins each year to form a new five year program. It will become indispensable to the efficient principal.

Some useful tools will aid the principal who hasn't done enough planning. S/he should never become so involved in the business of educational management that explicit goals are overlooked. It is not healthy to become so concerned (and justifiably so) about the alligators at one's seat that s/he forgets to drain the swamp, the initial objective. Thus, some work on goal setting is important for the principal to understand.

Brainstorming and Force Field Analysis are the final tools discussed in Unit 01. They will be helpful in the processing of data for the principal-planner. The means of determining the value of the brainstormed lists is especially helpful when decisions are made as to the efficacy of a program.

Problem Census is the neatest trick to be learned. It can be used for most any purpose in which a need for feedback has been discerned. It is a simple three question proposition that will be adopted and used extensively.

Each subunit fits into planning, in general, and can be read or studied or used in any order. There is no priority set by their listing within the text or in this introduction. Planning is always the first thing the principal will have to do at the beginning of each school session. The principal who plans is effective. Not to plan is planning to fail, howsoever indirectly the attempt. When the principal has accomplished some skills in this process for the job, s/he is all set to go to work to structure the office routine. If this unit is not taken seriously, the principal will be subjected to the following calf path*:

One day, through the primeval wood
A calf walked home, as good calves should
But made a trail all bent askew
A crooked trail, as all calves do.
That trail was taken up next day
By a dog that passed that way
And then a wise bellwether sheep
Pursued the trail o'er vale and steep
And drew the flock behind him, too
As good bellwethers always do.

And from that day, o'er hill and glade
Through those old woods a path was made
And many *men* wound in and out
And dodged and turned and bentabout
And uttered words of righteous wrath
Because 'twas such a crooked path
But still they followed...do not laugh...
The first migrations of that calf.
The years passed on in swiftness fleet
The road became a village street
And this, before men were aware
A city's crowded thoroughfare.

Each day a hundred thousand route
Trails that zigzag calf about
And o'er his crooked journey went
The traffic of a continent.
A hundred thousand men were led
By one calf near two centuries dead.

A moral lesson this might teach
Were I ordained and called to preach
For *men* are prone to go it blind
Along the calf-paths of the mind
They work away from sun to sun
To do what *other* men have done

14

They follow in the beaten track
And out and in and forth and back
And still their devious course pursue
To keep the path that others do.

But how the wise old wood-gods laugh
Who saw that first primeval calf.

* The calf-path was paraphrased from a poem written by Sam Walter Foss; original source is unknown to the author.

Although full texts have been written on management and the purpose of Unit One is not to assure the reader that he has become an expert planner, the goal of the unit is for the efficient administrator to realize that planning is not only an essential part of management but it is also the first role of management.

What exactly is management? Management is getting things done by and through others. The effective principal must be a good manager of others. To some in education, the term *management* has a negative connotation. This is because many in *management* positions are inefficient. The best way to promote efficiency is through planning.

There are many different types of planning. These include comprehensive, strategic, long-range, systems, operational, and forecasting, all of which apply to the educational situation. The uses of planning for which the principal is fully accountable include to monitor, control, and evaluate. For every hour spent in planning, the manager will save three or four in execution and improve upon results. The principal should not follow the lead of Alice. When Alice asked the Cheshire Cat, "Would you tell me, please, which way I ought to walk from here?" "That depends a good deal on where you want to get to," said the Cat. "I don't much care where---" said Alice. "Then it doesn't matter which way you walk," said the Cat, "if you only walk long enough!" And, that is not funny because some principals believe that as long as they are walking, they are getting some place in their plan. Principals must get their roadmaps in place, have a guide to work with, and go through each phase of the planning routines.

When getting prepared to plan, the principal should remember the following:

1. Plan your work; work your plan.
2. Work expands to fill the time available.
3. It is better to be defensible than to be on the defensive.
4. One cannot solve a problem once s/he becomes part of it.
5. Failure to plan is planning to fail.
6. Everything takes longer than it is planned to take.
7. If one doesn't plan his/her day, others will.
8. If the principal plans well, s/he can manage by exception.
9. The fate of each is the destiny of all.
10. Time is the first thing that must be planned and managed.
11. Execution time can be cut by good planning.
12. A good manager plans -- not operates.
13. People who have a half-hour to waste usually spend it with someone who hasn't!

The last statement is reminiscent of a manager who had a sign on his wall that said, "If you have nothing to do, please don't do it in here." This manager was well organized, planned well, and executed well.

The statements listed above are far more than cute or clever slogans which are to be read, grinned at, and then forgotten. They are truisms which ought to be committed to memory and practiced continually.

PLANNING TRAPS

Some managers allow themselves to fall into the following traps:

Not planning   Planning only partially
                   Planning for perfection

A good way to establish a base for planning to manage an operation is to take a couple of minutes to record the specific purposes for which one was hired. This provides a start. If the work has been completed, the principal should establish a new list. Typically, management work recurs rather than becomes totally eliminated.

PLANNING TIPS

1. Break big tasks into small, doable bits.
2. Weed out nonessential items; accomplish only the important.
3. Delegate those tasks unimportant to one's work.
4. Consolidate all fringe tasks into doable objectives.
5. State objectives specifically.
6. Rank objectives in order of importance and accomplish them in the order of priority.
7. Review past planning to reaffirm current actions.
8. Collect all necessary data *before* beginning.
9. Use all available tools to assist in planning.

Some starter lists for the principal to use in planning are those listed below. Each can be used for planning such topics as a report, a recommendation, or an instructional program. It is incumbent on the principal to survey the topic and decide which of the lists may be the most helpful to do the planning.

The Five M's of good management:

Men	=	Staffing
Money	=	Budget
Material	=	Supplies
Machines	=	Equipment
Minutes	=	Clock/Calendar

The Five Roles of Public Education:

Selection	Placement
Instruction	Custodialship
Socialization	

17

The Five Roles of the Building Principal:

Students   Staff
Instruction   Community Relations
   Business/Building Management

PLANNING TOOLS

Some of the more sophisticated tools which are used for planning include:

P.E.R.T.	Each of these will
Flowcharting	be covered in more
Gantt Charts	detail in other
Agenda Preparation	units whereas the
Force Field Analysis	final two are discussed
Brainstorming	later in this unit.

PLANNING -- ALONE OR COOPERATIVELY

Some planning must be done alone. Most, however, must be done in a cooperative effort with other faculty or staff members. One way to determine which type of planning a situation merits is by the availability of the necessary material. When the essential data are close at hand, planning singularly will save time. This should not become habit. Many good plans can be improved upon by calling good planners together for review and critique sessions. Teamwork is tantamount to success as the principal learns to work with his/her staff to improve the educational situation.

BARRIERS TO GOOD PLANNING

Planning can be enjoyable, and it is certainly productive. Time must be set aside for planning purposes alone. There are many barriers to planning. Dr. R. Alec Mackenzie lists the following reasons for not setting aside the time for planning. (176)

1. *Escapism* - doing something - anything - before sitting down to plan.

18

2. *Default* - becoming active in tasks no one else will
  do.
3. *Spur of the Moment* - racing off to do something.
4. *Habit* - staying in a rut and doing other tasks
  which are repetitive in nature.
5. *Precedent* - making sure to make the same mistakes of the last time.
6. *Others' Demands* - Doing what one is asked to do
  or told to do.
7. *Procrastination* - Delaying what must be done.
Many of these barriers will sound familiar to the
  principal.

Murphy, of Murphy's Law fame, has some fundamental laws which also apply and, although these may
appear to be designed out of humor, they are listed here
for their managerial content.

1. If anything can go wrong, invariably it will.
2. Nothing is ever as simple as it first seems.
3. Everything a person decides to do costs more
  than first estimated.
4. Every activity takes more time than one has.
5. By trying to please everybody, somebody will be
  displeased.
6. It's a fundamental law of nature that nothing
  ever quite works.
7. It is easier to make a commitment or to get involved in something than to get out of it.
8. Whatever one sets out to do, something else
  must be done first.
9. If one improves or tinkers with something long
  enough, eventually it will break or malfunc-
  tion.
10. By making something absolutely clear, someone
  will become confused.
11. Every clarification breeds new questions.
12. One can fool some of the people all of the time
  and all of the people some of the time, and
  that is sufficient.
13. Persons disagreeing with your personal facts
  are always emotional and employ faulty

19

reasoning.
14. Enough research will tend to support one's conclusions.
15. The greater the importance of decisions to be made, the larger must be the committee assigned to make them.
16. The more urgent the need for decisions, the less apparent becomes the identity of the decision-maker.
17. The more complex the idea or technology, the more simple-minded is the opposition.
18. Each profession talks to itself in its own unique language.

Apparently there is no Rosetta Stone.

BASIC ESSENTIALS TO GOOD PLANNING

There are three basic essentials to good and sound planning in the principalship. The principalship may be considered to be at the level of middle management to some, but the principal is akin to top management in the building where s/he reigns. Therefore, s/he needs to become both effective and efficient. The basics of good planning are three-fold. The principal must deal with the futurity of his/her decisions, with people - all members of the staff, and then take the most appropriate action. Each will be explained below as shown.

People: Human resources must be used in any task being planned. The manager must be cognizant of how many persons are able to accomplish the task and how skilled each is at doing what needs to be done. Numbers and abilities of people once assessed provides the manager with raw data for the completion of the project plan. The manager must consider people as the main point around which all plans rotate. Most subordinates can do very well that which they are assigned to do. However, the principal must leave the selection of the specific technique to do the job to the subordinate's own decision.

Futurity: It is usually thought of in three distinct parts. Short range = today, a week, or a month. Middle range = six months or a year ahead. Finally, long-range planning = two to five years. Once the time-lines have been determined, it is easy to think clearly and to plan productively. All good planning generates specificity in the outcomes. Methodology of accomplishing the plan is left to the person executing it. But one must also be aware that the future is where all one's living is done. It is that point in time that the children in school will be governing, passing laws, studying, and in general doing what needs to be done. What training and schooling will be needed? Only the concerned and competent will ever know because they will be working hard at making decisions which are futurology-based and not for this time only.

Action: Planning cannot be done in any other mode than that of action. If a task is worth doing at all, it must bring about some form of accomplishment. And this takes action. Action connotes the use of or expenditure of minutes, material, machines, and money, if only in the use of the fifth M of management, that of men or human resources. These resources can be disposed of routinely if a manager is first aware of them and then uses them and does not avoid them in taking action.

PLANNING QUESTIONS:

Three questions that need to be asked before planning is begun are the following:

1. Where am I currently?
2. Precisely what do I want to accomplish?
3. How can I best accomplish the task?

The number one question above calls for a real in-depth and sensitive look at oneself in the initiatory phase of any good planning session. If it is difficult to determine what the present situation is, one can soon become hopelessly lost. Self-assessment ought to take the least time in planning. Honesty is mandatory. Without it, it's like cheating at solitaire.

21

The number two question begins with the word *precisely* and that is the key to the whole process. If the manager doesn't know where s/he wants to be when s/he completes the task being planned, there is no way to determine when the project is completed. One seldom drives merely to Nevada, for instance. S/he would not only plan his/her route to Las Vegas but precisely to a specific casino and then to a specific room. When in room 222 of the Sands, s/he would realize that s/he had arrived -- not in Nevada, not in Las Vegas, not in the Sands, but -- in room 222. This is important because planning time can be cut on the third question if this second question is answered in a specific manner.

The third question is vital because every detail becomes completed to the fullest. The average planner frequently neglects to carry the plannng much beyond Nevada as in the illustration. But this is not about being a planner of average ability. One means of accomplishing any task being planned is not enough. Two or three means become the acceptable number to review. When these alternative means have been reviewed, the one selected as the top priority or most sensible is the one to follow.

If one has responded to the above three question before the onset of actual planning, here are four questions that need to be addressed at the time good planning is initiated.

　　1. What are the objectives?
　　2. What are the opportunities?
　　3. What are the resources?
　　4. What is the strategy to complete the plan?

In other words, the good planner (principal) must have the right questions in order to get the right answers from others.

THE MANAGEMENT PROCESS

"The Management Process" (132,80) defines terms and shows their relationship in management most appropriately and succinctly. The diagram is in actuality a "bowl" full of information for the manager. In the central point of the diagram, there are the three elements of management. These are: People, Things and Ideas. It is the element of Ideas that will be treated here. The rest of the "bowl" is discussed later.

Ideas have as the major task, that of **Conceptual Thinking,** defined as formulating notions. The *Continuous Function* of Conceptual Thinking is defined as analyzing problems, which means to gather facts, ascertain causes, and develop alternate solutions. The *Sequential Function* of Conceptual Thinking is to plan, which is defined as predetermining a course of action.
Planning activities are listed as:

(1) Forecasting - Establishing where present course will lead.
(2) Setting of Objectives - Determining desired end results.
(3) Developing Strategies - Deciding how and when to achieve goals.
(4) Programming - Establishing priority, sequence, and timing of steps.
(5) Budgeting - Allocating resources.
(6) Setting Procedures - Standardizing methods.
(7) Develop Policies - Making standing decisions on important recurring matters.

Bearing this all in mind, the effective principal must plan in four key operational levels. Here is a set of definitions to clarify the four key operational levels of the building principal. They are Management, Administration, Supervision, and Leadership. The following diagram was first presented earlier in this text but is expanded here.

The four key decision levels are presented in the form of a taxonomy for the purpose of clout. They can be used to assist the planner in determining who shall be involved in the planning process.

MANAGEMENT
Getting Things Done By and Through Others

ADMINISTRATION
Assisting groups to accomplish
organizational goals

LEADERSHIP | **SUPERVISION**
Assisting a group to accom- | Assisting others to improve
plish its own goals | his/her own skills

PLANNING WARNINGS:

1. Items which interrupt may be urgent but may
   not be important.
2. Don't plan because there is nothing else to do.
3. As all planning involves the future, don't wait
   for the future to plan.
4. It is easy to postpone difficult planning decisions.
5. Some managers, afraid of making a poor plan,
   don't plan at all.

Planning is an act which forecasts or predetermines a course of action. Basing decisions on that forecast, the principal must then construct programs. Forecasts should extend as far into the future as practicable. If s/he forecasts for a period of ten years, then the planning needs to be reconsidered every five years.

Here is a sign from the office of a secretary in Dallas, Texas:

Lack of Planning (on your part)
does NOT justify an emergency
(on my part).

SOME WORDS ON LONG RANGE PLANNING

Dr. Larry Hughes, now the Associate Dean of Education at the University of Houston, says that school administrators need three sets of goals for which appropriate objectives should be developed. These are a monthly plan, a one-year plan, and a five-year plan with guideposts set every six months for assessment.

If this is the case, the question that needs to be asked is "What are the faculty and administration going to be able to do 'down the road' with the students, teachers, administrators, management process and plant/parents/ public (STAMP) available to be programmed into a plan?"

One answer may be that the planner will have to be looking for the proper material/methodology, organization, sequencing and timing/ training (MOST) to be where s/he wants to be when finished planning.

A BASE FOR GOOD LONG RANGE PLANNING

Maynard's (137,3[48-60]) discussion of long range planning begins with these sound objectives which are shortened for use here.

1. The objective must be a guide to action and explicit enough to suggest certain types of action.
2. The objective should suggest tools to measure and control effectiveness.
3. The objective should be challenging.
4. The whole set of objectives should make sense.
5. Objectives, especially strategic objectives, must take into consideration external opportunities and constraints, and internal opportunities and constraints.

ITEMS OF CONCERN

In the same source, Maynard says that for the executive in planning (and educators must soon realize that they are executives and act accordingly), the concern is "to limit initial statements of objectives to questions which are quite recognizably of practical concern." Secondly, "regardless of the enthusiasm for the project, don't become overzealous as it is better to delimit the scope and cover it very well." The planner should "branch out later as the situation demands it."

Here is a six-part set of how to do it.

1. Develop goals.
2. Set subsequent objectives.
3. Plan some strategies to bring about the successful completion of the long range plan.
4. Identify possible outcomes of the strategies.
5. Evaluate the results of the strategies.
6. Select that course of action which appears to be best to follow -- bearing in mind the 5 M's of Management.

Six important things about long range planning in a building renovation program are:
1. The central office needs to manage by exception.
2. The building can manage by objectives.
3. Both levels need to be concerned about safety, health, and welfare of the students and staff.
4. Energy conservation needs to be planned for no more than a three to five year payback.
5. Preventive maintenance work calls for the cooperation of the district maintenance and building custodial staffs.
6. Outside (or inside if clearly visible) cosmetic work needs to be staged early so dollars being spent can be seen by all.

Everyone can become part of the overall plan and feel s/he is in the mainstream at the appropriate time and at the appropriate level. When this is accomplished, the plan will go very well.

Lastly, when planning for high schools, here is something on the lighter side which may help to determine what needs to be done.

WHAT IS A PUBLIC HIGH SCHOOL?

A school is where everyone must learn to learn
      -- from teachers who care and really discern.
A school is spelling C. A. T. and cyphering 2 plus 4
      -- is logrithms, equations, and a whole lot more.
A school is learning how to read and reading to learn
      -- is training to do work for money to earn.
A school is a slate, a scope, a shop, a lab
      -- a place to mope, cope, and learn not to blab.
A school is learning to type 60 words a minute or more
      -- and finding your requirements are a bore.
A school is tears and cheers
      -- is filled with love and fears.
A school is complex and simple
      -- is a 250 pound tackle and a cheerleader's dimple.
A school is headed by adults -- run by kids
      -- is kindergarten games and seniors on the skids.
A school is a place which observes all the right codes
      -- and students come in all types and modes.
A school is a house of intellect for all to use
      -- yet some come there just to abuse.
A school is where custodialship of the masses is done
      -- and the custodian's work is never fun.
A school is a place to flirt, to like, to love, and to fail.
      -- to find out what it's like to be a female or male.
A school is a social place with lots of grace
      -- a series of individuals, groups, cliques, and others
         to face.
A school is a place for the kids, all who can get there
      -- not a place for the adults -- they have but a share.

((Please see the exhibits for this entire poem.))

- INITIAL JOB ANALYSIS -

It is time to examine what a principal may do in a job. This actual response of a third grade girl who said that school was really fun, but that, "We just don't get enough time to think," is also the dilemma of the principal.

The examination of what current principals do may be important. It may be just as important to see what those same principals feel they would like to do or more succinctly what they feel they ought to be doing. To obtain this information, the following data were collected. They will show what is done and what could or should be done if principals were able to do what they feel they should do.

Each principal was asked to respond to the percentage of time s/he spent and would like to spend in the five categories listed below. All the results were tallied and the average figures were reported from the time audits. They are presented below:

	Desired	*Do*
1. Instruction	25.95	14.85
2. Students	26.29	20.68
3. Staff	33.15	26.99
4. Community Rels.	8.76	15.44
5. Business/Bldg. Mgt.	5.85	22.04

The data here not only provide a comparison of what principals are doing but show what principals desired to be doing. The principals surveyed had been in the principalship for an average of nine and one-half years and in education for over twenty years.

For the initial job analysis, the principal will need to make some decisions about which of the five categories above each task to be done will belong. After this is done, the principal can log tasks as they are done each month and use the data to study how they can better use the time available.

It is good to know what others are doing and what they would like to do if they had full control of their calendars and clocks. When one plans the year, each of the five categories must be addressed. Beyond that, the work that is done ought to be purposeful and directed to the role and operation of the principal as s/he would prefer it to be.

Consideration was given to that which prevents the principal from doing what s/he would like to do. A list of these consisted of one major element: people problems. When this was broken into the two categories of staff and students, the result was 80% for students' problems and 20% for staff problems. Data collected in high schools today will not be too much different. To control this, the principal must plan the work very carefully. S/he can begin to delegate as much as is feasible to others who work directly with the students. The principals can then manage by exception and improve upon doing that which s/he would prefer to do.

Another item that will require attention is the improvement of the individual school program. One needs to examine at least one key item in each of the five categories of his/her job and indicate what needs to be done. In the survey already cited, the following information was categorized according to need.

Category	*What was needed*
STUDENTS	An additional assistant was needed to allow the principal more time with the staff to develop an appreciation of new information on child growth and brain development.
STAFF	The principal needed to delegate more authority to department heads regarding the implementation of theories of learning and principles of teaching.
INSTRUCTION	Reduction in the size of classes espe-

cially in pilot programs was essential
so more could be started.

COMMUNITY   The appointment of an ombudsman
              is necessary to lighten the load of
RELATIONS   the principal and the appointment
              of an operations coordinator to han-
              dle the community use and other non
              instructional functions of the plant.

BUILDING/BUS. Computerization is needed so the ac-
               counts in the building can be tied
MANAGEMENT   directly to the central computer.

By examining these five areas through which a principal may analyze his/her performance, s/he may improve
upon the entire school program.

- PLANNING EACH DAY -

"Like other resources, time is either managed effectively or
it is mismanaged." Dr. R. Alec Mackenzie

The principal needs to develop a routine early so
that the bulk of the paperwork and hands-on work gets
completed somewhat easily. To do this, s/he can learn
from the following "Adopt Self-Management Routine."
The list prepared below provides an answer to the
dilemma of where to start in this confusing and complex
position called the high school principalship.

The procedure of utilizing a Daily Log will be a
great help in the planning of the work and working the
plan for managing the high school. First, there will be a
plan and second, it will be workable as the secretary learns
how to be protective of time and assists the principal by

keeping others away when they can easily organize the day in lieu of allowing the unplanned day to proceed.

The numbers on the left are the rank of importance the author has set from years of experience in being the chief executive officer of a high school. The routine fits most days of the operation and certainly all the routine days when an exception has not been sched-uled or does not occur. There will be many of them. The list is for the reader's initiation. It is not intended to be a panacea. The style of the principal is best set by how the operation is launched each day. Try this, reprioritize, sequence, or alter in a manner that fits the program. But, do something to plan the day, each day, or someone or something will do it anyway.

The second column contains blanks for the prin-cipal to be able to record the importance felt for each item as each is tested in the building and program being headed.

The third column is the initial of the first word in each task area. These initials have been extended to see the whole plan as an "Adopt Self-Management Routine." The contention here is that the principal must be a good manager of others to get things done; therefore, the word *management* is emphasized.

01 -**A** rrive early to get objectives prioritized for the day.

05 -**D** o verify that all faculty members are in their assigned
        rooms (for the liability it imposes if they
        are not).

04 -**O** rganize the day by locating only those materials
        needed to accomplish planned objectives.

03 -**P** lace notes on the subordinates' desks before they
        come in for the day.

08 -**T** ake time to verify that the rest of the staff and the
        supervisory personnel are at work.

06 -**S** ummarize minutes of the previous day's conferences and meetings -- closures and directions.

09 -**E** xamine the five OBJECTIVES for the day and make appropriate contacts to accomplish # 1.

24 -**L** ast item to do is to arrange tomorrow's Daily Log.

18 -**F** inalize the major OBJECTIVES for the day to record and report what is necessary.

= =

12 -**M** aximize secretarial performance by conferring at the same time each day.

19 -**A** ttend only necessary meetings.

20 -**N** eed to develop memo work which will be reviewed during the conference with the secretary.

13 -**A** llow time to have different contacts with everyone in the building weekly.

21 -**G** et to the classrooms to make observations on a meaningful schedule.

22 -**E** stablish contacts with out-of-building persons to al-low school to function best for kids.

14 -**M** ake all needed phone calls instead of waiting for them to interrupt planned schedule.

16 -**E** at lunch daily and be seen with different leaders daily.

07 -**N** ote places to visit.

17 -**T** ravel to selected meetings that have a significance for the school, even if not a member.

15 -**R** eceive (internal) calls on a schedule and not just
because the phone rings.

23 -**O** bligate schedule to manage the builing daily.

10 -**U** ndertake to call selected persons and places on a
predetermined schedule and roster.

2 -**T** erminate each conference with a solid closure.

11 -**I** nitiate stand-up conferences to control time.

1-25 -**N** ullify all time wasters.

26 -**E** liminate desk work before you go home. Learn not
to carry a "grief case" and impose your work
on the family.

= =

Planning will not only serve to get one organized
for the day but consequently for the week, month, and the
full year, day by day. It will even be helpful next year to use
as a guide for the days as they come at you one by one.
Most managerial work is cyclic so the smoothly established
routine can be repeated the next time   with only necessitated changes.   However, one needs not to reinvent the
wheel each year. The secretary must file (and log the location of) each of these Daily Logs when completed. Perhaps
a prime location is in the monthly buckets being prepared
at all times for quick reference this year and next year as
well.

Most of the topics or tasks listed above will be discussed later in the book. Suffice it to say, the list is not
only a starting place for a principal to plan a day but one
that can be used to plan the reading of the rest of the
material in the book.

Here are points about the way to PLAN THE WORK,
AND WORK THE PLAN.

1. Planning one's own day personally is mandatory.

2. Protect specific time to confer with the secretary to enable her to assist in accomplishing objectives of the day.

3. Complete the most important objective of the day before the second objective is begun, and so on throughout each day.

4. Receive internal calls at specific times.

5. Recognize the least productive part of the day, so the principal can plan some active task to do at that time.

6. Prepare for the next day at the end of the current day.

7. Complete all objectives each day and schedule work on them during the best time of day.

8. Leave the "grief" case in the office overnight.

9. Noncompleted tasks one day may not be a top priority the next day.

10. Failure to plan is planning to fail.

- THE DAILY LOG -

The daily log can become a tremendous aid in the organization of the office and help in planning each day. The principal should use it as a part of his/her management style to get organized. Once this is done, *the principal will no longer allow the urgent to crowd out the important.* Urgency usually is brought about by personnel (or paperwork) and can cause a loss of time so severe that one can't find time to do anything properly. The emphasis is placed on only those things which appear as "urgencies" rather than those that need to be completed, the important things. That is not an efficient means to manage time or the work that needs to be done.

The author has used this type of sheet for years. It is prepared on a legal sized pad of paper. It was designed into two columns with five to seven lines under each of the headings. As one moves from one level of administration to the other, the headings need to be relabeled according to one's needs. A discussion of each of the headings on the form continues below:

OBJECTIVES OF THE DAY
MEETING INFORMATION
PHONE CALLS EXPECTED/RECEIVED
PHONE CALLS TO MAKE
PEOPLE TO SEE HERE
PLACES TO VISIT
DEPARTMENT REPRESENTATIVES
ASSISTANTS
FOR REPORT TO THE STAFF
FOR THE CENTRAL STAFF
SECONDARY PRINCIPALS
FOR THE SECRETARY

The comments below for each of the items in the list are there to assist the principal in obtaining maximum effectiveness.

OBJECTIVES:
The priority item is one located at the top left. These blanks can be completed early each morning or (for the next day) as the last thing before going home in the evening depending upon one's style of managing time and people. It is also a good tool to use when something comes up during the day. Frequently, the next day's log will be partially filled by the end of the current day as things are noted and found to be necessary.

Some good time managers feel more comfortable listing their objectives as the first exercise of each morning. In a high school, the ability to do this just may not be available to the principal. In any respect, fill it in. It is vital to managing successfully both as TIME and SELF. In fact, Charles Schwab, once President of Bethlehem Steel, paid $25,000 in appreciation for this little tip to get more done and done purposefully. He asked a managerial consultant, Mr. Ivy Lee, how to get more done and the suggestion consisted of the above information. It is interesting to note that the executive was still searching for help even though he was regarded as highly competent.

There are five lines drawn in this category and drawn for a purpose. *Typically five daily objectives should be set.* They need to be prioritized for the day's activities. After prioritization, they can be written on the lines in the order in which they need to be completed. Some hints:

1. Don't start objective # 2 until objective # 1 is finished.
2. Don't expect that if # 5 is not done during the current day that it automatically will become # 1 tomorrow. This simply may not be true.
3. Don't record an objective for the day that can be put off until later. Every item on this list (whether there will be 1 or 5 objectives) must be done.
4. Don't state the process - state the result, e.g. *Staff letter written / not / Write the staff letter.*

The objectives constitute the prime item on the page. In fact, to ignore this one phase of the log is to acknowledge failure in the process to become organized.

To assure coordination of the entire year, month, week, and day on some sort of plan, the OBJECTIVES can best be made by examining the many charts which show progress in the major objectives of the year. Keep these charts on the wall or in a notebook. The secretary can be recording completed tasks, as they are done, on Action Demand Charts, Gantt Charts, PERTs, and CPM instruments. When the schedule of major activities has been put on such instruments, the Daily Log will be assistive to meet the specific work assigned for each day. This will prompt others to do the same thing. Both supervisors and subordinates need reminders. It is learning how to handle both that is the real skill in the principalship.

MEETINGS

It is good to have at least a single line on the DAILY LOG dedicated to each meeting or study group served. In high schools, subheadings on Policy, Activities, Staff Meetings, Assistants, Instruction, etc. are helpful. By using these lines and the scintillating six buckets (discussed later in this chapter), the secretary can be assisted in keeping track of each meeting separately.

If an item comes to mind during the day, it is good to record it so when the secretary comes in for the daily conference, it will be easy to relate them to her for future references. She can put it in the Tickler File or Meeting Bucket, whichever is proper and the item can then be brought to closure.

In another unit, some extensive material on the conduct of meetings will be offered. For the purpose here on the Daily Log, suffice it to say that the important features of meetings will be highlighted as topics to put on this part of the form: ANNOUNCEMENTS, ACTION ITEMS, DISCUSSION ITEMS, UPDATES, AND HANDOUTS. With these in mind, record the item or refer to it by its initial on the list for reference with the secretary.

PHONE CALLS EXPECTED AND RECEIVED

When someone "promises" to call on a given date, place a record of the incoming call on the proper daily log sheet when the promise is made, then make sure that the call can be taken when it does come.

PHONE CALLS TO MAKE - COMMENTARY

If a call needs to be placed to Tom O. McCormick - Carlton - on a given date, write it on the daily log sheet matching the date. A word on the purpose of the call will be helpful. Just because he is your best friend is enough.

37

It may be a good idea to use these sheets to make a roster of calls. A couple of important things from this log may become obvious:

1. Important contacts can be monitored so that everyone is called.
2. Calling each contact will be confirmed, and no one will be counted too frequently.
3. When someone is promised a call next week, or whenever -- record it on the appropriate daily log and then follow up on the call. Put the number, name, and purpose to assure a promise made is a promise kept. It may be helpful to record this call in green ink to make it more obvious when the day appears with this notation already on it.
4. At the end of the day, if all the calls are not completed, add the list to tomorrow's - always put "catch-up" calls on the next page (in red ink for emphasis) so they won't be missed the second time. When in red, GET AT IT.

PEOPLE TO SEE HERE OR THERE
These may be department heads, assistants, directors, coordinators, supervisors and all others ought to be able to visit without much preplanning on their part. Two criteria should be known first: (1) the contact is important and (2) the contact is best discussed directly rather than through an intermediary who may not communicate the exactness needed. In other words, as General Eisenhower is reputed to have said, "Anyone can come to see me, but they need to realize that what they have to say better be both urgent AND important." He always emphasized the need for the important and not just urgent.

These contacts, irrespective of their location, ought to be made while standing. In this way, control is not shifted to another. Be aware of the impact wanted before the determination is made as to where the conference will occur.

PLACES TO VISIT

Important persons in town like the Mayor, Police Chief, Council Member, and business owner are those who need to be visited on their turf. The group of businesses and industries that hire students, the providers of the goods needed to educate the students, and those who help staff and community are also viable candidates to be visited.

The school attorney, auditor, accountant, central office administrator, and the others who make the high school as good as it is also need to be visited. Schedule visits to them on their turf. Don't establish a pattern. There is nothing as foul as an "expected" visit which cannot be arranged.

The principal is the chief executive officer. Don't forget that it is mandatory to be seen in each of the rooms in the building periodically, beyond the formal and informal instructional observations made to assist the faculty. In this way, the students and teachers feel more comfortable and that the principal is part of the high school. They will remain loyal to the general purposes of the many programs if they feel involved and the leader's presence with them gives them this feeling. If the only time classrooms are visited is for formal observations and evaluative purposes, the observations will not be as purposeful as they would have been with occasional visits made throughout the year.

It is advisable to visit other principals on their own turf also. No one person ought to become an island unto her or himself even though s/he cannot ignore the plea Polonius made to Laertes, "To thine own self be true."

Set aside a couple of days each month to make these important visits. The execution of this important phase of the principalship (even for a brief five minute respite) is important to the parties involved.

DEPARTMENT REPRESENTATIVES

No matter what these persons are titled, they perform a vital function in the building. Their many tasks can be performed more easily when time is given to assist them. The principal needs to jot a note or two for this group as things come to his/her attention -- especially if an item in a journal seems to ring a bell.

ASSISTANTS
Communication is the most important part of the relationship to be established to make the job as pleasant as it can be. Good assistants need constant support and encouragement. The job is tough and the principal must be passing along both complimentary and directive notes all the time. Write items here that can be passed along to the secretary when she comes in for the conference or when an assistant drops in.

FOR THE NEXT REPORT TO THE STAFF --
CURRICULUM NEWSLETTERS
A good practice for any executive is to keep notes which may be later used in a document for the staff. As a time saver, it cannot be topped. Scan each daily log sheet from the date of the last report to the staff and the note will be a reminder of what was important to relay. When time is available, develop the note into a full-blown sentence or if a sentence, develop it into a paragraph so that the time used to prepare the final report will be greatly lessened. Have the secretary place the note in the appropriate Tickler File. When the time comes to "publish," the memo will be nearly done.

Personnel information (inhouse) is always available but to record it here will help considerably when the report is ready to be written. The reference on this sheet will keep the information available for the report.

CENTRAL OFFICE STAFF
The person who supervises the principal may be given one of many titles. So, whatever it is, this space is for items to be written down to pass along to him/her through the secretary.

OTHER SECONDARY PRINCIPALS

Colleagues can always use copies of the various agenda, notes to the staff, curriculum newsletters, and notes to the students as they are released. When the copies of written material are circularized, the payback will soon happen as others begin to send their material to the building. By receiving material from others, the communication gap becomes narrowed. The best way to get help is to offer it. Here is a start and a valiant purpose to get the link established.

FOR THE SECRETARY

Nothing slows a person more than unworthy interruptions. Rather than "buzz" the secretary at inappropriate times, jot the idea down in this space (lower right hand corner) and review it with her during the next daily conference -- or during one of the unscheduled interruptions during the latter part of the day. These statements or questions need to be discussed or asked given the time to do so.

It may be wise to save these notes to relate to the secretary the first thing in the morning or the last thing at night rather than to interrupt her day. The principal needs to have the secretary exchange messages when she checks-in as she arrives or prepares to leave.

- FIVE YEAR PLANNING -

The principal of a high school ought to have a plan for the next few years so that efforts are purposefully directed. It doesn't make any difference if the position is a new one or one that the principal is experienced at performing. A principal needs to know where s/he is headed. Without some "plan," there is no real direction as to where the program can be expected to head or the principal cannot

41

know when s/he gets there. The following brief unit is on setting the plan in motion. It is cyclic; therefore, the principal ought to be able to plan accordingly no matter how much experience s/he has.

YEAR ONE:

The first year in a principalship is best used to ask a lot of questions, some of which will be rhetorical. Others will need to be answered. These questions need to be asked of:

Parents
Other members of the residential community
Businesspersons and industrialists
Central office personnel
The staff in the building
The students in the building
Other principals in the district
The principal himself/herself

The questions should be asked about the following selected topics:

Community relations
Equipment to be repaired, replaced, or ordered
New material needed
Material that is good and needs to be reordered
Budgetary matters concerning both the resources
        and expenditures
Staffing the building for new courses
Clock and calendar and the limitations and support
        from each
Socialization processes used and those which ought
        to be used
Custodial aspects of the health, welfare, and safety
        for the occupants of the school plant and site
Research results about which the teachers are
        aware
Instructional breadth and depth, weaknesses and
        strengths
Business and building management concerns of the

42

staff and community

The goals and objectives of programs, departments, and the building in general

Issues and trends of education that need to be studied and/or reviewed

Extremes expected, sought, and met in the past six months or so

There are also categories like discipline, the cafeteria, and morale, among others. The principal must ask questions throughout his/her tenure in the building. There are many topics that will come to the attention of the leadership if listening skills are practiced. Questioning is a skill that must be fostered throughout the year. It is best when the parallel skill of listening is developed.

Questioning can be a form of determining needs. The issue here is the identification of the current status of the program as well as the desired outcome. That gap is defined as the Needs Determination.

YEAR TWO

It is up to the principal to set about designing a plan to answer most of the questions and concerns expressed by the staff. The plan must be workable, doable, and centered around the staff. The plan ought to follow the needs that are discussed by a majority of the audiences with whom the principal works on a daily basis.

One of the management axioms appropriate here is, "Plan your work, and work your plan." The working of the plan falls into the next year but must be kept in mind because it is more than the right thing to do. It is, indeed, the only way to go.

YEAR THREE

Implementation is the key to successful work in the total program. It must be done carefully. It must be firm but flexible. The purpose is to win. The plan, if it goes well, must be credited to the staff. The plan's failure, if it does not go well, must be accepted by the principal. The errors of omission run three or four to one to those of commission. This being the case, the best manner of implementation is to share widely the total picture and share only those specific applicatory parts necessary to obtain performance on that independent part with those who need it when they need it.

YEAR FOUR

This is the year of assessment. If the five years were well planned, the evaluation of each phase of the program which was implemented is relatively easy to do. Assessment will, of course, be functioning all the time. The total program, after a year of questioning, planning, and implementation, will be ready for someone from the outside to come in and give an honest assessment. The assessment may be done in one of two basic manners: 1) Goal Free (the type preferred by Dr. Michael Scrivens) whereby the goals are unknown by the evaluator until the study is completed and then the determined goals are matched with those supposedly in place. 2) The goals are written ahead of time and the program when implemented will either meet, or not, the goals and objectives as assessed.

YEAR FIVE

Recommendations and dissemination must be done based on the results of the evaluation of the study. The study will not be of any real value when completed unless it proposes some points to follow. The participants and the onlookers can base the accomplishments of the work done on the study and begin to correct whatever deficiencies are highlighted.

Once the recommendations are formulated, they must be disseminated to the community. The best definition of community is that group who has had contact with the building or any of its participants throughout the year or are affected by the results. THIS MAY BECOME A LARGE AUDIENCE.

SUMMARY

Year One = Ask questions to initiate a Needs Determination.

Year Two = Plan a program to narrow the gap identified
     in Year One.
Year Three = Implement the program.
Year Four = Study, assess, and evaluate the program.
Year Five = Make recommendations and disseminate the
     information.

   What has to be remembered now is that this is a full
five year cycle which begins every year. That is to say that
in year two the principal continues to ask questions but is
also planning based on year one. For years VI forward,
one would be performing all five functions. However, s/he
shouldn't attempt to do this without following all five steps
as outlined above. It is erroneous to assume that any level
of the cyclic planning can be ignored. One never has
enough experience to go without good input from colleagues. The following grid illustrates these points.

TASK\ YEARS	I	II	III	IV	V
ASK	A	A	A	A	A
PLAN	>	P	P	P	P
IMPLEMENT	>		I	I	I
ASSESS			>	S	S
RECOMMEND				>	R

- GOAL SETTING -

The goal setting process is easy to follow once it is
routinized. Principals are always goal oriented but when
queried about these goals some need to search hard to

45

determine what they are. Goals can be set for professional or personal purposes. Other categories of goals that can be set involve family, society, spirituality, career, finances, and community. Here is a plan for goal setting.

A. Set five year goal statements in place for long-range planning and make them easily defined.

B. Set one year goal statements in place for short range planning. Base these on the five year goal state ments already in place.

C. Set six month goals or shorter time lines which make the goals attainable within a time span which is comfortable.

D. Examine the goals set in "C" to affirm they have specific purposes.

E. Prioritize the goal statements in order of importance.

F. Generate tasks that need to be completed in order to accomplish the goals. Generate each of these lists on a separate page for each goal being addressed. When they are examined, it may be discovered that some tasks may be delegated.

G. Examine the activities one by one. Assess each for time to be committed to them to get them done. Make sure the time needed is available to work on the task.

H. Review the activities and rank them from first to last.

I. Rank all activities related to each goal into a single list of tasks to be done. Combine the three lists into a single list of tasks.

J. Assign activities to particular days (dates) to be accomcomplished. Set ALL the activities in a calendar book. DO IT NOW.

K. Approach each task by determining how it can be done to save time.

This goal setting plan is referenced as the MEGRID Plan.

One can fill in the grid's cells by using the 5 M's of good management as they are addressed across the top of the grid. The current situation is examined first using the top row. The goal is addressed in the middle row of cells. How to get to the goal is addressed in row three. The 5 M's are used because in any project in a high school they are vital.

A use of the grid may well be the initiation of a new program. In the Exhibits the program called IN-DIVIDUALIZED PROGRAMMING is explained. The Megrid would be an excellent tool to use to plan the program. The project is not long-ranged and can be posted in the cells since NO one cell is mandatory for the entire faculty to follow. Individualized programming is only best when used for individual students and/or individual faculty members. This yields the best program for each student.

The five roles of the public schools may be substituted for the five M's. Another alternative is to use the five roles of the building principal. For help on these, refer to the "Lists" section in the Exhibits.
= =

MEGRID GOAL SETTING

	MEN	MONEY	MAT'L	MACH.	MIN.
Present Conditions **Where Am I?**					
Future Objective **Where Do I Want To Go?**					
Best Route To Take **How Can I Get There?**					

In 1973 the following plan was initiated to set goals for a board of education in a medium sized school district. The same process was then adopted in each building within the district. The result is shown below. The ten steps have been used by Boards of Education and building principals in Michigan since 1973. Here are the ten steps which can be followed by a principal.

1. Establish the goal statements.
2. Assess the needs to accomplish the goals.
3. Identify the resources and restraints for accomplishing the goals.
4. Objectify goals and prioritize the statements.
5. Generate alternatives for each goal.
6. Analyze alternatives.
7. Select the best alternatives.
8. Develop and implement process objectives.

9. Evaluate process and performance.
10. Modify process and continue to
the next goal.

A principal must be cautioned not to "throw the baby out with the bath water." It may be that one's goals are good but the means of accomplishing them need some revision. Always look for the cause of the error as well as the effect of an error when doing good planning.

The last item for inspection is the proper orientation of goals into different levels. Here are the four levels of goals for a district and how they are assessed.

Level A Goal Statement:
(PHILOSOPHICAL GOAL STATEMENT)

These goals need to answer a question about what people want their school to accomplish. The logical question to be answered is, "What does the Board/community consider important to the children of the district?"

```
|Bd. of Ed./Comm. and Parents|    = 50 %
|Central Off.|.    .    .    .     = 18 %
|Bldg.Adms.|.  .    .    .    .    = 16 %
|Students  |.  .    .    .    .    = 16 %
```

This scale shows the weight of the different influence groups that affect goal development. The result of this input may well be something like this:

"Each member of the student body shall know his/her own body and how it functions."

Level B Goal Statement:
(OPERATIONAL GOAL STATEMENT)

These goals need to answer, "What can be done to meet the goals of the board and community within the budgetary constraints and staffing limitations that the school has?)

49

```
Bd. of Ed./Parents|.        .        .        = 25 %
Supt. + C. Office Personnel |.          = 50 %
Bldg.Admins.|.        .        .        .        = 13 %
Students|          .        .        .        .        = 12 %
```

This scale shows that the weight has shifted to the superintendent and central office directors to make the next level statement. The Board/community and parents are still involved, but their majority weight has been shifted to the central office. The building administrators have gained a significant amount of input as well. The statement from the superintendent may be something like this.

"The students should be able to identify the main functions of the eleven systems of the human body as evidenced by the course in 7th grade health, taught formally three days per week and fused into other curricula where appropriate."

Level C Goal Statement:
  (INSTRUCTIONAL GOAL STATEMENT)

These goals need to answer, "What can teachers do to structure a viable goal satisfaction with the health program as envisioned by the Board and central office?"

```
Bd./Parents|. .        .        .        .        = 18 %
Central Office|.        .        .        .        = 20 %
Building Admins./Teachers        |.        = 50 %
Students|.        .        .        .        .        = 12 %
```

This scale reflects that both the Board and central staff take less priority in the work to finalize the package in health education. The building administrators and teachers now have the influence on the program as it should be in the development of specifics for the goals to work with the youngsters at this point of time and in the community in which the instruction will take place.

"All seventh grade students upon completion of the course in health education in the American school system shall know the primary funtions of all eleven systems in the human body as proved by a teacher-made criterion referenced test from the course work established from the book: Gould, Gerald C. *Health is What You Make It and When You Can Get It.* Hillsdale, MI: Hillsdale Press, 1959.

Level D Goal Statement:
(CLASSROOM OBJECTIVE STATEMENTS)

These goals need to answer, "Given the test that will measure the success of the students in the program, what are some specific objectives which will satisfy the goal statements at all three levels of concern in the district?"

```
|Bd/Parents|
|  C.O.    |.    .      .      .      .    = 18 %
|Bldg.Adms |.    .      .      .      .    = 18 %
|Classroom Teacher Groups      |.    = 50 %
|Students|.    .      .      .      .    = 14 %
```

This scale shows the weight of the classroom teachers in the making of the finite decisions of the curriculum in which they were given representative assistance earlier but which now falls directly in the groups consisting of the professional classroom teacher with support from the central office and building administrators. Their work may take on the appearance of something like this in many statements.

"Trace the flow of blood through the pulmonary system of the human body and show the difference of arterial and venous flow."

This same format was successfully used by a high school principal by substituting levels shown below to level A - Total building, B - Three classifications of students, C - Departments, and D - Individual courses. It may be well to keep this in mind as the following is read. Please see the unit on Supervision for more information.

- BRAINSTORMING -

Brainstorming is a term used too loosely because literally *everyone* thinks he knows how to do it. The skill should be used wisely and with an earnest desire to communicate specific rules to follow and a process to which one should subscribe. To best learn how to define the term, one has to follow the technique to completion. It is the intent here to outline some specifics so that the reader can add this to a "tool kit" of management skills. It is expected that efficiency will improve once this skill has been learned and then practiced.

It is simply a means of obtaining as many creative ideas by "freewheeling" all conceivable items from within a group. The wilder the suggestion, the better. The purpose is to get as many ideas as is possible by having each participant "expand the brain" as much as he can and offer key words to stimulate the thinking of the rest of the group.

Some of the reasons a principal may wish to use this technique are:
- To initiate planning of a new project.
- To develop further, an ongoing program.
- To expand a single idea into a broader base of options.
- To plan, monitor, control, and evaluate a project.

Brainstorming can be taught easily and practiced constantly by students, staff members (all segments - or mixed segments in one setting), a team of persons who enjoy doing it, or just about any group that enjoys working together.

To do brainstorming well, there are some valuable tips for the chairperson to follow. Some of them are listed below:

1. Room color: Some psychologists indicate that

the best color of room in which to brain-storm is a room painted in a soft yellow.

2. Room location: Psychologists further suggest it may be well to locate the activity in a room not familiar to any of the participants, in other words, on neutral ground.

3. Best time: Determine best time of day for each person to be at his/her best.

4. Best people: A brainstorming group is not neces-sarily polite with each other, so the persons involved cannot "have thin skins."

5. Rules: There are not many, but each must be adhered to religiously. The group must un-derstand them and abide by them. There is no room for the "independent" member on this team.

      a. Select a chairperson for leadership.

to prevent criticizing -- the designed use of a small piece of red construction paper is good for the chair to "flag" the participants if they begin to criticize any suggestion and green to use when the chair wants them to continue.

to keep the comments flowing

to recognize inputs and make sure each is re-corded

to allow for the incubation of ideas, make sure the chair does not call the session completed until the *second* lull in the flow of ideas. The first lull comes, incubation oc-curs, then the second flow comes, albeit shorter in duration than the first, but still purposeful.

b. Phrase the item to be brainstormed in the form of a question. Make sure it is a *singular* problem. Make sure it is clear to each of the participants just what is being brainstormed.

c. DO NOT criticize any suggestion. Asking for clarity which can be given briefly is permitted, but DO NOT criticize.

d. HITCHHIKING on another statement is not only permitted, it is encouraged.

e. Choose groups of no more than from four to six persons to cooperate in the session at hand. A bigger problem does not dictate that a bigger group is necessary.

f. Select a recorder for visual reference to the many ideas being given. Be sure to audio tape the entire session to make sure each little kernel is included on the published list once the work is completed. Use large sheets of "butcher paper" on an easel with a felt tip pen to record. The participants do better when they see the items in front of them and can really "bounce" their brain off all the ideas already presented.

To involve the entire staff, it is good to form groups. When each has completed its session, the lists are exchanged between the groups. This does several things for the process: (1) it allows each to see what another group did and perhaps even add to the list, once the comments are seen from the other group, (2) it permits more of the members to participate, (3) it provides an opportunity to train the entire staff in the skill so perhaps they will use it in settings with the students, on committees and in general adopt it as the viable tool it is.

Once the groups exchange the lists and add their newly acquired comments if possible, ask them to separate (code) the items into four categories:

1. Immediate practical use   I
2. Study more   S
3. Needs clarification   N
4. Drop as it is stated   D

The principal then relists all the items into the four categories and publishes them to all participants for comment and clarity. This will assure more prompt participation next time.

The reason so much time is being spent on such an apparent simple task is that after the age of eight or nine, human beings begin to respect group pressure more than they do their own ability to think and be creative. The attitudes of others take precedence over what they think individually. In order to do creative problem solving, the rules as spelled out above are a great help. When some "rebels" have been identified who can really expound and expand on ideas, the principal should use them as frequently as s/he can to be the brainstormers for the staff.

One must shy away from the misoneist -- the hater of new ideas. S/he is easily identified by the constant reference to new ideas as, "It won't work here," "I'm ready, but the rest won't buy into it." A whole host of reasons (excuses?) emanate from such persons. (167,20)

Alex Osborn, the "father" of this management technique, used many categories for means of expanding the lists in brainstorming. When the staff brainstormers have been selected, it may be well for them to learn some mind expanding techniques which will enable them to do a better job. Here is a starter list to use.

- Put to other uses? --
- Adapt? --   Each of these categories
- Modify? --   can be broken down into
- Magnify? --   subheadings by the brain-

- Minify? --
- Combine? --
- Reverse? --
- Substitute? --
- Rearrange? --

stormers once they are designated to be THE team called upon to do this work.

Other terms used to reference this tool are "Creative Ideation," "Imagineering," "Idearamas," and "Buzz Sessions." Currently, the titles of "Creative Workshops," Idea Clinics," and "Incident Process" are each gaining popularity. They each go right back to Alex F. Osborn's initial conceptualization of the skill. He had a great idea and principals need to use it better than it has been used in the past.

- FORCE FIELD ANALYSIS -

Not to be confused with a student helper's interpretation who was once working with Dr. Lee S. Randall in Monroe, Michigan, when he was responsible for conducting a Force Field Analysis (FFA) with the staff. He asked the charming girl to come in and record the results of the Force Field Analysis as he read them off to her. The topic on the chalkboard that she wrote was "Field Forest Analysis."

FFA is a system used first by Kurt Lewin in The University of Michigan's Sociology Department. It is a process which brings about a list of brainstormed factors, each is evaluated and weighed, and then a decision is "forced" from the data which are collected.

It will serve to assist the decision maker in arriving at the best decision in the go, no-go determiniations of program planning, among others. It is a quick and efficient process to provide information from those who were involved in the evaluation. Most decisions have driving forces and restraining forces or facilitators and inhibitors. The FFA process will identify readily those forces which are impinging upon a given condition, problem, or concern and set in motion those solutions to the negative forces as they are identified.

Literally everyone can do it. The system is very simple yet yields in its finality an obvious decision or summary of the data used. Good brainstormers are the easiest group with whom to work because the major portion of the work will have been done once the lists are prepared.

FFA has a marked advantage in its application to difficult situations. It is that both positive and negative data are gathered or generated and listed accordingly. Always develop a list of recommendations which suggest a positive attitude toward the whole process before it is finalized.

When groups complete their projects, the principal can exchange their product with a different group to get:

1. concurrence
2. hitchhiked ideas
3. evaluation of significance

Each group needs to be reminded to report every comment to members of all groups and list all facilitators, inhibitors, and recommendations. Once done, the principal can easily verify each comment's intensity and provide a final, written report as soon as practicable to all participants.

Another technique may be to have the collated lists returned to the principal, by each staff member, when each has had sufficient time to rank the three most significant items on each list. Provide a factor to the ranked orders, multiply them by the frequency and use the products to establish the master list for distribution.

If the principal wishes to do a FFA of a program, it is wise to get it done as soon after the program is held as

conferences, it is good to have the staff remain for no more than a half-hour to go through this procedure. Freshness of thought is important so that the inhibitors and expeditors can be recalled.

The principal using FFA with the staff will:

1. Obtain total staff participation.
2. Set a definite goal statement.
3. Get all criteria for success/failures listed as feedback.
4. Rate each force's impact.
5. Gather valuable data.
6. Garner support from the staff for more involvement.
7. Improve a program.
8. Derive meaningful solutions to weak areas.

To do the analyzing, good brainstorming is important. One is encouraged to follow the rules presented in the preceding pages. Beyond this, the effective leader must call upon those who are good at Bloom's sixth level -- that of evaluation. The lists, once done, must be addressed. Rely on the Semones means of arithmetical process to come to the "forced" decision.

Here is a proven manner of completing a FFA.

1. Always begin by completing a brainstormed list of "things" which respond to the question of "What can be done to improve the 'program' just completed?"

2. Divide the brainstormed list into two separate categories: a. Those topics which the (sub) group felt inhibited the program from being as good as it could have been, and b. Those topics listed which the group felt expedited the program to be as good as it was.

3. Assign a (+) value to the expeditors and a (-) value to the inhibitors. These values will be in a range of 1 to 5, with (1) reflecting the low and (5) the high value.

4. Tally the two separate columns and determine the difference.

5. Analyze the results according to the scale shown below.

Once a FFA has been completed, the participants will be able to see and understand the value of its application. It is a fine tool to add to the "tool kit" of things to be learned to become efficient as well as effective.

Here is a case when the building staff felt the administration could help them more with an additional assistant principal.

Step I: BRAINSTORMED LIST

Curriculum work -- more can be done on time.
Money -- NOT in the budget.
Office space -- None is presently available.
Referrals -- Waiting list for students with needs
                    could be shortened.
Community -- Does not understand the need.
Union, Teachers -- Opposed to appointment of more administrators.
Parental Contacts -- Will be increased.
Sales Reps. -- Will not be bugging the principal.
Clrm. Observations -- Number and content will be
                    improved.
Curriculum Meetings -- More can be managed.
Must stay in dist. -- For level I appointments.
Bargaining -- Will be hampered.
Office set-ups needed for clerk and administrator.
Secretarial Union -- Supports additional administrative
                    staffing.

(The comments behind the dashes were added for clarity. This is an abbreviated list just to make the point necessary in this discussion).

STEP II. Distinguish EXPEDITORS (+) from IN-HIBITORS (-)

+ Curriculum work -- more can be done on time.
- Money -- NOT in the budget.
- Office space -- None is presently available.
+ Referrals -- Waiting list needs shortening.
- Community -- Does not understand the need.
- Union, Teachers -- Opposed to appointment of more
-     administrator
+ Parental Contacts -- Will be increased.
+ Sales Reps. -- Will not be bugging the principal.
+ Clsrm. Observations -- # and content improved.
+ Curriculum Meetings -- More can be managed.
- Must stay in district -- for level I appointments.
- Bargaining -- Will be hampered.
- Office set-ups needed for clerk and administrator.
+ Sec'l. Union -- Supports add'l. admin. staffing.

STEP III. ASSESSMENT OF THE VALUE OF EACH ITEM, RATED 5 DOWN TO 1.

+5 Curriculum work -- more can be done on time.
- 3 Money -- NOT in the budget.
- 4 Office space -- None is presently available.
+5 Referrals -- Waiting list for students shortened.
- 2 Community -- Does not understand the need.
- 1 Union, Teachers -- Opposed to appointment
+4 Parental Contacts -- Will be increased.
+3 Sales Reps. -- Will not be bugging the principal.
+4 Classroom Observations -- Number and content
       will be improved.
+4 Curriculum Meetings -- More can be managed.
+4 Must stay in district -- for level I appointments.
- 2 Bargaining -- Will be hampered.
- 4 Office set-ups needed for clerk and administrator.
+2 Sec'l. Union -- Supports add'l. admin. staffing.

EXPEDITORS separated from the above list.

+5 Curriculum work -- more can be done on time.
+5 Referrals -- Waiting list shortening.

+4 Parental Contacts -- Will be increased.
+3 Sales Reps. -- Will not be bugging the principal.
+4 Clsrm. Observations -- # and content improved.
+4 Curriculum Meetings -- More can be managed.
  Secretarial Union -- Supports additional administrative
+2
+27

STEP IV. INHIBITORS separated from the above list.

-3 Money -- NOT in the budget.
-4 Office space -- None is presently available.
-2 Community -- Does not understand the need.
-1 Union, Teachers -- Opposed to appointment.
-3 Must stay in district -- for level I appointments.
-2 Bargaining -- Will be hampered.
-4 Office set-ups needed for clerk and administrator.
-19

STEP V. TALLYING THE RESULTS OF THE LISTS:

EXPEDITORS =   +27
INHIBITORS =   -19
               + 8

DIFFERENCE = DIVIDE THE DIFFERENCE (8) BY
THE NUMBER OF ITEMS ON BOTH LISTS =

$$14 \overline{\smash{\big)}\ 8.00}^{\ 0.57} \qquad = 0.57$$

STEP VI. FITTING RESULTS TO THE DECISION. **

- to + .15 = Any negative number up to + .15 = Negligible reasoning for a positive recommendation being forwarded.

+.16 - .50 = Worthy of continued (inhouse) consideration for additional study before the recommendation goes forward for action.
+.51 up to 1.0 = Valuable and recommendation should be forwarded for further consideration.

** = Format for the FFA math was originally designed by Mr. Terry G. Semones, Director of Special Services in Monroe Public School, in Monroe, Michigan.

- PROBLEM CENSUS -

The Problem Census can be done to gather many types of information. It was first used when the author wanted to ask the students in a 2,500 student body what they thought of the school. There were some responses which were not exactly what was being searched. Here is the way the census is taken.

On a three by five index card, the questions, to which responses were requested, were printed. They were:

(1) THE THING I LIKE BEST ABOUT WTHS IS:_____

_____

(2) THE THING I LIKE LEAST ABOUT WTHS IS:____

_____

(3) IF I WERE THE PRINCIPAL, I WOULD:_____

_____

The results were very helpful to the administration and staff in the building. The only troublesome report was the suggested sixty-eight means for a principal to self-destruct! Anyway, once the cards were used by the administration and the students had had their opportunity to take an anonymous lick at the principal, the results were more helpful each time. Many of the topics listed in some material in the Exhibits had their origin from results of the Problem Census.

To make the cards even more helpful, color coding or the use of some other indicator for the different grade levels or sexes or phase of the staff or new/returning students, etc. can be used as a boost for the collation time.

The questions can be altered for the classroom teacher, the assistant principal, the department head, the student council president and any other person on the staff. The subject matter classroom teachers can use it all the time. Coaches in drama and athletics can use it quite comfortably and results will be helpful.

It may look simple -- cause it is. Don't be fooled. It is easy to use and reveals much needed information.

- UNIT TWO INTRODUCTION -
Self Management in the Office

Topics to be covered in this unit are:

Time Management - Myths, Principles, Savers, Wasters, Organizing, Analysis, Tips, and Audits,

Tickler Files
Scintillating Six
Secretarial Conferencing
Phone Usage
Correspondence - Incoming and Outgoing
Memo Work

Unit 02 deals with structuring the office routine to make it as personal as the principal wants it to be. How the great amount of paperwork is handled will determine how successful the operation is in the eyes of the staff and the central office. The principal will be amazed to discover that there exists a great number of people who thrive on paperwork. The time for paperwork is a luxury in the high school. The principal can ill afford to thrive on paperwork. The principal's job needs to be dedicated to the improvement of instruction. There is no other instructional leader in the building nor can the responsibility be delegated. The subunits in this chapter will certainly free time so that this prime responsibility can be accomplished.

The heart of the paperwork program is in the subunit on Tickler Files. These "buckets" hold the routine paperwork for each day of the month as the monthly buckets hold the paperwork for the upcoming and past months. The remembering of the countless tasks to initiate, monitor, or evaluate can be easily recalled when the secretarial conferencing is held daily.

The second important phase of the paperwork handling routine is the set of six "buckets" affectionately called scintillating six but referenced herein as the FARMER buckets. Each letter of the acronym stands in the place of the initial letter of the word they represent. The acronym consists of F ile, A ction, R oute, M eetings, E xpedite, and R eview.

The subunit on Secretarial Conferencing reveals that the SECRETary is the main person in the office. The principal will need to start the very first day with a secretarial conference. This will enable the secretary and the principal to determine the best means to launch the program of good paperwork management. On the first day, the principal can order the "buckets" (which are described in the units on Tickler Files and Scintillating Six) and begin to use the tickler file with regular folders. When the "buckets" come in, the contents of the folders can be transferred to the "buckets" for the Tickler File and the Scintillating Six (FARMER) buckets.

Paperwork will inundate even the best office manager if there is no system of controlling it. It cannot just happen; it must be planned. Taking charge is the first step, or it will be too late. It is a lot like geometry; if the first two or three theorems are missed, one may never understand the class.

The phone will also destroy time and well-planned routines. It should be used well. As the BOSS one can dictate how the phone will be managed. There are some valuable clues from an old timer on this topic. When a contact has been made (and most of them will be on the phone that need a record made), it is wise to complete a contact report and place it on file. There are some solid pieces of advice on this very topic which have been tied to the phone subunit.

Paperwork can be described as correspondence, whether or not it is external or internal mail. Everybody wishes to correspond with the principal whether or not it is in the form of a brief memo or a detailed report. This leads easily, almost automatically, into the unit on filing or storage of the mass of papers. It is good to have an immediate plan for its disposition and to handle it daily. The secretary must learn early that it will be greatly appreciated if DAILY filing is accomplished. Once material begins to be stacked, it is lost. The time it takes to locate "missing paperwork" will take more time than to file it daily. And this compounds with each time a search needs to be launched for that specific piece of paper. PAPERS SHOULD BE HANDLED BUT ONCE.

To convey what it is that needs to be conveyed precisely is a difficult task unless the following guides are kept in mind. Organizing memo writing into a routine is responsible administration.

- TIME MANAGEMENT -

All of these subunits are fully entertwined and with no apology. The topic is not necessarily complex, yet to keep each "clean" from the others would require much redundancy in the material. The list is below:

Time Management Myths	Time Usage Principles
Time Wasters	Time Audits
Time Savers	Time Organization
Time Management Tips	Time Analysis

The idea behind this unit is that the principal needs to TAKE time to understand that what s/he is doing at any moment is important and that time cannot be wasted or s/he will surely lose. Secondly, one needs to understand that the time not used well will never be returned. When these subunits are joined with the units on office management in the early sections of this book, the principal can see what is being done wrongly and how to correct the problems.

- TIME MANAGEMENT MYTHS -

Dr. R. Alec Mackenzie has identified the following myths of time management. They are being offered here so as not to have to take the TIME to "reinvent the wheel." Also, they are good ones and have been tested by Dr. Mackenzie in his consultancies. (176)

MYTH OF Activity -confusion of activity with good results

MYTH OF Urgency -don't crowd out the important

MYTH OF Higher Decision Level -decisions ought to be made at the lowest practicable level)

MYTH OF Delayed Decisions -the old "sit on it" philosophy -- referred to as the "hemorrhoid approach."

MYTH OF Delegation -it's quicker if I do it myself

MYTH OF Confidence -I can whip that off later

MYTH OF Unrelenting Hard Work -If I don't do it, it will
     not get done
MYTH OF The Open Door -I always have time for you

The question here is, "How many of them afflict the high school administration in the daily work of the school?" This unit will help alleviate the TIME trap most principals find in the school. The shocking part of this information is that one must blame himself for the situations he is in for the use of time. When one finds himself/ herself under pressure for time, s/he knows the trap was sprung by himself or herself. And, the only help one can get comes internally and not from anyone else.

After all, no one has enough TIME. The paradox of this last statement is, "Everyone has all there is and all have as much as the other." If the principal doesn't manage time well, someone else will. The use of a good system of management of time is the single most important task an executive can accomplish to improve personal performance. It is the simplest thing to learn. It requires no new talents or skills. It requires application of some very basic things which each person knows but has not yet packaged.

Peter Drucker says, "Nothing else distinguishes effective executives as much as their tender loving care of time." Here are some details on the application of the principles of good time management. A good place to start is with Voltaire's *A Mystery of Fate* when the Grand Magi asked Zadig,

> What of all things in the world is
> the longest and the shortest,
> the swiftest and the slowest,
> the most divisible and the most extended,
> the most neglected and the most regretted,
> without much nothing can be done,

which devours all that is little,
and enlivens all that is great?

The response was made by Zadig,

TIME.
Nothing is longer, since it is the measure of eternity.
Nothing is shorter, since it is insufficient for the
accomplishment of our projects.
Nothing is more slow to him that expects;
nothing more rapid to him that enjoys.
In greatness it extends to infinity,
in smallness it is infinitely divisible.
All men neglect it;
all regret the loss of it;
nothing can be done without it.
It consigns to oblivion whatever is unworthy
of being transmitted to posterity,
and it immortalizes such actions as are truly great.

Thus, this is the principle of good time management
as first discussed and written. The whole instance of
managing time before it becomes the manager is true.
Read Voltaire's passage again to understand the significance of TIME management. It is SELF management
at its best. And, self management is the real topic of this
unit. For if one cannot manage oneself, the problems of
managing others seems to magnify. They will grow much
like General MacArthur's analogy about the war machines
of the past and present when he said, "At first there was
merely the rifle to kill just one, then came the machine gun
to kill hundreds, the bomb to kill thousands and now the
atomic bomb to kill millions." We can apply this to mean
that the misuse of time will at first not bother. However,
the more it is misused, the more it will complicate management of the entire operation. Here is another statement
attributed to MacArthur: "To delay proper support is
mathematical, to wait a week will be geometrical, to delay
a month will be astronomical." This can be easily translated into the misuse of time by the manager. It is easy to
see what the delay can cost management of the organization.

If the principal visualizes him/herself as a manager and not just a principal (not a put-down) but one who must get things done by and through others then s/he is set to manage what must get done.

There will be skeptics. However, as Daniel Webster once said, "What is popular is not always right. What is right is not always popular." If time management is used, popularity will come from within the building and will surely come from peers as they begin to see that time is never a factor in the new image. It can be controlled. It must not be ignored.

- TIME MANAGEMENT PRINCIPLES -

Dr. R. Alec Mackenzie will be called-upon again for the assistance of his compiled list of 21 time management principles: (176)

1. *Equal Distribution.* No one has enough time. Yet everyone has all there is. This is the great paradox of time. It's the one resource which is distributed equally to all.

2. *Time Analysis.* A daily log of activities for at least a week, taken in fifteen minute increments, is essential as a basis for effective time analysis. It should be repeated at least semi-annually to avoid reverting to poor time management practices.

3. *Anticipation.* Anticipatory action is generally more effective than remedial action. A stitch in time saves nine, so expect the unexpected and plan for it. Assume if anything *can* go wrong, it will. (Murphy's third law)

4. *Planning.* Every hour spent in effective planning saves three to four in execution and gets better results. Both long-range and daily planning, formulated after business hours the previous day or early the same day, in conjunction with near-term objectives and events, are essential to effective utilization of personal time.

69

5. *Flexibility.* Flexibility in degree of scheduling personal time may be necessary to accommodate to forces beyond one's control. Time should not be over- or under-scheduled.

6. *Objectives and Priorities.* More effective results are generally achieved through purposeful pursuit of planned objectives than by chance. Time available should be allocated to tasks in ordered sequence of priority. Otherwise, managers will tend to spend time in amounts inversely related to the importance of their tasks.
(Parkinson's second law)

7. *Deadlines.* Imposing deadlines and exercising self-discipline in adhering to them aids managers in overcoming indecision, vascillation, and procrastination.

8. *Alternatives.* In any given situation failure to generate viable alternative solutions limits the liklihood of selecting the most effective course of action.

9. *Consolidation.* Similar tasks should be grouped within divisions of the work day to minimize interruptions (in taking and returning phone calls, for example) and to economize in the utilization of resources and in personal expenditure of effort.

10. *Pareto Principle/Concentration.* A critical few efforts (around 20%) generally produce the great bulk of results (around 80%). This principle, also called "the 20/80 Law" has led effective managers to concentrate their efforts on the "critical few" events. This increases the liklihood of their happening and, therefore, of achieving maximum results.

11. *Effectiveness.* Efficiency may be defined as doing any job right ... effectiveness as doing the *right* job right. Effort, however efficient, will tend to be ineffective if performed on the wrong tasks, at the wrong time, or with unintended consequences.

12. *Delegation/Decision Level.* Authority for decision-making should be delegated to the lowest possible level consistent with good judgment and available facts.

13. *Upward Delegation.* Managers tend to encourage upward (reverse) delegation unwittingly by encouraging dependence of subordinates upon them for answers. This results in their doing the work of their subordinates.

14. *Minimizing Routine and Avoiding Detail.* Routine tasks of low value to overall objectives should be minimized, consolidated, delegated, or eliminated to the extent possible. Managers should divorce themselves from unnecessary detail and selectively neglect all but essential information. This has been phrased "the need *not* to know."

15. *Limited Response and Selective Neglect.* Response to problems and demands upon time should be limited to the real needs of the situation. Some problems left alone go away. By selectively ignoring these problems which tend to resolve themselves, much time and effort can be conserved for more useful pursuits. (Also called the "principle of calculated neglect.")

16. *Exception Management.* Only significant deviations of actual from planned performance should be reported to the responsible executive to conserve his time and abilities.

17. *Visibility.* Keeping visible those things being worked on will increase the certainty of achieving the objectives. One can't do what one can't remember.

18. *Brevity.* Economy of words conserves time while promoting clarity and understanding.

19. *Tyranny of the Urgent.* Managers live in constant tension between urgent and the important. The urgent task demands instant action and drives out the important. Managers thus are tyrannized by the urgent and respond unwittingly to the endless pressures of the moment. In so doing they neglect the long-term consequences of more important tasks left undone.

20. *Crisis Management*. Managers often tend to manage-by-crisis, that is to treat every problem as if it were a crisis. This over-response syndrome causes anxiety, impaired judgment, hasty decisions, and wasted time and effort.

21. *Interruption Control*. Arrangement of and controls over activities should be designed to minimize the number, impact, and duration of interruptions.

The principles are brief and pointed. It may be well to have them copied and put under the glass on the desk to refer to as time becomes the essence in delegation, decision making, or use for the betterment of the school.

- TIME SAVERS -

Probably the most significant part of this unit will be learning how to determine the proper use of time. That will be done in time audits. For the second phase of this "struggle" to understand time and its impact on the principalship, the knowledge of ways and means to save time and correct time drains -- wasters -- is the logical unit to pursue. SAVE and WASTE time is the conflict. Some times when one feels time is being saved "for later on," s/he is actually wasting time NOW and will have to waste it AGAIN later. Here is the part of the exercise to help.

First, draw a prioritization grid and list the items on it for later ranking. On the grid, list the things that SAVE time. Then, list the things that waste time. Prioritize them on a one to ten basis for both the savers and wasters. Time Savers will be discussed first and then a discussion of Time Wasters will be covered. After that, the results of the personal listings can be matched with the results of over 1,000 principals.

When the lists are complete and prioritized for both SAVERS and WASTERS, turn the page and see what is listed there in three distinctive categories of Personal, Office, and Organizational Time Savers as perceived by over

1,000 principals that have worked this exercise in workshops earlier.

There are many practices which ought to become routinized in routines of self, office, other people, and organizational management. Time Savers can be listed in many categorical groups. They have been listed here as Personal Time Savers, Office Routine Time Savers, and School Position Time Savers using the format established by Dr. Mackenzie. Each management level may interpret these lists differently by habit and bad practices. By grouping the Time Savers, the busy executive can see, by categories, what has to be done to alter his/her style to get more done in the same length of time. In other words, to work smarter and not harder.

On the lists below, there will be a dotted line separating them into two segments to relate what happens to persons in leadership roles once they have been exposed to and learned to follow the self management information in this book. There is a bibliography of selected references on time management later in Part I.

CONSENSUS TIME SAVERS AS LISTED BY 1,000
PRINCIPALS

PERSONAL   OFFICE

Does proper delegating   Uses telephone
Provides complete info.   Schedules availability
Sets priorities   Organizes secretaries
Decides reasonably   Prevents interruptions
Listens and hears   Controls outside demands
Communicates well   Retrieves files well
Takes action timely   Controls paperwork
Makes timely decisions   Expedites mail service
Understands workloads
                SCHOOL
Delegates properly   Develops clear S. P. Bs.
Avoids duplication   Eliminates red tape
No overinvolvement   Staffs properly

73

Manages by exception

. . . .

Handles paper routinely	Separates important/urgent
Provides germane detail	Posts visual tools
Organizes daily routine	Logs mail
Knows limitations	Uses tickler files
Does not delay	Uses collection grids
Spreads workload(s)	Confers with Secretary daily
Allows for teamwork	Routes material
Is a realist-stretches	Uses color/number coding
Remains self-disciplined	Has information retreival sys.
Fosters consistency	Prepares agenda routinely
Assumes blame if needed	Displays Action Demand Charts
Has no special interests	Writes brief papers/letters
Assumes proper control	

SCHOOL

Designs grids properly	Uses planning tools
Hires for strength	Plans employee improvement
Structures all committees	Does long-range plans
Has clear chain of command	Is (de)centralized

    1. How many of the items listed appear on any of the sheets prepared before these lists were read?

    2. How many more ought to be there but were not thought of as time savers?

Once satisfied with a list, the principal needs to spend some time and develop strategies for their continuance and extension. Time savers can be perpetuated best once they are shared with both subordinates and supervisors so they can appreciate the fact that a good technique needs to be followed to save time. If each administrator in the school were to do the same thing, the productivity of the office staff, in general, would be greatly improved as each would soon be assistive to each other.

Typically the time savers listed most easily are those which would be placed on the lists of office and school time savers. Once some training has been done by reading and practicing good time usage in one's personal life as well, that list will be easier to manage.

- TIME WASTERS -

Below is the same type of list as prepared for the time savers. The compilation below is from the work of those same 1,000 high school principals who participated in workshops with the author. If one feels the need to regroup the items to understand them better, it is good to do that early in the reading.

PERSONAL	SCHOOL
Delegation confusion *	No Standard Practice Bulletins
Has personal problems	Upbucking prevails *
Incomplete information	Effort duplicated *
Too many details	Lacks priorities *
Lacks organization *	Poor communication *
Fatigue is obvious	Involves everyone
Makes snap decisions *	Understaffed in management
Fails to listen/hear	Uses committe decisions *
Pet projects emphasized *	Overstaffed
Special interests *	Overcontrolled
Poor Delegation *	Inconsistency *
Procrastination	Poor delegation
Errors-mental/physical	Manages by Crisis *
Unscheduled meetings *	No teamwork
Inability to say NO	Urgent not important *
Postponing decisions *	Lengthy correspondence *
Unrealistic time estimates	Tolerance for sloppy work
Blaming others	No file coding *
Outside activities	Too broad span of control *
Required socialization	No long range plan *
Lack of self-discipline *	
Special interests	

OFFICE

Red Tape abounds	Stacked desks
Telephone abuse *	Routes junk mail
Disorganization *	Allows interruptions *

Poor paperwork mgt.	Inadequate filing*
Delays in information	No file coding
No mail logs used	Drop-ins allowed
Improper schedules	

The items that were able to be eliminated after some concentration on the wasters identified are marked with an asterisk in the list above. This is the list that ruins the use of time. It must be studied. It will take hard work to rid them. By eliminating this list, time savers will increase considerably.

When the time savers have been extended and the time wasters have been eliminated, more time can be set to get at INSTRUCTION -- the prime role of the principal. Don't wait until the lists are fool-proof or it may be too late.

- TIME ORGANIZING -

The biggest item for the principal to work on is to stay away from operating and get to the role of managing. Remember that management is getting things done by and through others and the effective principal must do just that. High school principals need to wear four hats, but the two prime ones are those of the manager and administrator although the hats of supervisor and leader are also important.

Most individuals have the greatest training and experience in the area of teaching or coaching or leading and when asked to manage are a bit frustrated. The magic "cloak" of the principal soon is found not to be magic at all and the adjustment is hard to make.

A good deal of confusion exists between the managing, doing, or operating responsibilities...particularly for new managers or principals. When called upon, the principal is much more at ease with the role of doing than of managing. However, the greater the administrative responsibility, the greater devotion to time and timing must be exercised by the principal to manage, and the least amount of time must be assigned to operating.

Here are some items collected over the years while working with skilled time and self managers:

1. One can always get more financial and personnel resources but not more time --- it must be utilized more efficiently.

2. Nothing is easier than being busy ... the hardest managerial work is thinking. (R. Alec Mackenzie)

3. Alvin Eurich had a sign on his desk which read, "What is your recommendation?"

4. Thomas Prenkert had a sign in his office which read, "If you have nothing to do, please don't do it in here."

5. The cemeteries are full of indispensable people.

6. People who have a half-hour to spend usually spend it with someone who hasn't. (Raymond P. Bottom)

7. We are all losers at time management but some of us are better at it than others. (Terry G. Semones)

8. The heart of management is self management. (Gene E. Megiveron)

9. Time is the scarcest resource and unless it is managed, nothing else can be managed. (Peter Drucker)

10. Paradox of time: Few people have enough; yet everyone has all there is. (R. Alec Mackenzie)

11. There is one kind of robber whom the law does not strike at and who steals what is most precious to man ... time. (Napoleon)

12. Too often a manager is a puppet whose strings are drawn by a crowd of unknown and unorganized people. (Carlson)

13. A man who has taken your time recognizes no debt: yet it is the one he can never repay. (Seneca)

14. Like other resources, time is either managed effectively or it is mismanaged. (R. Alec Mackenzie)

15. I always seem to run out of the day before I run out of things that must be done. (Thomas E. Prenkert)

16. Of a thousand managers polled by Dr. R. Alec Mackenzie, only one in a hundred claims to have enough time.

17. We steal from our schools each time we do something of a lower responsibility than that for which we are being paid. (Gene E. Megiveron)

18. If we are to have our subordinates grow, they must have tasks delegated to them which are challenging and broadening of their skills. (Thomas O. McCormick)

19. To move is to gain; to stand still is to lose; to change is to grow. (Gene E. Megiveron)

20. It is sad to see a man with a potential and misusing it; it is sadder to see a man with a potential and not using it. (Terry G. Semones)

TO ORGANIZE YOUR TIME, ALL YOU HAVE TO DO IS:

Set at least three to five objectives to accomplish every day of the week and then go about getting them done.

Distribute the necessary workload to structure the day before everyone else structures it.

Adopt self management routine outlined in the unit on Planning Your Day.

Evaluate each day, at the end, BEFORE going home whenever possible.

Plan tomorrow today and develop objectives for tomorrow before going home today.

Do an audit at least semi-annually and stay on course with the results as corrected by the evaluation.

- TIME ANALYSIS -

The list below is of twenty-five tasks the high school principal has to perform. There are five tasks taken from each of the five basic roles of the principal during any given day. Check the frequency of performance of each of these tasks and see where the time audit and activities of any given week are aligned.

Once accustomed to the job, one could list ten or more in each category. Use this as a starter list. Keep a log of activities, or refer to Units 8 - 20 and select additional tasks for this survey. The results of a personal task list will be much more significant than any prepared list. The need to personalize the work for the school at this point of time cannot be over-emphasized.

Some good time managers assign the task of recording what they are doing to a subordinate for the audit. This may be fine, but the appreciation of the audit is best felt when the manager records on the form and then assesses it as the time moves along.

If there is a match with the regular time audit and the list below, it may be enlightening to see when the best time of the day or week occurs for the tasks which have to be done throughout the routine of the operation.

```
                                        ┌ANNUALLY
                                         ┌BY SEMESTER
                                          ┌MONTHLY
                                           ┌WEEKLY
                                            ┌DAILY
                                             ┌NEVER
INSTRUCTION                             |
1. Observe clrm instruction            |
2. Work with curr. comms.              |
3. Assist research projs.              |    |  |  |  |  |
4. Conference with dept.
      on programs.     .                |   |  |  |  |  |
5. Work with counselors
      on testing.     .                 |   |  |  |  |  |

COMMUNITY RELATIONS
1. Resolve teacher-parent
      conflicts.      .                 |   |  |  |  |  |
2. Arrange for field trips|             |   |  |  |  |  |
3. Develop a release for
      newspaper.      .                 |   |  |  |  |  |
4. Attend a social mtg.                 |   |  |  |  |  |
5. Go to office of a
      local official.                   |   |  |  |  |  |

BUSINESS/BUILDING MANAGEMENT
1. Analyze budget.   .                  |   |  |  |  |  |
2. Review inventory/order               |   |  |  |  |  |
3. Tour site/plant for
      safety items.  .                  |   |  |  |  |  |
4. Resolve room use.                    |   |  |  |  |  |
5. Review nutrition of
      foods.     .    .                 |   |  |  |  |  |

STUDENTS
1. Meet with student comms|             |   |  |  |  |  |
2. Conduct discipline
      hearing.   .    .                 |   |  |  |  |  |
3. Review honor rolls.                  |   |  |  |  |  |
4. Supervise student
      activities.                       |   |  |  |  |  |
```

80

```
5. Discuss problem census
      results.   .    .      | | | | | |

STAFF
1. Demonstrate new media.  | | | | | |
2. Hold faculty/staff mtg  | | | | | |
3. Interpret new policy    | | | | | |
4. Develop student mark-
      ing process.    .     | | | | | |
5. Publish a curr. newsltr | | | | | |
```

- TIME USE TIPS -

This is a summary of the tips already given in other units. They are listed again because they are perhaps missed when the topic is not directly that of time management.

1. Set and prioritize five daily objectives.

2. Don't list an objective that can be put-off until later.

3. Finish objective before beginning # 2.

4. Record completed tasks on Action Demand Charts, Gantt Charts, PERTs, and CPM material.

5. Arrive early to work and get the objectives prioritized for the day.

6. Locate all material necessary to get OBJECTIVES completed.

7. Organize the day by setting on the desk only those materials needed for accomplishing the identified objectives.

8. Meet with the secretary on a daily basis to go through an established routine.

81

9. Meet at the same time each day.

10. Attend only those meetings that must be attended.

11. Arrange to have different contacts for lunch each day.

12. Make all needed phone calls on schedule.

13. Note which places visits need to be made and record them on the Daily Log.

14. Receive "internal" calls on a schedule.

15. A workable day is designed and planned.

16. Failure to plan is planning to fail.

17. Handle each piece of paper only one time.

18. Do the planning during your best time of day.

19. Screen out needless interruptions.

20. Keep routed material moving along swiftly.

21. Have the secretary keep a collection grid to gain and maintain control of the paperwork.

22. Respond to correspondence as it is received.

23. Number all memo work and keep it in a notebook to make it easy to find.

24. Have the secretary respond to mail at every opportunity.

25. Respond on the original of correspondence whenever possible.

26. File both pieces of correspondence together.

27. Use color coding as an expedient tool for collating results.

28. Log all mail for easy location when needed.

29. Make sure memo work is timely.

30. Control the open door.

31. Learn to skim and scan material. Route it for a more concise treatment.

32. Make sure interruptions are both IMPOR-TANT and urgent.

The discussions above have been designed to prepare for the RIGHT way to handle the sea of semantics to which the principal is exposed. This may help: Tell me, I forget. Show me, I remember. Involve me, I understand.

- TIME AUDITS -

Once a "system" of handling paperwork and people is in place, probably six months into the new (or old) position for the year, be sure to sit back and "smell the roses." In that reassessment, over the long winter holidays, don't ignore the assessment of the use of time in the office. There are good and bad times to do things during the day depending upon the routine others have forced on the office. How the office operates over all is the tone set by the principal. In setting this style, one soon develops a use of time as well. To know whether or not efficiency is being achieved (doing things right), the principal needs to make a deliberate attempt to structure a time audit. The process below works well for a high school principal.

Perhaps the office is doing the running, and the principal is not in charge of the operation. Monday through Friday has little rhyme nor reason for the principal. But an audit needs to be done on some sort of planned schedule. Set the five days that can be scheduled to be "routine" and do the audit. It can last over a period of two weeks if this is best. Some weeks it would be highly impracticable for a high school principal to be concerned about a time audit. What started out as a routine week may have ended in chaos. To prevent this from happening, draw the blanks for one or two weeks and fill-in the information as the week progresses. When all ten half-days are completed, the audit is ready for study.

There is also an added element on the form as drawn below: There is a scheme to evaluate each fifteen minute segment. By doing this, a mathematical formula can be attained to more objectively judge the segment, compounding it to the day and to the week. Here is the form, abbreviated for the sake of space. The day of the high school principal often begins before 7:00 a.m. and ends most assuredly after 5:00 p.m. The form below is only intended to be descriptive of how to do a time audit and not for a typical day -- if there is one in the role of the high school principal. Some cells have been completed for clarity of how to use the form. The names of Semones, Randall, Objective and others are reflective of persons or performances which occur in the day of the principal.

If a: (3) = good purpose for segment
       (2) = not best, but good segment
       (1) = poor use of time segment

Some hints in interpreting and using the Time Audit:

1. If there is a (1), there are two things to consider: Either the (1) was brought about by the person, the object of the conference, or the time of day. So might the (3) rating be responsive to the same criteria. In any respect, the rating is the objective value of the use of the time of day. And the score of (1) is not a good use of that segment for the purpose it was used. If scheduled for that use, consideration may be given to place something else in that segment and try to use the time better than it was used.
======================================

84

MINI TIME AUDIT

	MON.	TUES.	WED.	THURS.	FRI.
7:00	Terry 3| |	Randall | | |1	Obj.#1 | |1	CallSupt | 2|	Semones 3| | |
7:15	Obj.1 |2|	Obj.#1 | 2|	Smith 3| |	Prenkert 3| |	Obj. 1 |2| |
7:30	Balfr | |1	| |	| |	| |	| | |
7:45	| |	| |	| |	| |	| | |
8:00	| |	| |	| |	| |	| | |

==

2. If there is a series of 3's for conferencing, it should indicate that the segment ought to be used for that purpose as much as is practicable until the time of year may alter it.

3. Some work on objectives for the day are done only where there is time. Examine the audit to make sure that the time of day they are worked on is assessed as a (3). If it is, that time needs to be protected to schedule work on the objectives.

4. Move the work around in the schedule so the best time of day is used for each purpose. Once a series of 3's show up in a row, the schedule need not be adjusted but rather protected.

5. The SECRETary can help the principal stay on course once this information is shared. She can control appointments to fit best the principal's schedule instead of everyone else's.

6. Take the little test of items (below) regarding use of time and then review the ratings given for TIME spent on the schedule.

A. The task I enjoy doing the most is:

_____.

B. The task I enjoy doing the least is:

_____.

C. I use my time well when I:

_____.

D. Others waste my time when they:

_____.

E. I waste other's time when I:

_____.

F. I need to delegate the:

_____.

G. My BIGGEST time waster is:

_____.

H. My BIGGEST time saver is:

_____.

I. My most significant task is:

_____.

J. I need to concentrate on:

_____.

When these are answered, a pretty good picture of an ideal day will evolve and the use of time within it will be sharpened.

Dr. R. Alec Mackenzie (131,27) asks nine questions regarding time audit analyzation. They are listed below because they are particularly good ones for the principal to use.

1. Did setting daily goals and times for completing improve my effectiveness? If so, why? If not, why?

2. What was the longest period of time without interruption?

3. In order of importance, which interruptions were most costly?

4. What can be done to eliminate or control them?

   a. Which telephone calls were unnecessary?
   b. Which telephone calls could have been shorter/more effective?
   c. Which visits were unnecessary?
   d. Which visits could have been shorter/more effective?

5. How much time was spent in meetings?

   a. How much was necessary?
   b. How could more have been accomplished in less time?

6. Did I tend to record "activities" or "results"?

7. How many daily goals contributed directly to long-range objective?

8. Did a "self-correcting" tendency appear as I recorded my actions?

9. What two or three steps could I now take to im-

prove effectiveness?

Answer these to become at least a conscious time user, hopefully eliminating time wasters and assuredly improving upon time savers.

- TICKLER FILES -

Tickler files are heavy duty fifth-cut index folders used to store the paperwork soon to inundate the principal. The functions of the folders, called "buckets" from here on, are:

1. To keep the paperwork for the year in a readily accessible place.

2. To contain important information on projects for later use.

3. To replace the piles of papers on the desk or credenza.

4. To hold the work for the day, month, and year in a manageable series of folders.

5. To hold smaller doable tasks in a bit-by-bit format.

6. To hold the daily or monthly work to be done by the secretary.

7. To tickle the memory to get things done on time.

8. To hold reminders of important dates for meetings, conferences, events, reports, contacts, and functions of a busy office.

9. To hold correspondence for later response.

10. To hold notes on calls to make or receive and on people to see.

11. To hold items to read.

12. To hold legal reminders.

13. To hold individual (3 X 5) index cards showing the event (or activity) that needs to be completed when taken from prepared schedules, PERTs, or action demand charts, even a grid or cube used in planning, controlling, or evaluating.

Tickler Files can be put in the office of the secretary, or they can be in the office of the boss. Experience dictates that the secretary is the better keeper of the daily and monthly files.

In order to get the Tickler File to perform in a manner which will be assistive in the office, the principal must buy five dozen fifth-cut heavy index folders. A good source is SMEAD # 405.

S/he will count thirty-one of them and mark them with Arabic numerals 1 to 31 inclusive to represent the days of the month. With one dozen more, the principal can write the names of the months for the fiscal year, July through June. This will use forty-three of the buckets. The others are put off to the side for proper labeling for use as the buckets for the Scintillating Six phase of this program.

To manage that "sea of semantics," lest one drowns, one must have a system. Most use **IN** and **OUT** baskets and leave everything in a pile somewhere in the office with no order whatsoever. A simple means of coding all this

material is to put the Arabic numbers of 1 to 31 in the upper right hand corner of the material as it is being handled. If it is for a specific day, encircle the number which tips the secretary that she is dealing with a piece of information which goes into the DAILY Tickler File.

After an agenda has been planned, a copy of it should be placed in the Tickler File for the date of the meeting. Or if the meeting is early in the morning of that day, one can file the agenda for the day preceding the meeting. All of this type of paperwork should be handled once.

As the secretary completes work during the day, she can put the finished material in the next day's daily Tickler File for disposition - if not noted - and for file, if the project has been handled. She can also place a copy a couple of days ahead of the due date, when appropriate, as a reminder to complete the task or to call a colleague on that date about the deadline set on the memo. This will establish a good relationship between offices and indeed help to ensure that work will not only be done but be done on time.

As for the monthly buckets, the same general application is made. When the material is something which will be done later in the year, a Roman numeral can be placed in the upper right hand corner to denote it is something to go into the monthly Tickler File. These monthly Tickler File buckets hold the major tasks, typically, in their entirety whereas the daily Tickler File hold the segments of the projects once the starting and ending dates of the preparation has been set. The agenda from last year's meetings, minutes, handbooks to be redone, scheduling information, and reports can all be placed into the monthly buckets. When the monthly tickler file contains complete agendas and/or minutes for annual projects, the file becomes indispensible for the busy principal. When the first of the month comes along, the secretary brings along that monthly bucket for the secretarial daily conference. The bucket is gone through and the material coded for a specific day of the month. Then this material is refiled into appropriate daily Tickler Files.

The new fiscal year is pretty well set once the process has been followed for a full cylce. The agenda, reports, etc. are in place and the planning is merely to make sure (because of the earliness of the dates) that the material is filed in the appropriate monthly tickler file. The PERTs when developed can be segmented into monthly buckets and the event cards appropriately filed into the daily bucket as the first of the month comes about.

The following is a mini-exercise to help develop skills in the application of the paperwork package just presented. The dates and hypothetical (albeit real from one day of actual application) items enhance the discussion and by application will make the material understandable.

Today is Monday, August 17th. The secretary is in the office to hold the daily conference. By the end of the week, according to the note in the tickler, a letter must be sent to all returning staff about an orientation schedule and the school calendar for the year. A note should be put into Wednesday's Tickler File, (19) to write the letter and get it in the mail before the end of the working day. (Now with the expansive use of the personal computers, each letter can be personalized by merging the names and addresses to the regular letter with appropriate changes in each letter). The letter used last year (located in the monthly bucket for August) was returned today in the tickler file as a reminder. When completed on the 19th, the secretary will place a copy in the August monthly tickler file so next year's letter will be easy to prepare. It will come back on the 1st of August for determination as to when to work on it.

The second piece of information to handle is a vacation plan for this month. The daily tickler file must be cleared for those dates and work done either before the vacation starts or immediately after it is over.

The third piece to discharge is a budget adjustment request from the central office. It should be placed in the October bucket if the information is to be based upon the membership count when school opens. The district's requirements can be determined now so this item will be appropriately filed).

The fourth piece of correspondence is a letter of resignation from one of the faculty. This should be put in the EXPEDITE folder (one of the scintillating six) to be handled today as soon as the conference is ended. The secretary needs to call the Personnel Director with this information and get direction as to the next steps to take to get this position filled.

A fifth piece of information is a request from another school for the records of the students of the Jones family, with no date of birth, past address, or any information to get the proper records to them. This either can be placed in the daily Tickler File that will be available when the Guidance Director reports, or the secretary should be instructed to call the school to get the proper information and then the letter can be placed in the daily Tickler File for the Guidance Director's use when s/he reports back on Monday. A (24) is placed in the upper right hand corner, and it is put away.

The sixth piece is a report from the summer school principal. The report shows which students completed work and the grades received. The Guidance Director will need these data for scheduling. Unless there is something unusual, the information ought to be handled routinely.

The seventh piece is a letter from a company scheduling assembly programs for high school students. This can be placed in the bucket for November |XI| to be dealt with by the student committee on activities when it convenes to plan next year's assembly program -- that is -- if the current year is already planned as it should be. If not, it can be placed in the Orientation bucket to refer it to the chairperson of the committe when s/he comes in for preregistration.

This completes the mini-exercise to learn to handle various pieces of information. It showed the use of the monthly buckets and the daily tickler files. Only practice will make this system easy to handle. And, of course, the whole paperwork package system consists of several parts. The tickler file is the stem of the plan so careful adherence to the rules of this part is most necessary.

- SCINTILLATING SIX -

To establish these files, or buckets, the principal will need to use the remainder of the Smead 405's. There are seventeen of these "buckets" left to use. Six can be used (just for the secretary) to initiate this phase of paperwork control. There are enough "buckets" to label for two sets should both the principal and the secretary wish to have a set of the Scintillating Six buckets. In any respect, these words should be used to label the folders:

F	ILE
A	CTION
R	OUTE
M	EETINGS
E	XPEDITE
R	EVIEW

The acronym FARMER will help you to remember the topics.

During the daily conference with the secretary (please read additional material on this conference later in this unit) when going through both the internal and external mail, there are some things that won't necessarily fit in either set of Tickler Files for daily or monthly consideration. In these cases, the principal or his secretary can use the FARMER buckets, affectionately referenced as the scintillating six.

Here is a breakdown of the types of material that go into each of the six buckets:

FILE:

These can be coded with an (F) in the upper right hand corner of the sheet and be given back to the secretary. Or the principal can confirm the code if the secretary has already gone over the mail before she brings the buckets for the conference.

Anything that is completed but is needed for later reference goes in here. The only danger here is "pack ratting" material. *One must be selective on what gets saved.* (Please read later in this unit the material on filing to understand clearly what is being said.)

ACTION:

The usual items can be placed in here. This includes those which are coded with a daily Tickler File reference as an indicator as to when they need to be completed, either with a (4) = daily, the 4th, or a (IV) = monthly, April, remember? This bucket is a most vital tool. It is the keystone to this whole package. Among the items to place in it, are:

Meeting notices to attend and/or prepare.
Bills to pay ahead of their due dates.
Notes to get back later for more time to review
    them.
In this case, place a numeral in the corner so it can
    be put in the proper daily bucket when the
    conference is concluded with the secretary.
Collected material after it has been pulled together.
Memo work that needs to be typed - either hand-
    written or taped.
Notes as to calls to make.
Places to visit.
Conferences to be scheduled.
Signed correspondence and other miscellany.

In other words, this is the "TO DO" bucket of old, but it is treated daily and emptied when the conference material has been gone over. When the secretary comes in, she will have all unfinished work from the previous day and all completed work in the bucket. In this way the secretarial objectives can be set for the day in ranked order in the ACTION bucket when she leaves.

ROUTE:
　　When items are to be circulated, a significant and routine route (Unit 2, later) should be developed for them to follow. Items to be placed in this bucket, for or during the conference, are:

Correspondence	Memos, typed and signed
Journal articles	Merchandise flyers
Reminders	Conference/convention flyers
Requests for data	Meeting agenda/minutes

　　In this bucket will be placed only those items which need to be routed. Some pieces may be circulated, and some may be circularized.

MEETINGS:
　　Primarily agenda items or material to backup or support an item are placed in the bucket. (The secretary can "subdivide" the bucket with a regular manila folder for each meeting responsibility, especially those being chaired.)　When the material has to be placed in the bucket during the conference, she can easily place it in a specific folder. When the day comes about to prepare the agenda for the meeting to be chaired, the secretary is all set to prepare the initial draft by using the contents of the folder with very little further direction. There will be announcements, action items, discussion items, handouts, updates, etc. See Unit 4 on agenda preparation.

EXPEDITE:
　　Into this folder should be placed that singular item that is to be done first -- before anything else is to be processed by the secretary.

REVIEW:

In this bucket will be placed those reports that are lengthy or articles that need to be read, back-up material for report preparation - or items the secretary is to scan. If the secretary needs to review material before its next disposition, whether it is route, action, or file, it is placed in here. On these sheets put the secondary location, like (F) = File, but it is placed in the Review bucket. She, after scanning the material, follows the secondary disposition noted on the paper.

Once the secretary learns how to handle the FARMER, she will wonder what she did before she had the system in place.

- SECRETARIAL CONFERENCING -

To the high school principal, the secretary is the most important person in the building. The job is tough, demanding, never-ending, and fills the most significant role in the building. Many questions come to the secretary in the course of any given day. Many times the principal cannot be available at a key moment, and the secretary sets the tone of the high school's program with her charm, knowledge, and answers. *It is imperative that the principal keep the secretary informed of all aspects of the TOTAL school program.* To do this best, the principal needs to meet with the secretary at least once each day in a formal, noninterrupted conference. The conference is best held when external demands are the fewest. A good time to meet is around 8:30 a.m. By this time, all students and teachers are in their rooms. They are busy in the instructional process. The mail has been delivered. The assistants are busy in the attendance process. The custodians are cleaning the corridors after school has opened. This is the appropriate time to set for the conference. At least thirty minutes should be set to get the day organized and share what needs to be done in the scheme of things, that is if the hours in the high school don't follow this sign which was posted in a Dallas business office:

====================================

OFFICE HOURS

OPEN most days about 8 or 9
occasionally as early as 7,
but some days as late as 12 or 1.

WE CLOSE about 5 or 5:30....
occasionally about 4,
but sometimes as late as 11 or 12.

Other days or afternoons we aren't here at all . . .
and lately we've been here just about all the time.

Except when we are someplace else,
but we should be here then, too.

THE MANAGEMENT
====================================

To make sure the secretary is as productive as she must be, the same specific time each day should be set to help get her organized. This will assure her that she will be doing those things which priorities dictate. If there are two secretaries assigned, the principal must meet with them both. If there are more than two secretaries, the principal can meet with the Office Manager. She will then distribute the work according to the skills of the staff when the conference is concluded.

STEPS IN THE CONFERENCE

1. *Exchange the contents of the ACTION bucket.* These buckets contain the work for the day as pointed out in the unit on Scintillating Six earlier in this chapter. One thing to add, perhaps, is that the bucket should contain all

the work undone from yesterday's conference forward until this conference. Remember, as in objective setting, the item not completed yesterday, may not be a priority item for today -- or it could well go into the EXPEDITE bucket. The main issue is that each item needs to be gone over in the morning to set the workload of the day properly.

2. *Check the day's schedules of both the principal and the secretary* so that both have identical items posted for conferences, meetings, phone calls, visits, and so forth. The principal can use the Daily Log notes as an aid for this.

3. *Check the next four days on the calendar* so that the next full week will be reviewed. (Even though the secretary does "all" of the scheduling, there are times that appointments need to be made when she is not available.) This check of schedules prevents double scheduling which, if done, can be rectified more easily early in the day.

4. *Assign the TICKLER file items for today.* The work that was placed in this bucket needs to be addressed. By checking it carefully, it will be more likely fit into the scheme of things.

5. *Go over the "inhouse" and external mail* received since the last meeting (yesterday!). When collecting information from several sources in response to a request, be sure to use the half page form to notify the sender that his/her mail was received. The secretary can fill this in easily when it is received. By then placing it in the folder with the others, it is easy to mark it on the collection grid before the conference so the principal will have a full prospective of the returns which have been received.

6. *Set/review/share personal objectives for the day* to make sure the "right arm" is aware of the priorities.

7. *Go over the innerworkings of the office* to hear the worthwhile "trivia" about peers or subordinates. (Not to the extent that Lyndon B. Johnson went though.) At times, the secretary can forewarn of attitudes of some of the staff

for their perceived good reasons. A personal "drop-in"
visit may just help heal the problem.

8. *Go through the other Scintillating Six buckets* in
order of their file space.

When all is done with the papers, *arrange the contents in the ACTION bucket according to priority* so that the
first thing to be completed is on top of the bucket as it is
opened.

HINTS

Here are some salient points about these conferences:

1. Follows a preplanned agenda.
2. Is held daily.
3. Is scheduled at the most appropriate time.
4. Is held at the same time each day.
5. Should never be interrupted -- if at all possible.

DISCUSSION OF THE HINTS

1. Follows a preplanned agenda -- The line-up to go
through daily is covered in the list of nine items above.

2. Is held daily -- This fact should not be ignored. It
is a simple truth that this is vital, and, therefore, if the office operation is to become organized, the conference must
be held.

3. Is scheduled at the proper time of the day. --
Once the mail delivery time is routinized, the time of the
day can be set. Most bosses prefer to get at it first thing in
the morning, but there are those who feel the last thing at
night is the best time to meet and review what went on to
plan the next day. It is dependent on style or personal
time clock or the uncontrolled innerworkings of the building. There is no absolute time for the conference to be
held. The most comfortable time is the best time.

4. Is held at the same time each day. -- It is important to be consistent whenever plausible. It is significant that this conference be held at the same time because those in the innerworkings of the office will respect this and not interrupt if avoidable. It is easy to schedule the conference if both parties know when it will occur. Because the external mail comes in at different times of the day, it is convenient if the mail is brought to the principal's secretary as soon as possible so it can be sorted and readied for the conference whenever it is scheduled to be held. However, this may not be plausible. In these cases, the secretary will soon learn to scan the mail and open just those pieces which are likely to need immediate attention. The rest can wait for the morning conference. The best time found for this conference to be held is the first thing in the day: always meet at 8:30 if the office opens at 8:00.

5. Should never be interrupted -- if at all possible. Once this conference becomes part of a standard day, persons in the building will respect the time and not use the phone to contact office personnel, schedule meetings, or come in for a "drop-in" conference. The idea is to get objectives set and the day planned for the staff. Typically in an office of several units, this practice spreads swiftly so this does not become a conflict with any single person's office.

To complete this section, here is the routine the secretary goes through when she returns to her desk. The secretary:

1. Examines and completes the EXPEDITE folder's contents.

2. Takes the ROUTE bucket to the mail center and distributes all items to appropriate mailboxes. (Please read the unit on the Scintillating Six to develop this routine).

3. Opens the ACTION bucket and works at it from the top-most item through to the last item.

4. FILES when a break in the routine is needed or when her day is not at its highest efficiency quotient. (Yes, secretaries have personal time clocks to honor as well as the principal).

5. REVIEWS bucket contents and disposes of it.

6. Sorts the contents of the MEETING bucket into the proper sub-folders. When time permits, she can add to the roughed-out agenda in each folder so that on the day these are to be distributed they can be brought into the boss for the secretarial conference.

Maybe it is summed here as in a principal's office, a secretary had this sign posted. It caused students to grin and relax.

RATE SCHEDULE

Answers $1.00

Answers which require thought $2.00

Correct Answers $4.00

Dumb looks are still free !

- PHONE USAGE -

Nine chances out of ten this "little black box" will be responsible for the abuse of time in which one had already planned to do something different than to talk to someone who has a need. There are many ways to learn to use this instrument of destruction. The effective principal soon learns to control it rather than have it become the controller.

HINTS TO FOLLOW IN USING THE PHONE

1. *The secretary should place all calls and answer the phone.* Many times the secretary can respond to the question or the call is for her anyway as other secretaries work their way through their respective days. This routine saves valuable time, and then it can be used much more fruitfully. Good phone use is a first step in proper delegating. If the secretary does not know how to screen calls properly, it remains the boss's fault and not hers. Some training by the phone company will be ever so assistive to her. When she makes the calls, it saves time. If the party is not there and a call-back is mandatory, personal time or routine will not be interrupted until a positive contact has been made.

2. *A specific time of day to receive calls from inside the building or the district should be set.* The principal must be available at that time to receive the calls. From experience, the best times to reserve for taking incoming calls are as follows: the first half-hour of the day, the last half-hour before lunch, and the last half-hour of the day. It is amazing at the brevity of calls when the caller has somewhere else to be -- and soon. This will save valuable time. Socializing on the phone is inappropriate during the busy instructional day, irrespective of who makes the call.

3. Meetings are sometimes held out of the office, other offices must be visited, and classrooms need to be visited. The principal needs to *tell the secretary where the meeting (or whatever) is being held and, more importantly, when the outside contact will be completed so the office will be covered again* so she can have calls returned or messages completed as contacts are made with her. This will save precious time. A clue was just mentioned here -- *STOP having the secretary tell people they will be called back.* This is the biggest time-trap. Instead, the secretary can ask the caller to call again when the schedule shows the call can be taken. It can go something like this: "Dr. Megiveron is out right now but will be back at his desk from 4:00 to 5:00. Could you please call him around 4:10 this afternoon?" The 4:10 time is **scheduled** as a conference. This will control the making of double appointments. It is not being

rude but primarily informative, and the skill of handling the caller grows as it is practiced. Failure to be available for the call-back is rude. The principal must be there when the secretary has scheduled the call to be returned. Thus, the importance of sharing precisely where the meeting is and the time of return becomes obvious when the principal leaves the office. This procedure is guaranteed to:

a. Cut down on the number of calls received because frequently the caller does not call back at a later time.

b. Allow the management of personal time on the phone.

c. Permit time to do other things outside of the office.

d. Complete the conversation if the caller does make a second call.

e. Eliminate the feelings of others that the principal hasn't returned their call even though the contact was attempted and they were not available. When involved in this situation, to them, the call was not returned.

4. *HOLD buttons should be avoided.*. Gads, this is frustrating. Better yet, when the secretary is placing the call, the principal will get on the phone as soon as the call is going through. The secretary can give a signal so the phone can be picked up as soon as the two secretaries have exchanged messages and the callee is being put on the phone by the second secretary. Ron Arnold's secretary used to tell me, "Mr. Arnold would like to talk to you," and then I would wait for her to get Ron to the phone. It was irritating to me. Therefore, when she used to say, "Mr. Ron Arnold would like to talk to you," I would

say "Thank you" and hang-up. After a couple of these exchanges, the lesson was learned, and when I got the message from my secretary that Ron was on the phone and switched to that line, he was on the line. This saved the two of us much time.

5. *If alone, after regular hours and the secretary is gone for the day, take the phone off the hook when the office will be empty for a few moments* . When an incoming call comes in, it will register as a busy signal. When the office is again occupied, the callback can be answered. It is far better than to have callers let it ring eight or nine times and think that the principal is not there and has left early.

6. *If the conversation is eroding into a one-way shouting match*, the principal should hang up on himself/herself. If the caller is really uptight, hollering and abusive, as soon as s/he can be interrupted, the principal should do so. S/he might interject that as soon as possible the conversation ought to be brought to a summary because the phone has been acting ..... and while talking, reach over and press the phone hook. If the call comes back, the caller can be reminded of the phone problem. If the caller is still abusive, the principal will hang up again as soon as s/he is doing the talking. If the caller gets hung up on when talking, it may well be double trouble. Seldom will the caller call back the third time. There is no reason to take verbal abuse on the phone. Nothing can be resolved that way so it is better to blame the abruptness of the end of the conversation on technology.

7. *Telephones should not be overused.* There seldom is an accurate record of what transpires on it. Unless there is a follow-up note to the caller of file, the agreements reached are hard to reference later. A file reference is always handy and should be made. For completeness of this form of communication, it is good to send the first copy to the other party so the communication can be verified. This need not be a long report, but a solid summary is vital. A copy of the report is shown below.

The form will help the principal to recall important items that transpire during the busy day whether the contact is in the office or on the phone. The key is to fill it in immediately upon returning to the office or getting off the phone. (The subunit on "Managing the Boss" shows a direct application.) The concern here is to remain informed and PUT IT IN WRITING. Once this process is followed, the files will soon be a valuable asset.

==

- CONTACT FORM -

Discussion re:_____ Date: __/__/__

Type of Contact: Phone _____ Meeting _____
Conference _____ Other _____

Location: _____

Persons Involved:

_____
_____

Items Covered:

_____
_____
_____

Further Action Necessitated:

_____
_____

Distribution To: By:_____

_____
_____
_____

file locater: ___ ___ ___ ___ ___
==

- CORRESPONDENCE, INCOMING AND OUTGOING -

To understand that there are time savers in this arena, the principal must be cognizant of the whole package. Correspondence is but one more means of becoming efficient in the operation of the high school. Here is a discussion of the better means for handling correspondence.

HINTS TO GO BY

1. *Respond directly on the copy received as frequently as is practicable* -- especially on the inhouse documents. (Be sure it has been logged in.) By having only one sheet of paper, filing space and time has been cut in half. Responding on the original sheet of paper usually forces brevity. Most short responses are sufficient. Hand written notes are effective and quick to complete the task. The secretary does not have to do any work on the response except copy it for filing. The one-shot photo copy will get both the request and response filed after being properly coded.

2. *Respond to letters the same day they are received.* It is far better to get correspondence completed and returned than it is to delay and eventually forget to send a response.

A rule to follow is to handle paperwork only once. To respond to letters or memos the day they are received is an excellent practice.

3. *Be on the alert for back-dated letters*! It is always good to date (and time) stamp all incoming correspondence -- and the outgoing responses for a reference later. Some agencies like to back-date mail and then call saying they sent a letter a couple of weeks ago and haven't received a response which is supposed to put guilt on the receiver. If the mail is logged in, a response is available. If there is no log for incoming or outgoing mail, it is easy to become defensive and at their mercy. *In management this*

is one more way to become defensible and not have to be on the defensive.

4. When material is circulated or circularized and a response is needed, *an additional copy should be put in the appropriate Tickler File.* This note will remind the principal to verify that the original letter has been handled.

5. *It is always good to number correspondence serially* (rather innocuously) and keep a set in a notebook. If a copy is placed in a notebook, it is more difficult to misplace the file copy. It is good to affix (staple) responses to the originals. Then the whole set of correspondence is in one place. On correspondence where only one side of the paper was used, it is good to photocopy the response on the reverse side for file purposes.

6. When correspondence simply cannot be responded to immediately, *a confirmation note should be sent.* A half-page form showing that the material has been received and what the disposition is at the time is presented below.

By putting the form, on the next page, in the mail immediately, the sender knows his/her information has been received. It's a polite way of dealing with people. The secretary can have a ready supply of these forms which she brings to the daily scheduled conference. Send this form immediately upon receiving the correspondence especially when it was requested or when this is but one return of a series expected.

7. *Most correspondence can be responded to by the secretary* with little, if any, prompting. The principal must trust her and have confidence in what she can do. Some secretaries actually enjoy preparing the correspondence replies or letters. The main point of this discussion is that correspondence can be completed more quickly if the secretary does not have to take dictation or read handwriting. (Both are time wasters.) And the principal doesn't need to spend the time to do something which the secretary can do very well.

===================================

CORRESPONDENCE RECEIPT CONFIRMATION

To: _____ Date__/__/__
From: Dr. Gene E. Megiveron
Subject: Your Memo #__ - __, dated __/__/__

1. Date Received ___/___/___ .
2. Disposition:

(__) Filed - No action Taken

(__) Held Until __/__/___ .

(__) Returned herewith, no further infor-
      mation needed.

(__) Routed to _____ for
      response.

(__) Needs to be compiled with other
      material; answer expected no
      later than ___/___/___ .

(__) Placed on the agenda for:
(__) General Staff Meeting (__) Ad-
      ministrative Council

(__) Department Chair Meeting (__/__/__)

(__) Secondary Admin. Council Meeting

(__) Endorsed as (dis)approved and for-
      warded to:_____

GEM/joe
===================================

    8. *Brevity is a key word in correspondence.* Apply
what has already pointed out earlier. A couple of moments set aside for planning will save threefold the time

108

for execution. No one ever got more credit for using more words than necessary.

9. *Responses to letters and memos can be delegated.* Frequently, the secretary will not have to go to others for information. The response may be within her area of responsibility. Or a subordinate may be able to develop the response. Letter writing should be delegated whenever possible or prepared for the principal.

10. *Time must be set aside to process all correspondence.*

11. *A response not made is actually a response.*

12. *Routed material must move very quickly.* It is sent according to the prescribed route.

13. *Avoid the use of personal pronouns in correspondence.* The pronouns to avoid are: WE, OUR, I, MY or MINE.

SUMMARIZING TIPS:

File in notebook or cabinet daily.
Use brief responses.
Negative responses are helpful.
Allow others to respond.
Respond on the original.
Number correspondence.
Allow secretary to respond.
Move routing swiftly.
Set a time for writing.
Initially skim/scan.
Stamp/log all mail.
Send receipt form.
Let the secretary prepare responses.
File letters/responses together.
Log all correspondence.

"It is better to have responded and erred than never to have responded at all!" Terry G. Semones

This means of communication is widely used in the principalship. Also, it is too often a poorly used means of communication by too many people. What needs to thought about in the preparation of any memo, primarily, is the receiver and how the message will be received. Here is an example of an OLD memo which apparently did not work.

===================================

MEMO RE: Recent statements to the press
TO: Her Majesty Queen Marie Antoinette
FROM: M. Reynaud, Reynaud Associates, Inc. Public
            Relations Experts
DATE: October 17, 1989

As you know, we're getting a lot of flack in the press about your recent off-the-cuff comment on the poor people of Paris. I know they bug you but "Let them eat cake" was just a little on the flip side as an answer to their request for bread.

In the future, I hope you'll give us a buzz before an important press conference so we can avoid any more boo-boos.

In these tough times, Marie, baby, the important thing is to keep your cool and not lose your head.

Marcel.
===================================

PROPER DEVELOPMENT

Once one is aware and conscious of the receiver, concern about three major facets of the proper development of a memo are next. These are:

1. What is the expectation?

2. Why the expectation?
3. What do you expect to be done about it?

To add to this, Mr. Terry G. Semones, an excellent administrator, once wrote this to use in an inservice program about memo work which floats around without proper preparation being given.

A memo is an innocent note.
Or so it appears when it is "wrote."
But closer inspection may lead to rejection
And cause a large lump in the throat!

AN ACTUAL MEMO:

The words enclosed in parentheses on the following memo were not on the original but are here for edification. Hopefully, by application, one can see the significance of the format and appreciate the brevity.

=================================
To: Dr. Seymour Samuels, Ass't. Supt. for Student Services
                                                    12/12/79
From: Dr. Gene E. Megiveron, Supt.   GEM #915
Subj: Liaison With T.R.A.P. (Truants, Runaways, And
                          Parents)

(expectation) Hopefully you will prepare your workload distribution and calendar so that you can attend the first and continuing meetings of this new group of parents and students concerned with truancies and runaways. The group is taking affirmative action through their individual failures/successes. It is mandatory that we have an agent of the school present -- preferably from your division -- and you, in person, if at all practicable. Until we know the sum and substance of the intent as being acted upon, not merely talked about, it would be appreciated if you worked with the new group.

(why) I feel we need to be represented by a trained psychologist with a child advocacy spirit. Our central administration, as an organization of student advocates, can

111

little afford to ignore a positve group (if indeed they are positive) helping kids in our beautiful city. Your personal attendance is significant because of the clout your office can carry in responses to concerns about our dedication.

(What) Please respond to this memo after you have called Mrs. Plutz, president, at 555-1212 and gone over the framework of the organization. You may be able to suggest a role we can fill.

It is vital for the superintendent to know the calendar of meetings and goals of the group. The news release was not particularly clear when I read the item in last night's paper.

Thanks, Seymour
cc: TF21/file TRAP/Bd. Letter
= =

Here are some statements to be assistive in preparing memos that work.

1. Know the recipient's style. Would a phone call or conference be better?

2. Be calm when writing a memo. "Cool off" before sending it.

3. Is the purpose to lecture, give a message, or make a request?

4. Develop a background if necessary to communi cate the message.

5. Make them brief, to the point, and necessary.

6. Be sure the subject is pertinent.

7. Use everyday language, not ponderous, polysyl- labic nonsense.

8. Be concerned about whether or not the person is a new or experienced subordinate. This goes

back to item # 1 above.

9. Write it to the position but don't ignore the person. Sometimes it makes a difference if one knows the recipient, but it is better yet to know how s/he operates.

10. Do not make it too brusque or too soft.

11. Be available to the recipient when the memo is received in case there is a question left unresolved in the content.

12. The message to get across is that a memo ought to reflect the sender because the sender needs to be perceived consistently.

13. Be sure it is dated when *sent* and not the date it was prepared. This is significant and should not be overlooked.

14. The format for a memo's heading as used for the memo sent to Dr. Samuels needs to be the standard format. Included are To, From, Date, Number, and Subject.

15. Communicate, communicate, communicate.

CONTENT HINTS

Dr. Carroll Munshaw, Professor Emeritus of Educational Administration at Wayne State University, gave the following advice a long time ago for writing memos.

1. Words should not exceed 3 syllables.

2. Sentences should not exceed 11 - 15 words.

3. Paragraphs should not be more than 3 sentences in length.

By experience, the author has added the following to Dr. Munshaw's list.

4. Memos should not exceed 3 - 5 paragraphs.

5. Written material should be kept to a single page whenever possible.

GUIDELINES

And to help even more, here are some guidelines developed through working with teachers over the years:

1. Introductory material should not exceed one-half page.

2. Summary and observation material should not be more than two pages.

3. Evaluative and report material should not exceed three to five pages.

Finally, the principal needs to bear in mind that no one can solve a problem once s/he becomes part of it. It is unwise to trap oneself or the receiver by what is said in a memo. If this is the very best way to communicate with that person, at that time, with the current circumstance, and his/her best style, then go ahead and write the memo. Don't just do it without thought. Consider the options before using this means of communication. Some people do best when talked to in person or being called on the phone, or written a memo or by going to their office or by having them come to the principal's. GET TO KNOW THE STAFF AND ACT ACCORDINGLY!

- UNIT THREE INTRODUCTION -
Structuring One's Own Niche

Unit 03 is steeped with information on becoming a singular individual and not just another one of the crowd. To establish one's own identity is a challenge. The busy principal must be able to wear four hats during the course of a few minutes. The hats are those of the manager, administrator, leader, and supervisor. The subunits in this unit are as follows and it begins with the four hats:

Management	Task Cards
Administration	Managing the Boss
Leadership	Conferencing
Supervision	Meetings
Table of Organization	Committees
Job Descriptions	Ranking of Priorities
(De)Centralization	Bldg. Safety Features

The four hats are most important in order to understand some of the rest of the material so they will be examined first. The definitions are given in the material but planned redundancy is often called reinforcement. Here are the isolated definitions for clarity.

MANAGEMENT is the skill to get things done by and through others.

ADMINISTRATION is the skill to direct others in the accomplishment of the institution's goals.

LEADERSHIP is the skill to assist others in the accomplishment of the group's goals.

SUPERVISION is the skill to assist others in improving upon their abilities.

With this differentiation in mind, it is easy to see how observation and evaluation are in conflict with the principal's roles. The other two roles are the means of accomplishing those administrivia that are necessary. The result is a finite line between roles. It is easy to do when the principal understands each as separate roles and then quickly merges them into the single role which is that of being the building principal. It is easy to understand that the biggest, direct role of the principal is that of supervision. Within this role, the most significant part is that of observation of the classroom instruction program. The subunit on supervision is written so that the principal can get some perspective on the role and do a much better job than s/he has been doing. The crux of the subunit is covered in the Exhibit area, where a complete observation form is included for reference to get it all done properly. To do observations properly, there are goals to be set for curriculum and instruction. An outline of a process is given from the Board of Education down to the building level. The process is important so substitution may be made if the building wants to work unilaterally. The emphasis here is on supervision as well, and the goal setting covered in other places is for the individual.

If there is no organizational chart, a Table of Organization must be developed for the building. Everyone should know the proper route for personnel to follow to expedite systematic transactions involving the principal, assistant principals, departmental chairmen, custodial hierarchy, secretarial grouping, and other staff members.

It is difficult to ascertain whether the Table of Organization or the job descriptions are completed first. In some respects the job descriptions can reflect the organized table of organization and in other situations, one needs to know how the organization is going to work before good job descriptions can be developed. It is wise to examine the availability of job descriptions with personnel in the central office, in the files the predecessor was using, the building handbook, building manual, or with the assistants who were in the program last year. It is crucial that each job description is written clearly with definitive

116

responsibilities delineated. These descriptions will reflect whether or not the philosophy of the building operation will be centralized or decentralized.

Whether or not to centralize or decentralize the administration of the high school is the option of the principal. The skills to master the roles necessary to fill the position of the principal change somewhat with this contrasting philosophy of operation. The object of the principal is to get the job done and ensure that all the students get the best possible education they can get. This subunit will help the principal decide in which manner s/he wishes to operate.

Task Cards ensure communication will be had between the principal and his/her assistants and staff. The task card is the best manner to bring about controlled work in the environment. These cards should be filed in the appropriate tickler file according to the project's commencement date. Then after the work is underway, they should be relocated to the file dated within a week of the project's estimated time of completion. This helps the principal to get work done on time and in the priority set earlier in the year. S/he can determine what each subordinate is doing in the next couple of days and whether or not new tasks can be delegated.

Managing the boss is a requisite for planning and operational style development. This is most easily accomplished by establishing set lines of responsibility and authority.

The principal confers a great deal. It is a special skill and so is written about separately. Conferences are not meetings or committees but are in fact a different set of circumstances which call for specific skills.

Meetings are usually stultifying in schools. Meetings are called because they are scheduled. Meetings, too, need to carefully planned. A good rule to follow is one which says that if the agenda for the next day's meeting is not in the staff mailboxes by the time they go home on the preceding day, there will be NO meeting. If not planned, it is better not to hold a meeting.

Committees are fine. Committees are good. Committees are a fool-proof means of getting convergence on issues by a representative group of staff. If a committee is structured properly -- before the fact -- it can be helpful. Some detailed work is outlined to make them effective.

How to decide what to do first is sometimes a real bore and borders on frustration. Here is a means to solve that problem. It works easily and takes very little time to complete. When done properly, it will force priorities to be set. At the bottom of the chart, when tallies are completed, the dozen or so categories will have been ranked by the forced choices made. It is drawn to make ten selections. Twenty items on a single grid can be prioritized with a great deal of success and as few as five or six can also be ranked. The beauty of the design is that the user is only ranking one object against a single other in each step of the process. More than twenty and fewer than five does not work well. It is a handy tool.

One of the roles of the school is that of custodialship of the students. The safety factors in the building are the responsibility of the principal. This subunit will address this most significant issue so that some ideas on what it is that needs to be examined will be carefully detailed.

- MANAGEMENT -
"Getting Things Done BY and THROUGH Others"

There is a great number of experts in the field of management. Some advocate "one minute management." Some are corporate consultants, and some are "paying their dues" by holding seminars wherever they can get ten people to sit all day and listen to the message from the hill.

One who has continued to write and present to stay in a leadership role over the past years is Dr. R. Alec Mackenzie. The author's first contact with Dr. Mackenzie was as one of the twenty-five persons attending the invitational Seminar on Relevance in Mobile, Alabama. Dr. Mackenzie is an expert known world-wide for his management skills. He has written extensively in books and in leading journals and has made presentations in countries as far away as Australia. The explanation below is a continuation of the part already covered in the subunit on Planning. (132,80)

- THE MANAGEMENT PROCESS - consists of three distinct ELEMENTS: ideas, things, and people. The section on ideas has been covered earlier.

The tasks of *things* fall into the area of ADMINISTRATION = Manage details of executive affairs. And the tasks for *people* fall into the area of LEADERSHIP = Influencing people to accomplish desired goals.

The continuous function of *Administration* is to make decisions = Arrive at conclusions and judgments. The continuous function of *Leadership* is to communicate = Ensure understanding.

The sequential function of *Administration* is to organize = Arrange and relate work for effective accomnplishment of objectives, and the sequential function of *Leadership* is to STAFF = Choose competent people for positions in the organization, to DIRECT = Bring about purposeful action toward desired objectives, and to CONTROL = Ensure progress toward objectives.

There are certain and definable activities which need to be addressed in good management. Mackenzie describes them as follows:

The activities for *organizing* include establishing organizational structure, delineating relationships, creating position descriptions, and establishing position qualifications. The activities for *staffing* are to select, orient, train,

119

and develop. The activities for *directing* are delegating, motivating, coordinating, managing the differences, and managing the changes. The activities necessary for *controlling* are to establish reporting systems, to develop performance standards, to measure results, to take corrective actions, and to reward.

Here are Mackenzie's definitions of the long list of terms just introduced. Because the list is so long, these definitions are categorized according to function.

Organizing

Establish organization structure = draw up organizational chart
Delineating Relationships = defining liaison lines to facilitate coordination
Create position descriptions = define scope, relationships, responsibilities, and authority
Establish position qualifications = define qualifications for persons in each position

Staffing

Select = recruit qualified people for each position.
Orient = familiarize new people with the situation.
Train = make proficient by instruction and practice.
Develop = help improve knowledge, attitude, and skills.

Directing

Delegating = assigning responsibility and exact accountability for results.
Motivating = persuade and inspire people to take desired action.
Coordinating = relating efforts in most effective combination.
Managing differences = encourage independent thought and resolving conflict.
Managing change = stimulate creativity and innovation in achieving goals.

120

Controlling

Establishing reporting systems = determine what critical data are needed, how, and when.

Develop performance standards = set conditions that will exist when key duties are well done.

Measure results = Ascertain extent of deviation from goals and standards.

Take corrective action = adjust plans, counsel to attain standards, replan and repeat cycle.

Reward = Praise, remunerate and discipline.

= =

In the original diagram by Mackenzie (132,80) the process is shown in an oval [a bowl] of information with concentric circles, each carrying a row as projected above. Therefore, Dr. Mackenzie uses the terms "at the center."

Dr. Mackenzie ascertains, ".... in education ... it is possible to have an outstanding manager who is not capable of leading people but who, if he recognizes this deficiency, will staff his organization to compensate for it. Alternatively, an entrepreneur may possess charismatic qualities as a leader, yet may lack the administrative capabilities required for overall effective management; and he too must staff to make up for the deficiency.

"We are not dealing here with leadership in general. We are dealing with leadership as a function of management. Nor are we dealing with administration in general but, again, as a function of management.

"The following definitions are suggested for clarity and simplicity:

Management -- achieving objectives through others.

Administration -- managing the details of executive affairs.

121

Leadership -- influencing people to accomplish desired objectives.

"The functions noted in the diagram have been selected after careful study of the works of many leading writers and teachers. While the authorities use different terms and widely varying classifications of functions, I find that there is far more agreement among them than the variations suggest.

"Arrows are placed on the diagram to indicate that five of the functions generally tend to be 'sequential.' More specifically, in an undertaking one ought first to ask what the purpose or objective is which gives rise to the function of *planning*; then comes the function of *organizing*--determining the way in which the work is to be broken down into manageable units; after that is *staffing*, selecting qualified people to do the work; next is *directing*, bringing about purposeful action toward desired objectives; finally, the function of *control* is the measurement of results against the plan, the rewarding of the people according to their performance, and the replanning of the work to make corrections -- thus starting the cycle over again as the *process repeats itself.*

"Three functions--analyzing problems, making decisions, and communicating--are called "general" or "continuous" functions because they occur throughout the management process rather than in any particular sequence. For example, many decisions will be made throughout the planning process as well as during the organizing, directing, and controlling processes. Equally, there must be communication for many of the functions and activities to be effective. And the active manager will be employing problem analysis throughout all of the sequential functions of management.

"In actual practice, of course, the various functions and activities tend to merge. While selecting a top manager, for example, an executive may well be planning new activities which this manager's capabilities will make possible, and may even be visualizing the organizational impact of these plans and the controls which will be necessary.

"Simplified definitions are added for each of the functions and activities to ensure understanding of what is meant by the basic elements described.

PROSPECTIVE GAINS -- of the diagram and the terms used in it.

A unified concept of managerial functions and activities.

A way to fit together all generally accepted activities of management.

A move toward standardization of terminology.

The identifying and relating of such activities as problem analysis, management of change, and management of differences.

Help to beginning students of management in seeing the 'boundaries of the ballpark' and sensing the sequential relationships of certain functions and the interrelationships of others.

Clearer distinctions between the leadership, administrative, and strategic planning functions of management.

"In addition, the diagram should appeal to those who, like myself, would like to see more emphasis on the 'behaviorist' functions of management, for it elevates staffing and communicating to the level of a function. Moreover, it establishes functions and activities as the two most important terms for describing the job of the manager." Each principal needs one of these diagrams.

All one has to do in education is to elevate his/her thinking to the level of the principal as a manager and the above will apply. The principal is called middle management, but more often s/he is the manager in the middle.

To escape the slings and arrows of those who are less informed about leadership, administration, supervision, and the umbrella under which they all fit snugly --- MANAGEMENT, principals must assume a more definitive posture as they go about intermixing all these skills on a daily basis.

Management, again, is getting things done by and through others. This is no easy skill to develop. One has to be more than conversant with delegation, decision-making, accountability, and recently the terms STRESS and BURN-OUT. By searching the contents of this reference for help to get started on the tough parts of becoming a good manager, one must automatically consider him/herself a manager or an executive. This reference is written to prove that the effective high school principal is both.

- ADMINISTRATION -

This is defined (as one of the four roles of the building principal) as directing others in the accomplishment of the institution's goals. As such, there are many things that fall into this arena as opposed to being tasks of leadership, management, or supervision. Each will be treated differently in this text.

Administrative skills include those of working with people in an evaluative role, such as working with students with learning and activities, staff with business and building maintenance, the community in relationships to explain the role of the school, and many, many more.

Jacob Getzels conceives of administration structurally, as the hierarchy of subordinate-superordinate relationships within a social system. And, functionally, this relationship is best described as that skill to allocate and integrate roles and facilities in order to achieve the goals of the school. (170,49) He conceived "the social system as involving two classes of phenomena which are at once conceptually independent and phenomenally interactive." (This is the complication of the principal and/or higher level administrators in the school system -- primarily public school system.) Those two phenomena are simply the institution with roles and expectations fulfilling the goals of the system AND the individuals with personalities and need dispositions who inhabit the system. The interaction between the two is called social behavior. (170,50)

The two dimensions are at the same time independent and interactive. Each dimension moves along the horizontal plane singularly. Each, however, is in conflict with the other role at the same point of the process. Individuals are in conflict with the institution, personalities are in conflict with the role of the institution, and, finally, the need disposition of the individuals is in conflict with the role expectations of the institution. This is to say that the nomothetic dimension can be thought of as requiring the members (teachers) of the organization (school) to perform certain roles in order that the goals and objectives (expectations) of the organization (school) are met. The ideographic dimension is seen as the individual's personality in combination with his/her desires to do or to be. The conflict of the principal is to do the following: S/he should strive to allow each staff member to satisfy his/her need disposition AND still complete or perform the expectations of the school which s/he is managing.

Getzels-Guba Model of Social Behavior

NOMOTHETIC DIMENSION

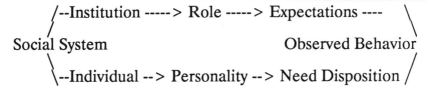

IDEOGRAPHIC DIMENSION

125

- LEADERSHIP -

The following statement is from *The Way of Life According to Loatzu*, written by Witter Bynner for Paragon Publishers in 1962.

A leader is best
When people barely know that he exists,
Not so good when people obey and acclaim him,
Worst when they despise him.
Fail to honor people, They fail to honor you;
But of a good leader, who talks little,
When his work is done, his aim fulfilled,
They will all say, We did this ourselves.

Leadership is any contribution to the establishment and attainment of group purposes and is defined consistently throughout this text as the skill in assisting others in the accomplishment of the group's goals. A definition that restricts leadership to persons in official positions is a denial of life situations. *Real leadership in a group may or may not be exercised by the officailly designated leader.*

Leadership is a quality of group activity. A person cannot be a leader apart from a group. It is the contribution that an individual makes in a group situation. A group and leadership are mutually dependent. Neither exists without the other. A group must have leadership. Unity must be established; otherwise the group remains a collection of persons with no positive direction. And, most importantly, there never is a vacuum of power.

- LEADERSHIP DETERMINATION -

The following questionnaire has been published in a small booklet by the N. A. S. S. P. In it, the authors prepared eighteen questions by which the user could determine whether or not people were more of a concern than the results of people actions in leadershp situations as indicated by the questions. What the Giammatteo questionnaire did was to allow the user to apply the results to a grid which is NOT shown here because their interpretation varies with the purpose of the work. Remember, for this text, leadership is the act of assisting a group in the accomplishment of its stated goals. The grid on which the scores were posted was labeled as: CONCERN FOR PRODUCTION" AND "CONCERN FOR PEOPLE." I would assume that the grid is not necessary as all that is being sought here is a decimal number which reflects the intent of leadership sytle with which the user of the questionnaire is most comfortable. Some explanations will follow.

As the questionnaire is being completed, the user is directed to please ignore the underlines and x's while responding. The purpose they each serve will be explained after the questionnaire is completed. Respond to the items as honestly as you can.

LEADERSHIP QUESTIONNAIRE

The following items were used to describe aspects of leadership behavior by Dr. Gerald Ubbens at the NISSA Conference in Reston, VA. conference in 1975. The instructions given were and are simple. Each participant is asked to respond to each item according to the way s/he would be most likely to act if a leader of a work group. The directions which follow were provided to the participants for scoring their responses.

"Circle how you would be likely to behave in the described way:

IF I WERE A LEADER OF A FACULTY IN A SCHOOL, I would.....

```
                          ┌──────(A) = Always,
                        ┌─┼──────(F) = Frequently,
                      ┌─┼─┼──────(O) = Occasionally,
                    ┌─┼─┼─┼──────(S) = Seldom, or
                  ┌─┼─┼─┼─┼──────(N) = Never.
```

A   F   O   S   N _1._ act as the spokesperson.
A   F   O   S   N   2. x allow members complete freedom
                          in their work.
A   F   O   S   N _3._ encourage the use of uniform
                          procedures.
A   F   O   S   N   4. x permit the members to use own
                          judgment in problem solving.
A   F   O   S   N   5. x needle members for greater
                          effort.
A   F   O   S   N _6._ keep the work moving at a rapid
                          pace.
A   F   O   S   N   7. x let the members do their work
                          the way they think best.
A   F   O   S   N   8. x turn the members loose on a job
                          and let them go.
A   F   O   S   N   9. x settle conflicts when they occur
                          in the group.
A   F   O   S   N 10. be reluctant to allow the members
                          any freedom of action.
A   F   O   S   N 11. decide what shall be done and
                          how it shall be done.
A   F   O   S   N 12. push for increased production.
A   F   O   S   N 13. assign group members to par-
                          ticular tasks.
A   F   O   S   N 14. x be willing to make changes.
A   F   O   S   N 15. schedule the work to be done.
A   F   O   S   N 16. x refuse to explain my actions.
A   F   O   S   N 17. persuade others that my ideas are
                          to their advantage.
A   F   O   S   N 18. x permit the group to set its own
                          pace.

           E   R
Put the totals here after reading the instructions
= =

I N S T R U C T I O N S

for

SCORING THE LEADERSHIP QUESTIONNAIRE

1. Place the number "1" next to each item IF: The S or N was the answer and the item number was underlined.

2. Place the number "1" next to each item IF: The letter A or F was the answer and the item number was not underlined.

3. Circle those "1's" when an X appears after the item.

4. Count all those "1's" which are not circled and put the sum at the bottom of the page for the (R) total, Concern for Production.

5. Count all those "1's" which are circled and put the sum at the bottom of the page for the E Total, Concern for People.

6. What you are searching for is a decimal number. This number will reflect your contrasting feelings toward the school and the felings you have for the people with whom you work. In school administration, you need to be high with the people number -- particularly.

7. The decimal number reflecting your instituional concerns perhaps ought to be low as it reflects the attitude of being a person more suited for ends and not the means of getting there.

8. If the number reflects the results for which there is comfort, do no more. If not, perhaps a change in attitude is needed.

= =

Here is what is being described. If the first number is greater than five, the results would show an attitude in leadership more toward the institution than for people. If the higher number is on the right, it would show the leader is concerned for people more than production. In the design of the questionnaire, a maximum score on either side of the decimal is that of 9.

If the decimal is 7.2, it reflects that the leadership sytle being followed is more toward ENDS rather than MEANS -- or people issues are taking less of a priority than is the school operation.

If the decimal used above is reversed, 2.7, it would reflect that the leadership sytle being followed is more toward MEANS -- rather than ENDS -- or people issues are taking more of a priority than is the operation of the school.

There are degrees of influence with each combination of numbers. For the simple purpose of using this particular formula, it stands to reason that the higher the number the more feelings there are for that portion of the position responsibility.

There is a source for much more intensive determiniation of leadership style. It is referenced in the bibliography as (14) work by Blake and Mouton. The grid used in the reference is easy to follow and has been used in industry all over the world,. The two sides of the grid are labeled as Concerns for Production and Concerns for People. The newest text is referenced. There has been three issues of *The Managerial Grid*.

The work that was referenced herein is by Michael and Dolores Giammatteo. The questionnaire used by these writers appear to have been taken from a pamphlet published by the N. A. S. S. P. It is probably sufficient for the principal who merely wants to examine his/her style just for the record. If, however, the principal wishes to make a full determination of style, the work by Blake and Mouton would have to be followed.

Leadership - the art of assisting groups to accomplish their preset goals is what this subunit has been about. It is not easy to share or give power away. The principal remains responsible - the bottom line.

- SUPERVISION -

The role of the supervisor is one that all principals play. Usually, "play" is the right word. However, it is a very serious role. It is defined as the skill in assisting others in the improvement of their skills. Without good supervision, the program in the building will surely erode and become less valuable annually. The goal of supervision, whether it is hidden or obvious, is the improvement of the program annually. Some principals stay too long. This often leads to atrophy of change. When this occurs and the program dies, the principal needs to leave.

The key role of the principal is that of a supervisor. The key role of the supervisor is that of developing the entire staff. For this text, concentration will be given to faculty development. Current practices of faculty development are criticized frequently. They are accused of being inadequate in that they seldom are established on the basis of need as perceived by the faculty. A competent principal is in the classrooms sufficiently to make sure the inservice work planned is not misdirected in its application. When done as suggested, the criticism of inadequacy or misdirection cannot any longer be true. There will be no evidence that relationships cannot be found between in-service and school program improvement. When a needs determination is designed on staff deficiencies, a staff development program is mandatory and CAN be conducted by the effective principal.

It perhaps needs to be emphasized that any good faculty improvement program needs to be initiated following a thorough needs determination. It cannot be developed on simple observation, perception, or on what the principal or an observer from the "head shed" *feels or thinks* needs to be done TO the faculty and not FOR them. Productivity is best when based upon developing resources of the faculty rather than on the development of more and more programs. "STEP-UP" needs to be the motto as designed by Wayne St. Pierre, a student working on his specialist degree, and the author this past summer. It stands for, "Synthesizing Teachers and Enriching Pupils, to Unleash Potentials." Identifying competency needs of *individual staff* members is a means by which an improved faculty development program can be designed if the principal knows her/his faculty well.

To get at the staff development program, the principal must specify purposes. Once established, they can be based upon the obviated needs so that the organization can arrange to provide the activities. The activities need to be planned in concert to achieve specific purposes. To get off this apparent circle of influence, faculty needs can be determined by the principal and faculty advisory group (building curriculum committee) by the good formative evaluation of individual faculty members on file. A contact with a neighboring university can yield some very good models for faculty development.

There is one role which cannot be delegated and which promotes a good year. It is the setting of instructional goals. To initiate the process, the principal must determine the distribution of the authority of the roles in the process. At this time, the principal must wear all four hats simultaneously. The goals will be supported best if a product of the team. So s/he must get others to actually write them as an act of management. Each subgroup becomes an entity as the goal statements wend their way to the final document. The principal must help others accomplish their own goals and that is the act of leadership. The means of assuring that the institution's (school's/district's) goals are met falls neatly into the role of administration. As each person works on the goal statement, each will perhaps need some help. As this role is accomplished, the work is that of supervision. Please see the introductory work on Goal Setting, found in Unit One.

a. It is necessary to identify *who is involved*:

Board	Administrators
Parents	Students
Taxpayers	Central Office Managers
	Teachers

b. Lines of *authority* in the process:

This should be done by levels as the goal setting routine moves along.

The Board of Education has the final authority over the goals as developed for any district. The Board usually sets the philosophical goal statements. From this point, some operational goals are developed by the central office cadre for each philosophical goal. At the building level, the staff gets involved with the process in the development of many of what is commonly termed curricular goals from each of the operational goals while the teachers develop many specific performance objectives to finalize the process. The process concludes with each level developing statements which spring out of the material prepared by the level immediately above.

c. Steps or *levels that need to be considered* are now discussed:

Step I. Board of Education sets district level philosophical goal statements. They are broad in scope and usually are developed in terms of societal expectations: read, write, compute, attain citizenship, develop morality, and such.

Step II. The Operational Goals are set by the central office administrators usually with broad representation of the school family. At this level, the goals are

133

stated in attainable, measurable, and specific areas of competency including and going beyond the basic skill areas of the Board of Education.

Step III. The building level goal statements all stem from the Philosophical and Operational Goals. The building members by virtue of application of the goals handed to them will be able to write statements with specificity.

Here is an example of how a history course would be put into this format and through *the process*.

I. The Board, in the area of U. S. history, may provide statements like the following:

"Students shall know the heritage of their country, learn to define Democracy, and learn by examples."

II. The Central Office, working under the direction of the Superintendent, may write something like this:

"Students shall understand at least the basic concepts in U. S. History which influence the study of Democracy."

III. The building administrators, working with the Assistant Superintendent of Instruction, will develop instructional objectives like the following:

"Students shall study the concepts of liberty, justice, equality, social class, self-government, economic systems and origins, and the influence of technology on the development of mankind." (23,156)

IV. The teachers working with the building principal will develop several performance objectives to teach the specific concepts.

"Students in the eleventh grade course shall learn the multiple means of the growth of liberty in the United States and explain it thoroughly to the questioner in no less than three weeks of instruction at at least 90 % proficiency."

The following goal setting process can be followed rather easily by the principal.

1. Establish specific goals to support stated purposes. Goals need to have just a few component parts to make them serviceable. They must be:

observable
clearly stated
measurable
concise enough to be understood

Also, for some, they must be of sufficient detail to be communicated meaningfully. In education, there are many purposes for operating the public schools which have been developed by national committees or commissions. Perhaps a glance at historical goal statements can be of some help to the principal. Here are some standbys to use at least as a springboard to further action.

Seven Cardinal Principles in Education (1918)

Health
Command of Fundamental Processes
Worthy Home Membership
Vocational Training
Civic Education
Worthy Use of Leisure
Ethical Character

Purposes of American Education (1938)

Objectives of Self-realization
Objectives of Human Relationships
Objectives of Economic Efficiency
Objectives of Civic Responsibility

White House Conference -- Aims of Education (1955)

135

Fundamental Skills of Communication
Appreciation for our Democratic Heritage
Civic Rights and Responsibilities . . .
Respect and Appreciation for Human Values
Ability to Think and Evaluate Constructively and
      Creatively
Effective Work Habits and Self-discipline
Social Competency as a Contributing Member of
      Family and Community
Ethical Behavior Based on a Sense of Moral and
      Spiritual Values
Intellectual Curiosity and Eagerness for Life-long
      Learning
Esthetic Appreciation and Self-expression in the
      Arts
Physical and Mental Health
Wise Use of Time, Including Constructive Leisure
      Pursuits
Understanding of the Physical World and Man's
      Relation to it as Represented Through Basic
      Knowledge of the Sciences
An Awareness of our Relationships with the World
      Community

2. Determine the importance of these goals.

The Prioritization Grid can be used to have several (individuals) (groups) react to the list of suggested goal statements by the Board, the Central Office, or the Building.

3. Make plans for action.

Once the goals have been prioritized and the decision has been made to develop them, each level will have to write the statements for consumption and action at the next lower level. The goal statements will eventually make a difference in the classroom -- the purpose of all goal statements.

4. Arrive at performance standards and measurement criteria.

As the goals are developed, means and strategies for their evaluation or assessment are finalized. If the goal statement is written properly, it will be easier to design how goals can be determined to be of value and are (or will) accomplish their intent.

5. State anticipated problems.

Within each statement the ogre (for some people) of CHANGE will rear its head, and with change there will be problems. It is well to attempt to anticipate these and work to narrow the impact into a manageable action program. Unanticipated problems are the ones which are haunting in the near future. Time to think through this phase of the process is best spent for what is labeled as Management by Exception.

6. Weigh the resources required to carry out the planned action.

Weighing, judging, and defining are all terms that could be used here. The principal must be cognizant that there is no such thing as a "free lunch" and work accordingly. The manner in which resources are expended to satisfy the goals will be the highlight of the process. The subordinates will undoubtedly have a different scheme in mind to be used. The principal must listen to them. S/he must be careful but diligent at the same time in "weighing" the resources to be used. These are not necessarily expendable.

7. Provide for the interaction of organizational and individual goals.

The faculty and the rest of the staff should be assured that the evaluation instruments used will reflect the goals of the organization (administration). The objectives (goals) each subordinate sets for him/herself will also be shown to be accomplished (leadership) by arranging small groups to operate collectively and cooperatively. They need not necessarily be in competition for time to spend in the need of assistance in completing their individual goals

137

properly. The whole art of assisting others to improve their skills (supervision) will be the means to use to bring about purposeful change.

8. Follow up with actual performance measurement and evaluation.

This may have been introduced in # 7, above, but the crux of the matter is that if the goals are just "nice" statements and not used after they are developed, they are of no value for the organization. Individual contributions to get them accomplished or written will have been wasted and lost. The documents over which managerial control has been used must relate back to the goal statements at every opportunity. In this way, supervisor(s) will be pleased, the faculty will be pleased, and the role of the person in the middle will be pleasing.

When this is put together with the observation and other roles of the competent supervisor -- leader -- administrator -- manager -- it will make more sense. The wearing of all four hats all of the time can be done. It is the perception of others that separates these into nice definable parts, and perception is, after all, reality to the perceiver.

- CLASSROOM OBSERVATIONS -

The observation process is a main skill area of the principal acting in the role of the supervisor. The principal that is comfortable with this role will make many positive strides with the faculty in gaining leadership posture. Below is a statement on the process.

PREOBSERVATION CONFERENCE TOPICS TO BE COVERED - Three cover sheets are used so the "main" part may have data recorded each time it is used during the year by the principal. There are twelve subheadings in this particular grouping. They range from definition of terms to the sociology of the classroom.

138

The preobservation conference sets the tone and the direction of the review about to be undertaken. The objectives ought to leap out during the lesson in the classroom. This may not happen. The principal needs to be prepared to understand (along with the teacher) where the class is going during that class period. The sociology of the class is significant also. Whatever it is that will be scrutinized needs to be understood by both the teacher and the observer. Without the preobservation conference, there is no way to assure this exchange will take place. If not, the setting may be more false than if both know what the other's role is so the class can continue as normal as it can with the principal in the room.

INFORMATION TO BE USED IN POST-OBSERVATION CONFERENCE

There are several items that the principal needs to observe even before the formal class session begins. These need to be listed on the form's cover sheet to be discussed in the post-conference setting. The first item to be observed is the entrance of the students into the classroom. Their reactions need to be observed, recorded, and discussed with the teacher. It is best to record both the teacher's and the students' reactions. The study of proxemics comes into play. How are the students greeted, how do they respond, how is the "climate" physically and mentally set for the learning which is to take place, and on and on it goes to an endless list of observable items which are so important to the entire class. The principal MUST BE THERE EARLY.

The second bit of information to be recorded is the controlled and uncontrolled variables which constitute the setting for the lesson. Each may or not be obvious to the principal. They are listed on the form as reminders of what is important to the lesson. These comments can be reacted to even before the formal observation takes place. There are fifteen comments under the category of Controlled Variables and another twelve Uncontrolled Variables to be considered.

With the variables attended to and record made of how the students enter the classroom, the next item to be addressed is how the class session is initiated. The first ten minutes after the bell rings is the MOST important time to record observations.

CLASSROOM OBSERVATION OF THE LESSON - There are over 200 items listed on the form in the Exhibits.

1. Class Initiation
2. Lesson Development
3. Teaching Strategies
4. Prof'l. Competence
5. General Flow
   of the Lesson
6. Closure/Bridging
7. Evaluation of the Students
8. Materials/Resources Used
9. Discipline Methodology
10. Appearance

Observation criteria can come from microteaching techniques, Flanders Grids, Grant and Henning's nonverbalness, or the Madeline Hunter program. Awareness of that great bulk of information is the key. As the lesson progresses, the astute observer makes notations and as much as possible makes terminal notes during the lesson's development. When the observation is completed, the paperwork should also be completed -- as much as is practicable.

USE OF BACKGROUND INFORMATION IN THE CLASSROOM

As the ten categories of items (some with many subheadings) are being observed, the observer needs to be apprised of what is going on within the twenty-three levels of the four domains: Cognitive, Affective, Psychomotor, and Perceptual. Use of the four taxonomies in the instructional process and especially in the daily/unit lesson plan is checked.

Beyond the domains, the use of Maslow's Hierarchy of Human Needs is also addressed on the form. To make sure the teacher is aware of the real motivation level of the students is a concern of the observer. This information when coupled with the teacher's knowledge and application of Dr. Herman T. Epstein's work on brain growth and development provides much significant discussion between the observer and observee. If the faculty has developed a list of survival, literacy, and competency vocabularies for the students to master, this work is also noted on the observation form.

POST-CONFERENCE TOPICS FOR DISCUSSION

Strengths of the Lesson   Flanders' Grids Discussed
Assistance Required   Teacher Commentary
Next Observation Scheduled

Are there discernible differences in the Flanders' Grids: (1) during the introduction of the unit, (2) during the development of the material, (3) during the closure or completion of the material? What information was posted to the Galloway grid for nonverbalness as well? What materials and resources were used for the lesson? What techniques were employed in discipline? Was the RED HOT STOVE considered: Did the teacher provide a warning, was she consistent, did she give immediate discipline, and did she show equality in the measures employed? What was the teacher's personal appearance like today? What was the setting the teacher provided? What alterations were used in the vocalization of the lesson?

The POST-CONFERENCE is the third link in the process. Some good material is covered by such writers as George Redfern, Dwight Allen, and Madeline Hunter in this arena. The basis for a successful post-conference is the pride instilled in all teachers after their lessons are completed. The observer should find something they did very well and build on it as a means of opening the door for constructive criticism at a later point. Once the tone has been set, The principal should move to the less than favorable areas and get the observee to thinking about what it is that needs some resource assistance -- either human or material. The material should be provided and in a week or so the principal should check to see that the teacher is trying the information provided.

The observation form contains more data than could be compiled in any single observation. The information contained is usually done over a full year or more and then in each post-observation conference the material, in composite, is gone over with the teacher.

Such skills for observation as listed above need to be learned by the supervisor -- the principal as a supervisor is not excused. S/he needs to understand (for application) the work done by Allen in microteaching, Ned Flanders in (verbal) gridding, Grant/Henning in nonverbalness, and Madeline Hunter's ITIP program. These specifics along with the taxonomy break-down of Benjamin S. Bloom for the Cognitive Domain (1956), David R. Krathwohl for the Affective Domain (1964), Elizabeth J. Simpson for the Psychomotor Domain (1966), and Maxine R. Moore for the Perceptual Domain (1967) are also necessary components for observation and conferencing later. To do this well, a rather extensive vocabulary has to be learned. and more importantly, applied. The issue of not knowing is not valid in a legal defense, nor is it of any value in an educational malpractice suit. The terms which are listed on the observation form are not explained there. It is expected that the user will have the proper background to understand them or will read the material presented in the text.

Beyond specificity in the terms and observable functions they allow to be recorded, there are the less than subtle items to be recorded. The path the teacher follows as s/he moves about the room is worthy of note. The study of proxemics is significant for cultural differences in society. As more Asians (and others) enroll into our U. S. schools, principals will have to depend on psychologists to instruct them on how to relate to the students so as not to cause discomfort on the part of the student or the teacher. The blacks, reds, browns, whites, and yellows are fairly well understood. The Far and Middle Eastern students are not. It is significant enough to merit some excellent in-service training for the entire staff should the school become one selected for education of these youngsters. (The Dearborn Public Schools in Dearborn, Michigan, has had to design several new programs to inculcate the newest tide of students from the Middle East. It is fairly well established by this time so a contact with the administration there will be helpful to get the program started in the school where students of new cultures enroll.) As new cultures enroll, the principal owes it to the profession to write some articles on newly developed programs.

Then there is the big word Closure. Not enough has been written -- or perhaps, practiced in this easy but made to be difficult phase of lesson development. One of the better works on this skill is Allen and Ryan's work called *Microteaching* and published by Addison-Wesley in 1967. Many of the terms one needs to use are defined in the text of their material. The definition for closure is as follows: *The act of summarizing a lesson and providing for the bridging of the lesson for continuation later.*

There is an observation form included in the Exhibits of the text. It may be well to examine it to help comprehend the material totally.

Other roles of the principal when s/he is involved with the supervisory part of the day might be:
1. *Student evaluation*
2. *Creating a positive atmosphere*
3. *Help people agree upon certain personal goals*
4. *Accepting responsibility for good staff morale*
5. *Increasing the creativity among the staff*
6. *Respecting personalities of each*
7. *Utilizing skills in group processes*
8. *Functioning in personnel tasks*
9. *Evaluating through facts and judgments*

Is there agreement with the following observation of one of the oldest members of the teaching profession?

TEACHER   EVALUATION   REPORT

Teacher: SOCRATES   Evaluator: Megiveron

ITEM   RATING   COMMENT

A. PERSONAL APPEARANCE

1. Personal Attire   X 2 3 4 5   Dresses in an old
                                   sheet draped over
                                   body
2. Self-Confidence   1 X 3 4 5   Not always self
                                   assured
3. Use of English   X 2 3 4 5   Speaks with a
                                   heavy Greek accent
4. Adaptability   1 X 3 4 5   Prone to suicide
                                   poison when under
                                   stress

B. CLASSROOM MANAGEMENT

5. Organization   1 2 X 4 5   Does not keep a
                                   seating chart
6. Room Appearance   1 2 X 4 5   Does not have
                                   eye-catching
                                   bulletin board

7. Use of supplies   X 2 3 4 5   Does not use *any*
                                   supplies!

C. TEACHER-PUPIL RELATIONSHIPS

8. Tact/Consideration
                     X 2 3 4 5   Places students in
                                   embarrasing situa-
                                   tions by asking
                                   unproved questions
9. Class Attitude   1 2 3 X 5   Class appears to
                                   be friendly

D. TECHNIQUES OF TEACHING

10. Daily Presenta- 1 X 3 4 5   Does not keep
                                   daily lesson plans
11. Attention to   1 2 3 X 5   Quite flexible--
    Course of   allows students to
    Study   wander to differ-
                                    ent topics
12. Knowledge of   X 2 3 4 5   Does not know.
    Subject Matter   Has to ask pupils
                                    for knowledge

E. PROFESSIONAL ATTITUDE

13. Professional   1 X 3 4 5   Doesn't belong to
    Ethics   PTA or any profes-
                                    sional organi-
                                    zation
14. In-service   X 2 3 4 5   Complete failure.
    Training   Has not even
                                    bothered to go to
                                    basic college for
                                    skill development
15. Parent Rela-   1 2 X 4 5   Needs to improve
    tionships   in this. Parents
                                    are trying to get
                                    rid of him. Gone
                                    to city.

==

This was published on the back cover of *The Kappan*, January, 1962.

- TABLES OF ORGANIZATION -

Golightly and Horst detail work on tables of organization in Maynard's book (137,2[33-44]). Some of their material

145

has been para-phrased and translated from business and industry terms to education.

The principal must understand that operationally a good *Table of Organization* in a high school is the one drawn from concentric circles. Other plans will be presented, but emphasis will be placed on the recommended plan, shown below:

WHEEL ORGANIZATIONAL CHART *
Besides the individual circles, if the department chairpersons report to a specific assistant or assistant to the principal, then color their sections of the circles the same as for the assistant and the chairpersons. In this way, it is clear who reports and to whom.

The center-most circle or smallest of all circles within the largest circle represents the building principal. Each ring will be consecutively numbered -- as follows:

1 - Building Principal
2 - Assoc. Principals, if any
3 - Assistant Principals
4 - Ass't to the principal
5 - Dept. Reps. & Teachers

5 - Head Custodian/Office /
    Mgr./Dietician
6 - Custodians/Secretaries/
    Cooks

The line or open space drawn through the circles to the innermost one is there on purpose. It shows that by revolving the circles properly and aligning them along the "pathway," anyone can go straight to the principal with no hesitation. The only comment here is that the reason needs to be not only urgent but important as well.

In Tables of Organization, the indicator of staff or line positions is the dashed or solid line, respectively. This can be done with the circles by the same indicators so there is really no reason to ignore this part of good chart planning.

There are other forms of developing charts as well. Here are the styles to consider before implementation of a specific design.

146

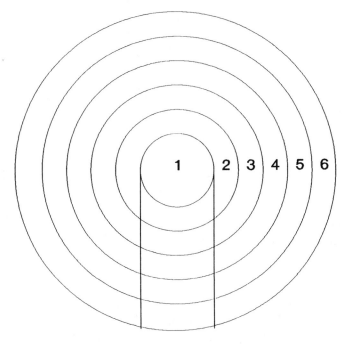

PRINCIPAL'S T.O.

A. Scaler:

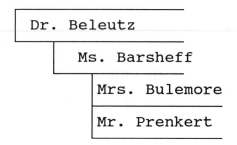

147

B. Line and Box:

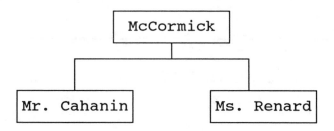

C. Functional Box Table:

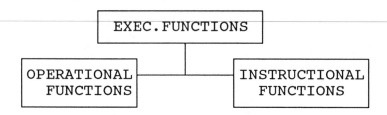

The idea of developing the Table of Organization is not new. However, it may be well to emphasize that one already in use may need to be altered or should be altered to express the new principal's leadership style.

- JOB DESCRIPTIONS -

"Written job descriptions are indispensable tools for effective school administration. Indeed, all of the many processes which are the concern of the school executive influence or are influenced by decisions about how work is divided into jobs and about how work is to be accomplished." (175,33)

148

The FIRST THING THE PRINCIPAL NEEDS TO DO IN HIS/HER JOB (See July list) IS TO DEVELOP A JOB DESCRIPTION AS FULLY AS S/HE KNOWS IT TO BE AT THE TIME. AN UNDERSTANDING NEEDS TO BE MADE THAT IT IS A TENTATIVE PAPER UNTIL THE PRINCIPAL AND HIS/HER SUPERVISOR MEETS NEAR THE END OF THE FIRST YEAR TO UPDATE IT TO REFLECT PRECISELY WHAT THE JOB DEMANDS. Some clues on inclusions will be given in the commentary on work in July in Unit 8.

In the principal's role, s/he must contact the personnel officer to ascertain what job descriptions are available for persons assigned to the building including him/herself. Also, it needs to be determined whether job descriptions as written are policy or rules and regulations.

It is well to remember that good job descriptions provide an accurate, yet not highly detailed description of the position, the organization, training and experience requirements, terms of employment, evaluation notes, and qualifications required and desired.

Job descriptions ought to provide information that will be helpful to the person filling the position and at the same time not be so restrictive as to preclude job alteration after employment. A valid means of developing job descriptions may well be to have broad participation of a range of staff who either will be expected to work with the person employed or who is currently working with them.

TERMS

RESPONSIBILITY: The *work* that is assigned to a position. In other words it answers the question of "what" is it that needs to be done.

AUTHORITY: This represents the *sum of the powers* and/or rights that are assigned to a particular position. Once this is clearly understood, it is much easier to

149

assume responsibilities. The clouding of responsibility and authority gets administrator into difficulty.

ACCOUNTABILITY: This can best be handled perhaps by saying it is the *obligation to perform the responsibilities and exercise authority* in terms of established performance standards within a building, or it is the sum of Responsibility and Authority.

EXAMPLES:

1. The Assistant Principal for Students shall be responsible for fire drills.
OR
2. The Assistant Principal for Students (i) shall be assigned student safety by the principal and by virtue of the State School Code, (ii) shall have the authority for sounding the exit alarm for ten (10) *called* fire drills, (iii) during the academic year (iv) with the time vacating the building being cut by a minimum of 45 seconds from the first to the fourth drill in a multiple floor building.

DIFFERENCE:

Here are the references to the small case Roman numerals in example 2:

    i = GIVENS = The APS has this
        authority to do the job.
    ii = EXPECTATIONS = That which is to
        be accomplished.
    iii = TIME LINE = When the work is
        to be completed.
    iv = PROFICIENCY, OR PERFORMANCE IM-
        PROVEMENT = How well the work is
        to be done.

Here are some delimiters that could be used in the GIVENS:

    1. No more than three drills shall be
        called in any one month.

2. Drills shall be called during each class period.

3. A least one drill shall be called when students are in a mass seating arrangement.

Hopefully, the difference is obvious between the two types of "statements," and the clarity of the latter is much more sufficient. Important work is itemized and clarified and less confusing when detailed in the second example.

The challenge for the assistant principal is done by using as few delimiters as is practicable allowing the assistant creativity even within the well-developed job description.

The principal must also be aware of duplication. This can be purposefully accomplished by developing a generic job description for assistant principals and/or assistants to the principal and then adding specific duties for specific roles or persons. The number of assistants determines the range of responsibilities for each.

The terms *assistants* and *assistants to* do not refer to the same title. The *assistant to* the principal usually has one word following the title, like instruction, attendance, or discipline. The assistant principal, however, is just that and needs to be ready to assume the role of building principal at any time.

Even with the best developed job description statements, no one should be misled. If the assistant assigned to do the fire drills does not do them, **the principal is still responsible**. The issue is that of assigning accountability, which is the sum of both responsibility and authority. As the principal, authority is granted to others through a good job description statement. But the responsibility can hardly be legally delegated in many cases. A management axiom for this is "People do better those things inspected rather than just expected."

In other words, the principal and an assistant may have duplicate statements but with a different accountability level indicated within the job description.

To make sure that subordinates remain motivated, the principal should, as items are completed, check them off each Friday and send a simple hand-written note to subordinates about the work that got done. When a significant accomplishment is finalized, it is good to send a carbon of a short memo praising the work to one's own supervisor. This is a little added reward for the subordinates.

To assist the principal in the preparation of the lists of tasks for the job descriptions to be completed, s/he should ask each of the assistants, "For what contribution should I hold you responsible -- how can I (we) best utilize your knowledge, ability, skills, and preparation?"

Assuming that the principal now has the entire list of responsiblities for subordinates in the building as well as him/herself, it is time to develop the job descriptions. On the cover page or at the top of page one, the appropriate headings need to be identified. They are as follows:

Position Title	To Whom the Employee Reports
Qualifications	Supervision Responsibility (people)
Mandatory	Position Goal
Desired	Employment Terms
Position Holder	Evaluation Comments

Beginning on page two, list the specific tasks for the subordinates to complete (with the four parts of each statement) carefully delineating precisely what needs to be done.

THE PRINCIPAL IS TO LET ALL SUBORDINATES KNOW SPECIFICALLY WHAT THEY ARE TO DO AND AGAINST WHAT THEY ARE TO BE EVALUATED AT THE END OF THE YEAR.

The principal should develop his/her own first, obtain approval of the immediate supervisor, and then go about developing those for the assistants with their aid when they return to school.

- (DE) CENTRALIZAION -

The term(s) are set for a reason. The effective principal will find as many means as is practicable to share in the "running of the school." However, there are times when s/he must pull back and actually centralize the operation. When to do either is the trick of the competent manager. The following is helpful in a form of taxonomy for this dilemma as the principal decides how to operate and how far to share the leadership.

Decentralization in the process of administration calls for specific guidelines. The list presented below will provide some for the effective principal.

1. Early success from citizen participation reinforces involvement.

2. Policies and actions will more likely be successful and lasting when they are democratically developed and implemented.

3. Involvement is enhanced when all people feel that they have an equal opportunity to influence the group and participate in leadership.

4. Involvement will be greater and more productive when work is done in intimate, informal, primary groups with the objective, of systematic truth-seeking.

5. Community response will vary according to the

degree of citizen involvement in study, planning, and action groups. All groups must be representative of a "mix" of people living in a community -- all ideas and interests must be considered.

6. The joining of new skills in communication, problem solving, and decision making increases citizen interest and involvement.

7. People become more involved and committed when they have an opportunity to evaluate and re-evaluate their objectives, methods, activities, and programs.

8. It must be recognized that initiative rests with the people; decisions are made by them out of their knowledge and convictions.

9. Objectives must grow out of a local situation and begin with conditions as they are - specific interests, concerns, and problems. (195,16-17)

Also in the report (195,17-18), the following list was printed as the result of a brainstorming session with members of the The National Task Force '74. The author has taken the liberty to add additional comments. They are located in parentheses.

1. Parents and citizens are confused by the growing complexity of the school system, (and find some sort of respite working within the individual school building. The high school is an interesting place to work and many "would" flock there if given the opportunity.

2. There are often no avenues by which citizens can register grievances. (This was intended to be for the district, but the high school must remain accessible.

3. Many educators are overly defensive in their responses to grievances when they are brought forward. (The principal has no known escape route being in "the first line of defense.")

4. Taxpayers have been alienated by the growth of the budget. (The building cannot escape this. In Michigan, the salaries, and other costs, spiralled upward when the Legislature passed the law for voluntary bargaining of public employees. Michigan has the distinction of being the first state to do so in July, 1965).

5. Increasing problems of vandalism and crime in the schools have led to a cynical view of the educational enterprise. (This occurs throughout the district but primarily in the high school.)

When authority is decentralized, one must not feel that a path "to the top" has been eliminated. Handling issues which come directly to the principal require delicate handling but must be done. The principal must make every attempt to allow the person involved at the lowest possible level to solve the problem. It is the best process even if a three-way conference is held at the time.

The principal should be prepared by knowing the policy manual of the district, attend Board of Education meetings, send memos to the central office, and, in general, share responsibility with whomever s/he can.

Lastly, here are the six viable reasons for decentralizing the operation as far as is practicable.

1. Decentralization increases public, staff, and student confidence in the school.

2. Decentralization takes schools closer to the people who pay for them. It definitely

155

leaves or puts the PUBLIC in public education.

3. Effective decisions are best made by those who have the problem.

4. Best educational decisions are made by those who relate them to "their" dollar.

5. It provides a vehicle for analysis of kids, programs, and product.

6. To truly lead a program, more and more final-type decisions need to be made at the program level.

A steering committee in the building is a good place to start this process. For help on how to (de)centralize, one should examine the units on agenda formulation, conferencing, meetings, and others. With these skills at hand, the principal is all set to be able to do what must be done. Here is an example of decentralizing.

1988-89
The principal plans the total building operation by working with a central administrator

1989-1990
The principal develops goals and approved plans for the total operation.

1990-1991
The Faculty Advisory Committee splits the goal work and gives it to the department heads as a single document.

1991-1992
The Department Chairmen each make plans for development and evaluation.

1992-1993
The teachers in year four submit plans to department for consideration to have incorporated into department plans.

- TASK CARDS -

The effective principal must be able to prepare definitive directions to the other members of the administrative cadre. These may include a variety of tasks, but subordinates must be aware of the criteria to be used for evaluation purposes. Typically, these task cards will be prepared either in late spring or early summer. They are best done following a brainstorming session with all key persons involved. Brainstorming for this purpose is best done annually, perhaps in May. Over two hundred items may be identified during a brainstorming session. After the brainstorming session is the best time to make the task cards for subordinates' tickler files as well as the principal's. Mr. Thomas E. Prenkert designed the first task cards used in school administration. He designed them in Monroe, MI as a means to show what information should be listed and according to the following categories which are numbered for the card below.

1. TASK STATEMENT OR TITLE -- Make sure that the statement is explicit and brief. Often in a brainstorming session, the tasks are listed as brief headings or even single words. Later it is hard to recall what was meant by them. Be explicit.

2. BEGINNING DATE (B.D.) and ENDING DATE (E.D.) -- When will the task begin? Even the collection of material is a beginning. Specify a day or date -- not just a week or a month. A helpful strategy is to avoid assigning Mondays or Fridays as task dates. It is much easier to initiate a task once the week has begun. Since

many routine activities culminate on Friday, this day should be avoided for ending dates.

3. PRIME PERSON -- That person assigned to be accountable (having been given not only the responsibility but the authority) to complete the task.

4. PURPOSE -- Why is it that the task needs to be done? In its simplest terms, why is it be accomplished?

5. INVOLVEMENT -- All others who may be helpers in the task's completion. It could be a list of titles or names. Preference is usually given to titles because names can change, but the title usually remains rather constant. It also will be assistive in scattering the load more evenly among the team.

When done properly, these 3 X 5 index cards can save a principal's professional life. They do provide direction, set restrictions regarding time, help to control the workload, and set daily objectives. (See unit on Planning Each Day and the one on the Gantt charts). By using the Tickler File, transposed to the Daily Log or recorded on a Task Gantt, the principal will always remember to begin those tasks that need to be done when all else is breaking loose in the building.

Once the cards are completed, they should be placed in the appropriate monthly tickler file for storage after being used for the development of a yearly Gantt for control and evaluation -- perhaps even planning. As the tasks are posted to the Gantt, the principal can visualize the necessity of adjusting time lines which would even out the load for any given length of time for key personnel.

When all of the subordinates have completed their Gantts and submitted copies, it will be easy to control the operation by exception throughout the remainder of the year. The secretary can superimpose all the assistant's work on a master Gantt or set up her tickler file so that when a task is to be completed by an assistant, she records it on the Daily Log for the principal's inspection. Here is a representation of an "actual" card.

TEPTASK CARD

```
| Merritt                                   | # 3
| DRAPERY PROGRAM FOR WEST WING             | # 1
| B.D. 3/10/87   E.D. 4/9/87                | # 2
|                                           |
| Purpose:  The west wing is exposed to     | # 4
| the hot sun during the times of 1:00      |
| forward for most of the months of the     |
| year making it nearly unbearable for      |
| the students or staff in the wing.        |
|  The sun must be controlled by some       |
| sort of glare/heat control.               |
|                                           |
|     Involved: Megiveron, Bulla &          |
| Maintenance  Dir.                         | # 5
```

- MANAGING THE BOSS-

An example to be used for managing the boss can be found in the subunit on conferencing. The unit on conferencing will be helpful after completing this topic. It is imperative that the princpal understands why the position is called one of middle management. The principal has a boss and is the boss. When this subunit is finished, the principal will know how to treat his/her boss and how the subordinates in the building ought to be treating him/her.

159

As long as one's workload is identified and the boss knows what it is, the administrator will frequently have the opportunity to manage him/her. But please *objectify the workload for each day.* The workload for the day should be identified by preset objectives. Having assumed both the role of delegator and delegatee, the author realizes the importance of selection when expertise is essential. Occasionally, the delegator is dismayed because s/he is greeted with, "Sure I can do it, Gene, but which of these objectives do you wish me to postpone?" The boss has just been managed. There is an alternative. The boss can either pick one or after examining the stated objectives carry the new task to another office to get it done. *This is a classic case of managing the boss.*

If one's boss becomes successful, his/her subordinates will enjoy success. Credit to the boss always returns (frequently, anyway). A good idea is best when credit is given to the boss. S/he can either express appreciation or return credit to its proper source. In either case the boss will be pleased.

The practice of managing the boss is vital in order to survive in the world of the building principalship. Everyone wants the principal to do things which will provide them a benefit. In most cases the principal will find that s/he can do the work very comfortably. The question is whether or not the work SHOULD be done by the principal. It is imperative to remember the difference between being defensible or being defensive. Do not wait to try to manage the boss at evaluation time with a series of "yabuts." The timing will be wrong. It will be difficult to expect the boss to recall "all" of those instances when any subordinate was given or had volunteered to do something beyond the rigid lines of the job description. Frankly, the boss should not have to do this. When a subordinate performs beyond the call of duty, he should record this performance directly on the mutually agreed upon evaluation document and forward a copy of it to his/her immediate supervisor for the record. In this way, s/he will be given credit at the year-end summative evaluation sessions. The goal is to manage the boss properly.

1. By routing a carbon of significant memo work (addressed to subordinates) to a superordinate, s/he will be apprised of the principal's progress or lack of it in the project addressed. The notation (cc) on the original for a carbon copy may be used. The principal may wish to note (bc) on the carbon copy to show there was a carbon forwarded but the one who received the original is unaware of a carbon going anywhere.

2. Some correspondence received is best responded to by the boss. If this is the case, prepare a response for the boss to sign or alter depending on his/her choice. But the principal can have the necessary material and information already collected.

3. The subordinate should be cognizant of the boss's objectives and make his/her work complement the boss's to ease both loads.

4. ALWAYS keep the boss informed verbally or in writing or on tape. If the boss's style is known, it is best to send information in the appropriate format.

5. Invite the boss to meetings for visibility and an honest show of continuity in the program.

6. Send copies of the agenda and minutes.

7. Invite the boss into planning sessions (not the mundane control/evaluation sessions) so that the information the boss would have more accessible information.

8. Involve the boss in the process of improving subordinates that report to the principal.

By practicing these, the principal will be more successful in his/her work with the boss who will either appreciate these good efforts, decide they are not necessary, or ignore the whole process. In any respect, the selective things being done are forwarded for her/his information.

The suggestions listed above will provide the principal with means of becoming a better boss as well as the principal's boss becoming better informed. A two-way street is good.

- CONFERENCING -

The conference presented below is called an example of the Authoritarian Conference (209,08).

"Kluge: But I absolutely cannot spare any units until this operation has been finished. We'll see how we can manage things afterwards.

"Hitler: You must see to it that you finish it as soon as possible. You will have to give up a few Panzer -- and a few Infantry Divisions --

"Kluge: Not Panzer ! I have - - -

"Hitler: Yes, we'll pull them out and they'll be refitted in the West.
"Kluge: But I can't do anything without Panzer Divisions!

"Hitler: But certainly you don't care about that junk. You can easily spare that.

"Kluge: What junk?

"Hitler: You yourself said, "That's just junk."

"Kluge: I did not say that!

"Hitler: Yes, it slipped out. That's why we're going to take them away from you.

"Kluge: No, my Fuehrer, I didn't mean that. I have so little left, just a little bit. What I wanted to indicate was that the situation is hardly tenable any more.

"Hitler: Yes, you have no Panzers. That is why I say they can be taken away and refitted in the West."

By reading the above carefully, one can see how Hitler used the conference as a means of communicating orders. He planted the word (junk) and then used it as a weapon with his favorite general.

Here is a chart to show how different conference types are set.

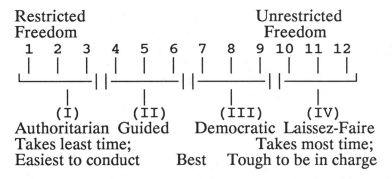

A conference is a mini-meeting with all the same rules and planning for a meeting. The issue is not what it is but rather that it is intended to serve a specific function. The skillful use of conferencing techniques can cut the number of meetings. A conference is usually called such when the membership has less than four and certainly not more than six participants. A conference is used to discuss one or two topics with specificity. Here are uses of a conference:

1. To develop a plan of action.
2. To analyze data.
3. To develop an understanding of policy.
4. To attempt reconciliation.
5. To coordinate an activity.
6. To brainstorm for creative solutions.

7. To call when time is of an essence.

When a conference is initiated for any of the reasons stated above, the first thing ought to be a brief statement as to the purpose of the conference to understand what the expected result will be. If the intent is to have a problem resolved, preparation needs to be given to present a suggested resolution or two. If conferences can be of contrasting views so much the better. This will stimulate the discussion so vital to a successful conference. Draw ALL participants into the conference discussion as soon as practicable. When an idea is heard, the principal needs to compliment the contributor as soon as practicable. This will help to get more suggestions.

Locale and physical arrangements are important in conferences. Conference can be held in the principal's office, another's office, or in the corridor. Are participants going to remain standing? Is the seating to be in comfortable furniture? Will participants sit on straight back chairs? Will there be visual aids needed for projection, distribution, or circulation?

Timing for the conference will also be important. Should it be early in the morning, just before lunch, right after lunch, or just before work is done? Check the subunit on Personal Time Clocks for more help on this, but be that as it may, the time a conference is held is important.

ONE ON ONE CONFERENCING

Here are some situations and a clue to follow when conferences are held. Let's assume a tough disciplinary conference needs to be held and the principal is the supervisor. In this scenario, seat the conferee straight across and at the boss's desk. To assure this happens, it is wise to remove other chairs from the immediate proximity so the choice is narrowed considerably. Hold this conference in the principal's office. If the tone needs to be softened, sit on the same side of the desk. To soften it even more, go to the office of the one being disciplined and hold the conference there. In this way, the supervisor can leave

164

anytime s/he wants rather than to be uncomfortable in discharging the one being disciplined.

As an item is discussed in a conference, as in a meeting, be sure to bring it to a sound closure. There must be no doubt as to what was meant in the discussion.

CONFEREE UPBUCKING

Many conference settings are concluded by "upbucking" taking place. If this word is unfamiliar, it is the art of delegating up to the supervisor that assignment that the subordinate feels could be better done by the boss. Don't "lift the monkey" from the subordinate's back. If something is delegated to be done, make sure it gets done by the delegatee not the delegator because personal work must be done. Some good advice is given on this topic under Unit 3 - Managing the Boss.

WHEN TO HOLD CONFERENCES

After having done a time audit (Unit 2), use the knowledge of personal time clocks to decide the best part of the day, perhaps the best day of the week, to schedule conferences. The conference may not be able to be called at the best time of the day, but certainly it ought not be called for the worst time or day either.

If the conference is set by a subordinate to seek further directions, the principal should not be too quick to advise. S/he must allow a sufficient time for discussion and then ask for alternatives that the conferee feels are available. Once declared, s/he should be allowed to select the best in his/her opinion. If one can agree, fine, if not, s/he should ask for some clarification of the issues this alternative would rectify. Frequently, the subordinate selects a different alternative, and it is somewhat more agreeable. See Unit 4 on Recommendations.

MULTIPLE TOPICS

A conference should not be arranged with a long

165

list of topics. If it is, on either party's part, it must move along swiftly. To do this, each item needs to be stated in the form of a question. One must stay on the topic at hand. It is easy to "wander." The principal won't let it happen. S/he should not only listen but hear what is asked. That will take some training. It will be well worth the time spent learning how to do this.

PERCEPTIONS

The two important questions that have to be thought through and not necessarily asked are:

Does everyone hear the same thing that you hear?

Does everyone understand the innerworkings of a conference?

What perception transpires between two people is the following:

The receiver's perception toward the sender.

The sender's perception toward the receiver.

The receiver's perception toward the statement to be considered.

The sender's perception toward the statement to be received.

The receiver's perception of the sender's perception.

The sender's perception of the receiver's perception.

COMMUNICATION SUFFOCATORS

One can understand why the smaller number of persons in a conference the better. Communication suffofocators abound. The greater number of participants, the more suffocators there are on a geometric scale. Here is a brief example using the formula (X times X-1):

One against One = 2 suffocators = 2 x 1 = 2
Three involved = 6 suffocators = 3 x 2 = 6
Four involved   = 12 suffocators = 4 x 3 = 12
Five involved   = 20 suffocators = 5 x 4 = 20

With technology as it is, the effective principal will soon be into teleconferencing (using the phone), using a fax machine, or conferring using the microcomputer by sending/receiving messages. This can be done best and with more purpose when the calling of a conference is impractical financially. The principal can check information with the phone company and with a computer headquarter's consultant for more direction.

When a conference is concluded, the principal should be sure that the one who called it sends the other party (parties) a brief memo stating precisely what was concluded in the conference. See the Contact Form provided in Unit 2.

- MEETINGS -

Some quotes for the topic will set the tone:

There are a number of common symptoms of poor organization which usually require no further diagnosis. There is, first, the symptom of *too many meetings* attended by too many people.   Peter Drucker

Meetings need to be called to solve problems -- not held just because they are scheduled.   Gene E. Megiveron

Effectiveness in building administration is attained by the principal calling the right number of meetings while the efficiency is measured by the meetings being called for the right purposes.   Gene E. Megiveron

It should be added that a good agenda, distributed ahead of time, is the keystone to all good meetings. If the chair has not taken the time to decide precisely what ought to be considered and by whom, the meeting will not only get started poorly, it will be conducted and culminated poorly as well.

To prevent overpopulating the meeting room, a consultant in time management recommends the placement of the following quote on the top of each agenda. It is titled, "Ericson's Law."

I have asked those noted to meet with me to discuss the items listed on the agenda below. Please come if you need first-hand information or want to participate in any discussion. As soon as practicable, minutes of this meeting will be distributed widely. They will indicate all actions taken. You are requested to make comments on the minutes and return them to the chairman.

While it may be said that this is going a little too far, most agree substantively with what is said. What do you think? It is not difficult to understand that too frequently the chairperson, two resource persons, and a good secretary can do in fifteen minutes what most meetings accomplish with fifty people in two hours. This is not a commentary on the topic as much as it is on the participants and the chair of the meeting. MEETINGS CAN BE PRODUCTIVE and ought to be given much more thought than they are given. Here is a selected list of thoughts about meetings:

The first goes into the preparation of a proper *agenda*.

The arrangement of the *seating* is important. Remember it took months to decide the shape of the table to bring the Korean Conflict to an end.

The real *purpose* of the meeting ought to be clear. There are too many "hidden" agendas in today's leadership operation.

Meetings ought not to be *scheduled* unless there is a reason. To many times meetings are held because they are scheduled or because it has been too long between meetings.

There is a list of good news/bad news items that are ignored:

GOOD NEWS	BAD NEWS
Starts on time.	Starts "anytime."
Agenda is made available early.	Agenda given AT mtg.
Selected mandatory attendance.	Y'all come now, here.
Purpose is clear before the meeting.	Unknown purpose.
Members remain defensible.	Defensive members.
Effective planning is done.	No planning is done.
Concrete issues are acted upon.	Abstract items are discussed.
Good closure is brought on all items.	Individual thought prevails.
Ends on prearranged time.	Allowed to disintegrate.
Minutes are taken, distributed.	NO summary is made.

There must be a defined process to bring items to closure in a good meeting. The very idea of the agenda being a process need not escape thought here. Discussion

169

items ought not be brought to a vote and action items must be voted upon. The flow of the meeting is controlled by the chair following the agenda precisely. The process of decision making could be, for example, majority vote wins, the chair will draw a consensus and take action accordingly, or representatives only will cast a vote. In other words, if there is no set means of resolving issues, set one. If there is no process in the meetings, set one. Process can mean different things to different persons. To assume a single process is the best for ALL people would be absurd but not as absurd as not having a defined process and that is the direction to give to the chairman. Perhaps the best conclusion to this thought is that one must realize that the actual decision is but a point in the process. It is not *the* process.

There are five pitfalls to being a good meeting participant that are generally accepted by writers in management. These are:

1. Avoid arguing from or for a personal point of view.

2. Do not assume that a win/lose outcome is the only one to have.

3. Do not alter thinking strictly for the sake of harmony.

4. Avoid majority votes, averages, coin-flipping, and bargaining.

5. Do not get uptight with differences of opinions.

The chart is shown below to enable the principal to see his/her staff or faculty in meeting settings. Some of the descriptors used by Bales are not included because not all of them apply. Please see the original source to understand all the items Bales felt were significant for his work.

INTERACTION PROCESS ANALYSIS

PROBLEM AREAS		REACTOR TYPES	
Communication	= a	A - Positive Reactions	= 1- 3
Evaluation	= b	B - Attempted Answers	= 4- 6
Control	= c	C - Questions.	= 5- 9
Decision	= d	D - Negative Reactions	= 10-12
Tension Reduction	= e		
Reintegration	= f		

```
Positive     (1. SHOWS SOLIDARITY,────────────┐
Social       (raises other's status,──────────┤
             (gives help───────────────────────┤
Emotional  ((2. SHOWS TENSION RELEASE,─┐       │
Area       ((jokes, laughs, is satisfied┤      │
             (3. AGREES, passive accept─┐│     │
             (ance, understands, concurs││     │

Task         (4. GIVES SUGGESTIONS, di─┐││     │
             (rections, implies ───────┤││     │
             (autonomy──────────────────┤│     │
           ((5. GIVES OPINIONS, ex─┐    ││     │
           ((presses feelings, analy┤   ││     │
           ((sis ───────────────────┤   ││     │
          (((6. GIVES ORIENTATION,─┐│   ││     │
          (((information, clarifies┤│   ││     │
Area                           abcdef
          (((7. ASKS FOR ORIENTATION┤│   ││     │
          (((information, clarity───┘│   ││     │
Neutral    ((8. ASKS FOR OPINION─────┤   ││     │
           ((feelings, analysis,─────┤   ││     │
           ((evaluation───────────────┘   ││     │
             (9. ASKS FOR SUGGESTIONS,─┐  ││     │
             (direction, ways of action┘  ││     │

Negative     (10. DISAGREES, passive────────┤│     │
             (rejection, formality,─────────┤│     │
Social       (withholds────────────────────────┤     │
           ((11. SHOWS TENSION, asks──────────┤     │
           ((for help, withdraws───────────────┤     │
Emotional    (12. SHOWS ANTAGONISM,────────────┤     │
             (becomes obstinate, asserts───────┤
Area         (self────────────────────────────────┘
```

171

Although this is TASK ORIENTATION for Group Participation, it can be applied to the role of others in groups and groups in meetings. One needs to know the roles different persons play.

There are several roles people play when in the setting of a meeting. In March's book (134,602) there is an interesting diagram of the roles people play in what he labels "Interaction Process Analysis." Roughly it says there are six problem areas and four sets of reactors in any group. Please see the previous page for the drawing for your study and understanding.

There has been a discussion of some problems in this unit. There are some which are really one-liners in content that need to be cleared. Here is a list of those problem areas:

Too many chiefs and not enough Indians -- everyone goes in different directions, but with authority.

Traffic in the setting -- too much movement within the room.

Personality conflict -- between the leader and the group.

Environment -- Room is too stuffy, warm, too much glare.

Avoidance -- "All is well" so no reason to face reality.

Leader manipulation -- gets what s/he wants.

Spinning wheels -- getting nowhere but making good time.

Unclear directions -- there are no goals.

Too many facts -- too much, too fast, too complicated.

Negative feelings -- can't do it anyway syndrome.

Late arrivers -- when repetition needs to be corrected.

Self-appointed experts -- never challenging themselves to a leadership role, but are experts in any respect.

The shotgunner -- blasts in generalities and never deals specifically with the issue at hand.

Sharp-shooter -- the toughest type to rectify. Call on them before they interrupt the meeting.
The misoneist -- there are always more reasons not to do something than there are to be a risk-taker.

The note-passer -- the worst type of participant because of disruption of whole setting.

There are many more categories to be covered, but the delimiters have been isolated in the list above. The know-it-all, the interrupter, pet, busy-body, backseat driver, interpreter, attacker, loudmouth, headshaker, dropout, broken record, and early leaver are all discussed in another source (42,107-117). It is a good reference dedicated entirely to meeting management.

MYTHS ABOUT MEETINGS

1. The leader is totally responsible for the success of the meeting.

2. The leader needs to have tight control.

3. Group participation is appropriate in all circumstances.

4. If everybody is courteous enough, the meeting is bound to succeed.

5. Touching base with everyone is good management.

These "truisms" ought to be copied and put in the flap of the notebook used for meetings. They are summative items whereas the people problems are somewhat formative.

173

Many meetings get boring. This is caused by either the leader or the participants. There are symptoms of restlessness that the effective leader must be able to see. In classroom observations, this is called *attending behavior.* Some successful techniques that have been used or observed are listed below. They are not profound nor are they intended to be panaceas. They are listed as a means for the principal to allow meetings to be productive in order that one can get over predictable lulls or low spots.

PREVENTING BOREDOM IN MEETINGS

a. Call for a break and walk away. Don't preschedule breaks, but call for them when they are needed. Get a cup of coffee and relax for just a moment. It doesn't take long.

b. Break up mass meetings into discussion groups to resolve a knotty problem or problems. If rooms are available, allow or structure different groups (attacking different problems) to go to different rooms.

c. Begin a "what if" session. Computerese now uses specific language in problem solving: IF -- THEN -- ELSE. What if I had a million dollars......then......else? What if I were in charge of the meeting......then......else? What if the biggest antagonist was in charge of the meeting......then......else......If the work is done this way, then the results will be positive else the administration will continue to muddle through.

The helpers will provide a time break, an action break, and get the meeting back on course. Summarily, the leader has to stay serious but not take it seriously. After all, meetings will end regardless of what happens even if they do "disintegrate" before they are over. The principal must be aware that there are **types** of meetings.

Finally, be aware and conscience of one of the psychology items learned years ago, perhaps. It deals with the word motivation.   One cannot be motivated unless s/he is physiologically secure and appeased. Once this has happened for or to him/her, one needs to feel secure, then a member of some unit, then can feel good about how one fits into the picture to become the best as a person.

Maslow's Hierarchy of Human Needs.

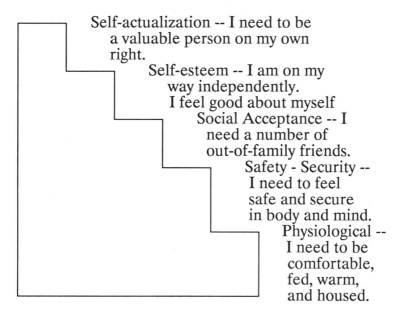

Self-actualization -- I need to be a valuable person on my own right.

Self-esteem -- I am on my way independently. I feel good about myself

Social Acceptance -- I need a number of out-of-family friends.

Safety - Security -- I need to feel safe and secure in body and mind.

Physiological -- I need to be comfortable, fed, warm, and housed.

The discussion leader must play many roles with most people coming to the meeting at least with level three being satisfied. Maybe level three is a little precarious, but one must assume that level four is where some concentration must be placed on leadership efforts. If persons are searching for self-esteem, what better way than "to take over" the meeting from the audience or even as a participant? There are ways of working with these people, like assigning them to chairmanships of subcommittees, calling on them for their opinion, thanking them for being responsive, etc.

If the person has achieved level IV, then s/he needs to run for an office or get into a leadership position in one way or the other. S/he will search for an appointment to good, strong leadership, and get involved in significant functions of the innerworkings of the building.

Davies and Herrold (39,17-24) list (and discuss) the following opportunities for staff development in working toward good staff meetings. These opportunities:

1. let you see yourselves as a team;

2. provide for economical communication of information;

3. help build a staff morale;

4. help greatly in the professional development of the staff;

5. help to develop leadership;

6. provide for speeding the exchange of ideas and for stimulating invention;

7. help to develop agreement on common goals and help to keep them in view;

8. help to strengthen and reinforce the best in the individuals.

As a means of closing the text on meetings, here is something on the key word of communication:

"I know that you believe you understand what you think I have said, but I'm not sure you realize that what you hear is not what I say!"

- COMMITTEES -

There is a poster which says:

*"Search all the parks in all the cities ...
You'll find no statues to committees."*

Perhaps this is not as humorous as it was intended to be. The doubts about the effectiveness of committees is deep-seated. The work on committees is often stultifying. At best, most committee work is boring. Many don't accomplish what they are formed to do simply because they are not structured correctly. This subunit is intended to be one of explanation and assistance. Here is an excellent way to operate committees.

A committee properly structured *should not be* "a collection of the unfit, chosen from the unwilling, by the incompetent, to do the unnecessary." The other popular comment about committees is the one that a camel is really a horse but put together by a committee. Putting all this aside, here is some good information about how to design committees throughout the year.

1. *Membership* should be listed first -- at least by categories, if not by name. As an example, if a cross-departmental committee needs to be structured, with representatives from each department, the membership list would be a list of departments to be represented.

2. *Responsibility* needs to be a statement indicating to whom the committee results will be forwarded.

3. *Function* covers a statement of exactly what needs to have been done by the committee when the work is completed. This sometimes is called the *Charge* to the committee.

4. *Duties* are listed by specific tasks to be accomplished. They should be precise, brief, and thorough.

5. *Significant Dates* ought to be listed. The list should include two types of dates. (A) Meeting dates are consistent in the selection of the time and days of the week to enable volunteers to be available for the times the meetings must be held. (B) The Interim Report date(s) and the date for the Final Report would also be listed.

With this format, *committees can be fruitful*. It happens because all members can contribute significant input through adequate preparation to serve on the committee. It will help to get committees organized before the first meeting is actually held. Too many committees meet and then decide what they are supposed to do, when they will meet, and who will chair/record the actions. All of this needs to be done AHEAD of TIME so that the work begins at the first meeting.

Secondly, for the first and subsequent meetings, *a well-planned agenda is mandatory*. Please see the comments earlier in this unit for help on agenda preparation. It works as well for committees as it does for staff meetings.

Third, *leadership is important*. The true leader (perhaps not the titular person appointed) understands *there is no vacuum of power in any organization* -- a committee fits into this. To manifest true "power," the leader must take charge of the committee and get the process to process. To do this well, the leader will understand that *there are small groups within the large group*. These will have to be identified as soon as possible and then dealt with. This is not to say they ought to be broken up; yet they must be controlled and then actually USED. A group, used in this context, may be one person.

Fourth, the leader must do the following:

- Arrange for the proper type of seating for the committee members is important. The shape of the table must also be considered. One must think about where

178

- Arrange for the proper type of seating for the committee members is important. The shape of the table must also be considered. One must think about where s/he wants adversaries, supporters, and those who are undecided to be seated. It makes a difference. No one should have his/her ego impaled because of the structured seating. Often this cannot be handled very well. If the chairperson is having trouble, s/he can arrange to come in at the same time as others and "force" seating as everyone is being seated.
- Provide for comfortable seating to be arranged when the purpose is one of deliberation. If it is a reporting session, the seating should not be too comfortable in order to stimulate brevity.

- The members should be informed of the leader's expectations.

- Here is the list of suggestions that can be "imposed" upon committee members:

- Committe members should come to all sessions prepared.

- They should study the agenda ahead of time and get the side conversation out of the way before the session is called

- Input should be kept short, direct, and pointed to the topic.

- The speaker should get everyone's attention before proceeding.

- The committee should make every effort to stay on the issue at all times.

- Although members criticize clearly and frequently while IN the room, they may agree/disagree, when all said and done, they must accept the results when a consensus is obtained.

- Each discussion should be brought to a firm closure, and this ought to be agreed upon by all in attendance.
- An agenda must be set for each meeting. For committees it is a good idea to ask for assistance of the other members by their placing items on the agenda any time but especially at the conclusion of each session for the next one as scheduled for the committee.

- Sessions must begin AND END on time. Waste of time by briefing a tardy member is the time lost times the number of those who were there promptly. It is unfair.

Here is an example of an actual committee appointment sheet for the potential establishment of an in-house radio station for applying on-air broadcasting techniques, production work, business operations, sales, and engineering experiences for students.
=================================
CABLE T.V. AND F.M. RADIO COMMITTEE

1. Committee Membership

- Kettering High School--Chairman
- Director of Secondary Education - or representative
- Director of Elementary Education - or representative
- An administrator from each of the other secondary schools
- Crary Jr. High   - Mason Jr. High
- Waterford Township   - Pierce Jr. High
- Mott Sr. High

2. Responsibility
This committee, through its chairman, shall be directly responsible to the Assistant Superintendent for K - 12 Instruction.

3. Function
To evaluate the feasibility of establishing a Cable

TV and/or FM Radio installation for the Waterford Public Schools and recommend its implementation, continued study, or dissolution at this time.

4. <u>Duties</u>
- To investigate existing Cable TV and FM Radio programs.

- To determine cost factors, initial and ongoing, for these programs.

- To investigate the possibility of a mutual operation with the local FM Radio Station and TV Channel 8.

- Others as identified by the committee.

5. <u>Significant Dates</u>
- Meetings   - Reports

September 17   (I) January 14
November 12   (I) May 13
January 14   (F) June 10
March 11
May 13   F = Final Report
June 10   I = Interim Reports
= =

That is all there is to it. When following this format, successful committee work can be completed in the high school. The evaluation form one can use for any type of meeting is shown below.

MEETING EVALUATION FORM

<u>AGENDA</u>

          High   Low

1. Received ahead of time ____ ____ ____ ____

2. Clear statements made ____ ____ ____ ____

3. Was prioritized correctly ____ ____ ____ ____

181

4. (a write in) ___ ___ ___ ___

___ ___ ___ ___

SEATING
1. Appropriate type ___ ___ ___ ___
2. Arranged for communication ___ ___ ___ ___

3. (a write in) ___ ___ ___ ___

THE MEETING
1. Started/ended on time ___ ___ ___ ___

2. Was necessary ___ ___ ___ ___

3. Effective planning evident ___ ___ ___ ___

4. Clear presentations 1. ___ ___ ___ ___
                     2. ___ ___ ___ ___
                     3. ___ ___ ___ ___
                     4. ___ ___ ___ ___

PROBLEM CENSUS FOR THE MEETING
1. The single thing I liked best about the meeting was:

_____.

2. The single thing I least least about the meeting was:

_____.

3. If I chaired this meeting, I would have improved it by:

_____.

_____.

182

- RANKING OF PRIORITIES -

There are many times when the expectations are such that the principal can quite honestly not know where to start or what to do first. If this happens, it is good to have a tool that can be of great assistance in determining what order the work or tasks need attention. The design in the Exhibits is as good a tool as there is available for the purpose of making rank-order decisions. The form shown has been used in many different situations as decisions plagued the better use of time or priorities which needed to be set.

To use the grid (171,05), in the Exhibits, list each project twice, once on a horizontal line AND in the vertical column of the same number. When completed, evaluate each horizontally listed item against each vertically listed item. If the horizontal item is *more* important, put an X in the cell where they meet. If the horizontal item is less important, leave the box blank or place a O in it. After all comparisons have been made, add blank spaces, (O) under each column and enter the total in the row marked "Vert'l Spaces." The X's are then totaled *across* and the row's total is placed on the row marked "Horiz'l X's" in the same order as they are now shown vertically. Add the two rows and place the sum on the row marked "TOTAL." The highest sum is the #1 priority and the lowest number equals the last priority. In case of a tie, redo the two comparisons.

The reason the above prioritization grid works so well and is so easy to complete is simply that the user only ranks one consideration against a single other at any one time. The formidable list of ten to fifteen items to be ranked is hard to approach. A practical list of "problems" for application below may be the resolution of some priority of internal or external articulation concerns the principal may have in terms of how best to arrange the programs or projects that need to be addressed. Two of the roles of the schools are addressed here. The roles of

SELECTION and PLACEMENT are very much involved in articulation. (The other three roles are: Instruction, Custodialship, and Socialization).

Articulation can be considered internally and externally. Internal articulation is the balancing of programs within the high school. External articulation references those programs between feeder junior high schools (or middle or even elementary) and other high schools in or out of the district. Out-of-district articulation is done when programs, kids, or faculty are being exchanged to make the programs better for all students in either or both of the schools. Both are discussed in detail following the prioritizing grid below.

INTERNAL ARTICULATION

This is often done rather unconsciously by the manner in which the courses are assigned in the grid which will become the master schedule. By manipulating (meant to be positive in this context) the courses horizontally, one can openly or inadvertently schedule some students OUT of particular classes. The use of conflict matrix will at least point these out to the principal before the schedule is "put to bed" in late spring. Of course, the matrix can obviously show how to schedule some courses and students IN by the means in which the courses are put on the schedule. The faculty is not to be lost here either. Some teachers are selected more quickly by students than other teachers are selected. By placing specific courses in specific periods and behind specific teachers' names, one can limit the enrollment or schedule some students IN or OUT of courses. The means of which courses are offered which semester or alternating years is also a manner of PLACING or SELECTING out some students. Another means of articulating the programs in the building is to examine the prerequisites for courses. To REQUIRE physical science before biology before chemistry before physics makes no sense whatsover. Perhaps articulating Algebra I concurrently or before chemistry makes some sense. Now examine the intelligence of REQUIRING Algebra I before geometry before Algebra II. What sense does this make?

In a limited action research over eight years, there could not be found any significant difference in the productivity or result of sequencing either of these departmental courses. Articulation between departments makes more sense than the ones within a department. Prerequistes need to be considered as non-mandatory guides by putting them to the test of the prioritization grid.

The program is one of serious consequences for the student. A case which is bordering on either external or internal articulation is the one of how courses are scheduled when there are limitations. If the district has but one high school or the distance to another precludes joint-enrollments, the principal needs to place courses on an alternating semester or year basis. When the frequency of offerings is reduced, it is much easier to fill courses when they are offered.

Internal articulation of programs can be considered in the treatment of the schedule. The effective principal must be aware of the arrangement of all courses and the approval of all programs before articulation can be considered as final in the process of scheduling.

EXTERNAL ARTICULATION

Programs in other district schools are to be considered when students are short-changed in their home school. In multiple high school districts, the principal needs to coordinate the scheduling calendar with his/her peers in the other buildings. For each principal to sit and close courses for insufficient enrollment when combining enrollments from two or more schools would allow the course to be offered borders on malpractice -- certainly misfeasance of duties. Students go through high school but one time and THIS IS THE TIME. It behooves each principal to be an advocate for them and arrange whenever possible to get for them what they feel they need.

One can't forget the parochial high school principals in the area. Often the enrollment in some courses is too low to offer or the availability of faculty is restrictive

185

(on either's part) and by joining forces the course can be taught to ALL students rather than not offer it in either location.

Two or three meetings in the winter or early spring between principals can correct many potential restrictions on the master schedule. It may be wise to alter the starting times of each of the potentially participating high schools to allow students to move from program to program without penalty of the preceding or succeeding classes in the home high school. In St. Clair Shores, MI, the three high schools altered their time schedules by only fifteen minutes each, and the programs were joined in several instances. The high school on the north end of town started its program fifteen minutes earlier than normal (whatever that means), the high school in the middle left its time the same, and in the south end of town, the high school started fifteen minutes later than normal. In this way, students could pass between schools (two miles apart each way from the central high school) and take courses that would have been dropped in each of the three buildings.

Articulation externally can broaden the programs in the high school if the principal and counselors agree with the plan and work to assist students in the program's offerings. Some union contracts get in the way with this temporarily, but those roadblocks can be hammered out once the benefits are shown for the students. The faculty is not really involved differently; in fact, some save their jobs when courses are saved.

SUMMARY

Whether or not the articulation bug has bitten yet, it will. There is usually a better way to do something. If the principal remains the strong student advocate s/he has to be, there will be few irresolvable problems that cannot be eliminated. There are at least a dozen examples of articulation concerns alluded to above. It may be a wise decision to either list these, add others, or augment them in other ways. The grid can be of assistance to the principal to help make some of those tough decisions.

-- SAFETY CONSIDERATIONS IN THE H. S. --
With deference to:
Mr. Leonard Mecca, New Rochelle CSD
Mr. Thomas O. McCormick, Carlton PS
Mr. Edward Bach, Lake Shore PS

One of the basic tenets of school administration, that of Health, Safety, and Welfare, is SAFETY. One of the roles of public schools, that of custodialship of the student body, fits into this nicely as well. The principal will be amazed by going on a rigid inspection tour of each room in the facility and recording what is amiss in each. The safety of the student body and staff is tantamount to a successful year. The potential advent of a student or a staff member being hurt on the job is indeed troubling. Here are some tips on what needs to be looked for in each room of the building. There are some tips on how to get this done in a timely manner.

1. Have each item recorded on a tape recorder for transcription into task lists for custodial/or maintenance work for the week or month.

2. Examine each wall, the floor, ceiling, then equipment and furniture in the room. Inspect the plumbing and electricity also.

A. Ceiling Lighting:

Are the lighting tubes covered in a plastic cylinder for protection? Are the fixtures secured tightly to the ceiling? Are the bulbs all working? Is the brightness at or above regulation? Is the paint peeling, moldy, cracked, dirty, or causing glare? Is there any danger of asbestos surfaces (untreated) becoming air borne? Any apparent structural weaknesses? Any sign of leaks?

B. Walls and Windows

Are there evacuation routes and instructions clearly posted on the wall of each room showing precisely how to

187

exit properly? If there are built-ons (cupboards, etc.), are they still secured to the wall and not in danger of loosening when the supplies are in place? Are there any "added-to" items which need tightening: the pencil sharpener, flag mount, shelving brackets, hinged table-tops, or others? Are the surfaces peeling, moldy, cracked, dirty, or in any means not as they should be? Is the moulding secure? Are there "board-like" strips on the wall to keep furniture from marking the surfaces? Are the electrical wall plugs covered when not in use? Are they wall-mounted or in the floor?

Do window hinges allow the windows to be opened inward? (These cause a hazard for students moving about the room.) Are they fixed to prevent injuries by opening too far to the outside on the first floor? Are the locks securely in place and usable? Are all the pieces of glass (plastic) in place? Are the codes met for wire (layered) glass on larger surfaces to prevent shattering? Is the "H" bar installed to separate large surfaces? Are the windows each fully closable? Is there a draft, dust, or water?

((A caution: Be sure to have the material used in the regular substitution of glass approved by your local fire marshall so as not to cause an inadvertent problem for the fire protection of the facility!!))

C. Floor and flooring

Is the "sealer" used on the wax, tile or terazzo flooring causing dust? Is it slippery when wet? Is it used around plumbing fixtures? Is it non-toxic when worn off? Is the safety factor being overlooked for aesthetics and appearance? If carpeted, what is the anti-flame rating? Is it snag/runner proofed? Are there metal edges (with screws) to hold the carpet in place? If a partial carpet is in the room, how is it affixed on the perimeter? Is the carpet subject to mildew and spores in the air for allergies? Are the colors non-irritating? How frequently and with what is it cleaned?

D. Equipment and Fixtures

Is each "surface" on fixtures free from stacked boxes or other items sitting atop it? Are the cabinetry and shelves properly supported, or are they too small to support the pieces stored on them? Is there any item cluttering the room? In the labs: Are there any frayed wires, non-operating equipment, safety fixtures not in place, bad flooring, non-skid strips or paint surfaces worn or not appropriately located, safety lines painted around equipment, and are toxic-volatile fluids all properly maintained and in place? Are there goggles for each machine or available for check out to students? Is the passing of germs from one to another prevented by proper treatment of the safety glasses between users? Are all hoses, wires, pipes, tubes, lines, etc. in good repair? Are color-coded, exposed pipes painted so that no one will misuse the content?

E. Equipment and Furniture

Are all pieces non-splintered? Are plasic tablet arms properly affixed to the metal supports? Are there left-handed pieces of furniture in each room? Are there left-handed scissors available for students? Are bulletin boards affixed snugly to each of the surfaces to which they are hung? Are the chalk boards affixed properly and snugly? Are the dust (chalk) trays rounded at each end? Are the corners of shelves rounded? Are there fire blankets, special fire extinguishers, and medical kits available in ALL lab settings from art to vocational labs? Are ALL of the fire extinguishers properly charged? Are storage rooms meeting these same requirements?

F. Athletic and Activity Program

Athletic and activity program equipment brings about a whole list of new questions. To inspect each piece of protective padding for each sport is not the job of the principal. However, the preparation of a form for the official recording by the coach or sponsor indicating that each piece of personally assigned and team-used pieces are of the quality to protect the individuals in the sport is

189

definitely the principal's responsibility. This is no laughing matter. If the equipment is bad and not repairable, GET RID OF IT. That "scrub" needs to be as safe as the "star" in any sport! Are the bleachers safe, the lighting poles, the concession stand, the benches, the fencing, and the guide wires? Are the fields lined with chalk and not lime, the paint safe, the fertilizer of an approved variety, and the bulbs for lighting all set on the scoreboard? Are the first aid pieces supplies and equipment up-to-date and proper? Are there an ambulance and a doctor available for sports activities? Is there anyone on call during scrimmages as well as during the game itself?

G. Sites

Sites need to be examined carefully also. Are there any broken glass, pieces of wire, sticks and twigs, or any other foreign substances on the playing fields or physical education facilities or general property? How often are weeds controlled so that no allergies bother children? Are the sidewalks, pavements, driveways, and all surfaces properly maintained? Are there any "pot-holes" (my Michigan experiences!) which could cause accidents by vehicles or walkers? Any icy surfaces? Are the wires hung properly between the poles and/or building so none will break or so low they might cause a dangerous condition? Are the drain covers secured and open for ridding the site of surface water? Fencing in general needs to be examined also. Is the insect repellant program in place to ward-off bites?

H. Safety planning

Safety planning inside the building is also mandatory. Evacuation or "storage" of students and staff need to be in place for hurricane, snow blizzards, flood waters, ice, tornadoes, or whatever weather elements plague the ongoing program of the school. Be awfully careful that the safety of the humans in the building is top-most in consideration when doing the job properly. Teach the head custodian how to use the prioritization grid so the work to be done can be carefully planned and meet the expectations of the building principal.

Remember that S A F E T Y stands for:

Sincere
Awareness
For
Energetic
Tours by
Yourself

-- CHAPTER TWO INTRODUCTION --
- Structuring the Office Routine -

There are four units in this chapter. The chapter and unit titles are:

Establishing a Managerial Aura

Management by Exception
Recommendations
Standard Practice Bulletins
Agenda Preparation
Cards to Carry
Master Schedule
Department Heads

Communication
Network
Conflict Management
Propaganda
Principal Contacts
Advisory Committees
Advocate-Ombudsman

Paperwork and People Aides

Evaluation of Textbooks
Fog and Smog Indices
Randall Plan of Employee Eval
Hardesty's 3 X 3 Evaluations

Case Study
Exceptional Students
Entrance Interviewing
Exit Interviewing

Preparation of Significant Statements

Critical Action Papers
Suicide Prevention Program
Misery Index

Wind Chill Grid
Curriculum Newsletter

Substructures for Sound Support

Closed Loop Fanout
Three Student Committees
Faculty Advisory Committee
School Volunteers and
Teacher aides

Progressive Honor Roll
Survival/Literacy/
Competency Vocabu-
lary

In these chapters and units, the principal can find some interesting and workable means to control the situations s/he finds daily in the schools of today. Chapter Four provides several units which were designed for easing

192

the management load. In this way, the principal can get to what the whole job should be about: to take care of the instructional program. Unit Five is provided to give the principal some help in evaluating the various programs and projects of the high school. The subunit on interviewing students as they exit or enter the high school is one which will involve students in their school and many sound practices came from this source. Unit Six will help the neophyte or experienced principal in the onerous job of writing papers to be of assistance in directing the operation of the high school. There are two subunits added here which the principal may wish to review and prepare significant material for the faculty. Two of the authors favorite writers are Hart and Epstein. Their work is placed here because some of the documents that need to be developed can easily start here as a practical base of action in curriculum. In the last unit, Unit Seven, the principal is given some information items which s/he needs to develop support systems within the organization.

Chapter Two is information to use to structure a base from which the principal can operate differently. Schools are either stasis or change oriented and if change is the mode of operation this chapter will provide the principal with several items to be of assistance to make that measurable difference.

- UNIT FOUR INTRODUCTION -
Establishing A Managerial Aura

The subunits in this management-dedicated part are:

Management by Exception	Communication Networks
Recommendations	Conflict Management
Standard Practice Bulletins	Propaganda
Agenda Preparation	Principal Contacts

Cards to Carry   Advisory Committees
Master Schedule   Advocate and Ombudsman
Department Heads in the H. S.

There really is no taxonomy to follow in learning or applying the tools presented in this subunit. The use of any of the tools is applied when THAT particular tool is needed. The application is a one-on-one proposition.

To manage everything in the organization is a big role the principal must assume as a key task of being in charge. It is nearly impossible to keep in mind all the details that are ongoing in a building with the many committees and routines established. This system of organizing a style of managing by exception will aid the principal in getting a wide range of tasks accomplished and under control.

Recommendations come to the principal many times during the year. To help keep the information in a usable pattern, this form can save time and energy for the busy principal. It shows conciseness and pertinent information to be examined. When it is used with regularity, the time saved and its value grows geometrically.

Standard Practice Bulletins (SPBs) will help the principal in the design of a series of significant papers. The outline is simple to follow. Once this technique is introduced to the staff members, the principal will see some submissions of suggested SPB's from them. It is one tool which can be referred to as "quick and dirty."

Agenda preparation can be a real drain on the energy of the principal. To keep track mentally of what needs to go on which agenda is a task that can be handled routinely. The principal will do well by reading the unit on the tickler files and scintillating six along with this subunit to get the whole picture. In any respect the careful design of an effective agenda will be a mark of the principal's ability to lead and must not be ignored.

194

Cards to carry is treated last. These 3 X 5 index cards can be used to convey messages between the principal and staff on a regular basis. The manner to use them for communication closure is highlighted in the subunit.

The subunit on the Master Schedule is more in line with some of the older philosophies than the other material but worthy of reading because when used, even today, these philosophies are worth the time to consider for the benefit of the student body. The master schedule is always a big concern and assuredly one in which the principal must always try to get assistance. The principal must not SCHEDULE THE PROGRAM; instead, the principal must PROGRAM THE SCHEDULE. The difference is not subtle. It makes a difference as to whether the principal is concerned about scheduling the faculty or scheduling the students. In other words, a principal can get the program in place and schedule it rather than to make a comfortable schedule and program it. Students need to be scheduled differently each semester or year. To design a "comfortable" schedule and then work to have the programs reflect it is wrong. There are many computerized programs on the market which provide assistance in this area.

High school departmental representatives are a necessity in any successful high school organizational structure. The principal needs assistance to accomplish the many tasks assigned and those others which seem to get completed automatically. Every faculty has to have internal leadership. Each principal has enough to do in the management of the enterprise to stay busy without the many tasks that each department can complete with a minimum of direction to finalize them. A ready and willing cadre of close supporters that is willing to help get the job done is good to have available. There is a management axiom that there is no vacuum of power. This is particularly true in a high school. If leadership is gradually taken by others not recognized in the formal hierarchy, it is not long and the formal hierarchy is not recognized as anything other than the titular heads of the enterprise.

How to develop a community network to get messages out and receive those the principal needs to know will be covered in this subunit. The method is simple. The routine of recording changes can be bothersome unless a schematic is developed for rumors in and rumors out.

Conflict is but a normal part of the principal's professional life. It is a real hassle unless one knows how to deal with conflict from defusing to "putting the water on the fire." One must manage it or someone else will.

How is the proper message gotten across to a diverse population when each of the many publics in the school community is different? It is a tough thing to do. The proper message is often times referred to as the "hidden message." It is called this even though it is not deliberately kept from an another but rather that it is that message that is sent whenever a contact is made with someone in the community irrespective of the message being given verbally. The unit on Propaganda will give the principal some ideas from an excellent psychologist-communicator, who assisted principals to become the type of principal the community wanted without their giving up any of their own personal principles.

The principal is being beseiged constantly by a wide variety of contacts. This chart may help to tell the story of the day in the life of a principal. It will be helpful for the principal to chart his/her own contacts to verify their routine.

Advisory committees are becoming more and more popular (Management's Theory Z ?) and, in fact, required or mandated with the distribution of allocated monies by an external source. This is one of seven factors which the principal must confront daily. See the LISTS section in the Appendix for the rest of these.

Advocate and/or Ombudsman fits most principals' philosophy as most are true advocates of kids. If, in fact, a principal is not, his/her job will create more stress or burn-out than it should. High school students are a great deal of fun despite their struggle to adulthood. The problems and concerns they have are serious to them irrespective of how they are perceived by the principal or staff member. Terry G. Semones says, "It may be puppy love to you, but it's important to the puppy."

- MANAGEMENT BY EXCEPTION -

MBE is not tough to understand conceptually. When one does some management work, and not all of it, s/he is doing management by exception. The issue here is to get things done through others for the "management" part and by not having to do everything all the time for the part of "by exception." However, another management axiom comes to mind here. It is that to manage by exception means one must also stay in charge, in control. To do this best, "One does better that which is inspected rather than just expected." So to assure this is being done, the effective principal sets some guidelines to get it done, and by exception only when a parameter is violated does s/he get involved with the day-to-day operation. S/he is ever-mindful that there is no vacuum of power. This concept is not to be confused with abdication.

Concentrating on what is important rather than all the urgent tasks a principal needs to monitor will be a time saver and another means of becoming effective in the principalship. Deviations from the norm are called to the principal's attention, and action is taken through the reference of the Five M's of Management:

Wo M en
M oney
M aterial
M achines
M inutes

They can be listed in any order as each is supported by the other four. The 5 M's can be used as reminders to the principal about action that must be taken. In other words, the one "M" which must be cared for is the one of minutes. To correct this problem when the appropriate schedule is found to be deviated, the principal can, by example, use additional staffing (men), approve overtime (money), provide more supplies (material), or secure more equipment (machines). Any combination of the four can correct the first.

There are several advantages to practicing some form of MBE. The key elements are as follows:

1. The best is the saving of the *principal's personal time*. S/he can spend more time on fewer problems; therefore, the work becomes easier on the tasks that really count. It will minimize the time-consuming work on what the author has affectionately labeled "manurtia," which clogs the wheels of true progress.

2. It will tend to *stimulate communication* which causes a better flow of opinions.

3. It lessens greatly the *frequency of decision making* because others will begin to accept their responsibilities. Once subordinates begin to realize that only the most severe situations should be brought to a principal's attention, they can relax.

4. It will allow the principal, no, force him/her to use *people more properly* than s/he is at the current time.

5. An effective principal can *increase the sphere of influence* s/he has because the *doing* is done by others and the principal is responsible for the overall direction or management.

6. Lastly, it will allow the principal to *spend more time where s/he needs it* and be more comfortable by *working on critical areas*. This allows the principal to *tackle promising projects*.

7. It enables inexperienced principals to handle assignments.

8. It alerts principals to opportunities as well as difficulties.

9. It identifies crises and critical problems.

10. It reduces distractions by keeping items under control routinely.

In instruction, MBE can be used for the control of such things as a responsibility of observations and evaluations. For students, it can be used for assessment of student marks. By merely choosing one word from each row and column, one will see that there are many machinations.

BY TEACHER
BY COURSE
BY SEMESTER
BY STUDENT
BY SECTION
BY MARKING PERIOD

An example of MBE might be a teacher's English report for a semester. If MBE is used, the exception would be selecting all English courses as one group. If the totals don't make any sense, the report would be asked for on a section by section basis. With the advent of the computer, it is easy to get MBE reports rather than a single, long, detailed report. To deal with it, the principal might request an exception report. This might be a report of all E's given or a report by percent or one by teacher or one by course or one by a specific department or one by level of ability, etc.

As for the evaluation process, the principal can get reports from the secretary as follows:

BY ADMINISTRATOR
BY MONTH
BY DEPT OR GRADE LEVEL
BY WEEK
BY TEACHER
BY TENURE LEVEL

For the responsibility of business management, MBE can be used by the bookkeeper for the expenditures from the budget. Budgetary applications could be reported on the following basis:

BY DEPTARTMENT
BY PERCENT ENCUMBERED
BY ACCOUNT NUMBER
BY TEACHER
BY MONTH
BY LINE ITEM

It is essential to remember to pick just one of the two choices from each column and each row to get the report prepared.

The principal can also ask for the reports to be filed in each of these categories by a specific number, like each third, etc.:

Disaster Drill Reports
Cafeteria Menus
Bomb Scares
Student Drops/Adds
Fire Drills
Tornado Alerts
Attendance Reports
Teacher Absences

Information is presented on what is referred to as the PARETO PRINCIPLE within this text. (131,52) To summarize it, "20% of the staff will cause 80% of the problems, or 20% of the students will cause 80% of the absenteeisms, etc. It is this trend for which the principal will be searching on a MBE basis.

When the secretary detects an exception to the norm, several things happen automatically:

1. The secretary notifies the overseer (assistant or principal) of the discrepancy.

2. The overseer examines the discrepancy and makes a judgment as to the action that can be taken.

   a. The secretary makes a notation on the chart as to how the discrepancy will be corrected, b. The overseer discusses the " shortage" with the person who has caused it so that the two of them can work toward a mutually satisfying resolution.

3. Corrective action is taken.

4. Necessary adjustments are made on subsequent agenda, etc.

Several tools fall into this routine. The names of them are listed below. In some cases, the tools listed below are not primarily management by exception tools but can be used for that purpose.

Action Demand Charts	Gantt Charts
Linear Demand Charts	Standard Practice Bulletins
Prog. Eval. Review Tech.	Force Field Analysis
Flow Charts and others	Prioritizing Grid
Standard Operating Procedures	

Perhaps this quote by W. J. Reddin will put this into perspective for Management By Exception:
An administrator's true worth to an organization can best be measured by the

length of time one could be dead in the office without anyone's noticing it.

- RECOMMENDATIONS -

One of management's good adages is "Don't bring me your questions; bring me your alternatives." The recommendation form will do just that. Other principal-managers say, "Tell me what you want, why, and what happens if you don't get it?"

Another adage is "If you don't have an objective, how will you know when you get there?"

The last adage which also tells the story is "I know that you believe that you understand what you think I said. But I'm not sure you realize that what you heard is not what I meant."

Far too much time is lost when skimming and scanning are not practiced. Principals need to develop these skills along with the skill of rapid reading. But to save a great deal of time before, during, and after these skills are learned, one should synopsize any report by designing a cover sheet. A good cover is a vital part of any recommendation. The sheet should be divided into these major categories:

1. Recommendation
2. Rationale
3. Best Alternative
4. Inhibitors
5. Endorsements

The form needs a proper heading. This was already pointed out in the subunit labeled as memo writing. It should be affixed to the major document, if there is one, to be forwarded. When the principal receives a recommendation, the same procedure should have been followed by the staff. The blank form follows the explanation.

Here is a brief explanation of the categories, why they are listed as such, and why they are in the specific order as above.

1. RECOMMENDATION

The first thing to relate is the recommendation. If the receiver agrees with the statement, the reading is nearly completed. These should be written in no more than three sentences and in sentences of no more than eleven to fifteen words. Also, each recommendation should be put on a separate page. The statements ought to be clear, concise, concrete, and complete. The wording ought to be simple, understandable, and should be able to stand independently should these cover sheets become unattached.

2. RATIONALE
If the recommendation is not clear or the receiver wishes some additional information, the rationale comes right after the statement of the recommendation for that purpose. These statements should be at least three in number with no more than five specific reasons to support the recommendation. They should say all that there is needed to be said about **why** the recommendation is being made. In an article (156,261) the following three categories were suggested as headings to be used for the rationale.

Each is explained later but for this purpose, suffice it to say, they were selected because (1) each clarifies and satisfies any intent of a recommendation, (2) each indicates a part of the principal's position, and (3) each identifies a list of categories in the life of a manager.

Purposes of Pub. Ed.	*Task Areas of Principals*
Selection	Instruction
Placement	Students
Instruction	Staff
Custodialship	Comm./Sch. Relations
Socialization	Bus./Bldg. Mgt.

5 M's of Management in Education

M en
M oney
M aterial
M achines
M inutes

Most frequently, when any one of the three lists is addressed, it will be found to be sufficient for clarifying the recommendation. Specific terms are defined in the introduction of Part I.

3. ALTERNATIVE

Yes, there is always one alternative -- to remain with the status quo. There are others also. Usually there are at least two; so the form calls for two. In other words, what can (should) or will be done if the recommendation is not carried out? Some thought on this will be helpful, and it is vital. The boss ought to know these.

4. INHIBITORS

Something will impede the natural progress even with the best recommendation made. Careful thought on this category may cause the savings of a great deal of time at a later date.

5. ENDORSEMENTS

There is space for endorsements because the final recipient ought to know who (dis)approves the recommendation. For example, unless they are shown, (1) some supervisors would not give their subordinates any due credit, and this is wrong, (2) no "level" ought to be ignored, and (3) the determination of each level's support ought to be shown.

If one was to put this management style into practice, it could be explained as follows using the standard practice format from the next unit.

PURPOSE: To establish a uniform format for personnel to use when a recommendation is being made to the principal of the building.

GENERAL: The idea of reading through pages and pages of material before one knows what is being recommended is time-consuming. The real point may well be lost in the verbiage.

RECOMMENDATIONS, to be helpful, ought to be briefly stated and supportable by evidence with major (when necessary) appendices affixed.

PROCEDURE: To forward a recommendation to the principal, one shall attach as a cover sheet:

a. The precise recommendation s/he is making.
b. A list of the rationale which supports the recommendation.
c. Alternatives to the recommendation.
d. The inhibitors listed to clarify information.

Lines and/or spacing may have to be adjusted to fit the situation when the following recommendation form is developed for use.

===

– RECOMMENDATION FORM –
VERMILION PARISH SCHOOL DISTRICT

TO:_____ Date:____/____/____
                                         GEM#12
FROM:_____ ____ # ____

RECOMMENDATION STATEMENT

_____

_____

_____

_____

RATIONALE

1. _____

_____

2. _____

_____

3. _____

_____

4. _____

_____

5. _____

_____

INHIBITORS

1. _____

2. _____

3. _____

4. _____

APPROPRIATE TIME LINE AS NEEDED

Initiate Project:___/___/___
Complete Project:___/___/___
Influence of time as it impacts this rec.

_____

_____

_____

PROJECTED COST FOR IMPLEMENTATION

Men: _____ Material: _____

Machines: _____

BEST ALTERNATIVE

_____

_____

_____

_____

_____

ENDORSEMENTS

1. Building Principal:_____ Date:__/__/__

2. Dir.:_____Date:__/__/__
(Dis)approved_____   return:_____ (See Back)

2. Cabinet Members' Action:__Date:__/__/__
(Dis)approved_____   return:_____ (See Back)

Superintendent:_____ Date:__/__/__
(Dis)approved_____   return:_____ (See Back)

==

- STANDARD PRACTICE BULLETINS -

These important documents save time and careers when prepared well. They are called bulletins because of their brevity. They stand in the place of policy because they are management tools and not necessarily work of the Board of Education.

What They Do:

1. They enforce continuity.

2. They describe an operation which then becomes a routine when prepared at any level of the hierarchy.

3. They function as "administrative policy" in an organization.

4. They save time by having all personnel know how things are to be done in set situations. In fact, they will soon accumulate as more SPBs are developed.

5. They provide directions for personnel in the operation of a complex system.

The SPBs are written in three major parts. The parts are:

(1) Purpose
(2) General
(3) Procedure.

The format of the SPB's described here was developed by Mr. Norman L. Bouche, Director of Business Operations of Monroe Public Schools.

The need for this type of bulletin arose when standardizing of practices was needed to direct some middle managers requesting equipment "on approval." The bulletin to control this practice in the Monroe Public Schools is used as an example. It is altered somewhat for this book.

I. PURPOSE:

To set forth procedures to be followed when it is desirable to obtain certain items, on approval, for examination by any staff member.

II. GENERAL:

It is sometimes necessary that an item be obtained for inspection before a decision can be or ought to be made as to the serviceability of the item to the particular application desired. Many vendors will ship merchandise on this basis.

III. PROCEDURES:

A. In the event merchandise should be ordered, use of a regular district purchase order is the only manner which will be approved.

B. All information regarding approval status shall be shown on the face of the order.

C. If and when items need to be returned, a letter shall accompany the merchandise when sent to the central warehouse.

D. All returned "purchase order items" shall be routed to the central warehouse and will be packed and shipped from that point only --- with the letter included.

E. A copy of the letter shall be sent to the Business Office (in the central office) and a carbon to the principal.

F. Personnel must follow this procedure explicitly or Board of Education or school building funds can not be used to pay for goods.

By following this bulletin's format, several things happen which improve management style and behavior, eliminate spurious charges being made to the high school's accounts, and save time as another form of MANAGEMENT BY EXCEPTION. When a process causes a SNAFU, a standard practice bulletin can outline the proper change to be made and everyone can gain from it.

An abbreviated format is shown below as printed and distributed to the staff members on which they can recommend a SPB.

To: The Staff of The Erna Obenaus H. S.　　GEM # F22
　　　　　　　　　　　　　　　　　　　　　　　　　15 Aug 65

From: Dr. Gene E. Megiveron, Principal
Subj: Format to be used when recommending a practice to become a standard for all staff to follow in the building.

STANDARD PRACTICE BULLETIN #____

To: _____   Memo # ____ - ____
From: _____, Dept. Date:___/___/___
SUBJECT:_____

PURPOSE TO SERVE: _____

_____

_____

_____

_____

GENERAL STATEMENT TO EXPLAIN ITS USE:

_____

_____

_____

_____

_____
PROCEDURES TO BE FOLLOWED:
1. _____

2. _____

3. _____

4. _____

5. _____

6. _____

7. _____

- AGENDA PREPARATION -

This essential tool for the principal is usually overlooked, making it difficult to know what is going to happen, what is needed, and what is important even to the one planning the agenda (or the meeting).

There are some glaring errors made in the planning of the agenda for meetings, and these need to be discussed. Some of the most egregious follow:

ERRORS

1. *Not getting the agenda to the invited membership at least twenty-four hours ahead of the meeting.*

This really bothers most participants because the agenda items can be resolved much more quickly and efficiently if the group knows what it is that is to be discussed. The meeting will serve all participants best once each has had an opportunity to think about the items on the agenda before the meeting is convened.

Some subordinates may have a valid reason to miss a meeting. They may well say something like, "I don't see anything on the agenda which is particularly fruitful for my operation. Is it all right if I use my time differently?" Most of the time respect can be shown to their request if they understand what it is that needs to be done in both situations -- the meeting and in their work. However, there will be times when they need to be at the meeting to give their input on an issue. Others may need to hear their thinking. In any respect, ALLOW THE MEMBERS THE COURTESY TO GET SOME BACKGROUND WORK DONE BEFORE THEY ARRIVE. THE MEETING WILL FLOW MUCH BETTER WITH AN ADVANCED AGENDA THAN IF THE PARTICIPANTS ARE SURPRISED WITH THE SUBSTANCE OF THE MEETING. Getting the agenda out ahead of the meeting is a real application of both the terms effective = doing right things and efficiency = doing things right.

2. *Not separating announcements, discussion topics, or action items.*

If the staff does not know how the chair wants to dispense with the topic, it can hardly be expected to know how to make contributions. A good agenda does not permit a meeting to drag on and on. It should have all items packaged and labeled. After all, delivery is the intent of a good meeting. This is best done by grouping the topics by categories or purpose. When done properly, the control of the meeting will more easily stay in the hands of the chair.

3. *Not requiring attendance at meetings.*

With the advent of the bargained union contract, there frequently is a limit on the number and length of meetings principals can call in the building. A way of not eroding the contract is to allow the staff to miss meetings. There is no limitation as to the accountability a staff members holds for the information exchanged at a meeting. If a staff member misses the meeting, all material covered can be acted upon by direction of those in attendance.

Big communication traps principals fall into are that they involve too many people or involve them in the wrong forum or at the wrong time. Creative thinkers should be invited to planning meetings or portions of meetings principals can call in the building. If a staff member is particularly adept at expanding ideas or developing them to their fullest, the principal should make sure that s/he is at the meetings where this is the goal. If some staff members are particularly adept at evaluation or assessment of something so it can be improved, these people should attend that form of meeting or portion of meeting. Because there is a variety of types of participants and a range of "mixes" within the group, few being "pure" types, each should be used properly. Once the realization hits that true involvement of each and everyone of the staff in each or all decisions is virtually impossible, it is advisable that the principal not fake his/her way through the leadership maze by inviting "all" the staff to every meeting that is called. However, a determination of the types of participants needed and the intelligent use of talents make the organization as efficient as it can be. The principal should involve each set of staff in the proper type of meeting or at the proper time in a meeting. There is a science of study on group participants. It is something which should not be ignored by the principal.

4. *Discussing items which are really announcements*:

The proposed format of the correctly determined agenda will explain these carefully enough. Each item has been numbered for reference. The agenda appearing on the next pages is a literal one which served the purpose of the meeting and required only thirty-two minutes for its completion. The staff numbers only thirty on the list, but in reality there were over one hundred participants. The names on the agenda are shown alphabetically for ease of recording the roll. Secondly, each name represents others. There are fifteen department representatives, three students, the head custodian, head dietician, office manager, director of transportation, an assistant superintendent, four assistants or assistants to the principal, the principal, all counselors and librarians. Others who attend will be recorded and reported. The ones listed are mandatory attendees to assure total communication throughout the building. Everyone on the staff has the "right" to attend. Everyone should also be held totally accountable for any actions taken by this group. The strange part of this whole administrative practice was that seldom did ANYONE want to miss a meeting and if absent s/he made sure someone had his/her proxy and took copious notes to read when s/he returned.

The next pages will carry an agenda with the actual headings of:

1. MEMBERSHIP
2. GUESTS
3. ANNOUNCEMENTS

4. DISCUSSION ITEMS
5. ACTION ITEMS
6. UPDATES
7. HANDOUTS
8. DATES/THINGS

====

WTHS Staff Mtg. # 38

PRESIDING_____

RECORDING_____

Choral Room - WTHS, "B" Wing

September 06, 1966   2:56 p.m. - 4:05 p.m.

MEMBERSHIP: till 3:00

Dr. Megiveron, Miss Bulla, Mr. Merritt -

Alcinda____	Lawless____	Rightly_____
Bottom_____	Mackenzie__	Smith_____
Bulla_____	McCormick__	Something____
Crumpton___	Megiveron__	Taylor_____
Emerick____	Merritt____	Truthout____
Gilmore____	Moffat_____	Ubetcha_____
Haus_____	Mollon_____	Vaughn_____
Kindred____	Paton_____	Wanta_____

GUESTS:

Welcome will be given by Dr. Megiveron to: Mr. Edward Bach, Director of Custodial Operations; Dr. Leonard Mecca, Insurance Matrix Planner; Mr. Thomas E. Prenkert, Budget Building and Control; Dr. John A. Beleutz, Supt.

ANNOUNCEMENTS: till 3:05

1. * Field Trips tentatively planned for

215

the year must be listed and returned to Mrs. Vaughn, Office Manager, by the end of the week for validation.

2. * Substitute Emergency Plans are still due from nine.

3. Planning for necessary adjustments due to inclement weather will be done in room 201 at 3:00 on Thursday. ALL ARE WELCOME.

4. Mr. Merritt, Miss Bulla, and Dr. Gilmore have birthday anniversaries soon. HAPPY BIRTHDAY TO EACH !!!

5. * Principal's 3 student advisory committees meet this next Wednesday. As usual, all faculty are welcome as spectators. See the Handbook (yearly schedule) for the place and time.

6. * Fire Drills are scheduled to begin next week. See the Handbook page (attached) for your specific duty.

7. Formal observations of faculty begin on October 3. SIGN UP NOW!!

DISCUSSION ITEMS: till 3:35

1. Custodial problems in the morning....   Dr. Gilmore
                                            Mr. Bach

2. Insurance determination of equipment..Mr. Semones
                                            Dr. Mecca
3. Budget building the building budget.. Dr. Megiveron
                                            Mr. Prenkert
4. * United Foundation drive .   .   Ms. Willing
5. * Main highway school crossing.......   Mr. Merritt
6. * Transportation for non-owner drivers Dr. Beleutz
ACTION ITEMS, recommendations: till 4:00

* P.R. # 09-026-65/66. . . . Dr. Megiveron
Move to approve forwarding the recommendation on the U. S. history text as approved by the faculty and Mr. Amell, Supervisor of social sciences.

* P.R. # 09-027-65/66. . . . Dr. Megiveron
Move to approve the calendar and schedule for MEAP
testing for all tenth graders.

* P.R. # 09-028-65/66. . . . Dr. Megiveron
Move to approve the purchase of ten (10) copies of the
book by Gene E. Megiveron. *The Role of Research in the
Classroom.*(East Lansing, MI: SDE, Res. Bulletin # 203,
1965.) Material to be assigned to each department and in
professional library. Cost not to exceed $250.00.

UPDATES: till 4:05

1. The schedule alteration recommendation we made to
the transportation department was accepted and is being
built into other recommendations the department received
From them and me, THANKS - YA DONE GOOD!

2. The report on the acoustics in the cafeteria has been
received by Mr. Geddis and is being placed on the next
BOE meeting for consideration by the entire Board.

HANDOUTS FOR THE MEETING:

H-1-A1. Field Trip Request Form -- those who have not
submitted one to date. Negative reports are essential.

H-2-A2. Emergency Sub. Outline -- to those who have not
submitted one to Mrs. Vaughn ASAP. Due ASAP

H-3-A5. Schedule sheet on Student Advisory Meetings w/
Dr. GEM

H-4-A6. Schedule on fire drill procedure from Staff Handbook

H-5-D4. UF Drive Explanatory Material authored by Dr.
Beleutz

H-6-D5. Safety Routes Augmentation Plan as detailed by
Dr. Gilmore

H-7-D6. Transportation Scheduling as drafted by Dr. Gilmore

H-8-R1. Book evaluation material for U. S. history (*not American history*) as submitted by faculty committee on curriculum

H-9-R2. Calendar and schedule of committee approved MEAP testing

H-10-R3. Book evaluation material for "Effectiveness" as submitted by steering committee

H-11   Minutes from last meeting

DATES AND THINGS:

1.   BOE meeting on this Thursday, 8:00 Administrative Center. We have a vested interest in the "Survey on Staff Welfare".   Representatives assigned to attend will be providing notes of the Board Members' comments. See Handbook for your upcoming assignment date.

2.   Next staff meeting scheduled is on September 13, same time, and same place as this one.

3.   The minutes from the last meeting stand as recorded with no objection from a staff member brought to the principal's attention *before the meeting is convened*. (If any objection does occur, the "corrected" minutes will be distributed at the meeting and placed on the agenda for staff consideration).

Each of the categories of the agenda need to be discussed. Thoughtful considerations of each item should be made before its inclusion on an agenda. Meetings need to be well planned. The results will be as planned.

The above agenda was a meeting when seemingly a little of everything was set to be handled by the principal, the faculty, and the remainder of the staff. From the opening information to the last item on the agenda, the meeting moved along swiftly and purposefully. Remember that it was in the hands of everyone (whose name appears on the face of the agenda) at a minimum of twenty-four hours before the meeting was scheduled to begin. This is not an insignificant point and, therefore, is repeated for clarity of its significance.

Each agenda has a specific heading. The number of the meeting is helpful later when referring to a particular set of minutes or a specific agenda. The person assigned to conduct the meeting is listed (on a line here because the administrators rotated this responsiblity among themselves). The recorder was assigned on the agenda on a rotating basis as well. However, it went through the secretarial/clerical staff on its rotation. The location of the meeting room was specific. The date and times were shown. It is important that a meeting start on time and as important that it end on time. Terry G. Semones says a good meeting conductor is done before the meeting attendees are. The ending time is posted so that all participants can plan their afternoon, riding pools, activities with kids, etc. One of the old adages used in management is helpful here.

"Work expands to fill the time available."

If there are two hours, the meeting, conference, or whatever will take two hours. In this agenda, the meeting was to end at 4:05. When the agenda has the "flow" of this one, it is easy to see that the heavies are listed last. Everyone wants to vote on the recommendations so the meeting moves along to get to that item. The starting time is not the typical "on the hour" setting. It is more noticeable if the meeting begins as this one shows: 2:56 p.m. or 3:02 p.m. so each will actually take notice of the time. It works! Also the amount of time for each heading was shown on the agenda as a guide.

219

MEMBERSHIP:

All of those who were to be in attendance were listed. The recorder had an alphabetized list of ALL staff members so if anyone came to the meeting, it was a matter of merely checking his name and he was included in the minutes. The minutes, by the way, only showed significant closures and actions taken. To understand all the inner-workings of the meetings, one had to be there. In the case of membership, most if not all of the staff participated. Remember that the seasonal head coach, the driver training program director, the heads of departments and staff groups, etc. were all expected to attend to make sure the entire staff was represented. The mandatories were alphabetized, again, for easy recording.

GUESTS:

Invited guests should be listed. The comments in the unit on secretarial conferencing or tickler files indicate how these names are NOT lost in the shuffle. When a guest is introduced, the conductor makes sure s/he is given a round of applause for attending. The guest is called upon when his/her item on the agenda comes around. Usually guests are invited for the discussion part of the agenda. Their items are listed first so they may leave if they choose to do that. They should not be forced to sit through a heavy agenda before being called upon to participate. It may be impractical to invite them for the vote on their topic (should one be necessitated) at the next meeting. Admittedly, they may return when the item does come for a vote.

ANNOUNCEMENTS:

These items call for NO discussion. If there are any questions, the staff is encouraged to ask them before the meeting so as not to take any time from the meeting itself. Some of them will reference a handout. The asterisk tells the reader there is an attachment for reference. The chair should not allow a discussion on any of these items. A good use of this agenda item is to list absentees and the reason so the remainder of those "required" to be there will not be uptight because "so and so" is absent. The substitute representative's name should be listed to alleviate any concern for the spokesperson in the discussion of topics later on the agenda. Follow-up notes on work can be introduced at this point of the agenda.

DISCUSSION ITEMS:

These are just that. They are to be discussed by any and all attendees. They usually are translated into ACTION items later so the discussion is serious. These topics bring the membership of the staff to the meetings. When closure is brought to these discussion topics, there is consensus gained, acknowledged, and recorded, but this is not a vote. The leader of the discussion is POSTED for all discussion topics and other segments of the agenda.

ACTION ITEMS:

A code is used here also. The code tells which item it was on which agenda and when it took place:

PR = Principal's Recommendation,
09 = September's Meeting,
26 = the number of the action item considered by the staff this fiscal year, and
89/90 = the fiscal year in which it was acted upon.

Coding is helpful when searching for a reference later in the year. Here is an example:

PR # 9-26-89/90

It is good to tell the staff in orientation that voting is important to the operation of the democratic administration of the building. In a half-kidding and half-serious tone, however, the principal reserves at least three times to call for a paper ballot to count the votes rather than have a show of hands. In other words, there may be a limited number of times when by virtue of the position held, the principal will not be able to necessarily go along with the

221

vote of the staff. Staffs like this, believe it or not. The have asked, "Is this one of those paper ballot discussions or action items, Gene?" If it was, I told them before the vote. But when discussing a "sticky" topic, they would be the ones wanting to place the burden of a decision on the principal. A principal should avoid putting anything on this part of the agenda which will result in a nonsensical vote. If the vote really won't make a difference, the staff ought to know it. Staff members will appreciate and be supportive of a position that needs to be taken when the majority or upper echelons of the administration want it this way, especially when their principal agrees.

The manner of numbering and the actual statement of the recommendation should be noted. It is important that specificity prevails. In fact, by the clarity and explanatory enclosures for the items, with twenty-four hours to consider them and plenty of time for discussion before the meeting, there will be more times than not in which the staff will use the consent agenda and adopt all three motions at one time. This will please the principal and serve as a good thermometer for the job being done. The name of the responsible party is listed for action items as they were in discussion items.

UPDATES:

These comments are not really announcements as such because they have been acted upon earlier usually in the ACTION format. Again, no discussion is needed, but these updatees are certainly worthy of being noted.

HANDOUTS:

These are listed in order of their appearance on the agenda. The items here have been coded for specific topics. The following will show the actual (only handwritten on the original for clarity) code used on each of the enclosures.

H - 1 - A1
Mtg. # 38
9/26/89

The first is the agenda level, (H-1-A1);
the second, the number of that series of meeting,
(Mtg. # 38); and,
the date of the meeting, (9/26/89).

With these on the sheet, it is easy to match the handout (later) with the actual agenda item to which it refers. Also if it becomes detached from the original packet, it is still easy to see when it was distributed to the staff and in what context. This will prove to be a GEM because those in executive positions will find themselves inundated with paperwork. This is another manner to learn to control it.

DATES AND THINGS:

The main feature to include is the date of the next meeting in order for material to get to the principal's office in time for consideration on the agenda.

Once the agenda is finalized, the meeting is held, and minutes are recorded AND accepted, the agenda should be put in the monthly tickler file marked September (in this case) so that all is set for the next year.

- CARDS TO CARRY -

When in those "miles" of corridors, the principal will be stopped many times. Questions are posed, situations explained, "upbucking" is attempted, and favors requested. Each is legitimate, but when the rounds are completed there could well be a half-dozen items for which the principal will be held accountable by various staff members. This may seem unfair to the principal who is the only one able to resolve many problems.

To eliminate this mental burden, the principal should carry 3 X 5 index cards in his/her coat pocket. When someone stops the principal and asks for something, the principal should hand him a card and request that he write a note and put it in the office mailbox or drop it off with the secretary. The use of these cards will save time from trying to recall every request. It will get to the point whereby staff will begin to carry cards for note-taking and when they see the principal, it will be easy for them to hand him/her the card.

A warning is in order about the use of the cards. Care must be taken to avoid the charge of seeming inhuman. It is wise not to use the cards until the reasons for using them have been covered in a general staff meeting. Staff members will become comfortable with them and understand that the procedure is not an attempt to "put them off." Depersonalization charges are very easy to make and very difficult to reverse irrespective of authenticity. After a discussion in a staff meeting, no one will mind the use of the cards.

A.V.O.* pads should be available in the main office. The staff should use the original (white copy) and leave it in the office mailbox when they have recorded their concern or question. If after a couple of days, they have not received a reply, they should put the yellow copy (carbon) in the principal's mailbox. The color will flag the principal that s/he needs to give the second request prompt attention. This procedure usually works fine unless there is a John Moffat in the building. He constantly put the yellow copy in first just to get the principal's attention. It worked a couple of times, and then he was "caught." To ignore the use of this type of management tool is in reality misoneism. It is easy to be critical until one tries it.

* = A void V erbal O rders

There are two distinctive philosophies of the principalship as the task of preparing the master schedule is approached. The philosophy is to either program the schedule or schedule the program. This is not just a play on words. Whether or not the schedule is developed once the needs of the students are known or the schedule is developed and students are put in the slots is the controlling difference.

Neither time nor space will be devoted to how to schedule a building or program. Instead time and space will be used to show some different angles the principal can use to make the schedule a working part of the instructional and staff program for the year. The work in administering the program is complex. Help and counsel is needed by any principal. Others decide the day and the year. The only hope is to make each day as profitable as can be.

If there are significant committees designed in the building, each member's conference period can be scheduled during the same class period. In this way, time can be allocated during the day for important meetings.

Departments being released for curriculum study is another good use of the conference time schedule. Although it is difficult to pull all the teachers from a single department into one conference period, it is not impossible. There usually are some part-time faculty members in departments who can occupy the unique or special room while the regularly assigned teacher is on conference if the need is there.

The personal time clock of the faculty is another consideration. Some teachers just are not early risers. Some teachers are not as sharp late in the afternoon as they are early in the morning. Some teachers cannot cope with a split class over the lunch period. Some classes are better taught in the morning than in the afternoon; some are not. Some pivotal classes must be taught so the potential availability is greater than during other class periods and on and on it goes.

A good conflict matrix can be the answer in designing the master schedule once the selections by the students have been made. The department heads can help with individual teachers' assignments for maximum efficiency, interim faculty (those who move between buildings), those who make some demands that need to be built into the schedule, coaches who may need sixth hour open (seasonally) for early departures for league contests, and other special demands that need to be known before the first class is put on the big board for possible offering. Pivotal classes (those offered but once) need to be addressed and some "natural" conflicts must be programmed early as well. If there are more courses than combinations of faculty and rooms can produce, the principal can use such techniques as "floating" a period by offering it at a different period each day by dropping that class for the day over whatever length of time is needed. Using this technique, the schedule is broadened and yet remains flexible.

The schedule must reflect the program. The program needs to be known early and definitively. The faculty's needs and wants, also must be available early. All of these things follow the student selection of courses. The schedule can reflect anything the principal wants it to reflect. The planning is up to the administrative team with lots of timely information on which to base decisions.

- DEPARTMENT HEADS IN THE HIGH SCHOOL -

The advent of department heads in not new. The proper use of them may be. The time that is required to develop

226

this team is worth it. It will require a great deal of effort on the part of the principal, but the advantages of working with a well-trained cadre makes the time and effort seem to pass along quickly. Following is a breakdown of a year-to-year approach to develop or redo the structure of the current department head team to make the program work.

THE BASES FOR DEPARTMENT HEADS:

1. To increase both interdepartmental and intradepartmental communication.

2. To improve the curriculum through cooperative studies.

3. To facilitate the administration of a large staff in more easily guiding the school program.

4. To provide a means for well-structured programming by a closely knit part of the total staff who would be cognizant of and continually dealing with problems which the department members feel are of primary concern.

5. To assure more intelligent decisions for the provision of adequate reference and text material for the better education of the student body.

6. To establish, at the teacher level, a governing body through which curriculum could be more realistically approached and developed.

7. To develop a council where building problems regarding scheduling and curriculum could be screened and in many cases solved.

TIMETABLE FOR IMPLEMENTATION:

Year One

Goals should involve the following:

227

1. Recommend job descriptions

2. Recommend manner of the selection

3. Suggest a pay schedule for these positions

4. Initiate work. Each teacher in the building will be given the opportunity to volunteer for the chairmanship by:

    a. preparing a list of needed reference material for the department.

    b. preparing a list of needed audio-visual material for the department.

    c. preparing material for Federal/State programs.

    d. preparing proper formwork for text selections.

    e. preparing recommendations for text selections.

    f. studying the need for summer courses.

To accomplish these goals, the staff, by departments, will meet at least twice each month during the time regularly scheduled for staff meetings.

Department members will work closely with the librarian, a consultant from an accredited college, a book company representative, and a State Dept. representative.

Year Two

Goals should involve the following:

1. Prepare descriptive material on each class as it should be taught within the department. This material would form the basis for a course of study

so that teachers could more intelligently make final recommendations for text adoptions.

Material to write would be: suggested prerequisites, homework assignments, out-of-class expectations, marking practices, course content, objectives to be met, use after high school, learning activities, and suggested delivery systems.

2. Finalize all lists initiated during last year.

3. Refer final recommendations to the administration for evaluation of work done by department representatives under the chairmanship of each member of the department.

4. Further study the summer school situation on basis of the previous summer's enrollments and needs.

5. Prepare terminal recommendation on release time, extra pay, and other means of compensation.

To accomplish these goals, all teachers, by departments, will be assigned conference periods at the same hour. This will promote at least weekly meetings of all departments during the regularly scheduled day. Teachers who will be assigned to work together are teaching in the following departmental areas at least three hours each day:

science	English
foreign languages	fine arts
social sciences	practical arts of
industrial education	business
mathematics	home economics

Year Three

Goals should involve the following:

1. Department heads will be appointed as recommended by the faculty through the principal and

superintendent to the Board of Education.

2. Requirements of department heads are:

   a. Attend all meetings of department heads.

   b. Chair weekly meetings of department.

   c. Prepare course of study, by grades, 7-12, for each department.

   d. Assist in screening all teacher applicants.

   e. Develop surveys for future needs.

   f. Be responsible for university and regional accreditation material.

   g. Re-evaluate summer school program annually.

   h. Recommend budget for supplies and equipment.

   i. Design departmental schedule annually for recommendation to the principal.

   j. Observe classroom teachers and develop observation dyads within all departments.

   k. Approve all requisitions from teachers.

   l. Attend at least four student-principal curriculum meetings throughout the year.

The administration should intricately schedule classes to release all department heads during same hour conference period as well as teachers in a department on a same hour basis as far as is practicable.

230

Money should be provided to release all teachers in a single department at least one day each semester for college library research. The principal will schedule students in large groups and conduct seminar work for the department.

Budgetary allowances shall be made to provide for material needed to carry out the program.

Year Four

Goals should involve the following for work to be done by the DHC through the departments:

1. Study enrollment projections for the purpose of making a five-year recommendation for class rooms.

2. Prepare material needed for influx of students.

3. Initiate, compile, and study surveys.

4. Continue evaluation of needed reference material and new texts published.

5. Study summer school program.

6. Upgrade departments to satisfy accreditation.

To accomplish these goals, the administration will follow the same manner of scheduling teachers' time as was done in the past year's schedule.

DEPARTMENT HEADS' RESPONSIBILITIES AND POSITION DEFINITION:

A. Responsibilities

1. To be diligent in supplying faculty with the latest subject matter material. Additional material from

the principal on the topics of learning theories, principles of teaching, and child growth and development will be circulated and discussed in departmental meetings.

2. To circulate material mailed to the building.

3. To gather and disseminate material on advance credit courses offered to students and faculty.

4. To refer any suggestions or material provided by department faculty to the building administration.

5. To employ proper foresight in recommendations so that both a sound rationale and alternatives are offered when a recommendation is passed through the DHC to the administration.

6. To chair all department meetings.

7. To choose an alternate in case of absence.

8. To take part in action to determine plight of other department head's recommendations before these are sent to the administration.

9. To develop plausible scheduling plans in order to initiate department's curriculum recommendations.

10. To contact universities or assembly agencies in order that an assembly may be held which is pertinent to the department.

11. To aid the administration in planning the total school program including the budget, staffing, programs, courses added/dropped, surveys, and master schedule.

B. Position Definition

1. A liaison between secondary and elementary teachers.

2. Delegated authority to represent administration in district-wide discussions of external/ internal testing, textbook adoptions or other pertinent curriculum matters that would affect the department.

DEPARTMENT HEAD COUNCIL (DHC)

A. *Membership* is inclusive with department heads and administrators appointed by the principal.
B. *Structure* will be that each department head will chair for six consecutive weeks on a prescheduled basis. Each member will have one vote on any item unless the voted outcome is challenged. In that case, each department will carry a weighted vote by the number of teachers in that department.

The second vote will be final. Vertical isolation departments will be prevented by each department being given a building-wide program each year like summer school, building policy review, enrollment projections, library scheduling, determining readability levels of books, examination of external tests, accreditation reviews for the building, community studies, discipline updates from the literature, reviews of journals, bulletin boards and display case emphasis on curriculum, articulation with the principal's student committees on Policy, Program, and Curriculum. The most important part of this structure is the alert and interested administrators that are trained in leadership.

C. *Removal* from the DHC can be done in one of three means:

1. A member must have a unanimous vote against their leadership from the other members of the council. The cause(s) must be specific and delivered to the principal by the acting chair of the council.

233

2. At least three-fourths of the faculty in a department can sign a petition and recommend that the DHC remove their chair from representation on the Council. A DHC recommendation must be affixed and given to the administration.

3. The building principal can remove any department head with or without cause. All department heads serve at the wishes of the principal.

D. *Appeal Routes*

a. Classroom teachers can appeal any decision of their department head to the DHC with a covering letter by the DHC member who will state the reason(s) for the action taken under appeal.

b. A single department head, only when in the majority of a vote taken, can submit to the administration an appeal for review of a decision of the council. This shall be forwarded to the principal with a cover letter addressed by the acting chair of the DHC.

c. The DHC can submit an appeal to the central office over the veto of the principal when the administration writes the cover letter to the superintendent.

E. *Miscellaneous*

1. Any business not addressed in this structure shall be placed on the first agenda of the DHC and a recommendation shall be dispatched to the principal for immediate action.

- COMMUNICATION NETWORKS -

An organized communication network is indeed an important part of administration in any high school. The number of rumors which run rampant in any comprehensive high school is astounding. Many of these are carried home for various reasons. When false messages are taken home, the parents get upset and start relaying what they heard, each time with a little more "gloss" than the initial story had. Pretty soon the building is housing drug addicts and dope pushers when in reality a conscientious teacher invited a police officer with a drug-sniffing dog into the class to show the students one means of detection that is gaining success. Yes, drugs were found in the school. The part of their being planted there for detection by the dog goes without being said.

To stop these wild accusations and inhibit the growth and spread of such vicious rumors, the principal needs to have developed a network throughout the attendance district of the building. To structure one, the principal first contacts all the leaders of parent groups in the building. There usually is a group representing the SPED's, athletics, band, choruses, foreign languages, and others.

The principal calls a meeting for the sole purpose of combatting rumors and controlling the news between the community and the school. It is well to point out to the parents at the top of the meeting that rumors only hurt their children's chances of graduating from a first class school and do no good whatsoever. Also, it may be a good idea to share that rumors once perpetuated flow in two directions and if they don't automatically believe what they hear, the school will take little stock in what is rumored to be going on in the community or homes of the parents.

During the meeting, phone numbers of each participant are collected. The addresses are indicated on a large map of the school attendance district so a visual guide can be determined and followed. As the houses are pinpointed with red push pins, the large gaps in area are easy to identify. At that point, the participants are asked if they know any concerned residents in the areas not covered by officers in the various school support groups. When their contributions are placed on the map, in yellow push pins, the map should be fairly well-filled with significant others.

Given that the map is now complete, a second meeting is called with everyone who has been identified to be a key communicator in the community and is posted with either a red or yellow pin. The participants in this meeting are asked to bring with them five addresses and phone numbers with permission to have them posted on the map. These five other persons would be willing to have their routine interrupted and participate in a fan-out of calls when necessitated by either a call from one in the community or the building principal. These expanded sources are posted with blue push pins and again the map is studied for gaps in areas or neighborhoods so that any message can be quickly handled to the benefit of all concerned.

The principal selects the five most available red pin communicators and assigns each of them five persons to call. Each of the twenty-five (25) are assigned five persons and so on until all the participants are on a call list. Then, when necessary, the principal calls his/her five contacts. Each of these persons calls his/her five contacts. The instructions to this system are to provide the brief, accurate information to eliminate the rumor and to instruct the person being called to call his/her five persons. In just this limited participation of three series of calls, the number of persons contacted will equal one hundred fifty-five in a rather short time.

Here is what happened to reach . . . . . 155 homes
The principal calls . . . . .5 homes
Each contact calls 5 homes which = . . 25 homes
Each new contact calls 5 homes = . . <u>125</u> homes
TOTAL 155 homes

The use of an answering machine is a real boon to communication and allows the principal to be selective as to whom s/he speaks directly with in the evening. When a "hot" bit of news comes in, the fan-out is then activated and in about 30 minutes, 155 persons know the facts, and the rumor is killed and the reputation of the school is protected.

This system is also good to get good information out to the community just as well as to defeat a rumor. Should one of the teams win the district or regional or any championship, it may be well to call and let the word get out as to the scores, the stars, and the highlights. If a student wins the national forensic championship, this is about the only means to let anyone know. By the time the papers put an article in the news, it will be old news to the principal's KEY COMMUNICATORS, who are so vital to the success of the program.

- CONFLICT MANAGEMENT -

S. I. Hayakawa, noted educator and member of the U. S. Senate, once said, "Underlying practically all our attempts to bring agreement is the assumption that agreement is brought about by changing people's minds -- other people's." The most poignant comment in conflict resolution is the quote by James M. Barrie: "I am not young enough to know everything."

The principal perhaps should feel like Mr. Barrie when in a conflict resolution situation. Whether or not it is conflict between oneself and another or conflict between two subordinates makes little difference on how it is handled. The biggest difference is the very important statement in good management, "You cannot resolve a problem once you become part of it."

237

Conflict management can be accomplished in many ways. Cooperation is learned and taught throughout life. Both cooperation and competition come about rather subtly from the old spell-down to the skills learned on the job in dealing with unions, student unrest, parental intrusions, central office enforcements, at the bargaining table, or whatever. Yes, even in athletics both conflict and cooperation are learned. However, conflict comes about in personal, social, as well as professional lives. The principal needs to be better at dealing with conflict than others, for it is the tone setting of the building which is at stake. The principal is constantly being thrust into conflict situations. In a book written by Herbert Cohen, the skills necessary to deal with conflict are delineated rather succinctly even though his application is for bargaining. The three parts of problem resolution are: INFORMATION, TIME, and POWER. However, not all three are always available so the effort to be exerted must be directed toward the situation by bringing it to a win/win conclusion. This is hard to do. There is a wide variety of conclusions that conflict can be brought to and a tremendous number of degrees in each conclusion. Here is a small four cell grid to show what the conclusions can be.

	YOURSELF	
	win	lose
OTHERS win	win/ win	lose/ win
lose	win/ lose	lose/ lose

Often too many conflict situations conclude in the lower right corner in a lose/lose outcome. A divorce is a good example of this. A union contract bargained, when there has been a strike by the teachers, is another good example. When either of these occur everyone suffers. There is seldom a friendship which evolves as a lesser relationship. To remain good friends with a person over an extended period of time, it is wisest to maintain a friendship relationship and not allow it to grow or erode from that level.

NUMBERS IN THE CONFLICT SITUATION

Remember that the number of possible communication suffocators in a group of people can be determined easily by this little formula: $X(X-1)$, where X equals the number of people in the communication structure. In other words, three people would potentially equal six communication linkages. With four people in the formula, there would be twelve linkages in the process. Just imagine two bargaining teams each with six or eight members. Sixteen in the process would equal sixteen times fifteen or a possibility of 240 blunders. One who has been involved in negotiations does not need anymore explanation than that example.

Atop this, public documents take away "information" (as one of the three vital parts of negotiating) from the Board team. As if this is not enough, the agrarian calendar precludes the element of "time." The conflict is loaded on the union side and thus is not practicable from the conflict stand-point and certainly is the stem of most of the conflicts in bargaining in education.

POWER

Power can be shifted several times in any conflict situation. When President Carter made the public (not private, as perhaps he should have) pronouncement that, "We shall not use military force to resolve the Iranian (Embassy captives) situation," he gave up a power base which perhaps brought about more than a year's captivity. The student in a principal's office has no power --- unless --- he again gains control. He loses his control when he enters the office. However, if he has been confronted in the corridors in front of his peers, he was allowed to maintain his power base, for he can act irresponsibly and the principal cannot when the gauntlet is thrown for consideration or challenge. Therefore, it is best not to confront him in the presence of his gang. In numbers there is perceived power. The other comment on power is

"There is no vacuum of power."

So, if the principal does not act in an authoritative manner during confrontation, the power shifts to the party who does act properly. It is well to know that abdication of the authority of the office of the princpal does not go unnoticed, howsoever insignificant it may be. Someone else will take over in that particular arena, and the power is lost, perhaps forever. Give away many of these power positions and the total power of the office is lost.

TIMING

The English relish in "having a spot of tea" when conflict arises. This is done to gain time -- then information comes to them -- then power becomes an element on their side. That is if all goes well. The principal often does not have the luxury of time on his/her side in conflict situations. To manage the conflict, it is good to seize the opportunity to take control (power) and set a time-line which makes sense in the conflict's resolution. In this way, the initial element of time being lost to the principal can be overcome.

TRAPPED?

Here is a technique used by a bargaining group of teachers in a setting where the consultant was called in to help "mediate" some years ago. They met the consultant at the airport in a limousine and provided first class treatment all the way to the hotel. It was grand. They were sociable and helpful by detailing what the situation was from their prospective. At the hotel counter, they asked the consultant for his ticket and if he wanted them to call and confirm his return flight. Not thinking, he gave the ticket to them. HE HAD JUST GIVEN THE ELEMENT OF TIME TO THE BARGAINERS. The mediation was not as successful as it perhaps would have been without this little error in or lapse of judgment. Come to find out, they had cleverly determined that he was to leave Wednesday at 5:00 p.m., and they "stone-walled it" up to and beyond that point because they knew when he had to leave. This was not too clever on the part of the consultant, for the base of TIME was given to one side and the mediator lost a substantial part of the POWER base.

TIPS TO GUARD AGAINST

Conflict is usually regarded as a negative situation between two persons or groups of persons. It does not necessarily have to be thought of in this manner. Conflict can, in fact, be healthy (and often is) in a relationship.

Here are ten tips to guard against, or follow, in conflict management:

The SUPERVISOR OR MANAGER

1. ...talks too much and does not listen enough.
2. ...retreats when s/he is right even when a clever counter is offered to what is said.
3. ...harbors a grudge.
4. ...fails to collect *all* the facts needed.
5. ...acts too quickly.
6. ...takes a position while personally angry.
7. ...fails to document items throughout the relationship then uses generalizations on unsubstantiated items.
8. ...does not use specificity in the "charge" to the subordinate --- either when the subordinate was assigned work or is being chastised.
9. ...does not listen (or hear?) to the other side of the story.
10. ...gets her/his personality involved in the conflict and does not remain impartial or worse yet impersonal.

DECISION-MAKING

Conflict Management sometimes needs to be used when the principal does not make key decisions in a timely manner or at all. This in itself is a deadly sin. There are some (viable) reasons for decision-making procrastinators and among them these select half-dozen are probably the most dependable ones to examine. Certainly, they are the ones that the lack of decision-making is attributed to for 90 % of the time. In fact, according to the 500 superintendents and/or high school principals surveyed, the claim is for these reasons:

1. Lack of goal setting --- or maybe finite objectives.
2. Fear of the untried.
3. The need to be "loved" by all.
4. Responsibility only and not the delegated concomitant authority has been delegated.
5. Newness and subsequent misoneism.
6. Lack of security.

Before the manager gets frustrated, s/he can eliminate this list by doing, in reverse, what has been outlined here. Get prepared before managerial decisions are necessary. If someone else does not give a decision that is vital for the operation, go back up the list and see where support can be given to eliminate these causal factors or understand which one (or combination) caused the no-decision and react appropriately.

CONFLICT REACTIONS

Here are the selected ways conflict is dealt with in terms of human behavior. Of course, the best means of managing conflict is through good education. Others, as selected, are as follows:

cheating	attacking	losing sleep
using logic	crying	punishing
drinking	laughing	griping
throwing	leaving	getting
withdrawing	denying	physical
manipulating	ignoring	clamming up

| telling lies | killing | seeking a |
| shouting | overpowering | referee |

It can be seen that the variety is difficult to comprehend. The principal must remain aware that conflict is the biggest part of perception between people. S/he deals with perceptions all the time. People react according to their perceptions. If the principal understands that the conflict is against the role of the principal and not against the person filling the role, it is much easier to control conflict situations in one's own perception.

CONFLICT ASSUMPTIONS

Any conflict assumption individually or in combination can be traced to a person's own experiences. The experiences may have been during one's childhood and not just in the professional life. David Freeman, principal at Mason Jr. High in Waterford, MI, says that some of the more valid assumptions in CONFLICT are that it:

cannot be avoided in normal human contacts.
is normal and should be expected.
frequently is brought about by many misconcep-
	tions, misunderstandings, or inaccuracies
seldom involves clear cut "right" and/or "wrong"
	issues.
can be dealt with in a healthy or unhealthy manner
	or constructive or destructive manner.
involves feelings.

What brings about conflict in education? The list is endless. Suffice it to say, there are literally thousands of opportunities for it to appear throughout any given day between and among students, teachers, custodians, administrators, secretaries, parents, and even more so between combinations of these subgroups. There is always the acrimony between the "professional" and "nonprofessional" persons --- (Don't get into this area.) All persons are professionally grouped into these really non-discriminating categories. Many competent managers prefer the use of certified and classified. Some managers

243

use faculty and staff. There are too many professional custodians and secretaries to call only the certificated teacher the professional.

Some "racial incidents" are actually conflicts between students who happen to be of different skin colors but are far from racially oriented. The good manager makes sure the problem is quickly defined and understood by those around the combatants. If verbal "attacks" are based on color, that conflict needs to be cleared right away as well as the physical aspect of conflict.

CONFLICT ARISING

In schools, conflict is brought about through many purposes. The list below will highlight the complexity. Some sets of behavioral traits are taught at home. The admonition of "Don't let the _____ push you around in school" is not only a pretty dumb attitude to hold but even a negative attitude inculcated into the judgment of another, especially a young child. All of the above "conditions" when crossed with the list of groups of persons with whom the principal associates can create (and often does) many variations and degrees of intensity.

possessions	students
school work	teachers
assignments	custodians
testing	administrators
evaluation	secretaries
appearances	parents
values	counselors
actions	librarians
discipline	monitors
attitudes	guards
feelings	drivers
equipment	cooks
timing	coaches
respect	clerks

Now it can be seen how these conflicts can occur when the middle area gets so crowded because of the social milieu being so frustratingly complex? Then change classes seven times a day and restrict the time each has to move from one point to the other.

Write any two of the conditions listed above on the blank lines across the top and the group name along side of the simple grid shown below. Then the principal can realize all four variables exist and so does conflict.

```
               win  lose
          Öáááááááéááááááá¢
        win° win/ ° lose/°
          ° win ° win °
          éáááááááéááááááé
   ———————° win/ ° lose/°
     lose° lose ° lose °
          âáááááááéááááááì
```

By putting one of the "things" (discipline, money, rules) on the blank line on the top and title of a role (custodian, teacher, student) on the side, one can see there is a potential of thousands of conflicts when using the small four part grid.

AVOIDING CONFLICT

To eliminate or reduce potential conflict in any situation, there are several things to be done. Here is a partial list to peruse, modify, and follow. THE PRINCIPAL MUST:

1. ...accept that conflict is a normal part of living between human beings.
2. ...learn to communicate verbally and nonverbally with all contacts.
3. ...learn to accept change, innovations, and flexibility.
4. ...understand that each person involved brings to any setting a finite list of character traits.
5. ...categorize that which is important or that which is petty.
6. ...be cognizant of compromise and depend on

"greyness." Give and take is essential.

7. ...AT ALL TIMES be open, honest, and develop trust and the three C's of compassion, confidence, and consideration.

8. ...never trap anyone. If this is done inadvertently, provide a "way out" of the conflict.

9. ...wait for the proper time to resolve conflict.

10. ...be prepared, learn, or satisfy conflict through the use of mutually acceptable alternatives.

11. ...be willing to listen to and at times even openly seek a third party if involved in the conflict.

Remember, in conflict as in problem solving, one cannot solve it if one becomes part of it.

12. ...listen and hear, listen and hear, listen and hear what is being said --- and more importantly --- what is not.

13. ...lastly, develop two layers of skin, an outer-most layer as a professional layer and the inner layer as a personal layer.

HANDLING PERSONAL ATTACKS = CONFLICT

First, go to rule 13. The outer (professional) layer of skin needs to be a coat of armor so that it can be scraped, bent, burnt, bruised, rubbed, chinked, etc. The inner (personal) layer can only be gored. If this is ever done, it is but a perception that it was done as no one outside the person can gore that layer. No one can literally do anything to another's mind. Only the person doing the ratonalization or thinking at the time is responsible. The principal must be defensible and not defensive in all contacts with others. Don't take professional attacks personally. The principal must remember that an attack is basically on the principal (the title) and seldom the person. If anyone else was in the same position at the same time with the same conflict, s/he would be under the same attack. IT IS NOT Gene Megiveron; it is the principal being challenged.

Second, conflict is normal and expected in institutions so when it arises, the principal should not be alarmed. There are three contexts in which conflict will arise. They will arise in the mode of the individual, the in-

246

stitution or the mix of the two as they clash on issues, the third context. The first two contexts are the most likely to bring about conflicts. The personality of the individual conflicts with the tone or philosophy of the school. It usually is centered around the perceived role of the individual as the individual perceives his/her role in the school and the role's impact on the situation.

In the same situation, one teacher may feel there are too many rules and looks for relief from them or their growing number; another may feel there are not enough rules and the school is operating on assumptions and without leadership. Perception is the key.

The only way one can become an "expert" in conflict resolution, is to become involved as a resolver -- not a participant, if at all possible. The techniques to control conflict cannot be observed and learned. They must be applied with the principal's own personality and feelings toward people, places, policies, programs, procedures, and practices.

The "Wall of Conflict" as first envisioned by Mr. Terry G. Semones of Monroe, MI, follows. It shows the various building blocks that can be put in place to fend off attacks on the position of authority. There are different blocks used by different individuals. A space has been left for this input.

The wall is a good capstone to this unit. There literally is a wall being built by the subordinates for each of their superordinates. The question which arises in graduate courses is "How can a new administrator prevent things from changing relationships between past good friends and colleagues on the faculty from which s/he took the promotion?" The response is to do everything one can to not change in attitude, posture, personality and then hope that continuity will permit "windows" to be put in the wall which most assuredly will be built. The wall which appears on the next page is not the relationship wall but can be used to deal with issues when conflict arises.

247

SEMONES' WALL OF CONFLICT KNOWLEDGE

BE AWARE OF COMPROMISE	THE OTHER GUY MAY BE RIGHT	ACCEPT CHANGE
USE GIVE & TAKE	REMEMBER YOU CARE	BE FLEXIBILE
SEEK A THIRD PARTY FOR RESOLUTION	CAN'T SOLVE IT IF A PART OF IT	EXAMINE ALL ALTER-TIVES

Be aware of and recognize the feel-ings and emotions involved --- and their intensity. Develop some safety valves -- ways for others to blow off

Classify Conflict and Consequences	Vital? Petty?
Try for Win/Win outcomes.	MAKE SURE THE FACTS ARE O.K.

Communicating and talking it out, is essential. Di-rect face to face is usually superi-or to other forms.	HEAR WHAT IS SAID	Schedule resumption at another time in a fair arena or forum

Listen - Listen

Tune In   For   Feedback

Recognize that conflict is normal and can never be totally avoided	There does not have to be any losers	DO NOT TAKE ANY ATTACKS PERSON-ALLY

248

- PROPAGANDA -

This subunit was developed by a personal friend, the late Dr. Kingsley Montgomery, an excellent school psychologist. His concern was that in the understanding of a community there were several things a principal needed to know. The following was Monty's draft of some of the highlighted concerns a principal ought to have. It was written when the schools were in the throes of change and the "melting pot" was being tested by "outsiders" moving into the communities. It was not a matter of skin color, religion, ethnicity, or any other current situation of conflict. It was a matter of change. It was the violation of stasis -- protected status quo. Here's Monty's paper:

"The propagandist surveys his audience for three psychological reasons:

(1) He must become acquainted with their auxiliary attitudes in order to have them perceive the propaganda;

(2) He must discover which personality responses he can conceivably evoke in order to relate them to the learning process, and

(3) S/he must seek to ascertain how strong those related responses are. "Thus, *if* a good proportion of our many publics can generally be described as:

1. Prejudiced,
2. Content to maintain the status
    quo in almost everything,
3. Upholding of private property,
4. Upholding of conventions and
    traditions,
5. Patriotic,
6. Stressing sexual restraint,
7. Upholding of religion,
8. Stressing of discipline in relation to educa-

tion, and /or
9. Politically conservative,

then, at least all written and spoken information emanating from and about the building should:

"1. Emphasize the possibility of being attached to another building or district as the size shrinks. De-emphasize everything that relates to the school sponsoring or school people being involved in such things as "Human Relations Councils," etc.

"2. Emphasize the possibility of being attached to another district; emphasize that local control will be lost; de-emphasize any innovations such as Initial Teaching Alphabet or the new math, or computer assisted instruction, etc. (This was in 1965.)

"3. Emphasize the district purchases vacant land for schools and seldom uses its condemnation power; sympathize with destruction of property at bus stops; elicit help from police on destruction of property; prosecute when possible any destruction of school property;

"4. Emphasize that we still concentrate on reading, writing, and arithmetic; emphasize that we take a dim view of physical violence and destruction by any dissenter.

"5. Say Pledge of Allegience at most gatherings called by the school people (e.g. at P.T.A. meetings; have the American flag prominently displayed whenever possible; play the National Anthem in the accustomed style at sports events.

"6. When addressing an audience, mention sex education not at all; publicize our dress code; never give cognizance to any pre-marital pregnancies; never mention venereal diseases. Never mention sensitivity training.

"7. Always open appropriate meetings with a prayer; publicize your interaction with ministerial associations; interact more often with ministers or groups of ministers; stress shared-time with parochial schools only to *accepting groups*.

"8. Have homework for all students; send work completed in school to the child's home via the child at least weekly.

"9. Never permit white or black panthers to talk to any class or use any school facility even after school hours."

This was the end result of Monty's report to high school principals. The report above is one which can be translated to fit current times and situations. The whole idea is that the principal must be aware of the many publics within the environs of that portion of the district the school serves. Small communities are sometimes more easy to work in than are complex institutions of the urban setting of today. The definition of the community more closely fits the type of program for which schools were founded. When the community becomes other than the "standard" type, the principal must be quick to adjust the communication from the building and in the building as well.

- PRINCIPAL CONTACTS - INTERNAL/EXTERNAL -

On a given day when school is in operation, the principal will meet and have to react to commentary, questions, recommendations, criticisms, pleas, ideas and contacts with many, many audiences. The audiences have their own agenda and the principal must be aware of this as the day progresses. The only disadvantage the principal has is that s/he simply does not know what the background is behind each contact made. This is a big fault of communication.

The *audiences* that may come in contact with the principal could well be those of parents or other community members outside the school. From within, the students, counselors, librarians, department heads, bus drivers, coaches, faculty, custodians, maintenance workers, nurses, other administrators in the building may well be seeking information or direction from the principal. Within the district and without the district, the central staff, superintendent, supervisors, directors, assistants, coordinators, and others in the world of academia may well be searching for responses to situations only the principal can contribute toward resolution. A businessman may be wanting to reach the principal to discuss a topic or it may be a president of a booster club, the new banker, a reporter, a college professor, chairperson of an internal committee in the district, a drop-out, the valedictorian for help with classes assigned and on and on it goes. Then there is the ever-present committee work that will have to be completd. Such groups like the secondary administrative committee, book review committee, the superintendent's administrative council, maybe even the central group of administrators working on building specifications will be necessary to be a part of during demanding times.

How does the principal get it all done? By compacting the conferences, meetings, contacts during the time S/HE can schedule them. In other words, being busy in the classroom and on other instructional tasks, is understandable by the many publics. To arrange for a short conference or meeting late in the day (after the students and faculty have gone home) or early in the morning will shorten the time allowed as others will need to get to the office and so forth. To understand what these demands are, here is a helpful diagram for the principal to show the number and variety of potential contacts s/he has in any given day.

There are many *types of contacts* with the principal: phone, memo work, letters, and personal. The *reasons for the contact* may be as wide a range of purposes as to enroll into the school to a suspension conference, selection of agenda topics for a committee, or subpoena from court.

252

The parent may be complaining or complimenting. Hopefully, the idea is now in place.

Each of the boxes in the chart in the Exhibits could well be interconnected with all other boxes in the chart. It is not intended to show the only relationship as connected. The principal is a fulcrum in many respects and in many others, is a conduit. Visualize this as a "matching" test item and draw the relationships as they occur. The original concept, by Dr. Jerry Blanchard, Waterford Schools, was drawn for a specific district. The author thanks her for the idea. The principal must have DIRECT contact with each category shown.

- ADVISORY COMMITTEES -

Teachers could use the advice of experts in the community. A way to get this assistance is to organize advisory committees for each discipline area. In some cases, each course may well develop a committee especially in the business and industrial education departments and others which have students assigned in co-op programs within the community.

In order for a principal to get good community representatives to join in this endeavor, there are a couple of hints to keep in mind: 1. Politicians may be able to provide assistance in getting good people to help in the work of these committees. They can advise in the appointing of consultants. They often know the industrialists, businessmen, and leaders in the work-a-day world. It would be good, politically, to ask the mayor to assist in this endeavor, and 2. The prinicpal may wish to check with the business manager in the central office for additional assistance in locating local firms which contribute by providing low-bid items as well as some items for which

253

there is no remuneration. 3. Don't forget the military service recruiters. They can get some word on significant purchases and advise on the enlistment changes which will affect seniors.

Some of the course areas which could benefit from community expertise are the departments of industrial education, art, business education, health, foreign language, and English. Individual courses are those which incorporate products of wood, plastics, metals, communication skills, word processing, commercial art, agriculture, and economics.

Advisory committees are best organized by the department chairpersons. What do the advisory committees do? The committees can locate some free or inexpensive teaching material or equipment. Locate and obtain such items as shelving, dash-board components, word processing equipment, leather, sponges, paints, paper for art work, industrial equipment being phased out, manuals for repair work, small engines, motors, and just about anything needed in the high school laboratory programs. It is not impossible to get more free equipment and supplies than can be budgeted and ordered in any one year. Advisory committee members can get personnel in the community to give the faculty good advice and direction in the evaluation of programs by sharing knowledge about community members who could be of assistance or by working with the teacher in the program evaluative process. The community members can be good communicators outside of the school. The committees' work needs to be widely proclaimed. Pictures of the membership in session are essential.

Each committee needs to meet at least monthly, and the agenda should be prepared so that times, dates, and discussion topics are published well in advance. (See the item on Agenda Preparation in Unit 4.)

The community members on the committees work as advisory persons. They will become formal members of the group in the form of support. The work with these community representatives can be one of the better programs in the building. The work can be the responsibility of several persons on the staff. Each person can prepare the work of "his/her" advisory committee in unison with other faculty members. If the agenda are prepared by the faculty representatives in concert with others, the program will move along smoothly. The teachers are good resources for this purpose.

Orientation must be done initially, and as membership changes, the new persons will need to be brought up-to-date as well. The agenda for these meetings may well show the following:

1. Introductions and tour of the facilities.

2. Explanation of the departmental curriculum to show how courses fits into the total structure.

    a. Introductory courses
    b. Developmental courses
    c. Culminating courses
    d. Expectations of the majors and minors to be earned by students enrolled in specific courses within the department

3. Staffing of the department.

4. Projections of student enrollment and competencies.

5. Employment of graduates as determined by the follow-up study.

6. Unmet needs in the curriculum, department, and courses.

7. Budgetary explanations and calendar.

8. Programming down the road and in the past.

9. What the emphasis is in the current marketplace.

10. The availability of student helpers.

11. What the student should know about the industry.

12. Guest speakers' orientation and invitation to come to classes.
13. Tax breaks for educational contributions.

14. The laws in the industry.

15. Adoption of programs by industry, businesses, and others.
16. Field trip availability.

This briefing is for application by some departmental representatives and the serious departmental student. The principal can enhance his/her total program by the careful organization of the advisory committees. Money that no longer has to be spent on supplies or equipment in these departments can be transferred to others and the whole curriculum is improved.

- ADVOCACY -- OMBUDSMAN -

There are several means of becoming a strong supporter of the students in a building. The role of a student advocate is one the principal will enjoy if the following means are implemented into the overall program. Each has been used in public high schools throughout the United States, but few principals have used all of them. It can be done if the principal has each in mind as s/he deals with the students and the staff as well as the community in explaining how the program can be helpful to individuals.

The unit number, if any, preceding the comments serves as a reference for locating more information.

Unit 05 - *Entrance Interviews* are an excellent means of determining who is enrolling, and they provide an opportunity of being able to meet every new student personally. These are best conducted with the assistance of other students in the building. When the interview has been completed, the principal can see what was or is happening elsewhere, what the student is looking for in this new school experience, and understand what the ever-changing student body is becoming.

Unit 05 - *Exit Interviews* will help to assess what the student body has lost in ever-changing membership as the students leave for whatever reason. The "reason" given unofficially may be different than the "official" reason given for the records. It is good to know what, if anything, can be done about it. By compiling some of the data, the principal can determine where some changes may need to be made.

Unit 05 - *Exceptional Students* are a good means of protecting every student in the building. After all, students come to school with the differences of style and needs that make the position of high school principal exciting and important to their lives. The effective principal regards the high school as a House of Intellect which s/he directs. It is not construed as a preparation for life but is, in fact, life itself as John Dewey said so long ago. To be a House of Intellect, the school must be where every child has his/her personal needs met, or at least, addressed. It is through the exceptional child card that the whole process of caring begins. It should be ever-present throughout all the processes of management in the high school.

Unit 05 - *Case Conferences* must be structured constantly by those on the guidance staff for the benefit of both the kids and the entire staff. The faculty must be aware of students' personal problems which have a need to be met if the faculty is going to work harmoniously with the students. Students are expected to produce as well as they can in the classrooms. Maslow says the human goes through a needs hierarchy beginning with the need for meeting the physiological drives, then to the need for

257

safety and security, then to the need for belonging. The higher level need can not be reached or attained until the lower has been fully satisfied. There is no motivation toward the fourth level, self-esteem, unless the three lower levels have been attained. The teachers assume these three levels are met when the child comes to school. This is NOT TRUE in too many cases. Society hears sickening cases of incest, rape, starvation indirectly by malnutrition, whole families sleeping in one room, etc. Love is a forgotten word in too many homes. The child comes to school where for the first time an entire set of adults is committed to assisting him in his attempt to reach toward self-esteem. A favorite motto which comes to mind here is "Don't trap kids." The author used it constantly with staff members so they could not forget to apply it.

When *Policies and Their Impact Statements* are written for the students, they need to be developed after the principal or the faculty listens to student concerns. After policies are written, the students are again "heard" through the use of impact statements. This is another vehicle which supports the students in the building. Policies must be developed to express a need to be satisfied. The Impact Statement tool can assist the principal in re-examining the policy to make sure students are NOT negatively affected by its wording or the concomitant actions of the staff.

Unit 05 - *Fog and Smog Indices* are a couple of ways that the principal can show the faculty and the students that there is real concern for the students. If the material being selected for use by the faculty is NOT material that the regular student can read and comprehend, then the students needs are not being met. Bloom's taxonomy is listed from knowledge to the upper level of evaluation. This needs to be reviewed so the faculty can understand that if the students can't read for knowledge or comprehension, a greater need must first be addressed. Some never reach the third or fourth level because they cannot read the material. The effective principal knows that the child learns to read from grades K - 3 and reads to learn from grades 4 - 12. If this is accurate, many high school students haven't successfully completed grade three reading.

Unit 05 - *Textbook Evaluation* is a subtle means of being the advocate for the students in one's building. The teaching material in the high school probably has not been assessed in the recent past, if at all, by the teachers that are assigned to the building at this time. Textbooks should be evaluated periodically by departments with the criteria mutually set by the faculty and the administration. These criteria should keep the students in mind. The form in the text is particularly broad for this purpose.

Student Failure results from the failure of the school to meet the individual needs of the students. It is true that the school cannot correct all of society's ills; thus, there will always be drop-outs. However, this can be minimized in a building designed with love, trust, respect, cooperation and competition, and all-around good will for the students. It is the responsibility of the principal to ensure that such a situation exists in his/her building. The effective principal recognizes that there will be some students who cannot be helped at the high school because they brought with them problems which just may be irresolvable by educators. However, it is not too late to seek the assistance these children need. It never is. The principal must make sure that each child is having done for him everything that can be done. The nation's goal of high schools to provide universal secondary education is a lofty one and is worth pursuing. However, it is just an experiment and not the law. Our many publics often get these confused. There can be no push-outs because of our faculty, rules, regulations, administration, policies, or other reasons. Society must realize that troubled kids in the public schools need help. Educators were not trained or educated to be clinicians. Educators are not educated as sociologists, psychologists, or doctors. Educators do a great job of instruction. Students will continue to fail as surely as people go to jail and die even when being assisted with the best minds in law and medicine. There are ways of preventing SOME cases of drop-outs and this unit will help in the understanding of them.

259

Unit 05 - *Safety Features* or care and feeding of the students in the building must not be ignored. The health, safety, and welfare of each student should be a prime concern. If the principal works with the class presidents when making a tour to inspect the facility, the morale of the students will be improved as they see one more expression of caring for them.

Curricular Applications by Leslie Hart, Bernice Mc Carthy, Herman T. Epstein, and Joseph Hill need highlighting. Concept work done by Elliot W. Eisner, John Goodlad, and B. Frank Brown need to be studied as well and are referenced to the faculty. If the assigned work is important for the student's future, then it must be done in an environment which is conducive to the student's welfare. There is much more to be put into a curriculum study than subject matter. To apply the subject matter takes time and much effort to place all the component parts into place. Methodology, child growth and development, principles of teaching, and the whole range of student interests and motivation must be considered in the theories of learning. The authors mentioned will help to bring into focus all of the elements of the curriculum.

Unit 01 - *Problem Census* is a successful means to get feedback from those over whom the principal has some control. The feedback necessary to make good changes is important to the principal. When used with the students in a high school of around 2,500 students, one can expect to receive more than twenty-five items which can easily translate into action programs. The suggestions which are given primarily fall in the area of individualized programming. Each could be introduced to the staff and student body before the second round of feedback is done. The second round can easily provide fifty more items for work by the staff, student committees, or the administration. It is vital to hear from students. To be their advocate, the principal must hear, not just listen to them.

Team Learning and other "different" programs are included so that school does not become all competition but becomes a place for cooperation as well.

260

Unit 07 - *Student Committees* can be divided into three areas: curriculum, policy, and activities. The committees ran surveys and came up with ideas based upon the results. These ideas for programs were researched and fully developed and then presented to the faculty.

Unit 07 - *Survival/Literacy/Competency* vocabularies are important to the student who will have to function one day without the help of the school, family, and friends. As the students' advocate, the principal must ensure that these vocabularies are included in the curricula. It is not enough to know what the curricula are, it is the principal's responsibility to know what the child is being taught. The vocabulary lists are designed to show what every child NEEDS to know and not what s/he OUGHT to know.

What is ADVOCACY? It is being there FOR the students and to represent them at every turn--even when the principal at first feels they are wrong, then especially when s/he finally determines they are indeed wrong and need more help. Girls get pregnant (not alone), boys wreck their dads' cars, both can get hooked on drugs or just experiment with them, failure is coped with, and honor is fleeting in too many places. These are just a sample of what students carry psychologically along with their school work. Errors or mistakes must be considered to be cues for the principal (the faculty) to the type of help students need. The students must learn to be responsible to themselves and not to anyone else. To become responsible, they have to fall down and at times even get dirty. The principal can lift them up when they need it. The principal is the one to HELP and not hinder the students' progress toward self-fulfillment, self-esteem, and self-actualization.

The principal is the ADVOCATE to be reckoned with by faculty, staff, parents, and other community members. S/he must be the one to go through when the issue is the student's welfare for now and for the future.

- UNIT FIVE INTRODUCTION -
Paperwork and People Aids

One significant and yet general task of the principal is that of being a good planner. To plan is but the first part of the process of total planning. Planning is the forecasting of events to take place. And around and around it goes. Once plans are finalized, the real world takes over for the work to do. Once planning is complete, then capable monitoring and eventually evaluation of all planned projects takes place. This series of subunits is the issue at hand now. This is the beginning of the end of the project, and that is all it is.

The subunits in this unit are grouped together because they provide skill areas needed for the effective principal. When put into effect, these skills help him/her to become more organized in working with the great students in the building. These subunits fit into the custodialship role of the school. They will set the principal aside from the regular administrator because each shows the attitude of caring. The subunits listed below will help the principal work better with the staff and student body by keeping him/her in contact with them.

Evaluation of Textbooks
FOG and SMOG Indices
Randall Plan of Employee Evaluation
Hardesty's 3 X 3 Evaluation
Case Study
Exceptional Students
Student Entrance Interviews
Student Exit Interviews

If the faculty (and principal) is not to be charged later with malpractice, then the evaluation of each textbook is a must in the principal's work for the year. A form can be used so the faculty is aware of the level of every source they use. It is of little value, though, if the faculty does not know what the reading ability is of each student assigned to them. Both speed and comprehension is important. It is assumed here that the reading level of each student is known.

The FOG and SMOG indices are two excellent sources to use for improved understanding of the texts and references used in the classroom and library. The principal should not be fooled by the simplicity of these indices. The value they hold is immeasurable.

A system of working with the portions of staff other than the faculty is the one by the jr. high principal, Dr. Lee Randall. Lee customized this from a program used in Washington by Dr. James Monosmith, to whom the initial credit must be given. Lee, however, refined it for his building and it worked very well for the purpose of the evaluation of the non-certified staff.

Hardesty can provide the principal assistance again and this time in the role of staff evauation or even the faculty portion. It is simplistic in its design and sound for the busy principal who needs to have work clarified and routinized as much as possible.

There are four important subunits covered so that the principal can show how much s/he cares for the students. The subunits are placed in pairs for discussion here. Case Studies/Conferences are held whenever a student is having problems and is referred for his own good. Exceptional Child Cards are kept in a select, locked file so the information is not generally available. When an existing problem is "activated," the cards are updated. Other cards are added to the file as new situations come to the forefront. The process is the important part of these subunits. Entrance Interviews are given to all students enrolling who have attended a different high school. Working WITH students can be exciting and when this occurs, the results of this "survey" will be helpful for the development of the many school programs on a continual basis. Exit Interviews follow the same process before students leave.

- EVALUATION OF TEXTBOOKS -

A modified version of the form designed and placed in the Exhibits has been used throughout Michigan. As new research becomes available, it has been altered to its current state. The form works.

It is the principal's prime responsibility in instructional leadership to ensure the community that the material provided for the students is not biased in any manner and is readable by the majority of the users. The textbooks of today need to examined carefully in order that the material presented therein is of the type that the students can use to learn and learn to use.

Teachers need to be involved in the selection process of all material. The text is the mainstay of the program in many high schools. The usefulness of the material must be guaranteed by the users and the consumers. When the form is used totally, it is a good one for the teachers to develop a knowledge about and use is then nearly assured by the faculty.

Students ought to be used to pilot the top two or three selections of the faculty committee before the final selection is recommended for adoption. It is through use that the material is given its final review. At times the student use of the texts will clarify which book needs to be suggested to be placed for adoption. It may *not* be the key reference which might have been recommended. The form will only provide a base for the adoption.

- FOG READABILITY FORMULA -

On April 24, 1970, Dr. Jerry Blanchard, then assistant principal at Pierce Jr. High in Waterford, Michigan, wrote the following position paper for action and consumption of administrators in the secondary division of a large suburban school district in Michigan. Use it. It is a quick, effective way to determine readability.

"School administrators are increasingly being called to account for their decisions regarding education: curriculum, materials, expenditures, student placement, evaluation, space utilization. The demand for accountability comes from parents, the local community, government, and assessment programs. Last year, for example, a school system was sued for malpractice. A young man's parents charged that school personnel knew their son could not read at the tenth grade level and yet had issued him tenth grade textbooks. They claimed that the school had not provided the correct learning materials for their boy and was culpable, therefore, for his failure.

"As school administrators we can be accountable for our decisions. We have the knowledge, skills, and experience to make critical educational decisions relative to the youngters for whom we are responsible. However, these decisions must be based on carefully defined rationale, objectives, and evaluative tools so that we will have the measurable evidence necessary to affirm our credibility.

"For these reasons, I take the position that all Waterford secondary school textbook selections should be subjected to a readability formula before a final decision for purchase is made by the Secondary Administrative Council. This would result in our having information about a text selection pertinent to its grade placement and reading difficulty. This, in conjunction with a careful diagnosis of student reading ability, would enable us to prescribe proper materials for individual students.

"I recommend that we use the *Fog Index* to ascertain the reading level of textbook selections. The *Fog Index* is described herein:

"The *Fog Index* was developed by Robert Gunning. The following are the steps in its application.

"1. Take several samples (at least three) of one hundred words each, spaced evenly through the article or book. Count the number of sentences in each sample. (Stop the sentence count with the sentence ending nearest the one hundred word limit.) Divide the total number of words in the passage (100) by the number of sentences. This gives you the average sentence length. Jot down this figure.

"2. Using the same samples, count the number of words of three sylables or more. Do not count the words (a) that are capitalized, (b) that are combinations of short, easy words (example: *bookkeeper*), or (c) that are verb forms made into three syllables by adding -ed, or -es (example: *created*). This gives you the percentage of difficult words in the passage. Jot down this figure directly under the figure obtained in step one.

"3. To determine the *Fog Index*, total the two factors just counted and multiply the total by .4 (four tenths). This gives you the approximate grade placement of the writing although it tends to run somewhat high with more difficult materials."

- SMOG READABILITY FORMULA -

In a journal about reading, the author of an article claims this formula is "quick and easy" and saves a great deal of time. In fact, it is so effective, there can be a simple computer program written to figure the results easily. Here is how the SMOG is completed to determine the reading level of the material used in high school buildings.

1. Count 10 consecutive sentences near the beginning of the text to be assessed, 10 in the middle and 10 near the end. Count as a sentence any string of words ending with a period, question mark or exclamation point.

2. In the 30 selected sentences count every word of three or more syllables. Any string of letters or numerals beginning and ending with a space or punctuation mark should be counted if at least three syllables can be distinguished when it is read aloud in context. If a polysyllabic word is repeated, count each repetition.

3. Estimate the square root of the number of polysyllabic words counted. This is done by taking the square root of the nearest perfect square. For example, if the count is 95, the nearest perfect square is 100, which yields a square root of 10. If the count lies roughly between two perfect squares, choose the lower number. For instance, if the count is 110, take the square root of 100 rather than that of 121. Most calculators have this key on them now.

4. Add 3 to the approximate square root. This gives the SMOG Grade, which is the reading grade level that a person must have reached if he is to understand fully the text assessed.

The article continues with some information which might be helpful, especially to those who are not particularly skilled in the process of READING. Here are some which will be helpful.

A. A readability formula is simply a mathematical equation derived by regression analysis.

B. The linguistic measures which have been found to have greatest predictive power are word and sentence length.

C. Fortunately there is no need to follow Flesch's (1948 in the *Journal of Applied Psychology*, 32, 221-233) system of counting every syllable in a passage in order to obtain a valid measure of its semantic difficulty. For practical purposes, the total number of syllables per 100 words may be calculated by this rule of thumb: multiply the number of polysyllabic word by 3 and add 112.

D. This system is called SMOG in tribute to Gunning's Fog Index.

- RANDALL PLAN OR EMPLOYEE EVALUATION -

Dr. S. Lee Randall used the folllowing system to work toward the improvement of the staff in his junior high in Monroe, MI. Dr. Randall worked this through after the author returned from a seminar in Nevada, where some information was exchanged between participants and lecturers. This was expanded as a program from a stencil copy by Dr. James Monosmith from Colville, Colorado High School.

The basic format for that which follows was taken from the handout which Dr. Randall wanted to use for his program. It is not easy to take something from paper to reality and have it work. Dr. Randall did an excellent job in this arena. The format below was completed by the evaluator and evaluatee meeting together and then being finalized by the evaluatee to get names and dates affixed before turning it in to the "boss."

The plan Dr. Randall instituted is as follows:

I. OBSERVED <u>PRIME</u> AREAS OF STRENGTH:

A. _____

B. _____

C. _____

II. AREAS OF IMPROVEMENT AS AGREED UPON:

A. _____

B. _____

III. AGREED UPON GOALS AND PERFORMANCE CRITERIA FOR FIRST SEMESTER:

Goal A. _____
what is to be done:

_____
performance indicator

_____
how to know when it is done

Goal B. _____
what is to be done:

_____
performance indicator

_____
how to know when it is done

IV. ASSISTANCE EXPECTED: peers, subordinates, superordinates

A. _____

B. _____

V. FEEDBACK COMMITTEE FOR EVALUATEE:
These 4 have agreed to serve.

A. _____
B. _____
C. _____
D. _____

VI. FEEDBACK DATES - Interim and Final:

A. Sixth week interim ___ / ___ / ___
B. Twelfth week interim ___ / ___ / ___
C. Six month interim ___ / ___ / ___
D. Final report on Mar. 1. ___ / ___ / ___

Signatures:
Evaluatee: _____

Evaluator: _____

Date of file: ___ / ___ / ___

= =

     This outline is brief and to the point. It borders both on Hardesty's 3 X 3 plan and the author's COATs program. It does not take into account the specifics of people as in Hardesty's plan nor the breadth of statements as in Megiveron's program. However, for the on-line administrator if reworked slightly to fit the overall plan of a district (where there is one), it can be helpful. It is not intended to show then only as a plan for classified personnel. It can be used for all employees.

     The system discussed above may prove to be a good starting point in working in evaluations. When this has been learned and is comfortable for the evaluator and evaluatee, the principal can then move to Hardesty's 3 X 3 plan and eventually into the COAT Program in a matter of three to five years. In any respect, try it before a decision is made not to use it. The newly found enthusiasm of the employees know what it is they are supposed to do and that there is help for them to do it properly will be a pleasant surprise.

- HARDESTY'S 3 X 3 EVALUATIONS -

The improvement of subordinates is one of the prime responsibilities of the good principal. It is worthy of note that when the principal leaves his/her position the assistant should be prepared to take the job and continue the many good things already started. After working in the public schools and doing a good deal of reading in the area of personnel evaluation and improvement, the author has found that Hardesty's material seems to be the most logical source to follow. It is worthy of purchase for the professional library for administration.

Hardesty and Scott (I-85,107-113) refer to their 3 by 3 People Improving Plan. This system like all of Hardesty's is simple -- meaning not complicated. It is explained below:

STEP I. List the names of all subordinates -- in rank order of their value by ability to perform. Be honest and do not regard personalities primarily. The supervisor should not (and really cannot) challenge this ranking when it is gone over with him.

STEP II. Examine the three names at the bottom of this list whether they are numbers 13, 14, and 15 or 4, 5, and 6. They are the three subordinates ranked to be least valuable. Consequently each needs assistance. Hardesty uses a quote in his material, "A manager is the first assistant to each of his subordinates." That being the case, as-

271

sist the subordinates so they can be of more assistance. Examine the bottom three names; fill in the three major problems each has which prevents him/her from moving up on the list.

STEP III. Write (in very brief words) what the solutions are to these problems -- one by one. Hardesty says, "Don't try to be a psychologist." Principals are in management and not in medicine. Don't complicate the resolutions. Write them in simple words.

STEP IV. Now -- and only now discuss the plan with the supervisor. Up to now, it has been a single effort. At this point, however, the supervisor can provide counsel and support. Don't be hesitant about seeking the advice. Get it and use it.

STEP V. The three people at the bottom of the confirmed list of employees prioritized by value to the program need much direct and significant attention now and more importantly to the specific resolutions to the identified problems. A common danger is that the principal gets so involved in the saving of others that his/her own effectiveness is weakened when time is taken to work with these people. Also, don't ignore other subordinates to help only the ones identified at the bottom of the list. Remain aware of the strengths of stronger personnel. There is an old adage in management, "Much more can be profited from strengthening strengths than from shoring-up weaknesses." It may be well to apply this here.

STEP VI. In sixty working days, repeat the whole process of listing employees one more time. The process may reveal the same personnel need attention, but it is likely that it won't. And, if it is, it should not be for the same reasons.

Of course, the system is best done when one has a full and adequate job description already in place. Please see the unit on development of such statements, Unit 3.

The Hardesty 3 X 3 works in many ways. First, it is quick. Second, it is deliberate and can be shared without destroying the subordinate in a manner from which s/he can rally and continue to do better work. Third, it is not time-consuming. Fourth, it "forces" re-examination of all subordinates on at least a quarterly basis to strengthen them for more positive action throughout the year. Fifth, the system can be shared and put into place quickly by others who have subordinates.

Shown below is an approximate form that T. Frank Hardesty distributes at his conferences and uses in his book. He encourages modification for personal use. The following has been modified for personal use in Monroe, MI. The names have been altered. The resolution of each is also shown.

There is some additional information in the reference noted above. The books are written in straight-forward language, and they are enjoyable to read and study. For the neophyte in management, the three volumes are recommended for the principal's growing library.

# Subordinate	Comments
1. Thomas E. Prenkert	Excellent performer great confidant
2. Terry G. Semones	Best Director. Smart, quick learner
3. Raymond P. Bottom	Has confidence of subordinates
4. Leo J. Perelman	Strong in community support - loyal
5. Lolly Lolliman	P1: Must learn to handle people P2: Decisions are

	made in haste P3: Erratic attend- ance S1: Working with Terry for good observation process S2: Take inservice course on decisions S3: Assign specific responsibilities
6. Mollie Plutz	P1: Uses feminine wiles on male subor- dinates P2: Irregular after 5:00 attendance P3: Unwilling to learn new tools S1: Discipline severely and ex- plain why S2: Rewrite charges to clear time S3: Provide self- help materials
7. Okie O'Goble	P1: Wastes too much time - not in office P2: Does not under- stand delegation P3: Uses poor ver- bal grammar S1: Complete time audit to show errors S2: Explain techni- que and follow-up S3: Reference Eng- lish textbook

Some other problems subordinates may have might look
like this:

lazy	talks too much	prevaricates
poor writing ability	wastes time	procrastinates
poor decision maker	makes excuses	spends too much
poor judgment	no dedication	time on details
poor attendance	"punches the clock"	or, whatever.

- CASE STUDY -

This process is used by the counselors to collect specific information when a student is referred to them by a teacher or information is needed by the guidance department. When a student needs help, the counselor can use these data once provided. The intent is to enable the students and teachers to work together more successfully. Many of the referrals for this service came from the use of the "Blue Card" program, which will be introduced for the benefit of the students in Unit 6.

    A form for the collection of data to use for the benefit of the student is shown below:

```
============================================
Date: __ /__ /__  CASE STUDY # ___ , _____
                                 Yr.   To Date
Staff Attendees: Teachers of
1st hr._____  2nd hr._____

3rd hr._____  4th hr._____

5th hr._____  6th hr._____

Counselor_____  Ass't Prin._____

Coach _____  Home Room_____

Sponsor _____  Others _____
```

275

Others_____ Others _____

1. Where does the student sit in class?

2. By whom does s/he sit in class?

3. Does s/he volunteer? Frequency?

4. Do you call upon her/him? Frequency?

5. Is there a "special friend?" student? staff?

6. What do you feel s/he likes best in your situation?

7. What do you feel s/he likes least in your contact?

8. Have you checked data in the cumulative folder?

What did it tell you that helped?

9. What didn't the folder tell you that you would have liked to have known to help this student?

10. Are you aware of any physical deficiency?

Heart?_____   Vision?____   Physical?__
Social?_____   Lungs?_____   Hearing?___
Mental?_____   Emotional?_____ Asthma?____
Ven.l Disease?__ AIDS?____   Drugs?_____

11. Rate this student's ability to perform. 1 = Highest, 5 = lowest

On Homework__ On Daily Work__On Projects__

On Tests_____ On Term Work___On Lab Work__

On Leadership functions____   On Tasks ____

On Cooperation projects___

12. What methodological approach seems to be best for cognition?

Visual ___ or Auditory explanations? ___
Psychomotor___ or primarily Tactile work? ___

13. On which types of questions is performance the best?
   Verbal (v) AND Written (w)
   General _____   Essay _____
   Specific _____   True/False _____
   High Order _____   Completion _____
   Probing _____   Matching _____
   Convergent _____   Divergent _____
   Multiple Choice _____

14. What has been the attendance record to date?

Number of Days Absent ____ of ____.
Day of week most likely _____

Number of times tardy ____ of ____.

15. What is the reading level of the material you use?_____ Use reverse side to list the material

16. What are the reading levels of the student?
Comp:____/Speed____

17. Is there a problem with incomplete work on tests?_____, on project work?_____, on daily work?_____

18. Are you aware of any social/emotional items which may help us if we each understand them? Yes____ No____
    Explain on back.

19. Is this student at all active in school matters?_____

20. Tell us anything else we need to know about this student.

_____

When a problem is discovered, generally the counselor assigned to the student calls for an immediate Case Study. It must be remembered that a mistake that a child makes is often to be regarded as a cue only. The case conference is called for the express purpose to discover what the cue is in the behavior with the child. When completed and the information has been compiled, the counselor relays the data to the participants. The conferees are staff members with whom the student has contacts in the building. No student name appears on the form, but file copies are coded. Remember that "staff" refers to all adults working in the building for the board of education. The attendees went beyond just classroom teachers. Each conferee completed the form as much as was practicable.

Whatever time of day the conference is held or whatever form is used to record the data is strictly up to the principal. If help can be given a student and s/he begins to progress fully, the reward is intrinsic.

- EXCEPTIONAL STUDENT CARD -

There are many students in the building about which the principal does not know all s/he should know. If this is questioned, chat with another principal who has had a student die in his arms as the author had happen in the early 60's. The parents were afraid that the school would treat their son like a "freak" if it was known that he had a rheumatic heart. So no one was told. It was discovered when the young man died because of over-exertion during a voluntary pick-up or "storage" basketball game in the gym during the noon recess. The EMS team could not revive him, and he was DOA at the hospital.

Exceptional student cards should always be available. The real push to get them accurate and complete

278

cannot be left to chance. The entire staff (beyond just the faculty) should study these cards intently and add information to them each semester when they are reviewed. Activity-type teachers need to concentrate on them. The entire staff is more knowledgeable and, thus, more competent.

Cards should be sent home for parent signature. Not ALL parents will be honest and provide full information, but it is the only way to assure accountability for the staff. If the card is not returned, the child should be sent home to stay until the card is signed and returned.

When ALL of the cards are collected, the staff will meet for the counselors' report. Each card needs to be computerized. Lists can then be provided for teachers by sections as they teach during the day. The physical education teachers will need to keep a total file as they typically are at the opposite end of the building and present for a longer time than regular teachers. The office staff needs to keep a separate list. In that way anyone can get rapid access to the information should it be needed during the extended day or anywhere in the building.

HERE IS THE CARD'S FORMAT

================================

Last Name_____ Home Rm___ Date__/__/____

First Name_____ MI___ Date of Birth__/__/___

Home Phone #_____ Emergency # _____

Information is on file for the following items as checked below. Please see the counselor assigned to this counselee.

Heart____	Lungs____	Posture___	Eyes____
Ears____	B.P.____	Speech___	Reading___
Birth____	Sinus____	Drugs____	Behavior__
Guardianship_____			

================================

By color coding the cards on file by counselor, it will be easy to know which counselor to contact for further information without having to check yet another list to make this determination.

Each teacher should be accountable for the students directly in his class each hour. The EXCEPTIONALITY information was made available to him on a semi-annual basis. The updated information lists are to be given out when the "old" list is returned so that no extra copies will be accessible in the building. In other words, the principal should insist on as much confidentiality as can be expected for the students. Only one copy of the cards should exist, and it should be kept in the counselor's office.

- STUDENT ENTRANCE INTERVIEWS -

The form which is located in the exhibits should be understandable following this brief explanation. It was used BY students to interview ALL new arrivals to the high school. The reasons for doing this are: (1) The new student learns about the program into which s/he is now enrolling, and (2) the students at the high school learn a great deal about the new enrollee and about other high school programs. When good ideas are learned from these interviews, the information is given to the principal or to one of the three student committees working with the principal. These committees focus on activities and athletics, curriculum and instruction, and policies and procedures. More information on these committees is covered in the subunit on Three Student Committees, Unit 7.

Kids talk to kids easily. The information to be gleaned from these interviews can be a real help and a constant input for consideration for program change.

Other principals are happy to share the good things going on in their buildings. Such information may be forthcoming during the interview by the students.

Some domestic student exchange programs were organized between high schools. Students, under the watchful eye of Mr. James Amell, went to several other cities in the United States on exchange visits and became hosts and hostesses when visits were made to the high school by the exchange visitors. Both the receiving and sending schools gained a great deal from these visits.

Many programs were introduced in the high school as explained or suggested by new enrollees. Some of the "Individualized Programming" options were learned from entrance interviews. And on and on it went. The students are the winners in this program.

- STUDENT EXIT INTERVIEWS -

The form which is a near duplication of the "Entrance" form is also found in the exhibits. It was used with students leaving the school program for ANY reason. The stated reason was not always the REAL reason for the official withdrawal as discovered when students talked to students. Students leaving related very well to students remaining in the building. They knew the answers given were going to be used to help others. The interviewers felt, each time, that the responses were sincere and as such they proved to be helpful to the administration, staff, and faculty.

- UNIT SIX INTRODUCTION -
Preparation of Significant Statements

There are several tools to use to be an effective principal. One of the concerns of the principal has to be getting information which is understandable to the staff and students. The papers as discussed in this unit are each self-explanatory, but a descriptive statement has been developed for each as a quick reference to the topic.

Critical Action Papers
Blue Cards for a Suicide Prevention Program
Misery Index
Wind Chill Grid
Curriculum Newsletter

Critical Action Papers are papers to be developed when something must be done. The format is interesting and substitutes for a memo and the formality of same.

Suicide prevention is serious business. But it is not new. In fact, the author applied for a principalship in a city in Ohio one year. The leading goal for the new principal to attack was stated by the chair of the interviewing committee, "We expect the principal will cut our 10-12 percent suicide rate in the senior class." The feelings were that of being totally flabbergasted. The program there indicated that they didn't want someone dedicated to work for and with ALL students. Their program needed so much reparation it could not be done in one year, if it could be done at all. It did not appear they were ready to make the changes necessary. Since the entire vocational program was housed in ONE room, apparently they were not. The program outlined in this subunit is efficient and releases tension when none is necessary.

Heat/Humidity and wind chill factoring are really the same problem for the principal but handled in different seasons. Coaches need to understand these and use good judgment when working with athletes outside at particular times of the year. Principals need this information to use for judgment on whether or not outside activities ought to be held.

Curriculum Newsletters are good means of keeping the faculty on the mission at hand: making the best possible program for the students in the building. The prime role of the principal is that of instructional leadership. It is easy for the principal to get buried in the myriad of assigned tasks which are seldom couched in instructional measures. Yet, the final word on success is how well the students did in their program. The principal is there for INSTRUCTION, and that is all there is to it. Most of the tasks which are not instructional can be done while the faculty and students are out of the building -- either before they are expected to be in attendance, or after they have gone home. That is the time to get the work done that the central office demands.

- CRITICAL ACTION CARDS -

The purpose of this type of communication is that it covers just what the title says it does: CRITICAL ACTION items. This process is used in business all the time when an executive visits outlying businesses and returns to report to the CEO. In educational administration it works well.

The object is to be succinct. This presentation will be succinct because the object is intense and self-descriptive. If administrators go into classrooms and see something which needs immediate action, such a paper can be prepared quickly and sent to the Head Custodian, the Office Manager, the Principal or whoever has the responsibility and can take the right steps to correct the concern.

The paper can be used for site visits, building inspections, meeting summaries by the principal's representative when s/he can't cover a meeting, summary of observation reports, discipline cases, case conferences, and many other items. The format is as follows:

```
============================================
To: Dr. Megiveron, Principal           BJM # 0014
From: Byron J. Merritt                      8/15/65
```

Subject: Critical Action Items <u>for school opening</u>

Room #   *Suggested Necessary Action*

101   The unit ventilator is filthy; the screen is blocked
103   The desks in the room are marking the tile floor
              Many (at least seven feet) lack plastic glides.
105   The water faucet is leaking (dripping) constantly
              and has been for some time causing stains
112   Molly is in a state of depression emanating from the
              recent death in her immediate family

```
============================================
```

Succinct "critical actions" have been passed along to the addressee to keep the building operating well.

The critical action statement makes no recommendation. It is an anecdotal record in and of itself. The recipient is the one to determine action. The administrator getting a critical action report is the one who is accountable for the subject of the contents.

- BLUE CARDS =
SUICIDE PREVENTION PROGRAM -

Here is a local parish's (district's) plan to inaugurate the Blue Card policy as described by Mr. Joseph Olmi, a graduate student who planned the program based on notes taken in class working on his specialist degree. Joe submitted this paper to a high school faculty recently as an example of application to one of the special programs learned in graduate school. Here is the paper as it went to the faculty for their use as prepared by Joe, the school psychologist.

THE BLUE CARD

Often times during the course of the school day, stress becomes a problem for both the teacher and student. Frequently, this stress is manifested in the form of a power struggle which places added stress on the situation causing the teacher to occupy a superior position with the student being placed in a seemingly inferior position. The situation can become compounded if the players do not wish to be in their respective positions. One method of contending with the stress brought into the classroom, by either the teacher or the student, is the "blue card."

RATIONALE

The rationale behind the use of the blue cards is that they will indicate to the teacher that a student is having problems that are significant enough to interfere with his/her ability to actively participate in classroom proceedings. The problems are such that the student does not choose to participate in the class activities. If these are frequent enough, then the counselor needs to become involved with the student and his/her parents.

SUGGESTIONS

1. After explaining the concept of the card, the teacher should discuss possible abuse of the card and the consequences of such action. Example: Disbanding use of the card or disciplinary action that will ensue.

2. Stress that the card cannot be used for sleeping.

3. Students should be reminded that no undue attention is to be given to students with the blue cards on their desk.

285

4. Teachers may wish to locate enrichment material (books, poetry, magazines, etc.) near the blue cards for the student to use during the class period.

Below is the contract as designed by the committee working with Mr. Olmi for use of the Blue Cards.
===
CLASS PERIOD_____ DATE____/____/____

STUDENT/TEACHER
CONTRACT

PURPOSE

The purpose of the "blue card" is to establish an opportunity for the student to choose not to participate in class proceedings. There will be no threat of reprisals from the teacher or the administration. Each classroom has blue cards, easily accessible, to be picked up by the student upon entering class. The student should pick up the card at the beginning of the class period. The teacher will record who picks up the cards. If within two weeks a student takes a blue card on three occasions, an automatic referral to a counselor will be made by the classroom teacher. The counselor will investigate the situation for the student's benefit.

AGREEMENTS

1. The card is a formal agreement between the teacher and student; it is formal in that it implies action on the part of both parties.

2. The agreement is also silent and nonthreatening to the student.

3. The obligation of the student is that he or she will not interfere with the other students or the proceedings of the class.

4. The obligation of the teacher is that s/he will not probe, question, or chastise in any way, nor will the student

286

be responsible for work during that class period. However, the teacher may offer encouraging comments at his/her own discretion.

5. The student is responsible for work assigned to be turned in at a date designated by the teacher.

6. The student is not able to use the blue card as a method of getting out of work assigned to be turned in on that particular day.

_____   _____

STUDENT   TEACHER

Although the above use of the card is not as it was initially envisioned and then practiced, it is a good means of showing the student body that the faculty is concerned about them.   It also shows that the teachers and administration are willing to work WITH them in an effort to alleviate their personal problems.

Statements such as "not sleeping in class," and "must record and report the third offering" were more student-oriented in the original plan.   Students have problems. The kids need help. They are calling out for help, and the staff must be there for their struggle to grow intellectually, socially, and emotionally.

- "MISERY INDEX" JUST HOW HOT IS IT? -

In USA TODAY, Thursday, July 23, 1987, page 9A carried a table of temperatures that busy principals can use. In the table, the considerations that are shown for the rows are Air Temperature by degrees Fahrenheit and across the columns Relative Humidity by percent. The introduction

287

says, "The thermometer may say 90 degrees, but the humidity can make it feel like 100. To read this chart, locate the air temperature on the left and the humidity on top, then find the apparent temperature where the columns meet."

The principal may wish to cancel field trips, athletics, or evening performances when the temperature is either too hot or too cold for human comfort.

The two tables that follow are for opposite ends of the index and show first the HOT index and then the wind-chill factor for (in some places) the "closing of school" recommendation that someone has to make to protect the children.

- "WIND CHILL" -- JUST HOW COLD IS IT? -

On a card distributed at a conference, a table of temperatures was printed for the busy principals to use in determining those times when school may well have to be canceled. It has been used by schools for years to determine the conditions outside the building. Superintendents use the wind chill table below to determine whether or not school should be closed because of the severe temperature for the rural (primarily) students waiting for the busses. While the high school principal does not call-off school in the district, the table is used for determining the type of activity for the students outside the building. In the table, the considerations that are shown for the rows are Air Temperature by degrees Fahrenheit, and across the columns Wind Chill by Miles Per Hour. The introduction says, "The chart shows how existing temperatures and wind velocities combine to produce the wind chill index shown as an equivalent temperature. For example, a temperatures of 25 degrees with 20 MPH winds equals a temperature of minus 4 degrees. Lines show combination of wind and temperature and the categories used describe them by the U. S. Weather Service."

It may be interesting to note that the relative humidity is reputedly of no influence on the danger of skin freezing. Although this is hard to fathom, it is not considered by the Air Force in Alaska when determinations are made for the troops. This information came from a retired general of the Air Force who said it was researched by the U. S. Gov't and no influence was found for the question raised on the humidity for freezing skin. The chart appears below:

Relative Humidity (%)

F /	0	5	10	15	20	25	30	35	40	45	50
140	125										
135	120	128									
130	117	122	131								
125	111	116	123	131	141						
120	107	111	116	123	130	139	148				
115	103	107	111	115	120	127	135	143	151		
110	99	102	105	108	112	117	123	130	137	143	150
105	95	97	100	102	105	109	113	118	123	129	135
100	91	93	95	97	99	101	104	107	110	115	120
95	87	88	90	91	93	94	96	98	101	104	107
90	83	84	85	86	87	88	90	91	93	95	96
85	78	79	80	81	82	83	84	85	86	87	88
80	73	74	75	76	77	77	78	79	79	80	81
75	69	69	70	71	72	72	73	73	74	74	75
70	64	64	65	65	66	66	67	67	68	68	69

Relative Humidity (%)

F/	55	60	65	70	75	80	85	90	95	100
105	142	149								
100	126	132	138	144						
95	110	114	119	124	130	136				
90	98	100	102	106	109	113	117	122		
85	89	90	91	93	95	97	99	102	105	108
80	81	82	83	85	86	86	87	88	89	91
75	75	76	76	77	77	78	78	79	79	80
70	69	70	70	70	70	71	71	71	71	72

==

```
                    Wind Speed in M.P.H.
  Temp./0    5    10    12    20    25    30    35    40
  +35   35   33    21    16    12     7     5     3     1
  +30   30   27    16    11     3     0    -2    -4    -4
  +25   25   21     9     1    -4    -7   -11   -13   -15
  +20   20   16     2   -06   -09   -15   -18   -20   -22
  +15   15   12   -02   -11   -17   -22   -26   -27   -29
  +10   10    7   -09   -18   -24   -29   -33   -35   -36
  + 5    5    1   -15   -25   -32   -37   -41   -43   -45
    0    0  -06   -22   -33   -40   -45   -49   -52   -54
  - 5  -05  -11   -27   -40   -46   -52   -56   -60   -62
  -10  -10  -15   -31   -45   -52   -58   -63   -67   -69
  -15  -15  -20   -35   -51   -60   -67   -70   -72   -76
  -20  -20  -26   -45   -60   -68   -75   -78   -83   -87
  -25  -25  -31   -52   -65   -76   -83   -87   -90   -94
  -30  -30  -35   -58   -70   -81   -89   -94   -98  -101
  -35  -35  -41   -64   -78   -88   -96  -101  -105  -107
  -40  -40  -47   -70   -85   -96  -104  -109  -113  -116
  -45  -45  -54   -77   -90  -103  -112  -117  -123  -128
```

A wind chill of negative 35 degrees freezes the ex
posed skin in about a minute. Therefore, most Boards o
Education close school if the transported children mus
wait for the bus at stops where the wind is bitterly cold. A
the high school, activities outside must be greatly curtailed

- CURRICULUM NEWSLETTERS -

After providing (writing and editing) curriculum newsle
ters for years with a large staff, feedback was constantl
sought so that the issues could be sharpened for a bette
focus. The faculty and staff should not be burdened wit
other than those items which they felt were appropriat
The following list is the result of the items selected by a
least eighty percent of the faculty:

Daffynitions	Chuckles
What Do You Think?	Dates to Remember
What Do You Want?	Journal Updates
Have You Seen?	For Your Information
Article summaries	Feedback on ___
Things in the Works	Quotable Quotes

The following material is presented for clarity.

Daffynitions: Some funny material to keep the staff loose, i.e. "A fine is a tax you have to pay for doing wrong; a tax is a fine you have to pay for doing right."

Chuckles: Some humor for the staff, i.e. "The Irish potato came from Peru; Greenland is not green; Camel's hair brushes are made from squirrels' hair; America was named by a German after an Italian navigator who was in the service of Portugal; Sauerkraut was originally a Chinese dish; Guinea pigs are from the rabbit family; the jugular vein is an artery."

What Do You Think? These items were of professional interest to the principal. Ones like those listed below were offered to the faculty as thought promoters.

1. Dr. Harl Douglass' list of twenty-four means to reduce the teachers' workload.

2. Faculty members application process for grant money to develop innovative programs for the students.

3. NASSP Spotlight reviews are good discussion stimulators.

Dates to Remember: Upcoming meetings, due dates for reports, upcoming days off, inservice programs, conferences or conventions.

What Do You Want? Usually alternatives the faculty could select from in terms of choices for curriculum or studies were listed. Another use was attachments for the staff to return to the administration.

Journal Updates: Whole issues were summarized by topics -- usually the table of contents was listed for the faculty to use.

Have You Seen? Particular pieces of software or equipment to use in the instructional process were highlighted. If a book seemed appropriate for any of the staff to read, it was mentioned here.

For Your Information: Feedback summaries, word from the "head shed" or another building, staff personal business, and other need-to-know facts were highlighted.

Article summaries: Self explanatory.

Feedback on ____: Results on requested information were given back.

Things in the Works: Equipment that had been ordered, supplies that were special ordered, master schedule for the next year for ideas from the faculty, policies being developed, minicourse (or other programs being developed) guidelines for feedback, student meeting minutes and the innerworkings of the staff were each covered here.

Quotable Quotes: Those comments made by important people in or out of the district were shared under this heading.

These newsletters were typed by the secretary and after a dozen or more of them, staff began to submit material to be included.

They were published biweekly, opposite the paycheck Fridays and began to be expected by all in the building. Each was published by using different colored paper to make it difficult to lose in the sea of white bulletins, etc. These were handy and especially good for the faculty to use to keep abreast of all that was going on in a comprehensive high school program.

- UNIT SEVEN INTRODUCTION -
Substructures for Sound Support

The help to decide the content of this special unit was given by a graduate class the author was teaching. The course was in Principles of School Administration. The following subunits were agreed upon to be significant to "shore up" the support needed by a principal in the building. Here is the list of topics selected.

Closed Loop Fanout
Three Student Committees
Faculty Advisory Committee
Progressive Honor Roll
Survival/Literacy/Competency Vocabulary
School Volunteers - Teacher Aides

Closed Loop Fanout is a design of a feedback instrument which is effective when the word must go out to the total staff and in a hurry. The author administered programs in the Northeast and as such was constantly in need of getting word to the staffs which they could use for delays or cancellation of regular school. The example here will be assistive to the principal.

The three student committees will become life savers and, -- in combination, a job saver. The kids in high school are pretty insightful and extremely helpful. The work they can do for a principal in curriculum, activities, and policy is amazing. The manner of their getting on the committees is left to the principal's discretion. However, by electing committee members students can see Democracy in action.

A Faculty Advisory Committee goes by many titles. The committee discussed in this unit is one used to orient the administrative program to INSTRUCTION, the key part of the job. Most questions can be answered by those in the classrooms and the members of this all important committee come from that audience. The committee will be extremely helpful to the neophyte or the experienced principal. The material on committees (1-3) and agenda (2-4) will be helpful if understood before reading the material for working with this significant body.

Progressive Honor Roll is a means of helping ALL the kids improve upon their self-concept as discussed by Maslow in Unit 25. It is amazing how popular this program will become with students, and it is simple to do. The program is now in several states as former students of mine take administrative positions and report to me that they have instituted the program in their schools.

Survival - Literacy - Competency Vocabulary Programming is a natural, considering the current emphasis on excellence and effectiveness. Students should know specifically what they will be required to learn. The lists are designed for a K - 12 operation. The lists can be accepted as they are or altered according to your staff's or/and student's input. Lists such as these can be designed strictly for the high school or the high school can become a finalizing agent for the district.

School volunteers are a big help to the entire staff. The program is outlined. There is a contrast shown between aides and unpaid volunteers.

- CLOSED-LOOP FANOUT -

One of the most frustrating events of a high school principal is to get a message from the central office and then try to pass it along to the staff for its full understanding and communication. To get the message out is not really a problem but to be assured that it is uniformly received and acted upon is something else. The last and first persons to hear the message ought to hear the same one. Once a message (brief, hopefully) is decided upon, the principal is in need of a network to get it across and accurately. A design that has worked successfully and with great relief to the principal is the Closed-Loop Fanout. Most executives use a fanout -- but few are assured that the message they started got delivered throughout the entire organization; this will permit such assurance.

ADVANTAGES OF THE CLOSED-LOOP FANOUT:

1. The principal and all others merely call two numbers and the entire staff is called routinely.

2. It is a rapid system of notifying an entire staff because the larger the number to be contacted, the more that become involved, but those on the chart still only have to call two persons.

3. The message being brief, written down each time, and then read to the next party, the chances are remote that the message to the "last" person will be any different than it was when it started.

BASIC RULES FOR OPERATING

1. ONLY ROWS ONE OR TWO MAY INITIATE THIS FANOUT AS IT IS FOR OFFICIAL SCHOOL PURPOSES ONLY.

2. Use the top phone number to call if during the day (work phone number) and use the bottom phone number to call after school hours and weekends (home phone numbers).

3. Put one of these in the official grade book, for security reasons, so it will be available during the day.

4. When the caller gives the message, do just two things:
      a. copy the message so it can be read back for verification and read to the parties to be called, and
      b. make the calls immediately.

5. If a contact is NOT available, call the numbers assigned to them so the message continues as rapidly as is possible. Keep going back to the party missed.

Broadening the range of the contacts (inserting a row) would add at least 24 names to this chart, as brief as it is. With a large staff of beyond the 42 or 43 places above, set the whole chart into departments. There are other examples in the Exhibits.

EXTRA CUES

1. The fanout needs to be distributed in the early part of the year. Whenever an emergency arises, all staff can be contacted. Here is a Closed-Loop Fanout:

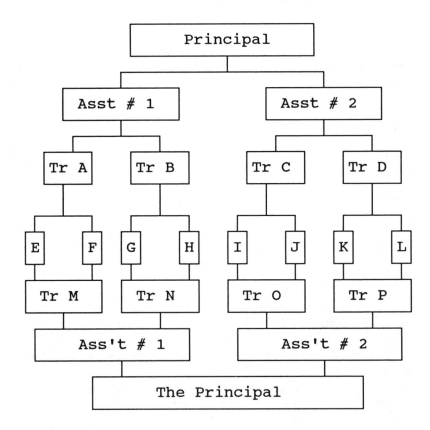

EXTRA CUES continued

2. If there are particular messages which need not go to the entire staff, but to a specific cadre, be sure to assign their names early in the chart and use it only to that level.

3. A dotted line across the page will serve the purpose of level indicators so all will know when the message is to be given only to a limited number.

4. The principal needs to have each staff member take a copy home because the message will frequently have to be run during the early hours of the morning when the school is either called off or delayed for inclement weather.

If there are any doubts as to what to do in terms of communicating with the entire staff in a hurry, reread the Halley's Comet item.

-THREE STUDENT COMMITTEES -

Three student committees which can really turn a principal's year around and get the student body working as part of the team in the building are the ones in the areas of:

Curriculum and Instruction,
Activities and Athletics, and
Policy and Programs.

These three student committees can find more good things to help the principal with than any other organized group. The purpose of their efforts is shared governance as the committees recommend items for consideration to the staff. When they come up with an idea or proposal to improve conditions for the student body, the recommendation is taken to the next staff meeting for discussion. The material for them to develop into "programs" or ideas can come from the problem census the principal takes throughout the year, surveys they conduct, homeroom discussions, class meetings, election campaign items, and others. (Please see the unit on Problem Census (1-1) for further information on this simple yet loaded means of obtaining information from any members of the total program over which the principal has jurisdiction.)

The committees, when working properly, take suggestions, concerns, questions, or other forms of input and go to work to resolve them in a favorable manner to be worthwhile for the students. They can perform a great service with the assistance of the faculty, the student body, and the administration in providing a continually improving program called school. The whole staff needs to get involved in the work of these committees. Initial involvement can be the "selling" of the Problem Census to those involved so that the questions are taken seriously and the responses are valid. Some faculty members will want to work directly with one of these committees. The principal needs to be careful in the assignment, if any, for supervision of one of these groups. They must be autonomous in their thinking and reflect the student body's attitude on issues and not a faculty member's attitude. If there is assurance that this can happen, it is good to have the committees sponsored because it not only builds improved staff-student communication, but it provides another avenue of staff-student cooperation.

Some of the ideas used in business/building management, community and public relations, instruction, evaluation and individualized programming for instruction can come from these committees. The committees need to meet at least biweekly, during school, and for a single class period. Any of the assistants, counselors, librarian, or the principal should meet with the committees unless the committee has requested a particular staff member or a staff member has asked to sponsor one of them. However, it is reserved as a major responsibility of the principal's in terms of time and a sense of a very real commitment to involvement, change, and innovation. At times, one of the committees may be meeting on a topic directly on the responsibility list of one of the assistants. Should this occur, s/he needs to be the one to meet with the committee to be helpful in problem resolution. The chairperson of the steering or advisory committee of the faculty needs to be free to meet with the students upon occasion. Here are twenty of the items brought to the attention of the committees while the author was a high school principal.

1. The establishment of an ombudsman's office.

2. Student input in teacher evaluations.

3. Arena scheduling for all students in the spring.

4. A study of the student body to determine what problems they had that may (not) be out of school yet solvable in the school.

5. Establishment of a student lounge and student council office.

6. Pregnant student program (in the 60's this was on the cutting edge and not too acceptable to the Board -- but was done).

7. Students in charge of the assembly program.

8. Refusal to give names and adresses of seniors to outside sources. (This was prior to the Buckley Amendment, but was honored.)

9. Establishment of a series of mini-courses (3 - 10 weeks long).

10. Credit toward graduation for community service.

11. Senior seminar courses developed on the basis

of concepts rather than chronology.

12. Participation in seminars for human relations, racism, and inservice work scheduled for the teachers.

13. Extension of the school day from 6:00 a.m. through to the time adult education classes began in the afternoon -- then allow the students to enroll in those classes they would not be able to take during the day.

14. Development of a Teacher-Aide and Child Care course for both sexes to work in the elementary and pre-school centers.

15. Permission for work in the Microteaching Clinic to count as credit toward graduation as service component.

16. Permission for students to sit in on the interview of new staff members.

17. Permission for student council to control all "internal" funds and provide the series for sales products for all groups in the building.

18. Organization of a host/hostess group to escort visitors.

19. Organization of a Pay As You Park plan for protection of student cars in the lot.

20. Permission for students to sit in on staff meetings and be called upon for input on items to which they can contribute.

All but numbers one and thirteen were completed successfully. The first was ruled outside the building's domain by the Board of Education and, therefore, such a position could not be established. (The students then appealed to the principal to be their ombudsman -- a position to which the author happily subscribed.) It led to a total student advisement program. This was accomplished by simply taking the entire enrollment and dividing it by the total staff in the building. The resultant quotient was around twenty (20). Each advisor met with his/her group at least weekly for a period of twenty minutes which was carved from the schedule and held as an extension of the first period of the day. Number thirteen was responded to by starting at 7:00, offering co-op classes in both morning and afternoon sessions, and allowing adult education classes to be taken for credit toward graduation by passing the "regular" school's final examination. The thirteenth worked for but a few of the students.

- FACULTY ADVISORY COMMITTEE -

In some places in the text, the faculty advisory committee may have been described as the Steering Committee. It performs that type of function. It is shared authority, and that is good in management. The idea of flex-time work and shared assignments came from a faculty advisory committee in the building. The programs, listed in a separate subunit called Individualized Programming, were each reviewed by this committee before they were submitted to the faculty at a faculty meeting. The recommendation of the committee carried a great deal of weight on the outcome of the program under discussion. The report of the committee below is developed following the committee development format, tied with the work of the Standard Practive Bulletins. In this way some of the work already covered in this text will be used as an example.

FACULTY ADVISORY COMMITTEE

I. PURPOSE (or) CHARGE

The recommended FAC is proposed to open communication directly with the principal acting as the agent of the Board through the superintendent. The committe is intended to bring about openness and non-combative conflict resolutions. The thrust of the work of the committee will be for discussions of the current thinking of the staff in the high school.

II. GENERAL

The current Professional Council is a bargained, forced group which does not permit a free exchange of ideas and information between the principal and the many parts of the staff in the building and is not necessarily representative of the entire staff and its components.

III. MEMBERSHIP

1. One teacher per 10 members from each course area (Basic Skills, Career Orientation, Soft and Hard Sciences, Physical/Mental Health, and Arts) in the high school and two members from each of the staff components of at least 10 employees will be chosen.

2. The assistant principals shall attend all meetings because of their breadth of responsibilities.

3. One teacher will represent the interim faculty members.

4. The three student class presidents will serve.

5. The Head Custodian, the Dietician, and Office Manager will be on the committee.

IV. RESPONSIBILITY

The principal shall report all information brought to a closure to the assistant superintendent of secondary education.

V. FUNCTION

1. To provide input on issues and concerns of the building as felt by the members to be valid.

2. To discuss issues and develop a consensus for eventual administrative application or information for the building administration.

3. To seek information on long-range planning under consideration by the building administrator or central staff of the district.

4. To develop a comfortable communication level between the Board's agent and the faculty.

5. To explore other topics as are felt to be significant to the group and placed on the agenda before it is published.

VI. DUTIES

1. To attend each meeting as structured by the committee at its first session.

2. To bring to the principal's attention all pertinent concerns of the staff before they become issues, whether they are being openly discussed or are in the "rumor" stage.

3. To take back to the respective represented groups of faculty/staff all pertinent information exchanged.

4. To call in other key personnel for responses which affect their department specifically.

5. To learn decision-making tools as used by the principal's cabinet and apply them when necessary.

6. To work at ferreting concerns so input can be given which is not based on personal whims or judgments.

7. To discuss and make recommendations to the general faculty and staff on all items sent to it by the three student advisory committees: Curriculum, Activities, and Policies, which meet the week prior to this advisory group.

8. To review the upcoming monthly calendar of activities, reports due, marking periods, project completions, and all other on-going tasks from the administration.

9. To make recommendations on conference applications, budgetary items, and public relation releases.

VII. DATES AND REPORTS

1. Monthly meetings will be scheduled routinely.

2. Written documents are to be prepared quarterly for the principal's consumption at the December, March, and June work sessions, currently scheduled for the second Thursday of each month.

3. Representatives of this advisory group were automatically placed on the Building Curriculum Committee, which sent representatives to the district's Central Curriculum Committee.

This committee served the building well. The administration became strengthened through the sharing of information and the advice given.

One of the author's favorite concepts which came to frui-
tion is the subject of this subunit. Following this brief introduction is an actual position paper sent to the high
school faculty to launch the program. The idea was the
result of a brainstorming session among two students and
their principal after they both sent in problem census cards
(See Unit # 01) in response to the item: If I were the principal, I would. . . Brent Barnes said he would ". . develop
broader, therefore better, means of student recognition
than ones we have in place now." Marsha Carnes
responded to the same item with: "I would design an honor
roll anyone in the building could get on by individual
effort." These two, by signing their cards indicating they
would be willing to discuss the idea with the principal,
were called in. The first item of business was to see if the
two items could be combined. It was agreed that they
could. They were combined as similar concepts. After
much thought and discussion, Marsha and Brent took it to
the Student Curriculum Committee.

The resultant idea was given to the student government. The results were as follows:

Committe on Impending Legislation: Approved - 03 - 0
House's Education and Curr. Comm.: Approved - 05 - 0
House Vote: Approved - 74 - 2
Senate Vote: Approved - 20 - 0
Faculty (Vice President)   Approved

Here is the position paper sent to the staff.

================================
To: Staff of Kathryn Bulemore High School
From: Dr. Megiveron
Subject: Progressive Honor Roll

Introduction:

This paper is being presented to you as a handout for our next staff meeting when it will be discussed. Brent, Marsha, and the SCC chairman will present it to you. Following that session, the paper will be rewritten, as altered and/or confirmed, for general student discussion in your advisee settings some time early next month.

BACKGROUND AND POSITION TAKEN:

Too many excellent kids are being ignored because the great amount of effort exuded in their studies does not bring about qualification for our Platinum, Gold, or Silver Honor Rolls with the God-given ability they have. Our Honor Rolls are determined by the following point averages for all subjects taken:

4.0 - 3.9 = Platinum 3.8 - 3.6 = Gold   3.5 - 3.2 = Silver

Therefore, the school should adopt an honor roll designed to meet the needs of the audience of the hard working - low ability student. It should supplement, not supplant, the current honor rolls in existence at this time, at least in my perception. What I am attempting to do is have a program which will allow a student to compete with himself and not against other students.

We each know that students who are able to get on and stay on the honor rolls are usually blessed with a good home, good environment, and, if nothing else, a good attitude toward school. Mix this with a very kind, loving, and considerate teacher during their schooling and they are on the honor roll.

HOW TO GET ON THE PROGRESSIVE HONOR ROLL:

1. The second and each subsequent report card period will be used to determine eligibility to be placed on the honor roll. The first report's marks will be the base for honor roll attainment.

306

2. Eligibility shall be the maintenance or improvement of the overall grade point average from one report card period to the next.

3. Each time cards are distributed, the homeroom teacher shall examine each report card after distribution and the appeal is made by the student to get (stay) on the honor roll. Should a student's total grade point average be maintained or improved, the student's name shall be placed on the sheet labeled PROGRESSIVE HONOR ROLL RECIPIENTS. The list is then sent to the main office for consolidation into a single list by grade level.

4. Should a student's grade point average decline once they are on the Progressive Honor Roll, their names shall be deleted from the roll.

5. Once the Progressive Honor Roll is prepared in a single list, the list shall be distributed to each teacher who will make alterations on it rather than to have to record each name, every time.

Please study this proposal and be ready to take action on it at the next staff meeting.
= =

Progressive Honor Rolls are now available to students in several states as the author's past graduate students are becoming administrators and putting the practice into place. It is a means of assisting ALL students in the building. The program is representative of many others which can be put into place if the principal is listening and hearing his/her student body and staff.

- SURVIVAL-
LITERACY-
COMPETENCY-
VOCABULARIES -

These words, phrases, and symbols must be learned to avoid danger and/or acute embarrassment. Learning proficiency is first checked at the fifth grade level and *mastery must be obtained* at the twelfth grade level. The lists are one district's attempt to set in writing what was important to the students. The principal and faculty need to determine what is their list of words. In this subunit, there are three lists. They have been grouped into categories as shown in the title of the subunit: Survival, Literacy, and Competency.

- SURVIVAL VOCABULARY -

Acid	Falling Rocks	Off
Antidote	Fire:	On
Area	Alarm	One Way
Beware	Escape	Out
Bridge Out	Extinguisher	
	Flammable	Poison
Caution		Poisonous
Cold	Gasoline	Posted
Combustible	Go	Private:
Contaminated		Property
Corrosive	High Voltage	Road
Cross Here	Hospital	Proceed at
	Hot	Own Risk
Danger		Prohibited
Deep Water	In	Pull
Do Not:	Inflammable	Push
Breathe Fumes	Irritant	Radiation
Enter		Road Ends
Inhale Fumes	Keep:	Smoking
Open	Away	Steam
Operate	from Heat	Step Down

308

Push	Closed	Stop
Shove	Off	
Stand Up	To Left	Telephone
Take Internally	To Right	Thin Ice
Use Near Heat		Turn Off
Use Near Open Flame		
	Live Wires	Use:
Drugs	Look	Before
		../../..
Dynamite	Look out for	In Open Air
	Low Gear	
Emergency Exit	Men	
Exit		Walk
Exit Only	Next:	Warning
Explosives	window	Women
External Use	Gate	

No: Diving
    Exit
    Fires
    Smoking
    Swimming
    Trespassing
Not For Internal Use
Noxious

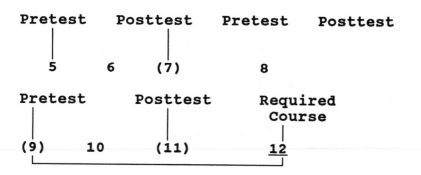

Proficiency tests are to be administered in June of the grade levels as noted above -- the proficiency level is 100%.

- LITERACY WORD LIST -

These words go a level beyond the absolute survival lists above. They are necessary words, phrases, and symbols to function at a level of understanding of the most common terms and signs. Proficiency is first checked, for most students, early in the seventh grade, and hopefully can be terminated at the ninth grade in the month of May. It is suggested that 80% proficiency should suffice but the work is mandatory to be followed in the high school if the list cannot be mastered ahead of time.

Again	Instructions	Railroad
Authorized		(R. R.)
Personnel	Junction 101A	Crossing
Only		Rest Area
Church	Keep Out	Restrooms
Closed		Resume Speed
Dead End	Ladies	Right Lane
Deer (Cattle)	Lane Ends	Must turn
Crossing	Left Lane	Road Closed
Detour	Must Turn	
Dim Lights	Left Turn on	School
Dip	Signal	Stop
Do Not	Left Turn O.K.	Zone
Cross	Look Out For	Shallow
Use Tunnel	Fork Lift	Water
Handle	Lost	Shelter
Refreeze		Slide Area
	M. P. H.	Slippery
Ear Protection	Men Wanted	When Wet
Area	Menu	Slow Down
Elevator	Merge Left	Slow Traffic
Emergency	Merge Right	Keep Right
Station		Keep Left
Vehicles	NO	Stairs
End	Admittance	Steep Grade
Construction	Bare Feet	Stairs
Exhaust	Pets	Stop
Exit Speed 30	Allowed	Again
Eye Protection	Hunting	Ahead
Required	Left Turn	Motor

Minors

First Aid Parking This End Up
Four Way Stop Passing This Side Up
Fumes Right Turn Three Way
Turns Light
Gentlemen U Turns Tickets
Go Slow
One Way Street Track
Handle With Care Traffic
Hands Off Out of Order
Hard Hat Area Unloading
Help Pavement Ends Zone
Hospital Zone Ped X ing Use Other
Pedestrians Door
Prohibited
Police Wanted
Police Station Winding Road
Station
Precinct Yield
Right of
Way

- COMPETENCY WORD LIST -

The student who masters these words and symbols has the knowledge to read and understand at a level to adequately function in present day society. Formal instruction begins, for most students, in the ninth grade and concludes in the eleventh. Students are post tested at the end of their junior year in high school. Proficiency level is 70%. Those who fall below this standard will be required to take a nine week course in Essential Word and Symbol Skills. Students may test out of this course at any time they score 70% over the entire subject matter area. Those finishing, before the nine week unit is completed, will be given experiences or study in the alternative pro-gram. The instructional plan will be worked out between each principal and staff. However, especially at the secondary level, it becomes imperative that the plan include specifically assigned departmental responsibilities. After development, each plan will be committeed to paper with copies disseminated to teachers, appropriate director, and assistant superintendent.

Adults Only
All Cars Stop
All Trucks
    Stop
Ask Attendant
  for Key

Beware of Dog
Bus
      Only

Floods When
    Raining
Found
Fragile
Freeway

Garage
Gate

Information
Inspection

Office
Open

Playground

Post No Bills
    Office
Receptionist
Registry
Reserved
Restaurant

        Station
        Stop
Bridge May
    Ice in Cold
    Weather
Cafeteria
Construction
    Zone
Curve

Delicatessen
Dentist
Diner
Doctor (DR.)
Do Not Crowd
Don't Walk
Down
Drive Slow

Employees Only
Entrance
Escalator
Express

Fallout Shelter
Flooded

    Station
Last Chance
      for Gas
Library
Local

Manager
Mechanic On
      Duty
Men Working
Merging
    Traffic
Military
  Reservation
Money Orders
NO
      Checks
        Cashed
    Credit
    Dumping
    Fishing
    Loitering
    Standing
    Stopping

Not a Thru
    Street
Nurse

Safety First
Speed Check
  By Radar
Station
Subway

Taxi Stand
Terms Cash

Up

Violators
  Prosecuted

Waiting Room
    Wet Paint
Watch Your
  Step

These lists are not to be considered to be carved in stone. Certainly, if prepared in Louisiana, the words would be different than if they were prepared in Michigan. Bayou, Crawfish, and many more probably would be added. The purpose of these lists is to assist the reader with the preparation of lists of his/her own.

The idea is sound. The lists must be tempered for regions and maybe even by states. The lists when distributed to the students and the teachers explained them to fellow staff members got more activity in reading and writing going fast. The lists proved to be very convenient for teachers to use in assignments and students to use in themes and reports or spelling lists.

The high school cannot escape responsibility in the preparation of such lists for the district's students. Remember, ALL of them show up to the high school sooner or later.

- SCHOOL VOLUNTEERS - TEACHER AIDES -

The principal will assess the need for volunteers during the first year when his/her prime concern will be asking questions.

There are a great number of volunteers available if the principal looks for them. Grandparents, certified teachers not currently working, college students, central office personnel and other persons in business, industry, military constitute a large audience for work with a special group of kids on a limited basis. Perhaps it is an item that the Advisory Committees can help with when the need is known and the work properly described.

313

Needs and resources of a building will dictate what volunteers do in the building. It is hard to distinguish the functional difference of volunteers and aides. One way to understand the difference is that the aide ought to be assigned to instructional work, and the volunteer is used in any area whch improves the personal service to members of the faculty/students in the building. The prime difference between aides and volunteers is that volunteers are unpaid, and the usual practice is to pay the aides.

There are several areas of service in which these fine people can perform. Here are the most popular ones as distributed to the author while taking post doctoral graduate work.

In the high school, the work of either volunteers or aides is of great help in the community relations program just as it is in the instructional and activity programs. By the involvement of the members of the community IN the school and its many programs, the staff and programs become much more visible and when the need arises for explanations of what is ongoing, a whole new cadre of persons is available to tell the school story.

If the principal plans to use volunteers or aides in the school program, s/he should be sure to put someone on the full-time staff in charge of the coordination and administration of same. The coordinator should be aware of the following for a successful program:

1. Work with the entire staff in the establishment of procedures, rules and regulations of the program. It should not be launched until there is far more than just consensus on the staff of its value. Background work is essential to bring the staff into the thinking of the value of such a program.

2. There is much information from the USOE and several of the state offices of education throughout the United States. The source, *National School Volunteer Program of the Public Education Association*, has packets of

of information already prepared. The address of this organization is: 20 West 40th St., NYC., NY 10018.

3. Receive Board of Education tentative approval to structure a program. When the structure is completed, go back to the Board with the final plans and get approval formally. Financing of the program cannot be ignored in the initial or certainly the final program plan as approved formally by the Board.

4. Provide an active program of recruiting and surveying of the community-at-large. There are many wonderful resources in the community of a high school who will be participants if asked and others who are not comfortable about volunteering. The younger child is also available to assist. Send flyers home about the decision to organize such a program. This single act will likely bring many to the ranks. Be sure to include all homes in the area. At this time many communities have only 30 % of the homes represented in the school.

5. Give orientation to all participants. This must happen all throughout the year. Part of this would be introduction of all the aides and volunteers at a very next staff meeting so all will be aware of the service being provided.

6. Arrange for constant and continued training of the aides and volunteers. Do not expect them to grow in the education world without good assistance and explanations from the ones in education who can use their assistance.

7. Provide synthesis for the entire program to utilize all resources in the building and the community.

- SELECTED REFERENCES -

1. ASCD. *Current Thought on Curriculum*. Alexandria, VA: ASCD, 1985.

2. Adler, Mortimer J. *The Paideia Proposal: An Educational Manifesto*. NY: Macmillan, 1982.

3. Amidon, Edmund J. and John B. Hough, eds. *Interaction Analysis: Theory, Research and Application*. Reading, MA: Addison-Wesley, 1967.

4. Austin, David B. and Harry L. Brown. *The Assistant Principalship*. Reston, VA: National Association of Secondary School Principals, 1970.

5. Bair, Medill. and Richard G. Woodward. *Team Teaching in Action*. Boston: Houghton-Mifflin, 1964.

6. Barbe, Walter B. and Raymond H. Swassing. *Teaching Through Modality Strengths: Concepts and Practices*. Columbus, OH: Zaner-Bloser, Inc, 1979

7. Barnard, Chester I. *The Functions of the Executive*. Cambridge, MA: Harvard Univ. Press, 1938.

8. Beggs, David. *Decatur-Lakeview High School: A Practical Application of the Trump Plan*. Englewood Cliffs, NJ: Prentice-Hall, 1964.

9. Bell, Terrel H. *A Performance Accountability System for School Administrators*. West Nyack, NY: Parker, 1974.

10. Bent, Rudyard K. and Lloyd E. McCann. *Administration of Secondary Schools*. NY: McGraw-Hill, 1960.

11. Berle, Peter A., Chairman. *Making the Grade*. NY:

Twentieth Century Fund, 1983.

12. Besag, Frank P. and Jack L. Nelson. *The Foundations of Education: Stasis and Change.* NY: Random House, 1984.

13. Bittel, Lester R. *Essentials of Supervisory Management.* NY: McGraw-Hill, Inc., 1981.

14. Blake, Robert R. and Jane S. Mouton. *The Managerial Grid III.* Houston, TX: Gulf, 1987.

15. Blanchard, Kenneth and Spencer Johnson. *The One Minute Manager.* NY: William Morrow & Co., 1981.

16. Bloom, Benjamin S. *Human Characteristics and School Learning.* NY: McGraw-Hill, 1976.

17. _____. *Taxonomy of Cognitive Domain. Hdbk I.* NY: David McKay, 1956.

18. Blumberg, Arthur and William Greenfield. *The Effective Principal: Perspectives on School Leadership.* 2nd ed. Boston: Allyn and Bacon, 1986.

19. Blumberg, Arthur. *Supervisors and Teachers.* Berkeley, CA: McCutchan, 1974.

20. Boyer, Ernest L. *High School: A Report on Secondary Education in America.* NY: Harper and Row, 1983.

21. Brandt, Ronald S., ed. *Content of the Curriculum.* Alexandria, VA: ASCD, 1988

22. Brown, B. Frank. *New Directions for the Comprehensive High School.* West Nyack, NY: Parker, 1972.

23. _____. *The Nongraded High School.* West Nyack,

317

NY: Parker, 1963.

24. _____. *The Reform of Secondary Education.* NY: McGraw-Hill, 1973.

25. Brown, Donald J. *Appraisal Procedures in the Secondary Schools.* Englewood Cliffs, NJ: Prentice-Hall, 1970.

26. Burrup, Percy. *Modern High School Administration.* 2nd ed. NY: Harper, 1963.

27. Callahan, Michael G. *The Effective School Department Head.* West Nyack, NY: Parker, 1971.

28. Caplow, Theodore. *How to Run Any Organization.* Hinsdale, IL: The Dryden Press, 1976.

29. Castillo, Gloria A. *Left-Handed Teaching: Lessons in Affective Education.* NY: Praeger Publishers, 1974.

30. Cetron, Marvin and Thomas O'Toole. *Encounters with the Future: Forecast of Life into the 21st Century.* NY: McGraw-Hill, 1982.

31. Chernow, Fred and Carol Chernow. *School Administrator's Guide to Managing People.* West Nyack, NY: Parker, 1976.

32. Coleman, James C., chrm. *Youth: Transition to Adulthood.* Chicago: University Press, 1974.

33. Cook, Desmond C. *Educational Project Management.* Columbus, OH: Charles Merrill, 1971.

34. _____. *Program Evaluation and Review Technique.* Wash., D.C.: U. S. Gov't. Printing Office, 1966.

35. Cooper, Joseph D. *How to Get More Done in Less Time.* Garden City, NY: Doubleday, 1971.

36. Culver, Carmen M. and Gary J. Hoban (eds.) *The Power to Change: Issues for the Innovative Educator.* NY: McGraw-Hill, 1973.

37. Cunningham, Luvern L., Walter G. Hack, and Raphael O. Nystrand, *Educational Administration.* Berkeley, CA: McCutchan, 1977.

38. Darling, Arthur. ed. *Seminar on Relevance.* Dayton, OH: IDEA, 1971.

39. Davies, Daniel R. and Kenneth F. Herrold. *Leadership in Action.* New London, CT: Croft Publications, 1954.

40. _____. *Make Your Staff Meetings Count.* New London, CT: Croft Publications, 1954.

41. Douglass, Harl. *Modern Administration of Secondary Schools.* Boston: Ginn, 1963.

42. Doyle, Michael and David Straus. *How to Make Meetings Work.* NY: Wyden Books, 1976.

43. Drucker, Peter F. *Management Tasks, Responsibilities, Practices.* NY: Harper and Row, 1973.

44. _____. *Technology, Management, and Society.* NY: Harper and Row, 1958.

45. _____. *The Practice of Management.* NY: Harper and Row, 1954.

46. _____. *Managing for Results.* NY: Harper and Row, 1964.

47. _____. *The Effective Executive.* NY: Harper and Row, 1966.

48. Dunn, Rita and Kenneth J. Dunn. *Administrator's Guide to New Programs for Faculty Management and Evaluation.* West Nyack, NY:

Parker, 1974.

49. _____. *Educator's Self-Teaching Guide to Individualizing Instructional Programs.* West Nyack, NY: Parker, 1975.

50. _____. *Practical Approaches to Individualizing Instruction.* West Nyack, NY: Parker, 1972.

51. Dunn, Rita and Shirlely A. Griggs. *Learning Styles: Quiet Revolution in American Secondary Schools.* Reston, VA: NASSP, 1988.

52. Dunn, Rita. "Learning Style: State of the Science." *Theory Into Practice.* XXIII, (Winter, 1984), 10-19.

53. Dunsing, Richard J. *You and I Have Simply Got to Stop Meeting Like This.* NY: AMACOM, 1978.

54. Eisner, Elliot W. *The Educational Imagination: On the Design and Evaluation of School Programs.* NY: Macmillan, 1979.

55. English, Fenwick W. ed. *Fundamental Curriculum Decisions.* Alexandria, VA: ASCD, 1983.

56. Epstein, Herman T and Conrad F. Toepfer, Jr. "A Neuroscience Basis for Reorganizing Middle Grades Education." *Educational Leadership*, 35 (May, 1978), 656-660.

57. Epstein, Herman T. "Brain Growth and Cognitive Development." *Educational Leadership*, 41 (February, 1984), 72-75.

58. _____. "Growth Spurts During Brain Development: Implications for Educational Policy and Practice." *NSSE Yearbook*, 1977, Part 2, 343-370.

59. _____. "Learning to Learn: Matching Instruction to Cognitive Levels." *Principal*, 60 (May, 1981), 25-30.

60. _____. "Some Biological Bases of Cognitive Development." *Bulletin of the Orton Society*, 30 (1980), 46-62.

61. _____. "Stages in Human Brain Development." *Developmental Brain Research*,XXX (1986), 114-119.

62. Erickson, Donald and Theodore Reller. *The Principal in Metropolitan Schools*. Berkeley, CA: McCutchan, 1979.

63. Federal Electric Corporation. *A Programed Introduction to Program Evaluation Review Technique*. NY: John Wiley & Sons, 1963.

64. Feinberg, Mortimer, Robert Tanofsky, and John Tarrant. *The New Psychology for Managing People*. Englewood Cliffs, NJ: Prentice-Hall, 1975.

65. Flanders, Ned. *Analyzing Teaching Behavior*. Reading, MA: Addison-Wesley Publishing Co., 1970.

66. Flory, Charles D. *Managers for Tomorrow*. NY: New American Library, 1965.

67. Fox, Robert S. *School Climate Improvement: A Challenge to the Secondary School*. Bloomington, IN: Phi Delta Kappa, 1977.

68. Fuller, Jocelyn K. and James G. Glendening. "The Neuroeducator: Professional of the Future."

    Theory Into Practice. XXIV, (Spring, 1985), 135-137.

69. Gardner, David P., chrm. *A Nation at Risk*. Wash,

D.C.: Gov't. Printing Office, 1983.

70. Gellerman, Saul W. *Managers and Subordinates.* Hinsdale, IL: The Dryden Press, 1976.

71. Gerhard, Muriel. *Effective Teaching Strategies with the Behavioral Outcomes Approach.* West Nyack, NY: Parker, 1971.

72. Glueck, William F. *Organization Planning and Development.* NY: American Management Association, 1971.

73. Goldhammer, Robert, Robert H. Anderson, and Robert Krajewski J. *Clinical Supervision.* 2nd ed. NY: Holt, Rinehart and Winston, 1980.

74. Goodlad, John I. et al. *The Conventional and The Alternative in Education.* Berkeley, CA: McCutchan, 1975.

75. Goodstein, Leonard D. and William J. Pfeiffer. *Annual Handbook for Group Facilitators.* San Diego, CA: University Associates, 1983.

76. _____. *Annual Handbook for Group Facilitators.* San Diego, CA: University Associates, 1985.

77. _____. *Annual Handbook for Group Facilitators.* San Diego, CA: University Associates, 1987.

78. Grant, Barbara M. and Hennings, Dorothy G. *The Teacher Moves.* NY: Columbia Univ., 1971.

79. Green, Edward J. *The Learning Process and Programmed Instruction.* NY: Holt, Rinehart and Winston, 1962.

80. Gregorc, Anthony. "Style as a Symptom: A Phenomenological Perspective." *Theory Into Practice.* XXIII, (Winter, 1984), 51-55.

81. Griffiths, D. E. *Human Relations in School Administration.* NY: Appleton-Century-Crofts, 1956.

82. Gronlund, Norman E. *Measurement and Evaluation in Teaching.* NY: Macmillan, 1985.

83. Guthrie, James W. and Reed, Rodney J. *Educational Administration and Policy.* Englewood Cliffs, NJ: Prentice-Hall, Inc., 1986.

84. Handy, H. W. and Hussain, K. M. *Network Analysis for Educational Management.* Englewood Cliffs, NJ: Prentice-Hall, Inc., 1969.

85. Hardesty, T. Frank and Scott, W. Wayne. *Action Tools for Increasing Individual Management Productivity.*, Vols. 1-3 Clarkston, GA: Janco, 1976.

86. Harris, Ben M. *Developmental Teacher Evaluation.* Boston: Allyn and Bacon, 1986.

87. Hart, Leslie. *How the Brain Works.* NY: Basic Books, 1975.

88. Hart, Leslie. *Human Brain and Learning.* NY: Longman, 1983.

89. Hennings, Dorothy G. *Smiles, Nods, and Pauses.* NY: Citation Press, 1974.

90. Hentoff, Nat. *Does Anybody Give a Damn?* NY: Alfred A. Knopf, 1977.

91. Hentschke, Guibert. *Management Operations in Education.* Berkeley, CA: McCutchan, 1975.

92. Hill, Joseph E. *The Educational Sciences: A Conceptual Framework.* W. Bloomfield, MI: Educational Sciences Research Foundation, 1981.

93. Hodgetts, Richard M. *Management: Theory, Process and Practice*, 3rd ed. NY: CBS College, 1982.

94. Hosford, Philip L., ed. *Using What We Know About Teaching*. Alexandria, VA: ASCD, 1984.

95. Hostrop, Richard W. *Managing Education for Results*. Homewood, IL: ETC, 1973.

96. Hoy, Wayne K. and Patrick B. Forsyth. *Effective Supervision: Theory into Practice*. NY: Random House, 1986.

97. Hoy, Wayne K. and Cecil G. Miskel. *Educational Administration: Theory, Research and Practice*. 3rd. ed. NY: Random House, 1978.

98. Hughes, Charles L. *Goal Setting: Key to Individual and Organizational Effectiveness*. NY: American Management Association, 1965.

99. Hunkins, Francis P. *Questioning Strategies and Techniques*. Boston: Allyn and Bacon, 1972.

100. Hunt, David E. and Jane Gow. "How to Be Your Own Best Theorist II." *Theory Into Practice*. XXIII, (Winter, 1984), 64-71.

101. Hunt, Herald C. and Paul R. Pierce. *The Practice of School Administration*. Boston: Houghton-Mifflin, 1958.

102. Jensen, Richard N. *Microteaching: Planning And Implementing A Competency-Based Training Program*. Springfield, IL: Thomas, 1974.

103. Jones, Beau F., et al., eds. *Strategic Teaching and Learning: Cognitive Instruction in the Content Areas*. Alexandria, VA: ASCD, 1987.

104. Jones, John E. and William J. Pfeiffer. *Annual Handbook for Group Facilitators*. San Diego, CA: Univ. Associates, 1973.

105. _____. *Annual Handbook for Group Facilitators*. San Diego, CA: University Associates, 1975.

106. _____. *Annual Handbook for Group Facilitators*. San Diego, CA: University Associates, 1977.

107. _____. *Annual Handbook for Group Facilitators*. San Diego, CA: University Associates, 1979.

108. _____. *Annual Handbook for Group Facilitators*. San Diego, CA: University Associates, 1981.

109. Keefe, James W. "Assessment of Learning Style Variables: The NASSP Task Force Model." *Theory Into Practice*. XXIV, (Spring, 1985), 138-144.

110. _____. *Learning Style Theory & Practice*. Reston, VA: NASSP, 1987.

111. _____. *Profiling & Utilizing Learning Styles*. Reston, VA: NASSP, 1988.

112. Kepner, Charles and Benjamin Tregoe. *The Rational Manager*. NY: McGraw-Hill, 1965.

113. Killian, Ray A. *Human Resource Management: An R.O.I. Approach*. NY: Amacom, 1976.

114. Kimbrough, Ralph B. and Michael Y. Nunnery. *Edu- Educational Administration: An Introduction*. 3rd ed. NY: Macmillan, 1988.

115. Kohler, Mary Conway. *New Roles for Youth in the School and the Community*. NY: Citation Press, 1974.

116. Koontz, Harold and Cyril O'Donnell. *Principles of*

Management: Analysis of Managerial Functions. NY: McGraw-Hill, 1959.

117. Korda, Michael. *Power: How to Get It, How to Use It*. NY: Ballentine, 1975.

118. _____. *Success*. NY: Ballentine, 1977.

119. Kourilsky, Marilyn and Lory Quaranta. *Effective Teaching*. Glenview, IL: Scott, Foresman and Co., 1987.

120. Krathwohl, David R., Benjamin S. Bloom, Benjamin S. and Bertram Masia. *Taxonomy of Educational Objectives. Hdbk II*. NY: David McKay, Inc., 1964.

121. Kuttner, Monroe S. *Managing the Paperwork Pipeline*. NY: John Wiley, 1978.

122. Lancaster, Eileen H. "A Study of Herman Epstein's Brain Growth Theory." *Unpublished paper for independent research*, USL, 1987.

123. Larson, Knute and Melvin R. Karpas. *Effective Secondary School Discipline*. Englewood Cliffs, NJ: Prentice-Hall, 1963.

124. Latterner, C. G. *A Programmed Introduction to PERT*. NY: John Wiley, 1967.

125. Lawson, Douglas E. *School Administration Procedures and Policies*. NY: Odyssey Press, 1959.

126. Layden, Milton. *Escaping the Hostility Trap: The Sure Way*. Englewood Cliffs, NJ: Prentice-Hall, Inc., 1977.

127. Leggett, Stanton. *Managing Schools in Hard Times*. Chicago: Teach'em, 1981.

128. Lewis, James, Jr. *Differentiating the Teaching Staff*.

West Nyack, NY: Parker, 1971.

129. Loen, Raymond O. *Manage More by Doing Less*. NY: McGraw-Hill, 1958.

130. Love, Sidney F. *Mastery and Management of Time*. Englewood Cliffs, NJ: Prentice-Hall, 1978.

131. Mackenzie, R. Alec. *The Time Trap: Managing Your Way Out*. NY: American Management Association, 1972.

132. _____. The Management Process in 3-D," *Harvard Business Review*. (November-December, 1969).

133. Marburger, Carl. *One School at a Time*. Columbia, MD: NCCE, 1985.

134. March, James G., ed. *Handbook of Organizations*. Chicago: Rand-McNally, 1965.

135. March, James G. and Simon, Herbert A. *Organizations*. NY: John Wiley, 1958.

136. March, James. *Handbook of Organizations*. Chicago, IL: Rand McNally, 1965.

137. Maynard, H. B., editor-in-chief. *Handbook of Business Administration*. NY: McGraw-Hill, 1970.

138. McCarthy, Bernice. *The 4Mat System*. Arlington Heights, IL: Excel, 1980.

139. McCay, James T. *The Management of Time*. Englewood Cliffs, NJ: Prentice-Hall, 1959.

140. Mc Greal, Thomas L. *Successful Teacher Evaluation*. Alexandria, VA: ASCD, 1983.

141. Medley, Donald M., Homer Coker, and Robert S. Soar. *Measurement-Based Evaluation of*

Teacher Performance: An Empirical Approach. NY: Longman, 1984.

142. Megiveron, Gene E. "A Process of Critical Inquiry," # IV. Random Thoughts Series. Monroe, MI: Board of Education, 1976.

143. _____. "A 'New' Cognitive Mapping Program," # XI. Random Thoughts Series. Monroe, MI: Board of Education, 1977.

144. _____. "Future Thinking for MPS Purposes/ Goals," # XIII. Random Thoughts Series. Monroe, MI: Board of Education, 1979.

145. _____. "Improvement of Instructional Quality- Part 2," # VI. Random Thoughts Series. Monroe, MI: Board of Education, 1975.

146. _____. "Improvement of Instructional-Part 2," # VI. Random Thoughts Series. Monroe, MI: Board of Education, 1975.

147. _____. "Instructional Inquiry," # VI. Random Thoughts Series. Monroe, MI: Board of Education, 1976.

148. _____. "Inquiry-Phase 2," # VI. Random Thoughts Series. Monroe, MI: Board of Education, 1976.

149. _____. "Learning Styles," # XVI. Random Thoughts Issues. St. Clair, MI: Board of Education, 1982.

150. _____. "Promotion, Retention, Acceleration, and Demotion," # XVII. Random Thoughts Issues. St. Clair, MI: Board of Education, 1982.

151. _____. "The Improvement of Instructional Quality," # II." Random Thoughts Series.

Monroe, MI: Board of Education, 1975.

152. _____. "The Three Major Issues in Education Today - Finance - Bargaining - Equal Ed. Opportunity," # I. Random Thought Series. Monroe, MI: Board of Education, 1975.

153. _____. "The Work Ethic & Mastery Learning," # VII. Random Thoughts Series. Monroe, MI: Board of Education, 1976.

154. _____, ed. *Catalog of Policies, Practices, and Programs in Instructional Supervision.* Alexandria, VA: Association Supervision Curriculum Development, 1986.

155. _____. "Time Audits," *Michigan School Board Journal.* 25, (February, 1979) 21.

156. _____. "Communication Via A Recommendation," *School Business Affairs*, (August, 1978), 261.

157. _____. "Fifty Measures of Your Professional Attitude." *Selected Articles on the Teaching of Reading*, Barnell Loft, 1978.

158. _____. "Five Dozen Good Things You Can For Your Kids," *Selected Articles on the Teaching of Reading*, Barnell-Loft, 1978.

159. _____. "Time and Self-Management," *Michigan School Board Journal*, 25, (November, 1978) 27-28.

160. _____. "Planning Your Day," *Michigan School Board Journal*, 26, (March, 1979) 27-29.

161. _____. "Tickler Files or 'T' Files," *Michigan School Board Journal*, 26, (April, 1979) 19.

162. _____. "The Scintillating Seven," *Michigan*

School Board Journal, 26, (May, 1979) 25-28.

163. _____. "Time Saver: Agenda Preparation," *Michigan School Board Journal*, 26, (June, 1979) 25-28.

164. _____. "We've Got to Stop Meeting Like This," *Michigan School Board Journal*, 26, (July, 1979) 25-28.

165. _____. "Planning," *Michigan School Board Journal*, 26, (September, 1979) 25-28.

166. Megiveron, Gene E. and Terry G. Semones. "Guidelines for the Aspiring Misoneist." *Responsibility Newsletter*, IL SBE, 1976.

167. Molnar, Alex and John A. Zahorik. *Curriculum Theory*. Alexandria, VA: ASCD, 1977.

168. Montague, Earl J. *Fundamentals of Secondary Classroom Instruction*. Columbus: Merrill, 1987.

169. Moore, Maxine Ruth. *A Proposed Taxonomy of the Perceptual Domain*. Princeton, NJ: ETS, 1967.

170. Morphet, Edgar L., Roe L. Johns, and Theodore L. Reller. *Educational Organization and Administration*. 4th ed., Englewood Cliffs, NJ: Prentice-Hall, 1982.

171. Morrisey, George L. "Decisions, Decisions," Oct. 25, 1976. *Nation's School Report*, pp. 5-6.

172. Myers, Donald A. *Decision Making in Curriculum & Instruction*. Dayton, OH: IDEA, 1970.

173. NASSP. *Student Learning Styles*. Reston, VA: The Association, 1978.

174. _____. *Student Learning Styles and Brain Be-*

havior. Reston, VA: The Association, 1982.

175. National Association of School Boards. *The School Personnel Management System: Administrator's Handbook*. Wash, D.C.: The Association, 1976.

176. Notes taken or material distributed at the Seminar in Relevance in Mobile, Alabama in 1971. Conference sponsored by /I/D/E/A/, NASSP, and Danforth Foundation.

177. Odiorne, George S. *How Managers Make Things Happen*. Englewood Cliffs, NJ: Prentice-Hall, 1962.

178. Odiorne, George S. *Management Decisions by Objectives*. NY: Englewood Cliffs, NJ: Prentice-Hall, 1969.

179. Odiorne, George S. *Management and the Activity Trap*. NY: Harper and Row, 1974.

180. Ouchi, William H. *Theory Z*. NY: Avon Books, 1981.

181. Peterson, Penelope L. and Walberg, Herbert J. eds. *Research on Teaching: Concepts, Findings, and Implications*, Berkeley, CA: McCutchan, 1979.

182. Peterson-Dillon, Betty. ed. *Staff Development/ Organization Development*. Alexandria, VA: Association Supervision Curriculum Development, 1981.

183. Pfeiffer, J. William and John E. Jones E. *Annual Handbook for Group Facilitators*. San Diego, CA: University Associates, 1972.

184. _____ . *Annual Handbook for Group Facilitators*. San Diego, CA: University Associates, 1974.

185. _____. *Annual Handbook for Group Facilitators.* San Diego, CA: University Associates, 1976.

186. _____. *Annual Handbook for Group Facilitators.* San Diego, CA: University Associates, 1978.

187. _____. *Annual Handbook for Group Facilitators.* San Diego, CA: University Associates, 1980.

188. _____. *Annual Handbook for Group Facilitators.* San Diego, CA: University Associates, 1982.

189. _____. *Annual Handbook for Group Facilitators.* San Diego, CA: University Associates, 1984.

190. _____. *Annual Handbook for Group Facilitators.* San Diego, CA: University Associates, 1986.

191. Pollock, Ted. Managing Creatively: *A Practical Guide to Managing Yourself.* Boston, MA: CBI Publishing, 1982.

192. Popham, W. James. *Educational Evaluation.* 2nd ed. Englewood Cliffs, NJ: Prentice-Hall, 1988.

193. _____. *Evaluating Instruction.* Englewood Cliffs, NJ: Prentice-Hall, 1975.

194. Popham, James W. and Eva L. Baker. *Classroom Instructional Tactics.* Englewood Cliffs, NJ: Prentice-Hall, 1973.

195. Porter, John W., chairman. *The Adolescent, Other Citizens, and Their Schools.* NY: McGraw-Hill, 1975.

196. Raths, Louis E., Merrill Harmin, and Sidney B. Simon. *Values and Teaching.* Columbus:

Merrill, 1966.

197. Read, Donald A. and Sidney B. Simon. *Humanistic Education Sourcebook.* Englewood Cliffs, NJ: Prentice-Hall, 1975.

198. Redfern, George B. *How to Appraise Teaching Performance.* Columbus: School Management Institute, 1963.

199. Reller, Theodore L. *Educational Administration in Metropolitan Areas.* Bloomington, IN: Phi Delta Kappa, 1974.

200. Richards, Max and William Nielander. *Readings in Management.* Franklin, TN: South-Western, 1958.

201. Rickards, Tudor. *Problem-Solving Through Creative Analysis.* Epping, Essex: Gower, 1974.

202. Rioux, William. *You Can Improve Your Child's School.* NY: Simon and Schuster, 1980.

203. Roberts, Arthur D., ed. *Educational Innovation: Alternatives in Curriculum and Instruction.* Boston: Allyn and Bacon, Inc., 1975.

204. Rollins, Sidney P. *Developing Nongraded Schools.* NY: Peacock, 1968.

205. Rosenbloom, Paul C. and Paul C. Hillestad. *Modern Viewpoints in the Curriculum.* NY: McGraw-Hill, 1964.

206. Rosenthal, Robert and Lenore Jacobson. *Pygmalion in the Classroom.* NY: Holt, Rinehart and Winston, 1968.

207. Rutherford, Robert D. *Just in Time: Immediate Help for the Time Pressured.* NY: John Wiley, 1981.

208. Sabine, Creda. *Accountability: Systems Planning in Education*. Homewood, IL: ETC Publication, 1973.

209. Sattler, William M. and N. Edd Miller. *Discussion and Conference*. Englewood Cliffs, NJ: Prentice-Hall, 1954.

210. Schleh, Edward C. *Management by Results*. NY: McGraw-Hill, 1961.

211. Sergiovanni, Thomas J. ed. *Supervision of Teaching*. Alexandria, VA: Association Supervision Curriculum Development, 1982

212. _____. *The Principalship: A Reflective Practice Perspective*. Newton, MA: Allyn and Bacon, 1987.

213. Sergiovanni, Thomas J. and Fred D. Carver. *The New School Executive: A Theory of Administration, 2nd. ed.* NY: Harper and Row, 1980.

214. Sheive, Linda T. ed. *Leadership: Examining the Elusive*. Alexandria, VA: Association for Supervision and Curriculum Development, 1987.

215. Shoup, Barbara J. *Living and Learning for Credit*. Bloomington, IN: Phi Delta Kappa,1978.

216. Sizer, Theodore R. *Horace's Compromise: The Dilemma of The Amerian High School*. Boston: Houghton Mifflin Co., 1984.

217. Stein, Mark L. *How to Understand Time & Use It Right*. NY: Peter H. Wyden, 1976.

218. Stewart, Donald. *Educational Malpractices: The Big Gamble in Our Schools*. Fountain Valley, CA: SLATE Services, 1971.

219. _____. *Instruction As A Humanizing Science: A Behavioral Learning Systems Approach to Instruction: Analysis and Synthesis.* Vol. II, Fountain Valley, CA: SLATE Services, 1975.

220. _____. *Instruction As A Humanizing Science: Creating An Emphasis on Learning: Quality Control, Productivity, and Accountability.* Vol. I, Fountain Valley, CA: SLATE Services, 1976.

221. _____. *Instruction As A Humanizing Science: The Changing Role of the Educator: The Instructioneer.* Vol. I, Fountain Valley, CA: SLATE Services, 1975.

222. Terry, George R. *Managing Office Services.* Homewood, IL: Dow Jones-Irwin, 1966.

223. _____. *Office Automation.* Homewood, IL: Dow Jones-Irwin, 1966.

224. _____. *Office Organization and Motivation.* Homewood, IL: Dow Jones-Irwin, 1966.

225. _____. *Office Systems and Procedures.* Homewood, IL: Dow Jones-Irwin, 1966.

226. Tuttle, Edward M. *School Board Leadership in America.* Chicago: Interstate, 1958.

227. Tyler, Ralph W. *From Youth to Constructive Adult Life: The Role of the Public School.* Berkeley, CA: McCutchan, 1978.

228. Uris, Auren. *Mastery of Management.* Chicago, IL: Playboy Press, 1968.

229. Van Fleet, James K. *Power With People.* West Nyack, NY: Parker, 1970.

230. Wahlquist, John T. *et. al. The Administration of Public*

Education. NY: Ronald, 1952.

231. Walberg, Herbert J. *Improving Educational Standards and Productivity*. Berkeley, CA: McCutchan, 1982.

232. Wallace, Daisy G. ed. *Developing Basic Skills Programs in Secondary Schools*. Alexandria, VA: ASCD, 1981.

233. Wang, Margaret C. and Herbert J. Walberg. *Adapting Instruction to Individual Differences*. Berkeley, CA: McCutchan, 1985.

234. Wayson, William W. *Handbook for Developing Schools with Good Discipline*. Bloomington, IN: Phi Delta Kappa, 1982.

235. Webb, L. Dean, et al. *Personnel Administration in Education*. Columbus: Merrill, 1987.

236. Webber, Russ A. *Time and Management*. NY: Van Norstrand, 1972.

237. Weinstein, Shelly and Douglas E. Mitchell, eds. *Public Testimony on Public Schools*. Berkeley, CA: McCutchan, 1975.

238. Weinstock, Ruth. *The Greening of the High School*. NY: Educational Facilities Laboratories, Inc., 1973.

239. Weisselberg, Robert C. and Gowley, Joseph G. *The Executive Strategist*. NY: McGraw-Hill, 1969.

240. Wheelwright, Steven and Spyros Makridakis. *Forecasting Methods for Management*. NY: John Wiley, 1973.

241. Whiteside, Lynn W. *Managing Yourself and Others for Executive Success*. West Nyack, NY: Par-

ker, 1971.

242. Williams, Richard C., *et al. Effecting Organizational Renewal in Schools*. NY: McGraw-Hill, 1974.

243. Wirt, Frederick M. and Michael W. Kirst. *Schools in Conflict*. Berkeley, CA: McCutchan, 1982.

244. Wittrock, Merlin C. *Handbook of Research on Teaching*. 3rd ed. NY: Macmillan, 1986.

245. Wood, Charles L., Everett W. Nicholson, and Dale G. Findley. *The Secondary School Principal: Manager and Supervisor*. Boston: Allyn and Bacon, 1979.

246. Wylie, H. C. *Office Organization and Management*. NY: John Wiley, 1953.

PART II

THE PRINCIPAL'S TASKS
THROUGHOUT THE YEAR

WHAT to do and WHEN to do it

- PART II - INTRODUCTION -
- THE SCHOOL YEAR'S TASKS -

Chapter 3. Work in the Summer Months
Chapter 4. Work in the Fall Months
Chapter 5. Work in the Winter Months
Chapter 6. Work in the Spring Months

Part II is all about what to do and when to do it. It will provide lists of tasks so that the principal initiates, develops, and finalizes them on time. It will show that there is no mystery in managing a great school if some planning is done. Unit I provided information on how to plan, and this part will indicate what to plan.

Part II is the guts of the book. The introductory chapters and those which follow will be assistive in accomplishing what is listed on the task lists and more. Part I was designed to prepare the principal for the onslaught of the year and to teach some basic items. Part II is for use by the practitioner to assure him/her that ALL will be done and, more importantly, that it will be done on time.

The principal is a busy person. This is certainly an understatement. It makes no difference whether s/he is at work in July or January. There always is something to do. The chapter on the summer's work is important no matter when one assumes the job of principal. The listing of tasks to complete should be done in the summer. If this is not possible, the tasks still have to be done. The school year will begin just before or after Labor Day whether the work is done or not.

There are five lists of tasks to accomplish each month. The sets of tasks are listed in the five essential functions of the principal in the numbers as shown below in the grid. The lists for each month are in the categories of Instruction, Students, Staff, School/ Community Relations, and Business/Building Management, the order followed in each of the Chapters 3 - 6.

By ranking the most to the least number of activities or tasks to be completed, it comes as no surprise that the greatest number falls in the listing of the Business and Building Management category. However, in most instances in the other four lists, each task is unique whereas many of the BBM tasks are duplicated, routinely, for each month. However, the principal is a manager, right? Of course. The main job is instructional leadership. If classroom observations, each month, were counted as single tasks, the area of instruction would far outweigh any of the other lists. So be it. The summary of this grid shows the following ranking from (1) the highest to (5) the lowest ranking according to just the numbers of tasks to complete.

1 = 517 = Business/Building Management
2 = 502 = Instruction
3 = 387 = Students
4 = 251 = Staff
5 = 237 = School/Community Relations

	I	Stu	Stf	S/C	B/B	Total
July	20	23	26	18	55	142
August	37	33	27	17	51	165
September	50	34	23	23	42	172
October	45	34	16	18	39	152
November	43	32	22	20	46	163
December	38	35	22	20	37	152
January	41	35	18	18	38	150
February	45	32	19	16	37	149
March	48	26	18	20	39	151
April	38	29	16	22	36	141
May	45	34	17	25	43	164
June	52	40	27	20	54	193
	502	387	251	237	517	1,894

It is up to each principal to add to these lists as s/he performs the tasks for the year. Good luck on an exciting year ahead.

The listings of material in Part II were gleaned from spiral appointment-calendar books after ten years in the high school principalship. The material is listed to satisfy the ever-asked question in graduate classes, "Now that we know what to do, how do we get it all done -- started, developed and completed -- and on time?" The response is here. If the school calendar is different than the "normal" year of Labor Day to mid-June, adjust the listings. However, before the work begins, make the adjustment in the summer months and the rest ought to fall into line comfortably.

The listings within each category are not in priority as presented. The intent is to have the principal read the whole list of tasks and set his/her own time-line and priority as tasks are placed in the assigned tickler file as explained in Unit 2.

What is recommended to make these lists work best is to have someone copy each of the tasks on a 3 X 5 index card and drop them in the appropriate monthly tickler bucket. Please see Chapter 1, Unit 2. The first of the month is the time to scatter them into the appropriate daily Tickler File for action on that given date. Whatever other tasks the principal may have ought to be treated in the same manner. Color coding set of tasks by using the five divisions of the principal's workload may be helpful.

It is important to put tasks on the Daily Log so that both the principal and his/her secretary have a convenient and ready list to verify as the day, week, or month progresses. The principal is expected to delegate some of the tasks that are listed, especially the operational duties. In some cases there will not be a person with the title as listed in the task lists. If this title does not exist, it is incumbent on the principal to then meet with his/her assistants to ensure the work to be done gets assigned. Whether delegated or personally attended to, it is not expected that all of the tasks will be started at one time. This breeds anxiety, and anxiety turned inward causes depression. The principal doesn't have the luxury of suffering from either.

The lists are intended to be starter lists, albeit a good start in the many tasks the principal will have to complete month by month in the school year ahead. This work is PRIMARILY for the months as indicated in the headings. In no way can anyone visualize every task for every high school principal in every setting. Use the list as a basic one and go from there. The numerals behind some of the tasks which appear as [2-07] are there to show the reader that assistance for the topic can be located in a specific chapter and unit. The example 2-07 would indicate Chapter 2, Unit 07.

These lists will continue to be revised as the work with other principals in the "trenches" continues. The lists are here for initiatory help in planning. Substitutions and additions can be made throughout the experiences gained each year in the job. Keep them updated for next year's planning.

The last subunit in Chapter 6 is the one entitled "End of School - Closing." The part of the closing-out of school is that information the principal should be formulating throughout the year. S/he really could make a separate task in each category in each month to update the year-end form so that when the end comes -- and it most certainly will -- s/he will not forget noted items.

There will be a reference in the lists for the meeting with the directors of special and satellite programs. The following list is the one from a high school when a full program was in operation.

Special and satellite programs include the following:

Homebound	Night School
Substance Abuse	Volunteers/Aides
Cooperative Educ.	Restaurant
Community College	Correspondence

	Credit
F-M Radio Station	Teacher Aide-
	Child Care
Talented and Gifted	Special Education
Vocational Educ.	Suicide Prevent
Enrollment in	Individualized
other H.S.	Programming
Middle Group	Univ. Attendance
Assistantships	Int./Ext'l. Tests
Scholarships	Placement
Mainstreaming	Student Council
Adult Educ. Liaison	

This short list of specific terms which follows is not an attack on the reader's intelligence. Instead it is offered as a means of clarifying some regularly used terms. The term is not defined if it has been emphasized in preceding units.

NAMES AND TERMS THE PRINCIPAL NEEDS

Allen, Dwight The father of microteaching as it is known today.

AEW American Education Week

Affective Domain Developed by David R. Krathwohl in 1962. relationship and complexity of the domain. From the simplest to the most complex, the levels are: Receiving, Responding, Valuing, Organization, and Characterization by a Value or Value Concept.

Beggs, David Was doing some interesting work on the length of time students could concentrate in the classroom without some sort of intervention. Work at the high school proved that twenty-eight minutes is the longest to expect a high school student to concentrate on a single topic without change.

Brainstorm

1-01

The use of specific skills to develop lists of items in response to a question. Properly trained personnel can build on suggestions given and finalize an exhaustive list for the moderator to use.

Building Curriculum Committee

A committee of interested faculty with the core members being departmental representatives that meet with the principal on a monthly basis to discuss the instructional program from budget to schedule, teacher instructional program from budget to assignment to student evaluation.

Cognitive Domain

Developed by Benjamin S. Bloom and committee to show the relationship of cognition skills by levels. From the simplest to most complex, the levels are: Knowledge, Comprehension, Application, Analysis, Synthesis, and Evaluation.

Curriculum Newsletter

2-06

This is a three or four page "memo" addressed to the faculty for instructional directions in basically the same parts throughout the year.

DTLF

Douglass Teaching Load Formula - a formula which will develop a factor of the total load assigned to a teacher for the purpose of leveling classes based upon the total assigned load for the staff.

Dunn, Rita/ Kenneth

Work at St. John's University in learning and teaching styles provides instrumentation to determine how children learn through the visual, auditory, tactile, kinesthetic, and olfactory senses.

Faculty Advisory Committee

A group of representative teachers elected by other members of the faculty to sit with the principal at least twice per month and discuss the operation of the non-instruction-

2-07	al program in the school.
Flanders	Dr. Ned Flanders, father of Interaction Analysis - a means of recording the verbalizing in the classroom during a lesson.
FOG Index 2-05	A readability formula for secondary texts. Simple to use and yet significant, especially for comparisons of books in a committee to select material for instruction.
Force Field Analysis 1-01	A tool to determine the inhibitors and ex peditors of a program. Follows brainstorming by a group.
Four Domains	Cognitive, Affective, Psychomotor, and Perception.
Grant, Barbara	Dr. Barbara Grant, developed material in the non-verbal category for observers to as sist teahers to improve skills. Work is done in concert with her sister, Dr. Dorothy Grant Hennings.
Gregorc, Anthony	Professor in Connecticut who has developed Joe Hill's material into four basic areas for clarity and application. The areas are: Abstract Sequential, Abstract Random, Concrete Sequential, and Concrete Random.
Hart, Leslie	A consultant working out of New Rochelle, New York, who has developed and labeled the Proster Theory for explaining how the brain works. Testing theory now in schools in the East. Finding success.
HVAC 1-03	Stands for Heating, Ventilation, and Air Conditioning.
Hill, Joseph	The guru of learning/teaching style differentiation. Dr. Hill developed what he termed "Systems in Education." Work continues in

Bloomfield, Michigan, after his untimely death.

Impact Statements   Documents returned in criticism of a potential policy before it is considered for adoption. Can be either supportive or nonsupportive of the statement.

Issue Paper   A response to another document provided by the administration or colleague following specific rules set aside by those involved. Format follows the headings of: Statement, Issue Involved, Resolution Preferred, Recommendations, Rationale, Alternatives, Support.

Krathwohl, David R.   Developed the Affective Domain taxonomy in 1962. Levels from easiest to most complex are: Receiving, Responding, Valuing, Organization, and Characterization by a Value or Value Complex.

Linear Demand Chart   A chart which details (by numbers) along lines, the total count of tasks to be done in several categories so that a visual control can be made by the careful monitoring of several functions at a time.

Maslow's Needs Hierarchy   Work done by Abraham Maslow to determine levels of motivation in a taxonomy from most basic to most sophisticated. From the most basic level upward: Physiological, Safety and Security, Belonging, Self-Esteem, and Self-Actualization.

McCarthy, Bernice   Works within workshop settings to present a solid means of lesson planning to use her program on the four types of brain functions and on hemisphericity work. The four types of learners as presented are: Innovative, Analytic, Common Sense, and Dynamic. While teaching is done in the analytic mode, clearly 70% of the learners are not in that mode.

MEAP In Michigan, the state department's testing, required program for all 4th, 7th, and 10th graders. To be given in early fall for students in specified subjects.

Micro-teaching A set of skills to be learned through pre- through presenting to a small group for a short period of time and using basically a single skill to develop sound techniqes.

Moore, Maxine Developed taxonomy for the Perception Domain in 1967. Levels from simplest to most complex are: Sensation, Figure Perception, Symbol Perception, Perception of Meaning, and Perceptive Performance.

Orientation

3-10 A year-round task to assure that all newcomers to the program are aware of the possibilities for excellence in the school.

Pareto Principle A situation which shows that when there is a cause and effect, 20% will cause 80% of the problems. Example, 20% of the employees will be absent 80% of the absenteeisms in the unit.

Perceptual Domain Developed by Maxine Moore in 1967. The levels from simplest to most complex are: Sensation, Figure Perception, Symbol Per ception, Perception of Meaning, and Percep tive Performance.

Personal Time Clock Reference to the best and worst time of the day or week to accomplish tasks which call for concentration and energy. Each person has a personal clock which allows him/her to be most productive.

P.E.R.T. Stands for Program Evaluation and Review

Technique. Is a scheduling technique best used for interrelated strands of tasks to be shown visually for planning, monitoring, and control.

Porter's Hierarchy Work done to parallel the work of Maslow for the human being. Porter's work is for the professional - adult needs hierarchy. Drops level I from Maslow, inserts the word *autonomy* between self-esteem and self-actualization to discuss his work.

Position Paper A brief paper giving the readership a view of a topic which the writer either supports or denounces. An effective principal needs to keep the staff alert to changing times through this medium.

Problem Census A three part brief questionnaire to be given to any audience to get instant feedback on a 1-01 range of activities.

Progressive Honor Roll An honor roll on which anyone can get credit for work done irrespective of ability. 2-07

Psychomotor Domain The taxonomy used extensively in the development of objectives for courses in schools. The levels of the taxonomy are: Perception, Set, Guided Response, Mechanism, Complex Overt Response, Adaptation, and Origination.

QWL Committee A committee structured for the improvement of the quality of work situations in an organization.

Satellite Programs Programs which are not housed in the building but where students are being instructed. Usually programs in an earn-learn or serve-learn environment.

Simpson, Prepared the taxonomy of the Psychomotor

Elizabeth Domain, 1970, which is used extensively in the development of objectives in the practical arts courses. The levels of the taxonomy are: Perception, Set, Guided Response, Mechanism, Complex Overt Response, Adaptation, and Origination.

SMOG Index A readability formula for secondary texts.
2-05 Simple to use and yet significant, especially for comparisons of books in a committee on selection of material.

Standard Those procedures which call for subordinate
Operating attention throughout the year and with no
Procedures variation. When the S.O.P. is adhered to rigidly, the function of the organization is much better than if it is ignored or violated by the subordinates or superordinates.

Stewart, Don President of SLATE in Westminister, CA. Developed his work on Boredom Factor, Instructional Effectiveness, and Instructional Efficiency along with Educational Malpractice. Popular writer in the late 1960's who conducted workshops on getting technology into educational decision-making.

Student In Michigan, the high school verifies the
Work birthdate of applicants for work when under
Permits the age of 18 and in search of work limited in scope by laws which are policed by the Department of Labor.

Study Can be teachers working to collect informa-
Groups tion on a theme for the building, nongradedness, educational television, team teaching, microteaching, Epstein, the four domains or whatever interests the faculty for program improvement.

Survival / A program designed by teachers for teachers
Literacy/ to teach a basic set of words for all children
Competency in school to learn at differing levels of

348

Competency Program 2-07	in school to learn at differing levels of mastery as they progress through school and become contributing citizens.
Wind Chill Chart 2-06	A chart used by administrators to determine when the activities of a school should not be conducted outside the school plant. Wind speed and degrees of coldness determine the time it would take for the exposed skin to freeze.
Yearbook Dance	An evening dance where the admission was the receipt for the yearbook's purchase. It occurs right after camera night, which is structured for picture taking of all groups which will be representing the school during the year in activities and athletics.

-- CHAPTER THREE INTRODUCTION --
- Work in the Summer Months -

In July and August the principal will be responsible to do two major things for the year ahead: 1. finish the work from the previous year, and 2. initiate the new year. It is a great time as the building and equipment are being repaired and renovated to get everything set for the new year. This usually causes much debris in the corridors as all the furniture is taken from the rooms so they can be cleaned and sanitized properly. There is the summer cadre of custodians, secretaries, and a handful of main-tenance personnel staffing the facility. Kids start to drop by. Mail starts to pile high. The showplace of the district is being prepared for the district's biggest student enroll-ment. Soon the largest staff in the district will be back. The community is still out there and can't be ignored as they are the stockholders. Lastly, the business of heading one of the larger corporations in town still has to be done.

Handled separately, the subunit on orientation is special as all the work in the summer leads to this all important phase of launching a successful school year. The work begins as soon as school is out.

- UNITS EIGHT, NINE, AND TEN INTRODUCTION -
July's and August's Tasks Plus Orientation

For the lists of tasks below, each principal may not wish to do precisely what is suggested. The titles of significant papers may be substituted for personalizing the work. However, direction to write a specific type of paper should not be ignored. Communication is the key to a successful principalship. These lists are directed to that end.

- UNIT EIGHT -
July Work in the Form of Task Lists

PRINCIPAL'S JULY TASKS IN INSTRUCTION

1. Compile Achievement-Ability studies; use as part of annual report.
2. Write Annual Report (see June for proper collection of material).
3. Present Annual Report to the Board of Education.
4. Write curriculum newsletter for faculty consumption
2-06
5. Prepare journal abstract listings for departments and others to do monthly to report to the staff in the curriculum newsletter.

350

year.
7. Develop material for Faculty Advisory Committee 2-07
8. Meet with Building Curriculum Committee (BCC) to set goals for instruction and complete a curriculum review.
9. Write position paper on Individualized Programming.
10. Finalize study groups for the staff for the year.

11. Finalize order for inservice programs for the year.
12. Pull files for summer school enrollees; prepare to enter results.
13. Review grading reports from each teacher, and compile composite for inspection by teachers when mailed this summer.
14. Assure that process for field trip application is in hand book.
15. Evaluate all satellite programs and their impact on total program.

16. Review activity program in relation to the instructional program.
17. Plan educational assembly program from notes on Year End Report.
18. Monitor summer school program.
19. Study groups of teachers assigned the same conference/planning periods for proper assignments of work to be done.
20. Meet with Faculty Advisory Committee (FAC) to alter building handbook and align activities and program of studies.   2-07

PRINCIPAL'S JULY TASKS WITH STUDENTS

1. Contact all dropouts of last year for career planning or school.
2. Plan student orientation with student volunteers.
3. Assess discipline policy in terms of numbers in each category.
4. Evaluate student activities for the year.
5. Study retention policy with aim of possible elimination.

6. Initiate and verify new student scheduling.

7. Check senior schedules against graduation require-
    ments.
8. Flag folders and prepare list of seniors in question of
    graduating on schedule.
9. Verify that student handbook was updated and sent for
    printing.
10. Send letters of thanks to various student committee
    and group memberships.

11. End first summer session driver training program.
12. Verify eligibility for fall athletes already on roster.
13. Hold entrance and exit interviews with students. 2-05
14. Implement student recruiting to get more kids back
    into school.
15. Handle due process proceedings for summer school
    discipline.

16. Verify report from counselors on acceptance of seniors
    in college.
17. Verify student working permits as students need them
    authorized.
18. Initiate new session of summer driver's training
    program.
19. Send reminder to student body of upcoming yearbook
    dance.
20. Place on school calendar (as listed on staff year-end
    reports) all activities scheduled for next year.

21. Verify that planned help is being given to "special" kids
    on nurse's and/or social worker's lists.
22. Finalize preparations for Yearbook Dance next month.
23. Study results taken from entrance/exit questionnaires.
                                                    2-05

PRINCIPAL'S JULY TASKS WITH STAFF

1. Update teacher certification check completed in June.
2. Review/rewrite job descriptions based on need and
    performance.   1-03
3. Notify Personnel Department of all known staff
    vacancies.
4. Post vacancies for all staff positions known.

5. Fill vacancies for all staff positions.

6. Plan orientation sessions for new and returning staff.
                                                               3-10
7. Review teacher/staff handbook based on year end
    reports.
8. Publish regional meetings for staff to attend.
9. Meet with fall coaches to verify safety of all equipment.
10. Meet with custodial staff to review summer work done.

11. Meet with new hires and explain their worth to the
    program.
12. Recruit new teacher aides.
13. Observe to evaluate summer school faculty.
14. Report on preliminary Douglass Teacher Load Formula (DTLF).
15. Schedule staff meeting topics to cover each month's
    meeting.
16. Prepare yearly calendar for scheduled meetings.
17. Assign assistants to meet with specific groups.
18. Assign assistants to work with specific depts.
19. Assign assistants to work on specific committees.
20. Assign assistants to specific district committees.

21. Determine tasks for teachers on conference periods.
22. Review work of Quality of Work Life Comm.
23. Design/develop material for QWL Committee.
24. Prepare "Randall" evaluation material for staff. 2-05
25. Design 3 X 3 Evaluation material for next year. 2-05

26. Meet with nurse and social worker regarding students.

JULY TASKS IN SCHOOL/COMMUNITY RELATIONS

1. Provide information for press release this month.
2. Write monthly position paper on summer school.
3. Establish phone network for communication and rumor
    control.   2-04
4. Send thank you letters to PTA officers.
5. Send letter to community businesses to survey what student product they can use or display and what serv-

5. Send letter to community businesses to survey what student product they can use or display and what services school can provide.

6. Improve philosophy on school community relations.
7. Develop philosophy to improve interschool relations.
8. Send thank you letters to commencement guests.
9. Attend local community organizations.
10. Send thank you letters for social/fraternal assistance.

11. Do a needs assessment of community-parents-staff.
12. Identify dept. advisory committee members.   2-04
13. Send commendation letter to summer school students on their commitment to excellence.
14. Send letter to staff and student committee members.
15. Send letter to all staff highlighting their strong efforts.

16. Send letters to spouses of assistants for the time given.
17. Send letters to parents of questionable, timely graduation.
18. Mail newsletter to school patrons.

PRINCIPAL'S JULY TASKS IN BUSINESS/BLDG MGT

1. Monitor planning of transportion, custodial, secretarial, and cafeteria programs.
2. Prepare weekly calendars for the month -- distribute each Friday.
3. Review field trip arrangement procedure for possible improvements.
4. Inform staff of new material and equipment received -- file copy for summer newsletter, orientation, and departments' readiness.
5. Control budget and internal accounts.

6. Supervise cumulative records in all areas for students.
7. Attend School Board meeting.
8. Supervise staff certification, transcripts, evaluations, observations, commendations, etc.
9. Prepare local, state, federal reports for:_____.
10. Interpret law and school policy as necessary.

11. Maintain adequate supply of materials.
12. Supervise selection of supplies, equipment, materials.
13. Order, invoice, inventory, control supplies/materials.
14. Supervise lunchrooms/noon hour activities of students.
15. Supervise student traffic on site.

16. Monitor school master/time schedules for summer.
17. Prepare planning, control, and evaluation tools:
    (Action Demand Charts, PERTs, Gantts, and
    Linear Demand Charts).
18. Monitor community programs and facility use.
19. Examine effectiveness of fire/civil/weather processes.
20. Check with custodial staff on safety in building.

21. Inspect site/building for needs in maintenance/ clean
    liness.   1-03
22. Draw Table of Organization for next year.   . 1-03
23. Develop material for secretarial staff to meet needs
24. Follow up suggestions made by staff.
25. Inspect equipment safety/boiler room/HVAC/labora-
    tories.   1-03

26. Evaluate last year's grievances from sections of staff.
27. Refine Standard Operating Procedure for this year.
28. Inspect kitchen weekly.
29. Check safety and protection lighting.
30. Verify building and special room equipment security.

31. Check for forms of vandalism.
32. Meet weekly with Dietician, Hd. Custodian, Dir. Trans.
33. Write standard practice bulletins as needed. . 2-04
34. Verify room equipment is in proper repair.
35. Check athletic facilities and equipment.

36. Implement or monitor vehicle registration procedures.
37. Place incoming goods in inventory.
38. Establish calendar of conferences for all staff.
39. Receive senior class yearbooks.
40. Verify inventory of all building equipment.

41. Select commencement location for mid-year.
42. Establish building use schedule for upcoming year.

43. Establish schedule for parent group "coffee hours."
44. Verify summer work of custodians and maintenance.
45. Call a meeting with yearbook dance committee.

46. Conduct Initial Job Analysis.   .   .   1-01
47. Attend principals' meetings.
48. Verify photographer is set and scheduled for IDs.
49. Write information bulletins for staff as things occur.
50. Plan the monitoring of new policies.

51. Develop and copy Policy Manual; make adjustments.
52. Develop and copy recommendation forms for staff use.
                                                    2-04
53. Set priorities for work to be done each month.
54. Review personal goals and rewrite (?) job descriptions.
                                               .   1-03
55. Develop and print yearly school forms.

- UNIT NINE INTRODUCTION -
August Work in the Form of Task Lists

The principal is as busy in August as in any other month of the year. This chapter on the summer's work is important no matter when a principal receives the appointment. The listing of tasks will have to be done.

PRINCIPAL'S AUGUST TASKS IN INSTRUCTION

1. Write position paper on Learning Styles and Elements using Hill, McCarthy, and Dunn material.
2. Finalize schedule preparation of students.   2-04
3. Coordinate instruction with special program directors in Talented and Gifted, Special Education, Vocational Education, Co-op Education, etc.
4. Finalize in-service programs for the year.
5. Meet with Building Curriculum Committee with representatives from each discipline.

6. Establish goals for improving instruction - review with BCC.

7. Write Information Bulletin on the giving of E's, F's, I's.
8. Plan for curriculum review with staff through BCC.
9. Develop charges for curriculum review with staff.
10. Develop charges for BCC in basic 6 areas: Basic Skills, Career Orientation, Hard and Soft Sciences, Physical and Mental Health, and Arts and Humanities.

11. Verify that all incoming students' credentials are available to counselors.
12. Replace full set of teachers' textbook editions in the library.
13. Prepare selected material to establish Microteaching Clinic.
14. Verify senior credit standing for commencement at mid-year.
15. Conclude summer school program.

16. Review gifted and talented program.
17. Finalize yearly calendar.
18. Review July and August journals for faculty.
19. Prepare material on socialization of students for staff.
20. Review program for slow learners.

21. Prepare to (re)select all BCC members.
22. Review Survival/Literacy/Competency Program report.   2-07
23. Review programming for "middle of the road" students.
24. Write curriculum newsletter to be mailed to staff.   2-06
25. Write position paper on study groups' relationships.

26. Develop explanation of "Impact Statements" to be used by staff.   2-06
27. Prepare agenda for first orientation meeting.   2-04
28. Design teacher evaluation and observation plans.   1-03
29. Review with supervisor the progress on personal goals.
30. Provide review of statistics for teacher's classroom use.

31. Run "FINAL" DTLF.
32. Review Exceptional Kids' Cards.   .   2-05
33. Organize Department Head Structure.   .   2-04
34. Design report format for student marks each period.
35. Meet with FAC regarding S. O. P. and activity program

in the fall.   2-07

36. Prepare material on Maslow's Hierarchy.
37. Review Achievement/Ability Study information.

PRINCIPAL'S AUGUST TASKS WITH STUDENTS

1. Update files for summer school students.
2. Meet with new students about problems and needs.
3. Review graduate surveys received.
4. Verify 9th (10th) grade credentials.
5. Assign lockers. Maintain assignments for returnees.

6. Finalize student schedules.
7. Evaluate last year's attendance patterns (sex/grade/ months/days).
8. Issue diplomas to summer school graduates.
9. Finalize, with students, agenda for orientation.   3-10
10. Verify foreign exchange students' housing/schedules.

11. Verify that student schedules are being mailed.
12. Verify facilities and schedule set for taking IDs.
13. Verify supervision is set for student groups in building.
14. Verify list is completed from cumulative records and year-end forms for all exceptional students.
15. Attend yearbook dance.

16. Verify arrangements made for physicals for athletes.
17. Conduct entrance/exit interviews.   .   2-05
18. Prepare WELCOME BACK sign.
19. Verify that planned help is being given to "special" kids.
20. Finalize schedule of student activities.

21. Verify completion of student handbook.
22. Monitor student recruiting.
23. Prepare student group for entrance/exit interviews.2-05
24. Verify bus routes, pick-up and drop-off times.
25. Monitor plans for student orientation.   .   3-10

26. Verify student working permits are being processed.
27. Finalize plans for substance abuse program.
28. Meet with athletes on scholarships, rules, and expecta-

tions.
29. Meet with incoming students -- transfer and promotion.
30. Attend all due process hearings on student discipline.

31. Attend to due process proceedings with students.
32. End second driver training summer session.
33. Study information from entrance/exit questionnaires.
2-05

PRINCIPAL'S AUGUST TASKS WITH STAFF

1. Plan staff observation/evaluation schedule blank.
2. Post staff vacancies.
3. Work to fill ALL staff vacancies.
4. Hold separate orientation meetings for new families
   and staff groups.   .   .   .   3-10
5. Make emergency changes for teacher assignments. Run
   new DTLF.

6. Formulate a sub-list from input by staff.
7. Print all handout materials for first day staff meetings.
8. Design new personnel file system to meet bargained
   contract stipulations.
9. Meet with Comm. Ed. Dir. re: night school program.
10. Send letters to notify teachers of opening school.

11. Finalize staff handbook for publication.
12. Send letters to teacher aides and others for opening
    school.
13. Send letters to non-teaching staff for opening school.
14. Research attendance patterns to diminish the Pareto
    Principle.
15. Send letters to coaches with expectations for athletes.

16. Send letters on housing and orientation to new staff.
17. Meet with sport and activity coaches.
18. Collect substitute information at orientation of staff.
19. Assign staff activity duty calendar based upon DTLF
20. Distribute yearly calendar of scheduled meetings.

21. Complete list of exceptional students. .   2-05
22. Develop list of potential school volunteers.   2-07

25. Meet with counselors re: seniors who MAY not graduate. Set case conferences on schedule to review findings with faculty.

26. Notify personnel dept. of known vacancies on staff.
27. Meet with nurse and social worker re: special students.

AUGUST TASKS IN SCHOOL/COMMUNITY RELATIONS

1. Send news release to notify students of school opening.
2. Attend school planning committee meetings.
3. Provide information for press releases.
4. Attend community organization meetings.
5. Publish bus schedules and calendars.

6. Plan orientation releases for all staff groups.
7. Publish fall sports calendar.
8. Develop CHARGE for communication committee.
9. Organize a camera night to be followed by a dance.
10. Distribute (year round) yearbook after camera night.

11. Send letters to welcome staff back for the year.
12. Publish/distribute news releases for school beginning
13. Write principal's newsletter for September.
14. Recognize outstanding summer staff member/student.
15. Plan orientation for foreign exchange students.

16. Recruit community/parent volunteers for hall, library, and lunchroom duty. . . 2-07
17. Visit businesses in area to arrange for monthly display of student work.

AUGUST TASKS IN BUSINESS/BUILDING MGT.

1. Monitor cafeteria, custodial, secretarial, and transportation program planning.
2. Prepare weekly calendars for the month (distributed

tation program planning.
2. Prepare weekly calendars for the month (distributed each Friday).
3. Review field trip arrangement at meeting with Director of Transportation.
4. Inform staff of new material and equipment received.
5. Control budget and internal accounts.

6. Review all planning, control, and evaluation tools.
7. Supervise cumulative records in all areas for students.
8. Supervise staff cumulative personnel files for inclusions.
9. Prepare local, state, federal reports for:_____.
10. Interpret law and school policy.

11. Maintain adequate supply of materials.
12. Supervise selection of supplies, equip., and materials.
13. Order, invoice, inventory, and control all supplies/ materials.
14. Personally check emergency lighting in the corridors.
15. Supervise student traffic on site.

16. Monitor time schedules for year.
17. Monitor community programs and facility use.
18. Review fire/civil defense/inclement weather drills.
19. Check building safety with custodial staff.   1-03
20. Inspect site/building for maintenance and cleanliness.

21. Develop material for secretarial staff to meet needs.
22. Review of receipt of all supplies -- notify staff.
23. Inspect equipment safety/boiler room/HVAC/labs.
24. Evaluate all grievances from each section of staff.
25. Inspect kitchen weekly.

26. Complete check on all safety and protection lighting.
27. Verify building and special room security provisions.
28. Check building and site for vandalism.
29. Meet weekly with Dietician, Hd Custodian, Dir. of Transportation.
30. Verify room equipment in proper repair.

31. Monitor vehicle registration procedures.
32. Verify orders that have been completely filled.

33. Re-order back-ordered materials or cancelled items.
34. Meet with parent groups for fund raising programs.
35. Orientation begins for all staff. .   .   3-10

36. Sort/assemble/stack all supplies.
37. Make a roster of all extra duties and responsibilities.
38. Make sure labels are on all rooms.
39. Orient new staff/students to building. . .   3-10
40. Prepare building for opening.

41. Prepare building for student registration.
42. Attend Board of Education meeting.
43. Attend all principals' meetings.
44. Prepare task cards for self and subordinates.   1-03
45. Prepare humidity index material for staff.   . 2-06

46. Duplicate philosophy/objectives for orientation.3-10
47. Develop SPB to explain "Issue Papers."   . 2-04
48. Verify that all emergency signs are posted in each
        room and corridor.
49. Prepare and duplicate teacher "policy" manual.
50. Prepare audio-visual cards for use this year.

51. Inventory all incoming supplies, materials, equipment.

- UNIT TEN INTRODUCTION -
Orientation Planning

In the lists for monthly tasks already covered, as well as in
some of the lists yet to be read, there is a list of over 1,800
tasks that need to be addressed by the principal for his/her
orientation planning. There are many specific items which
call for orientation -- even with the experienced staff that
is returning. One point of clarity at the top of this unit
ought to be that *orientation is NOT a one-time of the year
project or task*. In a high school of today, there are always
changing memberships on the part of all staff segments
and literally hundreds of them within the student body.
Quite typically, orientation is done in late August or early
September. The orientation is usually done so well, in fact,

that most think it will be another year before it has to be done again---WRONG.

What is outlined here is a series of topics to be covered in an orientation program. It is divided into five parts, and each is addressed in segments of the population that need to be oriented. A staff with no changes can be oriented one time. How many times does that happen? A student body with no changes since the last orientation could be oriented one time. That never happens. The material, therefore, is presented in many segments: students new to the building, students new to high school, returning students, staff new to the building, staff new to the high school, and returning staff. Staff, all those who are employed by the Board of Education (or, better yet, those who work in the building including aides and monitors and others who volunteer but are not paid by the Board), will be broken into their units -- at times. It is wise to meet with the custodians-maintenance personnel in one group but to go over very few topics. The cooks, dieticians, bakers, and monitors can be met with separately also. Here are some lists of groups to meet:

GENERAL STAFF ORIENTATION WITH LITERALLY EVERYONE THERE AT ONE TIME

Teachers new to teaching   Teachers new to the building
Teachers returning from last year Teacher Aides
Custodial-Maintenance Team   Cooks-Dieticians-
Monitors-Bakers   Secretaries-Clerks-
Stenographers-Aides   New Teachers

=============================
GENERAL STUDENT BODY ORIENTATION WITH ALL STUDENTS IN ATTENDANCE

Students new to the high school level
Students new to the building
Students returning from last year

With these groups in mind, how does the effective principal orient all the people coming to the building for an education program? It is wise to start with the mass in terms of the staff and then keep narrowing the numbers down to the point of a very small group. For the students, it is just the opposite. Start with the smallest group and move to the total student body if physically possible. DON'T excuse any students -- including the football team, cross country, etc. Have ALL of the students in the orientation program.

================================

The various agenda appear on the following pages. Please refer to Chapter 2, Unit 4.

================================

- ORIENTATION PLAN # 1: STAFF - GEN'L. MTG. -

MEMBERSHIP: All adults working in the building for the school year

ANNOUNCEMENTS:

1. Welcome: Principal and Central Office Representative
2. Introductions: New Staff, Dept. Chairs, Administrators
                                              --Ass't # 1
3. Plans for lunch are announced   --Principal

DISCUSSION:

3. Philosophy/Objs. of BOE/building   --Ass't # 2
4. Orientation Plans for students   --Ass't # 3

UPDATES:

5. Review of the Handbook -- Changes only --Principal
6. Review of Curricular Changes   --Ass't # 2
7. Master Schedule --- for the fall   --Ass't # 1
8. Student Handbook -- Changes   --Ass't # 3

364

9. Staff/Student Recognition Plans --
    Progressive and Regular Honor Rolls,
    attendance, Students of the Month,
    election to three Advisory Committees,
    student council, Staff Member of the
    Month, Teacher of the Month, athletic
    awards, academic awards   --Principal
10. Constitution of the student body
    elections and government credit   --Principal
11. Building alterations for the new year --Director
12. Equipment received in the facility
    backorders   --Ass't # 4
13. Supplies received, short--on backorder--Ass't # 4
14. The building budget   --Bookkeeper
15. Comm'y Relations/Volunteers/Assembly Programs/
    Parent Involvement/P.T.A./Newspaper and Media
                                       --Principal
16. Building Governance   --Principal
17. Cafeteria Operation   --Dietician
18. Building Use for activities   --Ass't # 4

ACTION: Nothing on this agenda

HANDOUTS: (If not listed, staff is referred specifically to
a page number in one of the handbooks distributed the day
before the meeting. These are listed on an attached page.
Some are here for POSTING in the various classrooms.)

D-03. Philosophy and Objectives of the BOE and building
D-04. Orientation Plans for students
U-05. Changes in STAFF Handbook
U-06. Curricular Changes for the year
U-08. Changes in Student Handbook
U-11. Building alterations for the new year
U-12. Equipment received and workable in the facility and
      on backorder
U-17. Cafeteria Operation Report
U-18. Custodial/Maintenance Report
= =

- ORIENTATION PLAN # 2 - STAFF - NEW TO BLDG. -

MEMBERSHIP: List the names on the agenda of those who are to attend.

ANNOUNCEMENTS:
1. Welcome: Principal
2. Introductions: Custodian/Maintenance Hd, Dietician, Office Manager, Guidance Personnel, Librarians, Administrators present

DISCUSSION:
3. Accomplishing the Board and building philosophy and objectives
4. Details for Orientation Plans for students --Ass't # 3
5. Review of the Staff Hdbk -- Minus Changes --Principal
6. Review of total curr. (District-wide)   --Principal
7. Master Schedule --- Implications   --Principal
8. Student Handbook -- Significant items --Ass't # 3
9. A word on the 3 student Advisory Committees
                                        --Principal
10. Building tour you need to know about --Stu.C'l.
11. Equipment inventory for clrm assignments--Principal
12. Supplies -- how to get and treat   --Ass't # 4
13. The building budget--how to draw upon funds
                                        --Ass't # 4
14. Cafeteria Operation --special requests   --Ass't # 4
15. Building Use for activities -- spec. requests
                                        --Ass't # 4

This agenda will be important when completed properly. If a buddy system is in place, have the new staff and their buddies at the meeting. Be sure to have gone over orientation planning, generally, in the summer letter to the staff so that this series of meetings won't surprise any of the employees. It is also a good time to continue to establish the philosophy that all of the adults are important. All staff groups need to work together.

=============================

- ORIENTATION PLAN # 3 - NEW TO TEACHING -

MEMBERSHIP: List the names on this agenda for easy checking and later use.

ANNOUNCEMENTS:
1. Welcome: Principal with administrative team
2. Introductions: New staff by departmental areas with a thumbnail sketch of credential for communication

DISCUSSION:
3. Philosophy/Objectives of the BOE/bldg --Principal
4. Student Orientation Plans -- Role of teachers
                                                    --Principal
5. Significance of the student handbook
        impact on students/staff.   .   --Ass't # 2
6. Master Schedule --- explanations and understandings
7. Staff Handbook -- Expectations for staff --Ass't # 3
8. A briefing on the committees to meet with the prin-
        cipal, student council, Staff of the Month, Teacher
        of the Month, athletic awards, academic awards.
                                                    --Principal
9. Equipment -- how to order / inventory   --Ass't # 4
10. Supplies --how to order, inventory, store--Ass't # 4

The agenda for those new to teaching is significant as the general orientation topics have now been covered two additional times. It is called planned repetition and not redundant to assure the new folk that the institution is a vital part of their lives now and that they MUST know how and what to do and even more important - WHEN to do it.

= =

- ORIENTATION PLAN # 4- NONFACULTY NEW TO BUILDING

MEMBERSHIP: List, by name, who is supposed to be in this meeting.

ANNOUNCEMENTS:

DISCUSSION:
1. Governance
2. Roles to be carried out by each of the team partners
3. Complaints from other staff -- processing
4. Regular meetings with the admin. on a monthly basis
5. Student "handling" when conflict arises
6. Use of the building, all facilities
7. Inclement weather days
8. Safety in the building and on the site
9. Cleanliness and help from other staff and students
      Work on the area of student involvement

Secretaries	Custodians	Maintenance
Aides	Drivers	

===============================

ORIENTATION PLAN # 5 - STUDENTS - GENERAL - MEETING -

MEMBERSHIP: List home room or some other group.

ANNOUNCEMENTS:
1. Welcome: Principal
2. Introductions: New Staff and Administrators--Ass't # 1
3. Review of Curricular Changes for the year   --Ass't # 2
4. Master Schedule -- Scheduling Changes   --Ass't # 1
5. Student Handbook -- Changes from last year --Ass't # 3
6. Student Recognition Plans --
      Progressive/Regular Honor Rolls, attendance,
      Students of the Month, election to three
      Advisory Committees to meet with the princi-
      pal, student council, athletic and academic
      awards.   --Principal
7. Constitution of the student body =
      elections and government credit   --Principal
8. Building alterations for the new year   --Director
9. Community relations -- Parent Involvement --Principal

10. Building Governance   --Principal
11. Cafeteria Operation - lunch period planning--Ass't # 4
12. Building Use for activities   --Ass't # 4

This meeting with the students will set the tone for all mass meetings during the year. Politeness, respect, responsibility, and all that goes with socialization as a determiner of the tone in the building will be monitored here. Don't do it as if it were routine; it is NOT.

==============================

ORIENTATION PLAN # 6 - STUDENTS NEW TO BLDG
- GENERAL MEETING -

MEMBERSHIP: List the numbers, at least, that are to be in attendance

ANNOUNCEMENTS:
1. Welcome: Principal and administrative team
2. Introductions: Dept. Chairs/Guidance team--Ass't # 1
3. Review of curriculum in the building   --Ass't # 2
4. Master Schedule --- Scheduling Changes   --Ass't # 1
5. Student Handbook--Intent for governance   --Ass't # 3
6. Constitution of the student body = elections
        and government credit   --Principal
7. Building Tour for acquaintance   --Director

This meeting with the newest students will set the tone for all mass meetings during the year. Politeness, respect, responsibility, and all that goes with the desire to provide for them a good socialization experience will be launched in this assembly. This is a tone setter for the building's operation.

REQUESTED CHANGES
IN THE HIGH SCHOOL
AS SEEN BY STUDENTS

For orientation planning, here is something that the principal may wish to use in planning what needs to be gone over with the teachers when they come in before school actually opens. The list may be a good background of what to do with the agenda of the advisory committees of students with whom s/he will be working during the year. It actually came to the author's attention when a fellow principal shared it as the results of his students presenting a petition. Here are the "*demands*" they were making. It was initially in the form of a questionnaire used for his teachers. When it was used where the author was principal, there was no printing on the right half side of the page so the staff could react to any or all items directly opposite the comment. For the sake of space here, both sides are printed with the statements.

DIRECTIONS:

"Circle all numbers with which you find agreement if the area is one that we could comply with now in school. Then, circle (a-j) those areas in which you feel we ought to be permitting students to learn for credit. You may add others. On the right hand column, please list the administrative practices and rules that we have that you could agree to eliminate if you wanted to work without them or that you feel would correct or compensate the item on the left-hand column."

1. Establish an ombudsman office.

2. Stop intimidation of students.

3. Give students an important role in shaping and implementing curricula.

4. Allow student input in teacher evaluations.

5. Eliminate tension and rigidity from the schools.

6. Hire educators and researchers to examine

370

deeply what effect the school system has on a student's self-concept, creativity, and desire to explore and learn.

7. Eliminate the bias of letter grades.

8. Encourage and allow teachers to respond to the individual needs of their students.

9. Allow students to exercise control over what happens to them in school.

10. Replace rigid class periods in secondary schools.

11. Grant students the right to print and distribute their own publications.

12. Allow students the freedom to decide what they want to print.

13. Provide for outside speakers.

14. Refuse to provide the names and addresses of high school students to any organization.

15. Develop relevant courses to meet student interests.

16. Consider the use of the community as a classroom for "service learning."

17. Allow students to arrange voluntary seminars, or mini-courses, to be held during the school day.

18. Expand resource range.

19. Inform students of rights.

20. Eliminate restrictions having to do with student dress.

21. Hold seminars for teachers in the areas of human relations, racism, and progressive teaching methods.

22. Integrate into classes such as United States history and problems of the 20th century material which thoroughly explores all cultural minorities and minority viewpoints.

23. Allow school board hearings for students.

24. Elect students to participate in school board meetings.

Atop this, they listed service oriented learning areas in which they would like to participate.

a. hospital work
b. homes for the elderly
c. fire department volunteers
d. elementary teacher assistants
e. high school slow learners
f. public health
g. welfare department
h. nursery schools
i. executive internships
j. yours_____

- UNIT ELEVEN -
September Work in the Form of Task Lists

As in the last chapter the following is still a starter list as it continues for the work to be done. The months of September, October, and November, the fall months of the school year, will be covered in this chapter. Later months will be listed in later chapters. Please reread the introduction to the lists covered for the months of July and August, for that information has not been repeated here.

PRINCIPAL'S SEPTEMBER TASKS IN INSTRUCTION

1. Emphasize learning styles at inservice meeting.
2. Post the Observation Scheduling Form for teachers.
3. Prepare review of journal articles.
4. Supervise the beginning of classes.
5. Prepare mainstreaming lists for faculty special session.

6. Supervise homeroom climate establishment.
7. Level classes for controlling class overloads.
8. Verify distribution of teacher loads with DTLF.
9. Distribute Instruction-Yearly Calendar.
10. Present information to staff about library program.

11. Assign showcase display to librarians for month.
12. Distribute teacher evaluation/observation information.
1-03
13. Review Emergency Lesson Plans for faculty.

14. Meet with dept chairs on textbook evaluations and
    initiate four domain grid on taxonomies.
15. Verify distribution of course/marking requirements.

16. Plan MEAP testing (St. of Mich. mandatory testing
    program) external testing program.
17. Review beginning of new programs.
18. Review testing and evaluation process, standardized/
    teacher-made.
19. Review discipline as it relates to instruction.
20. Construct field trip schedule.

21. Review School Board instructional policies.
22. Plan for in-school and out-of-school visitations.
23. Review NCA (Reg'l Assoc.)/U of M (St.) evaluations.
24. Review student eligibility for co/extra-curricular
    activities.
25. Implement Homework Policy.

26. Discuss/implement homebound assignments.
27. Implement special programs: (Teacher Aide-Child
    Care, Individualized Programming, Talented and
    Gifted, Middle Students, Special Education, Assis-
    tantships, Internal--External Testing, Scholarship,
    Placement, Mainstreaming, Student Council, etc.).
28. Meet with supervisor concerning personal goals. 1-01
29. Prepare for first Open House for parents and patrons.
30. Initiate concept that the school is a house of intellect.

31. Meet with BCC on studies and suicide prevention.
32. Examine for use the material on FFA.   1-01
33. Assign Eng. Dept. professional journals report.
34. Review Maslow's Human Needs Hierarchy for faculty.
35. Monitor special programs.

36. Present new teaching method at faculty meeting.
37. Discuss position paper on Learning Styles with faculty.
38. Review Observation Record Form with faculty.
39. Develop Information Bulletins for: FOG, SMOG, and
    Flesch.   2-05
40. Balance class sizes.

41. Publish material on marking and student evaluation.
42. Review journals to share with staff in newsletter.
43. Write curriculum newsletter.   .   .   2-06
44. Write position paper on topic obviated during orientation.
45. Monitor satellite programs' initiation: Co-op (a.m. and p.m.), attendees at other high schools, correspondence credit, community college attendance, university attendance, and homebound.

46. Meet with conf./planning pd. committees on orientation.
47. Review activity program in relation to instructional program.
48. Serve on district-wide committees.
49. Hold educational assembly program.
50. Meet with FAC at a bite and gripe breakfast regarding activity program and building committee reports.

51. Review "programs" for slow learners, middle group, and talented.

PRINCIPAL'S SEPTEMBER TASKS WITH STUDENTS

1. Hold class level assemblies (student orientation).
2. Update state required vaccination records.
3. Implement student orientation material for all groups.
4. Handle schedule changes requested by faculty/students.
5. Meet with student groups.

6. Verify ALL sports' physicals have been taken.
7. Announce formulation of 3 student committees. 2-07
8. Identify bilingual students for special programming.
9. Verify availability of ext'l testing materials, dates, etc.
10. Implement the fourth Friday count (st. count for membership finances, is the fourth Friday after Labor Day in Michigan -- check to see state guidelines and insert in appropriate month.)

11. Meet with treasurers and activity officers of student

groups.

12. Plan homecoming activities with student (summer) committee.
13. Implement substance abuse program infusion into all programs.
14. Maintain and monitor the enforcement of rules established in the student handbook.
15. Attend student co-curricular and extra-curricular activities.

16. Work closely with guidance staff to assist students with personal problems.
17. Maintain discipline program with fairness.
18. Verify eligibility for each student participant in athletic/extra-curricular program.
19. See that students begin entrance and exit interviews.
2-05
20. Examine results of entrance and exit interviews. 2-05

21. Verify plans for fall drivers training program.
22. Handle due process proceedings for student discipline.
23. Implement "Blue Card" Philosophy after full discussion at faculty meeting.   .   .   .   2-06
24. Generate positive morale.
25. Verify student working permits.

26. Initiate Student of the Month program.
27. Approve start of fall sports programs.
28. Attend student activities as listed on yearly calendar.
29. Verify that seniors' regular and scholarship applications are being processed expeditiously.
30. Meet with new students.

31. Meet with newly elected presidents of activity groups.
32. Verify incoming students' credentials match schedules.
33. Assign procedure of screening new student credentials
34. Verify records of summer driver training program.

PRINCIPAL'S SEPTEMBER TASKS WITH STAFF

1. Distribute management job descriptions to staff. 1-03

375

2. Define yearly goals for staff.   .   .   1-01
3. Collect emergency lesson plans.
4. Collect emergency personal information (address, phone,etc.).
5. Establish closed loop fan-out phone list.   2-07

6. Meet with custodial staff.
7. Distribute staff/faculty handbook.
8. Meet with school nurse concerning student health problems.
9. Conduct staff meetings: Substance Abuse, Bloom, Maslow, explain all programs, detail observations and evaluations.
10. Do Problem Census and FFA on school opening.1-01

11. Plan staff inservice program.
12. Develop routing list.
13. Verify special help being given with nurse and social worker.
14. Report exceptional children to staff.   .   2-05
15. Initiate Quality of Work Life Committee.

16. Develop staff evaluation form to assess administration.
17. Recognize and support excellence.
18. Interview to fill staff vacancies.
19. Select Teacher of the Month and Staff Member of the Month.
20. Meet with fall coaches and extra/co-curricular coaches.

21. Meet with secretarial work force.
22. Notify central office of staff vacancies - known and pending.
23. Post all staff vacancies.

SEPTEMBER TASKS IN SCHOOL/COMMUNITY RELATIONS

1. Provide information for press releases.
2. Attend community organization meetings.
3. Write monthly position paper on community relations.
4. Attend monthly PTA meeting.

5. Attend school planning committee meeting.

6. Prepare/distribute monthly newsletter of student and staff summer accomplishments. Recognize new programs, dates, and citizen support.
7. Organize and schedule a back-to-school open house for parents.
8. Work through PTA to gain support for upcoming millage/bond issue.
9. Schedule orientation for ninth graders and parents.3-10
10. Invite church leaders and non-profit social agencies into school for coffee.

11. Meet w/ community, students, and staff to develop and coordinate charity drives for needy and crisis families in area.
12. Participate in fall community and school clean-up campaigns.
13. Invite grandparents to pay a visit to the school.
14. Issue gold cards to allow free admission to all events at school.
15. Invite a speaker for upcoming assembly.

16. Inservice staff on community relations.
17. Send mid-marking period failure reports to parents.
18. Publish dates for SAT, PSAT, ACT testing.
19. Complete schedules/register for adult education program.
20. Meet with leaders of Booster clubs.

21. Meet with leaders of social and fraternal organizations.
22. Hold Open House for all parents and community members.
23. Mail mid-marking period failure notices to parents.

SEPTEMBER TASKS IN BUSINESS/BLDG. MGT.

1. Solicit needs from staff regarding supplies and materials.
2. Attend School Board meeting.
3. Monitor transportion, custodial, secretarial, and

cafeteria programs.
4. Prepare weekly calendars for the month (distribute each Friday).
5. Review field trip arrangement procedure with faculty.

6. Inform staff of new material and equipment received.
7. Control budget and internal accounts.
8. Attend Principals' meeting at central office.
9. Supervise cumulative records for health, testing, behavior, etc.
10. Supervise staff certification, transcripts, evaluations, observations, commendations, etc.

11. Prepare local, state, federal reports for:_____.
12. Interpret law and school policy.
13. Maintain adequate supply of materials.
14. Supervise selection of supplies, equipment, and materials.
15. Order, invoice, inventory, and control all supplies/materials.

16. Supervise students in lunchrooms during noon hours.
17. Supervise student traffic on site.
18. Monitor school master and time schedules.
19. Review all planning, control, and evaluation tools.
20. Monitor community programs and facility use.

21. Implement fire/civil defense/inclement weather drills.
22. Verify building safety with custodial staff.   1-03
23. Inspect site/building monthly for needed maintenance and cleanliness.   .   .   .   1-03
24. Develop secretarial staff to meet needs of program.
25. Finalize community "rumor control" fanout for school.
                                                         2-04

26. Follow up suggestions made by staff.
27. Inspect equipment safety/boiler room/HVAC/labs.
28. Tabulate and assess all grievances from each section of staff.
29. Inspect kitchen weekly.
30. Check safety and protection lighting.

31. Verify building and special room security provisions.
32. Check for vandalism.
33. Meet weekly with Dietician, Head Custodian, Director of Transportation.
34. Verify that room equipment is in proper repair.
35. Check athletic facilities and equipment at least semi-monthly.

36. Monitor vehicle registration procedures.
37. Adjust budget after state membership count is verified.
38. Inform department heads of budget alterations.
39. Have staff verify materials received.
40. Meet with student treasurers and distribute student account books.

41. Review district policies with staff.
42. Finalize community "rumor control" fanout for school.

2-04

-- CHAPTER FOUR INTRODUCTION --
Work in the Fall Months

This Chapter continues what has been detailed in the prior units for the summer months. Each month will be detailed for the five areas of activity for the building principal. The work to be done, at this time of year is crucial for it launches the "programs" so vital to a good year for the students and staff in the building. This, in turn, launches an excellent year for the effective and efficient high school principal.

- UNIT TWELVE -
October Work in the Form of Task Lists

PRINCIPAL'S OCTOBER TASKS IN INSTRUCTION

1. Observation of teachers begins on schedule.

2. Prepare review of journal articles for the month.
3. Hold discussion on preparation of Honor Roll(s).
4. Present English curriculum at staff meeting.
5. Monitor homework policy implementation.

6. Review position paper on Bloom's Taxonomy.
7. Assign Sci. Dept.to review journals for faculty.
8. Assign showcase use to English Department.
9. Construct field trip schedule.
10. Initiate grid development of four domains (Dept Hds.)

11. Meet with BCC on research in field/trends in schools.
12. Identify all "special" students in and out of school.
13. Complete MEAP testing.
14. Provide updated mainstream list to classroom teachers.
15. Hold fall Open House.

16. Initiate textbook evaluations for the next year.   2-05
17. Review utilization of guidance staff in core functions.
18. Schedule professional conferences.
19. Develop instructional master teacher concepts.
20. Plan teacher-led instructional workshops.

21. Serve on district-wide committees.
22. Develop incentive program for student achievement.
23. Plan progress reports for all newly entered students.
24. Review marking process for first report cards.
25. Review grids for first marking period grades.

26. Hold first outside educational assembly program.
27. Prepare a review of journals for the staff.
28. Meet with curriculum review groups.
29. Meet with dept. reps. on Team (Cooperative) Learn-
     ing Concepts regarding student marking and 4
     domain grid.
30. Emphasize Flanders' and Grant/Hennings' work.

31. Develop position paper on Allen's microteaching.
32. Review activity program in relation to instruction.
33. Discuss Progressive Honor Roll for students.   2-07
34. Write curriculum newsletter.   .   .   2-06
35. Meet with Faculty Advisory Committee on Progressive

Honor Roll, learning styles, building committee
reports. 2-07

36. Post both honor rolls. . . . 2-07
37. Monitor satellite and special programs.
38. Meet with hourly study groups during conference
periods on six curricular areas.
39. Monitor special programs.
40. Develop information bulletin on a teaching method.

41. Prepare paper on *Selection* in the Public Schools.
42. Distribute form to collect data on Survival/Literacy/
Competency Program. . . 2-07
43. Collect marking period I marking grid from teachers.
44. Present new teaching method at faculty meeting.
45. Review "programs" for slow learners, middle group,
and talented.

PRINCIPAL'S OCTOBER TASKS WITH STUDENTS

1. Finalize homecoming preparation.
2. Attend homecoming activities.
3. Verify compliance of activity programs with handbook.
4. Conduct a student evaluation of homecoming activities.
5. Review procedures for honor roll(s). . 2-07

6. Identify informal student leaders by staff input.
7. Attend student activities as listed on yearly calendar.
8. Attend class organization meetings.
9. Meet with all homeroom (elected) reps. for November's
election to senate and executive offices.
10. Monitor the enforcement of student discipline policy.

11. Meet with newly elected members of Students' Policy,
Activities, and Curriculum Advisory Committees. 2-07
12. Meet with all elected student presidents.
13. Organize assembly program for remainder of year.
14. Plan College/Career Night with guidance staff.
15. Verify SAT/ACT testing review program for students.

16. Verify student eligibility for all athletic/activity
programs.

17. Read information from entrance/exit interviews. 2-05
18. Attend (when appropriate) all case conferences.
19. Verify upcoming dates on PSAT testing for juniors.
20. Initiate fall drivers training program.

21. Handle due process proceedings for student discipline.
22. Generate positive morale.
23. Verify student working permits.
24. Monitor substance abuse program.
25. Distribute Problem Census # I to students/staff 1-01

26. Verify preparation for MEAP testing -- grade 10.
27. Verification for distributing report cards to students.
28. Select students of the month.
29. Initiate Suicide Prevention Program.   .   2-06
30. Students conduct entrance/exit interviews.   2-05

31. Meet with all new students.
32. Monitor new student credentials.
33. Monitor substance abuse program.
34. Arrange for physicals to be given for mid-year sports.

PRINCIPAL'S OCTOBER TASKS WIH STAFF

1. Select Teacher and Staff Member of the Month.
2. Plan staff appreciation day for AEW.
3. Schedule new teacher/employee conferences.
4. Meet with winter coaches.
5. Interview to fill staff vacancies.

6. Distribute and explain grading forms.
7. Review inclement day procedures.   .   2-07
8. Meet with school advisory groups.
9. Meet with fall coaches and sponsors.
10. Notify central office of known vacancies.

11. Conduct staff meetings on student marking, honor
       rolls, studies in progress, and district committee
       reports.
12. Meet with nurse and social worker on students with
       problems.
13. Recognize and support excellence.

14. Meet weekly with Dietician, Head Custodian, and Office Manager.
15. Post all known staff openings.

16. Meet with Quality of Work Life Committee.

OCTOBER TASKS IN SCHOOL/COMMUNITY RELATIONS

1. Publish monthly newsletter.
2. Provide information for press releases.
3. Attend community organization meetings.
4. Attend monthly PTA meeting.
5. Attend school planning committee meeting.

6. Meet w/ community, students, and staff to coordinate application for grant monies.
7. Sponsor a "Back to School" program for community members so they can be students for a day.
8. Send press release publicizing homecoming which has been coordinated with booster club and alumni association.
9. Check w/ counselors on progress of planning for this month's college/ career night.
10. Publicize and campaign for school millage/bond issue.

11. Meet with Chapter I/Article 3 advisory committees.
2-04
12. Meet with vocational advisory committees   2-04
13. Send thank you letters to community members who supported Homecoming.
14. Be visible at parent-teacher conferences.
15. Support school-wide United Fund Drive.

16. Contact speaker for upcoming assembly.
17. Write monthly position paper on "How to Talk to Reporters"
18. Publish honor rolls in local newspapers.

OCTOBER TASKS IN BUSINESS/BLDG. MGT.

1. Attend Board of Education meeting.
2. Attend principals' meetings.
3. Monitor transportion, custodial, secretarial, and cafeteria programs.
4. Prepare weekly calendars for the month (distribute each Friday).
5. Monitor field trip arrangements.

6. Inform staff of new material and equipment received.
7. Control budget and internal accounts.
8. Supervise cumulative records for health, testing, behavior.
9. Supervise staff certification, transcripts, evaluations, observations, commendations, etc.
10. Prepare local, state, federal reports for: _____.

11. Interpret law and school policy.
12. Maintain adequate supply of materials.
13. Review all planning, control, and evaluation tools.
14. Supervise selection of supplies/equipment/materials.
15. Order/invoice/inventory/control supplies/materials.

16. Supervise lunchrooms and noon hours.
17. Supervise student traffic on site.
18. Monitor school master and time schedules.
19. Obtain feedback on month's activities.
20. Monitor community programs and facility use.

21. Implement fire/civil defense/inclement weather drills.
22. Check with custodial staff on building safety.   1-03
23. Inspect site/building for needs in maintenance/cleanliness.   1-03
24. Develop secretarial staff.
25. Check City Hall for use of voting machines.

26. Follow-up suggestions made by staff.
27. Inspect equipment safety/boiler room/HVAC/lab.
28. Evaluate all grievances from each section of staff.
29. Inspect kitchen weekly.

30. Check safety and protection lighting.

31. Verify building and special room security provisions.
32. Check for vandalism.
33. Meet with Dietician/Hd Custodian/Off. Mgr. weekly.
34. Verify room equipment is in proper repair.
35. Check athletic facilities and equipment semi-monthly.

36. Monitor vehicle registration procedures.
37. Conduct force field analysis on Open House.
38. Receive materials ordered for staff.
39. Monitor policies through impact statements.

- UNIT THIRTEEN -
November Work in the Form of Task Lists

PRINCIPAL'S NOVEMBER TASKS IN INSTRUCTION

1. Plan for AEW (American Education Week).
2. Meet with curriculum review groups.
3. Meet with dept. reps. on faculty handbook and spring
    semester offerings.
4. Meet with conference planning period committees on
    roles of the public schools.
5. Present report of science department at staff meetings.

6. Develop position paper on Leslie Hart's Proster
    Theory.
7. Assign journals to report on by Mathematics Depart-
    ment.
8. Plan parent teacher conference FFA report.   1-01
9. Initiate team learning program.
10. Compare marking reports for two periods for staff.

11. Construct field trip schedule.
12. Post both regular and progressive honor rolls.   2-07
13. Assign showcase to Science Department.
14. Continue observation of teachers.   .   1-03
15. Plan college night for seniors.

16. Verify special plans for Thanksgiving.
17. Prepare review of journal articles for the staff.
18. Initiate lay curr. comm. to study proposed changes.
19. Visit with teachers who had a "negative" marking trend.
20. Monitor plan for recognizing academic achievement.

21. Present new mode of teaching at staff meeting.
22. Monitor new programs.
23. Monitor plans for teacher-led workshops.
24. Hold parent-teacher conferences.
25. Monitor textbook evaluations. .   .   2-05

26. Develop position paper on student concentration.
27. Work with BCC on Emergent Curriculum Package and
     marking.
28. Monitor special programs.
29. Emphasize Allen's work at inservice meeting.
30. Post honor roll(s) for second marking period.

31. Collect, tabulate, and report on marking period II.
32. Present new teaching method at faculty meeting.
33. Monitor satellite programs.
34. Meet with directors of special and satellite programs.
35. Write curriculum newsletter.   .   .   2-06

36. Meet with FAC on list of teaching methods, activity
     program, and building committee reports.   2-07
37. Continue to work on four domain grid on taxonomies.
38. Review Survival, Literacy, Competency Program. 2-07
39. Serve on district-wide committees.
40. Conduct assembly program.

41. Review activity program in relation to instructional
     program.
42. Monitor suicide prevention program.
43. Review "programs" for slow learners, middle group,
     and talented.

PRINCIPAL'S NOVEMBER TASKS WITH STUDENTS

1. Conduct entrance/exit questionnaires. .   2-05
2. Verify eligibility of athletes for state tournaments and regular program.
3. Meet with athletes of winter sports re: scholarship expectations.
4. Attend student activities as listed on the calendar.
5. Meet with Policy, Activities, and Curriculum Advisory Committees.   2-07
6. Meet with all student presidents of activitiy groups.
7. Read information garnered from entrance and exit interviews.   2-05
8. Attend (when appropriate) all case conferences--or delegate.   2-05
9. Verify student working permits.
10. Monitor substance abuse program.

11. Handle due process proceedings for student discipline.
12. Generate positive morale.
13. Collect cards for Problem Census I. .   1-01
14. Evaluate responses to Problem Census Survey I 1-01
15. Present to staff the data from Problem Census I 1-01

16. Finalize fall drivers training program.
17. Attend marching band competition.
18. Meet with senior class to initiate planning for commencement.
19. Verify administration of PSAT test to juniors.
20. Verify implementation of workshops on SAT/ACT testing.

21. Attend College/Career Night.
22. Finalize plans for fall sports program banquet.
23. Meet with new students.
24. Inform students of winter recess dates.
25. Hold election to offices of Senate and House for student council.

26. Orient new students and staff. .   .   3-10
27. Monitor student discipline program.
28. Meet with counselors on kids with problems.

29. Monitor new student credentials.
30. Select students of the month.

31. Attend student organization meetings.
32. Read information gleaned from student questionnaires.

2-05

PRINCIPAL'S NOVEMBER TASKS WITH STAFF

1. Select Teacher and Staff Member of the Month.
2. Purge lists of substitutes in all staff areas.
3. Implement staff appreciation day.
4. Prepare for inservice day.
5. Prepare custodial schedule for vacations.

6. Observation of staff continues -- check schedule.
7. Conduct staff inservice program.
8. Evaluate coaches of all sports.
9. Evaluation of fall coaches and sports.
10. Meet with nurse and social worker for students.

11. Meet with winter coaches.
12. Encourage staff to evaluate administration.
13. Provide non-tenured faculty with first warning.
14. Submit recommendations for mid-year tenure and continuing probationary status.
15. Recognize and support excellence.

16. Notify central office of known staff vacancies.
17. Meet with Quality of Work Life Committee.
18. Interview to fill staff vacancies.
19. Hold meeting with counselors on senior failure prospects.
20. Meet with Hd Custodian/Dietician/Off. Mgr. weekly.

21. Conduct staff meetings on Flanders, Grant-Hennings, Stewart, Problem Census I, Student Marking, District Committee Reports.
22. Post all known staff openings.

NOVEMBER TASKS IN SCHOOL/COMMUNITY RELATIONS

1. Inform parents of winter recess dates.
2. Publish monthly newsletter.
3. Provide information for press releases.
4. Attend community organization meetings.
5. Attend monthly PTA meeting.

6. Meet with parent curriculum committee.
7. Plan Veterans' Day activities for alumni of the school.
8. Attend school planning committee meeting.
9. Meet with Chapter I/Article 3 Advisory Committees.
                                                    2-04
10. Meet with reps of Vocational Advisory Committee.2-04

11. Publicize American Education Week.
12. Publicize special winter events, athletics, and upcoming recess dates.
13. Check on food basket drive for the needy.
14. Support the Black United Fund Drive.
15. Write monthly position paper on "What Should Be Done With Community Pressure Groups Who Place School in Promoting Group's Self-interest."

16. Provide wind chill information to community.   2-06
17. Invite church and social leaders into school for coffee.
18. Send mid-marking period failure reports to parents.
19. Publish winter sports calendar.

NOVEMBER TASKS IN BUSINESS/BLDG. MGT.

1. Monitor transportion, custodial, secretarial, and cafeteria programs.
2. Prepare weekly calendars for the month (distribute each Friday).
3. Monitor field trip arrangements.
4. Inform staff of new material and equipment received.
5. Control budget and internal accounts.

6. Supervise cumulative records for health, testing, behavior.
7. Supervise staff certification, transcripts, evaluations, observations, commendations, etc.
8. Prepare local, state, federal reports for: _____.
9. Interpret law and school policy.
10. Maintain adequate supply of materials.

11. Supervise selection of supplies/equipment/materials.
12. Order/invoice/inventory/control supplies/materials.
13. Supervise lunchrooms and noon hours.
14. Supervise student traffic on site.
15. Monitor school master and time schedules.

16. Monitor the sports programs.
17. Monitor community programs and facility use.
18. Implement fire/civil defense/inclement weather drills.
19. Check with custodial staff on building safety.   1-03
20. Inspect site/building for cleanliness and maintenance needs.   1-03

21. Develop secretarial staff to meet needs of program.
22. Attend School Board meeting.
23. Follow up suggestions made by staff.
24. Inspect equipment safety/boiler room/HVAC/labs.
       1-03
25. Evaluate all grievances from each section of staff.

26. Inspect kitchen weekly.
27. Check safety and protection lighting.
28. Verify special room security provisions for equipment.
29. Check for vandalism.
30. Meet weekly with Dietician, Head Custodian, and Office Manager.

31. Verify room equipment is in proper repair.
32. Check athletic facilities and equipment at least semi-monthly.
33. Monitor vehicle registration procedures.
34. Meet with parent groups for support of winter sports/activities.
35. Review snow removal contract/maintenance proce-

dures.

36. Institute winter maintenance of facility.
37. Distribute inclement weather policy.
38. Develop winter recess work schedule.
39. Collect and place orders for second semester items.
40. Check on winter safety supplies.

41. Establish mid-year graduation ceremony supplies.
42. Check on maintenance of air handling equipment.
43. Attend principals' meeting in central office.
44. Monitor policy implementation.
45. Initiate planning on mid-year graduation.

46. Review all planning, control, and evaluation tools.

- CHAPTER FIVE INTRODUCTION -
Work in the Winter Months

During these months, the flurry of the year begins. Seniors begin to panic, holidays dot the calendar, first semester marks are being entered, students who may not graduate on schedule are being identified, parents are taking trips, and the general mood of the building is predictably getting into a fever pitch with the band and vocal concerts over the holidays. It is a fun time to be the principal of this magnificent program in the public schools.

There is much to do as others begin to add to their busy schedules. The principal must remain diligent in the exercise of the management of the buildings and its many programs. These winter months are exciting and busy. There are numerous tasks to complete. Some have been identified on the lists which follow. The more mundane tasks are listed -- the new ones will be completed because there are a great number of persons involved. The tasks listed below are the grid work on which all other things are suspended.

- UNIT FOURTEEN -
December Work in the Form of Task Lists

The following is a list of tasks, albeit only a start for MOST principals, that needs to be completed during the winter months of the school year. The lists are divided into the five roles of the principal and then subdivided by months from December through March for this chapter.

PRINCIPAL'S DECEMBER TASKS IN INSTRUCTION

1. Prepare position paper on Krathwohl's material.
2. Assign the Soc. Sci. Dept. to review journals for faculty.
3. Re/develop material for the faculty on pass/fail for 2nd semester enrollment into courses.
4. Construct field trip schedule.
5. Monitor homework policy application.

6. Hold educational assembly program.
7. Meet with BCC on spring semester preparation and field trips.
8. Present personal goals for review with supervisor.
9. Meet with curriculum review groups.
10. Meet with department representatives on SLC Vocabulary and four domain gridding.　　2-07

11. Review journal articles.
12. Present report of Math Department at staff meetings.
13. Assign showcase to Mathematics Department.
14. Continue observation of teachers.
15. Review instructional budget for second semester.

16. Verify the credit standing of seniors.
17. Emphasize Beggs and Hart's material at inservice.
18. Prepare material for registration for second semester.
19. Continue to work on four domain grid of taxonomies.
20. Monitor textbook evaluations. .　　.　　2-05

21. Report on a teaching methodology at faculty meeting.
22. Finalize schedule for second semester.
23. Finalize requests for second semester curr. changes.
24. Prepare first DTLF for second semester loads.
25. Publish closing bulletin for first semester including exam schedule.

26. Monitor satellite programs.
27. Write curriculum newsletter.   .   .   2-06
28. Meet with FAC on budget for this/next year, activity program, and buiding committee reports.   2-07
29. Meet with directors of special and satellite programs.
30. Meet with conference planning period committees on marking, discipline, and learning.

31. Collect, prepare, review marking period II marking reports.
32. Hold College Night.
33. Prepare material on PLACEMENT for staff.
34. Develop evaluation reports for mid-year faculty.
35. Serve on district-wide committees.

36. Monitor special programs.
37. Monitor suicide prevention program.
38. Review "programs" for slow learners, middle group, and talented.

PRINCIPAL'S DECEMBER TASKS WITH STUDENTS

1. Review student attendance patterns.
2. Attend student activities as listed on yearly calendar.
3. Meet with Policy, Activities, and Curriculum Advisory Committees.
4. Meet with all student presidents of activitiy groups.
5. Read information garnered from entrance/exit inter views.   2-05

6. Attend all case conferences or delegate to assistants.
7. Verify student working permits.
8. Monitor substance abuse program.

9. Handle due process proceedings for student discipline.
10. Generate positive morale.

11. Verify athletic/activity eligibility of students.
12. Have students conduct entrance/exit interviews. 2-05
13. Monitor student discipline program.
14. Attend fall sports program activities.
15. Check on progress of winter sports program.

16. Plan for mid-year commencement.
17. Conduct assembly program preceding winter recess.
18. Verify student use of building during winter recess.
19. Review attendance policy with students.
20. Meet with student reps and senior class advisor(s).

21. Initiate second session of driver training program.
22. Meet with new students.
23. Contact last/this year's student losses for returning to program.
24. Direct the structuring of student workshops on SAT/ACT testing.
25. Notify parents of seniors who may not graduate on schedule.

26. Have students evaluate faculty.
27. Verify distribution of report cards to students.
28. Prepare Wind Chill Chart for students. 2-06
29. Initiate planning for prom.
30. Monitor counselor report on list of seniors in credit difficulty.

31. Monitor new student credential formulation.
32. Attend student organization meetings.
33. Orient new students and staff. . . 3-10
34. Select Student of the Month.

PRINCIPAL'S DECEMBER TASKS WITH STAFF

1. Interview to fill staff positions.
2. Select Teacher and Staff Member of the Month.

3. Review absenteeisms of staff for possible patterns.
4. Assist in preparation for winter party for staff.
5. Mail appropriate <u>holiday</u> cards to staff members.

6. Review plan of non-instructional personnel for winter break.
7. Verify needs for staff for second semester.
8. Finalize second round of new teacher observation summaries.   1-03
9. Conduct student evaluation of staff.
10. Post all openings on staff.

11. Recognize and support excellence.
12. Meet with winter coaches.
13. Hold staff meetings on Allen, emergent curriculum, district committee reports.
14. Meet with nurse/social worker for special students.
15. Notify personnel department of staff needs.

16. Hire staff needed for next year and semester replacements.
17. Meet with Off. Mgr., Dietician, Hd Custodian weekly.
18. Meet with Quality of Work Life Committee.
19. Finalize first round of all teacher observations. 1-03
20. Write part of faculty's evaluations for reporting to central office.
21. Prepare Wind Chill Chart for staff to use.   2-06
22. Develop DTLF for "scheduled" loads for next semester.

DECEMBER TASKS IN COMMUNITY/SCHOOL RELATIONS

1. Publish monthly newsletter.
2. Provide information for press releases.
3. Attend community organization meetings.
4. Attend monthly PTA meeting.
5. Attend school planning committee meeting.

6. Meet with Chapter I/Article 3 Advisory committees.
            2-04

7. Meet with Vocational Advisory Committees' reps. 2-04
8. Publish next semester's adult/continuing education
   program offerings.
9. Coordinate next semester's building use calendar.
10. Notify parents of inclement weather procedures and
    radio stations to be used.

11. Arrange for broadcast of school athletic events on local
    TV.
12. Check plans for student visitations to nursing homes
    and hospitals.
13. Attend special December winter programs.
14. Prepare announcement--closing/opening of semesters
    and exam schedules.
15. Verify food basket delivery plan.

16. Write monthly position paper on "What is School Role
    of the community in the Interview Process on
    School Personnel"
17. Attend and be visible for second round of Parent-
    Teacher conferences.
18. Meet with Parent Curriculum Review Committee.
19. Prepare Wind Chill Chart for parents to use.   2-06
20. Publish honor rolls in local press.

DECEMBER TASKS IN BUSINESS/BLDG. MGT.

1. Attend Board of Education meeting.
2. Attend principals' meetings held at the central office.
3. Supervise transportion, custodial, secretarial, and
   cafeteria programs.
4. Prepare weekly calendars for the month (distribute
   each Friday).
5. Monitor field trip arrangements.

6. Inform staff of new material and equipment received.
7. Control budget and internal accounts.
8. Supervise cumulative records for health, testing, behavior, etc.
9. Supervise staff certification, transcripts, evaluations,

observations, commendations, etc.
10. Prepare local, state, federal reports for: _____ .

11. Interpret law and school policy.
12. Maintain adequate supply of materials.
13. Supervise selection of supplies/equipment/materials.
14. Order/invoice/inventory/control supplies/materials.
15. Supervise lunchrooms and noon hours.

16. Supervise student traffic on site.
17. Monitor school master schedules for summer and
     regular year.
18. Review all planning, control, and evaluation tools.
19. Monitor community programs and facility use.
20. Implement fire/civil defense/inclement weather drills.

21. Check with custodial staff on building safety.
22. Inspect site and building monthly for needs in main-
     tenance and safety.   .   .   .   1-03
23. Develop secretarial staff to meet needs of program.
24. Check on winter maintenance.
25. Follow-up suggestions made by staff.

26. Inspect equipment safety/boiler room/HVAC/labs.
27. Evaluate all grievances from each section of staff.
28. Inspect kitchen weekly.
29. Check safety and protection lighting.
30. Verify building and special room security provisions.

31. Check for vandalism.
32. Meet weekly with Dietician/Hd Custodian/Off. Mgr.
33. Verify room equipment is in proper repair.
34. Check athletic facilities and equipment at least semi-
     monthly.
35. Monitor vehicle registration procedures.

36. Prepare staff for budget process.
37. Write and distribute winter recess memo to staff and
     community.

- UNIT FIFTEEN -
January Work in the Form of Task Lists

PRINCIPAL'S JANUARY TASKS IN INSTRUCTION

1. Develop position paper on Simpson's work for teachers.
2. Journals reviewed by Physical Education Department.
3. Meet with BCC on SLC Vocabulary, Internal-External testing.
4. Hold educational assembly program.
5. Construct field trip schedule.

6. Meet with curriculum review groups.
7. Meet with department representatives on FOG, SMOG, 4 Domains. .   .   .   2-05
8. Review journal articles for staff.
9. Present report of Soc. Sci. Dept at staff meetings.
10. Assign showcase to Social Sciences Department.

11. Continue observation of teachers.   .   1-03
12. Continue work on four domain grid of taxonomies.
13. Present teacher-led workshops.
14. Begin first semester evaluation of instruction.
15. Level class sections as far as is practicable.

16. Verify DTLF for second semester.
17. Finalize departmental offerings for the next year.
18. Monitor progress of seniors toward commencement on schedule.
19. Meet with committee for honors' assembly.
20. Request all curriculum revisions.

21. Initiate plans for summer school.
22. Marking period III ends.
23. Emphasize Krathwohl's Psychomotor Domain at inservice meeting.
24. Present curriculum relevancy report to central office.
25. Emphasize service groups for staff.

26. Collect marking period III grids for tabulation.
27. Discuss specific teaching methodology with faculty.

28. Close out first semester.
29. Supervise beginning of new semester.
30. Monitor textbook evaluations.

31. Monitor progress in special programs.
32. Monitor satellite programs.
33. Write curriculum newsletter.
34. Meet with conference planning pd. comms. on styles, Maslow, Hart, Epstein, and activity program.
35. Meet with directors of special and satellite programs.

36. Prepare material on INSTRUCTION of students for staff.
37. Serve on district-wide committees.
38. Meet with FAC on programs as scheduled, activity program, building committee reports.
39. Review activity program in relation to instructional program.
40. Monitor suicide prevention program.

41. Review "programs" for slow learners, middle group, and talented.

PRINCIPAL'S JANUARY TASKS WITH STUDENTS

1. Attend student activities as listed on yearly calendar.
2. Meet with Policy, Activities, and Curriculum Advisory Committees.
3. Meet with all student presidents of activitiy groups.
4. Conduct student entrance/exit interviews.   2-05
5. Attend (when appropriate) all case conferences.

6. Verify student working permits.
7. Monitor substance abuse program.
8. Handle due process proceedings for student discipline.
9. Generate positive morale.
10. Verify athletic/activity eligibility of students for second semester.

11. Monitor student discipline program.
12. Attend student organization meetings.
13. Monitor prom planning.

14. Verify honor graduates for mid-year.
15. Verify total credits for graduating seniors.

16. Plan registration for second semester.
17. Meet with new students.
18. Attend party for graduating seniors.
19. Verify workshops/registration for ACT/SAT testing.
20. Verify adjustments made in schedule for 2nd semester.

21. Verify testing for scholarship exams.
22. Verify with counselors that PSAT scores have been gone over with juniors.
23. Review MEAP results. (State of Michigan state-wide tests).
24. Assess student evaluation forms of faculty.
25. Distribute Problem Census II survey for students.

26. Verify distribution of report cards to students.
27. Verify accuracy of student attendance records.
28. Students conduct entrance/exit questionnaires. 2-05
29. Select the Student of the Month program (by grade level?).
30. Monitor new student credentials.

31. Check with counselors on senior credit standing.
32. Conclude driver training program for semester.
33. Orient new students and staff.
34. Meet with counselors about kids with problems.

PRINCIPAL'S JANUARY TASKS WITH STAFF

1. Determine second semester load factor DTLF.
2. Meet with school nurse/social worker about students.
3. Hold staff meetings.
4. Hold meetings with winter coaches.
5. Hold faculty meetings on Hart, SLC Vocabulary, district committee reports.
6. Meet with spring coaches.
7. Select Teacher of the Month and Staff Member of the Month.
8. Notify central office of known vacancies on staff.

9. Check on staff needs for next fall.
10. Report on student evaluation of staff.

11. Meet weekly with Dietician, Head Custodian, and Office Manager.
12. Meet with Quality of Work Life Committee.
13. Post all openings of the staff.
14. Conduct feedback discussion for staff relationships.
15. Welcome new staff members at semester change.

16. Recognize and support excellence.
17. Initiate plans for staffing fall semester.
18. Interview to fill staff vacancies.

PRINCIPAL'S JANUARY TASKS IN THE AREA OF COMMUNITY/SCHOOL RELATIONS

1. Publish monthly newsletter.
2. Provide information for press releases.
3. Attend community organization meetings.
4. Attend monthly PTA meeting.
5. Attend school planning committee meeting.

6. Meet with Chapter I/Article 3 Advisory committees.
   2-04
7. Meet with Vocational Advisory Committee Rep. 2-04
8. Announce semester closing/opening and exam schedules.
9. Write monthly position paper on "Uses of Cable TV."
10. Plan/organize recognition of Martin Luther King's Birthday.

11. Schedule picture day for winter and spring concerts.
12. Schedule/organize a recognition assembly for students, parents, staff, and community.
13. Send congratulatory letters to parents of students who excelled during first semester.
14. Invite a speaker from the community to speak at winter assembly.
15. Publish honor roll, progressive honor roll, attendance

awards.

16. Meet with parent curriculum review committee.
17. Invite church leaders to review past recess period activity.
18. Send mid-marking period failure notices to parents.

PRINCIPAL'S JANUARY TASKS IN THE AREA OF BUSINESS / BLDG MANAGEMENT

1. Supervise transportion, custodial, secretarial, and cafeteria programs.
2. Prepare weekly calendars for the month (distribute each Friday).
3. Monitor field trip arrangements.
4. Inform staff of new material and equipment received.
5. Control budget and internal accounts.

6. Attend Board of Education meeting.
7. Attend principals' meetings.
8. Review all planning, control, and evaluation tools.
9. Supervise cumulative records for health, testing, behavior, etc.
10. Supervise staff certification, transcripts, evaluations, observations, commendations, etc.

11. Prepare local, state, federal reports for: _____.
12. Interpret law and school policy.
13. Maintain adequate supply of materials.
14. Supervise selection of supplies/equipment/materials.
15. Order/invoice/inventory/control supplies/materials.

16. Supervise lunchrooms and noon hours.
17. Supervise student traffic on site.
18. Monitor school master schedule for regular year.
19. Monitor sports and recognition programs.
20. Monitor community programs and facility use.

21. Implement fire/civil defense/inclement weather drills.
22. Check with custodial staff on building safety.   1-03

23. Inspect site and building monthly for needs in main-
     tenance and safety.   .   .   .   1-03
24. Develop secretarial staff to meet needs of program.
25. Review and evaluate, with staff, last year's budget.

26. Follow-up suggestions made by staff.
27. Inspect equipment safety/boiler room/HVAC/labs.
       1-03
28. Evaluate all grievances from each section of staff.
29. Inspect kitchen weekly.
30. Check safety and protection lighting.

31. Verify building and special room security provisions.
32. Check for vandalism.
33. Meet weekly with Dietician/Hd Custodian/Off. Mgr.
34. Verify room equipment is in proper repair.
35. Check athletic facilities and equipment at least semi-
     monthly.

36. Monitor vehicle registration procedures.
37. Review expenditures.
38. Distribute budget survey forms.

- UNIT SIXTEEN -
February Work in the Form of Task Lists

PRINCIPAL'S FEBRUARY TASKS IN INSTRUCTION

1. Prepare position paper on Moore's Taxonomy.
2. Monitor homework policy being followed.
3. Construct field trip schedule for staff use.
4. Have journal reports by Fine Arts Departments.
5. Meet with BCC on material acquisition for all levels of
    ability.

6. Meet with curriculum review groups.
7. Meet with department representatives on community-
    advisory committees' reports.
8. Review journal articles.
9. Present report of Physical Education Department at
    staff meetings.

10. Assign showcase to Physical Education Department.

11. Continue observation of teachers.
12. Review and draw comparisons on three sets of marks earned during the first semester.
13. Publish marking statistics for students and teachers.
14. Publish first semester scholastic/progressive honor rolls.
15. Monitor senior credentials.

16. Meet with honors assembly committee.
17. Begin class section preparations for next year.
18. Solicit supplies and other requests for next school year.
19. Verify in-service program for March.
20. Prepare for academic games, science fair, etc.

21. Emphasize Simpson's Taxonomy at inservice meeting.
22. Finalize grid of four domains on taxonomies with department chairpersons.
23. Develop summer school planning.
24. Hold second Open House.
25. Prepare for fourth marking period.

26. Present a different teaching method to faculty.
27. Monitor textbook selections.
28. Select members for student leadership forum.
29. Finalize commencement plans.
30. Finalize DTLF.

31. Monitor satellite programs.
32. Meet with Faculty Advisory Committee on resources for staff, activity program, building committee reports.
33. Meet with conference planning period committees on thirty-nine teaching methods.
34. Monitor special programs.
35. Finalize first semester evaluation of instruction.

36. Distribute form to collect SLC Vocabulary information.   2-07
37. Prepare rough draft schedule for fall semester.
38. Serve on district-wide committees.

404

39. Meet with directors of special and satellite programs.
40. Collect achievement/ability study information.

41. Write curriculum newsletter.   .   .   2-06
42. Review activity program in relation to instructional
     program.
43. Conduct assembly program.
44. Monitor suicide prevention program. .   2-06
45. Review "programs" for slow learners, middle group,
     and talented.

PRINCIPAL'S FEBRUARY TASKS WITH STUDENTS

1. Hold educational assembly for students.
2. Attend student activities as listed on yearly calendar.
3. Meet with Student Policy, Activities, and Curriculum
     Advisory committees.   .   .   2-07
5. Meet with all student presidents of activitiy groups.
5. Conduct student entrance/exit interviews..   2-05

6. Attend (when appropriate) all case conferences. 2-05
7. Verify student working permits.
8. Monitor substance abuse program.
9. Handle due process proceedings for student discipline.
10. Generate positive morale.

11. Verify eligibility of student activities and athletes.
12. Monitor student discipline program.
13. Attend student organization meetings.
14. Orient new students and staff.
15. Post winner(s) of Student of the Month program.

16. Prepare senior ranking for initial list of top ten.
17. Verify with counselors that seniors' applications are
     being processed properly at the colleges.
18. Initiate pre-enrollment procedures for fall semester.
19. Compile follow-up on students from who entered/
     dropped this year.
20. Meet with new students.

21. Meet with spring athletes on rules, expectations, and

scholarships.
22. Attend band sectional rating and competition.
23. Verify plans for winter sports banquet.
24. Verify plans for spring drivers training program.
25. Monitor seniors' activities.

26. Collect cards for Problem Census II.
27. Evaluate responses to Problem Census Survey II.
28. Present to staff the data from Problem Census II.
29. Monitor senior prom committee.
30. Read information from entrance/exit questionnaires.
     2-05

31. Monitor new student credentials.
32. Initiate graduate follow-up study design.

PRINCIPAL'S FEBRUARY TASKS WITH STAFF

1. Meet with nurse and social worker regarding students
    with problems.
2. Meet with winter coaches.
3. Hold staff meetings on Simon, affective domain,
    Problem Census II, district committee reports.
     1-01
4. Meet with counselors about exceptional kids.   2-05
5. Review Simon's Participation Hypothesis with staff.

6. Notify central office of staff vacancies.
7. Start recruitment of new teachers.
8. Conduct inservice day for staff.
9. Hold meeting with spring coaches.
10. Collect teachers' requests for master schedule.

11. Interview and fill vacancies within the staff.
12. Post all known staff openings.
13. Meet with Quality of Work Life Committee.
14. Meet weekly with Dietician/Hd Custodian/Off. Mgr.
15. Assist staff in parent and teacher conferences.

16. Complete FFA on parent conferences.   1.01

17. Recognize and support excellence.
18. Meet with spring coaches.
19. Select Teacher Staff Member of the Month.

FEBRUARY TASKS IN COMMUNITY/SCHOOL RELATIONS

1. Publish monthly newsletter.
2. Provide information for press releases.
3. Attend community organization meetings.
4. Attend monthly PTA meeting.
5. Attend school planning committee meeting.

6. Meet with Chapter I/Article 3 Advisory comms. 2-04
7. Meet with vocational advisory committee rep.   2-04
8. Write position paper on alumni relations.
9. Invite a speaker from the community for the monthly assembly.
10. Develop a video or slide/tape presentation for eighth grade recruitment / orientation.

11. Meet with parents for curriculum review committee.
12. Invite guest speakers and community for Black History month program.
13. Plan second semester orientation for new families and staff.   3-10
14. Organize a plan for parent/teacher conferences and review last FFA.   .   .   .   1-01
15. Publish semester break and spring recess schedules.

16. Send mid-marking period failure notices to parents.

FEBRUARY TASKS IN BUSINESS/BLDG MGT.

1. Supervise transportion, custodial, secretarial, and cafeteria program.
2. Prepare weekly calendars for the month (distribute each Friday).
3. Monitor field trip arrangements.

4. Inform staff of new material and equipment received.
5. Control budget and internal accounts.

6. Monitor cumulative records for health, grades, testing, behavior.
7. Supervise staff certification, transcripts, evaluations, observations, commendations, etc.
8. Prepare local, state, federal reports for: _____ .
9. Interpret law and school policy.
10. Maintain adequate supply of materials.

11. Supervise selection of supplies/equipment/materials.
12. Order/invoice/inventory/control supplies/materials.
13. Supervise lunchrooms and noon hours.
14. Supervise student traffic on site.
15. Monitor school master schedule for regular year.

16. Monitor sports and recognition programs.
17. Monitor community programs and facility use.
18. Implement change on fire/civil defense/inclement weather drills.
19. Check with custodial staff on building safety.   1-03
20. Inspect site and building monthly for maintenance/ safety needs.   1-3

21. Develop secretarial staff to meet needs of program.
22. Attend principals' meetings.
23. Follow up suggestions made by staff.
24. Inspect equipment safety/boiler room/HVAC/labs.
25. Evaluate all grievances from each section of staff.

26. Inspect kitchen weekly.
27. Check safety and protection lighting.
28. Verify building and special room security provisions.
29. Check for vandalism.
30. Meet weekly with Dietician/Hd Custodian/Off. Mgr.

31. Verify room equipment is in proper repair.
32. Check athletic facilities and equipment at least semi-monthly.
33. Monitor vehicle registration procedures.
34. Distribute budget request forms.

35. Meet with parent support groups for spring sports/ activities.

36. Attend Board of Education meeting.
37. Review all planning, control, and evaluation tools.

- UNIT SEVENTEEN -
March Work in the Form of Task Lists

PRINCIPAL'S MARCH TASKS IN INSTRUCTION

1. Review curr. flowchart for development of course work.
2. Review fourth marking period reports and watch for "trends."
3. Prepare position paper on program/personnel evalua-tion.
4. Construct field trip schedule for staff.
5. Conduct educational assembly program.

6. Emphasize Maxine Moore's work on the Perception Taxonomy at inservice meeting.
7. Design information bulletin material on individualizing programing.
8. Meet with curriculum review groups.
9. Meet with department representatives on budget review and design summer workshops.
10. Assign Guidance Department to review journal articles.

11. Review journal articles for staff.
12. Present report of Fine Arts Depts. at staff meetings.
13. Assign showcase to Fine Arts Departments.
14. Meet with BCC on resources in community/ univer-sities.
15. Continue observation of teachers.   .   1-03

16. Finish student class selections--preregistration for next year.
17. Computerize course selections.
18. Order material for commencement -- finalize all plans.

19. Monitor progress of seniors.
20. Send budget requests to the superintendent.

21. Review current budget for instructional materials.
22. Attend academic games, science fair, etc.
23. Plan for MEAP Recognition Day.
24. Review computer services for testing.
25. Plan parent-teacher conference program.

26. Prepare recommendations for textbook purchases.
27. Present microteaching critique to staff meeting.
28. Prepare for NHS induction.
29. Verify enrollment projections.
30. Finalize plans for summer school.

31. Prepare material to establish microteaching clinic.
32. Forward textbook evaluation comm. recommendations.
   2-05
33. Collect material on marking period IV from teachers.
34. Post both honor rolls.
35. Write self-evaluation regarding personal goals.

36. Write curriculum newsletter.   .   .   2-06
37. Meet with FAC on professional library, activity
       program, building committee reports.
38. Present material on a different teaching method.
39. Visit to monitor satellite programs.
40. Meet with directors of special and satellite programs.

41. Meet with conference period planning and study
       groups on program individualization.
42. Prepare position paper on student team learning.
43. Review SLC Vocabulary program report.   2-07
44. Serve on district-wide committees.
45. Monitor special and satellite programs

46. Review activity program in relation to instructional
       program.
47. Monitor adolescent suicide prevention program.2-06
48. Review "programs" for slow learners, middle group,
       and talented.

PRINCIPAL'S MARCH TASKS WITH STUDENTS

1. Attend student activities as listed on yearly calendar.
2. Meet with Policy, Activities, and Curriculum Advisory Committees.
3. Meet with all student presidents of activitiy groups.
4. Read information garnered from entrance/exit interviews.   2-05
5. Attend (when appropriate) all case conferences. 2-05

6. Verify student working permits.
7. Monitor substance abuse program.
8. Handle due process proceedings for student discipline.
9. Generate positive morale.
10. Verify athletic/activity eligibility of students.

11. Monitor student discipline program.
12. Attend student class organization meetings.
13. Initiate pre-enrollment process in feeder schools.
14. Verify scheduling of spring sports.
15. Attend winter sports banquet.

16. Arrange for physicals to be given for spring athletes.
17. Meet with new students.
18. Have Student(s) of the Month selected.
19. Monitor senior prom committee.
20. Verify the start of spring drivers training program-3rd session.

21. Orient new students and staff.
22. Students conduct entrance/exit interview questionnaires.   2-05
23. Monitor new student credentialling.
24. Verify senior credit standing for those in doubt of commencement.
25. Verify credits entered for driver training students.

26. Meet with counselors about kids with problems.

PRINCIPAL'S MARCH TASKS WITH STAFF

1. Hold staff meetings on Psychomotor domain, morale boost, district committee reports.
2. Meet with custodians regarding spring vacation schedule.
3. Send recommendations to superintendent for tenure/ probationary teachers.
4. Evaluate winter coaches and sports.
5. Finalize all evaluations for Board recommendations.

6. Interview to fill positions on the staff.
7. Select Teacher and Staff Member of the Month.
8. Recognize and support excellence.
9. Meet with spring coaches.
10. Meet with winter coaches.

11. Meet with nurse/social workers on students.
12. Review feedback tools used with staff.
13. Check for staff needs for next year.
14. Notify personnel department of potential openings for next year.
15. Evaluate the performance of winter coaches with students.

16. Post all openings on the staff.
17. Meet with Quality of Work Life Committee.
18. Meet weekly with Dietician/Hd Custodian/Off. Mgr.

MARCH TASKS IN COMMUNITY/SCHOOL RELATIONS

1. Publish monthly newsletter.
2. Provide information for press releases.
3. Attend community organization meetings.
4. Attend monthly PTA meeting.
5. Attend school planning committee meeting.

6. Meet with Chapter I/Article 3 advisory committees.2-04

7. Meet with vocational advisory committee reps.   2-04
8. Write monthly position paper on negativism in the community.
9. Invite a speaker from the community for the monthly assembly.
10. Publish honor rolls.   .   .   .   2-07

11. Check on production of video for orientation and recruitment.
12. Plan for displays of student work in county fairs, libraries, shopping malls.
13. Plan for and publish information on parent-teacher conferences.
14. Visit eighth, ninth grade classes, public and non-public, to discuss high school.
15. Work with committees in preparation for the June millage issue.

16. Meet with parents on Curriculum Review Committee.
17. Inform parents and students of spring recess dates.
18. Publish spring sports information and calendar.
19. Publicize upcoming special student programs--concerts, plays, fashion shows, and other means of recognizing students.
20. Invite church leaders and agency directors for coffee.

MARCH TASKS IN BUSINESS/BLDG. MGT.

1. Attend Board of Education meeting.
2. Attend principals' meeting held in the central office.
3. Supervise transportion, custodial, secretarial, and cafeteria programs.
4. Prepare weekly calendars for the month (distribute each Friday).
5. Monitor field trip arrangements.

6. Inform staff of new material and equipment received.
7. Control budget and internal accounts.
8. Review all planning, control, and evaluation tools.
9. Supervise cumulative records for health, testing, be-

havior, etc.
10. Supervise staff certification, transcripts, evaluations, observations, commendations, etc.

11. Prepare local, state, federal reports for: _____.
12. Interpret law and school policy.
13. Maintain adequate supply of materials.
14. Supervise selection of supplies/equipment/materials.
15. Order/invoice/inventory/control supplies/materials.

16. Supervise lunchrooms and noon hours.
17. Supervise student traffic on site.
18. Monitor school master schedules for summer and regular year.
19. Monitor sports/recognition programs.
20. Monitor community programs and facility use.

21. Implement fire/civil defense/inclement weather drills.
22. Check with custodial staff on building safety.   1-03
23. Inspect site and building monthly for needs in main tenance and safety.   .   .   .   1-03
24. Develop secretarial staff to meet needs of program.
25. Meet weekly with Dietician/Hd Custodian/Off. Mgr.

26. Develop spring recess work schedule for noninstruc-tional staff.
27. Follow-up suggestions made by staff.
28. Inspect equipment safety/boiler room/HVAC/labs.
29. Evaluate all grievances from each section of staff.
30. Inspect kitchen weekly.

31. Check safety and protection lighting.
32. Verify building and special room security provisions.
33. Check building and site for vandalism.
34. Verify room equipment is in proper repair.
35. Check athletic facilities and equipment at least semi-monthly.

36. Monitor vehicle registration procedures.
37. Prepare budget and forward to central office.
38. Meet with student treasurers for their work with ac-tivity funds.

39. Use impact statements to monitor new policies.

- UNIT EIGHTEEN -
-April Work in the Form of Task Lists

A continuation of the listings of the work to be done. This list is for the months of April, May, and June. All five areas of the principal's duties are included in this order: Instruction, Students, Staff, School/Community Relations, and Business/Building Man-agement.

PRINCIPAL'S APRIL TASKS IN INSTRUCTION

1. Prepare position paper on microteaching clinic.
2. Hold an educational assembly program.
3. Monitor homework policy implementation.
4. Meet with BCC on budget review and field trips.
5. Construct field trip schedule.

6. Assign the For. Lang. Department to review journals.
7. Meet with curriculum review groups.
8. Meet with department representatives on fall semester offerings and the faculty handbook for suggested revisions.
9. Prepare summary of journal articles.
10. Present report of Guidance Dept. at staff meetings.

11. Assign showcase to Guidance Department.
12. Continue observation of teachers.
13. Prepare first draft for commencement program for printer setting.
14. Evaluate participation in academic games.
15. Attend induction of NHS students.

16. End marking period V and collect material for marking grid.
17. Verify the credit standing of seniors.
18. Hold parent-teacher conferences.

19. Emphasize student team learning at inservice meeting.
20. Serve on district-wide committees.

21. Verify planning for honors assembly.
22. Plan for teacher turn-over for next year.
23. Attend MEAP recognition day.
24. Meet with conference, planning period study groups on observation, evaluation, and resources for learning (students & staff).
25. Attend Co-op Banquets.

26. Present a different teaching method at faculty meeting.
27. Order textbooks as recommended.
28. Write curriculum newsletter.
29. Meet with Faculty Advisory Committee on graduate offerings in the summer, activity program, and building committee reports.   .   .   2-07
30. Monitor special programs.

31. Monitor satellite programs.
32. Prepare material on CUSTODIAL role of the public schools.
33. Meet with directors of special and satellite programs.
34. Work toward design of fall master schedule of classes.
35. Review activity program in relation to instructional program.

36. Develop position paper on Program vs. Personnel Evaluation.
37. Monitor adolescent suicide prevention program.
38. Review "programs" for slow learners, middle group, and talented.

PRINCIPAL'S APRIL TASKS WITH STUDENTS

1. Attend student activities as listed on yearly calendar.
2. Meet with Policy, Activities, and Curriculum Advisory Committees.
3. Meet with all student presidents of activitiy groups.
4. Read information from entrance and exit interviews of

students.
5. Attend (when appropriate) all case conferences--or
   delegate.   2-05

6. Verify student working permits.
7. Monitor substance abuse program.
8. Handle due process proceedings for student discipline.
9. Generate positive morale.
10. Verify athletic/activity eligibility of students.

11. Monitor student discipline program.
12. Attend student class organization meetings.
13. Distribute Problem Census III forms. .   1-01
14. Complete orientation for new students and staff.
15. Finalize spring drivers' training program.

16. Hold annual elections for student council and class
    officers.
17. Meet with new panels of elected representatives for
    student council.
18. Meet with newly elected class officers.
19. Verify beginning of spring sports.
20. Monitor seniors in academic trouble.

21. Meet with new students.
22. Implement pre-enrollment from feeder schools.
23. Verify preparations for commencement.
24. Students continue to complete entrance/exit question-
    naires.   2-05
25. Post selection of the Student(s) of the Month.

26. Monitor new students' credentials.
27. Monitor senior prom committee.
28. Monitor graduate follow-up study design completion.
29. Notify parents of senior students who may not
    graduate.

PRINCIPAL'S APRIL TASKS WITH STAFF

1. Meet with Quality of Work-life Committee.

2. Survey for faculty sponsors for extra-curricular activities.
3. Make staff dismissal recommendations to central office.
4. Hold conferences with employees affected.
5. Conduct informal survey of staff plans for retiring.
6. Remember secretaries' week.
7. Review all coaching assignments for next year.
8. Submit list to central office for teachers to be on either tenure or continuing probationary status.
9. Select Teacher and Staff Member of the Month.
10. Recognize and support excellence.

11. Meet with spring coaches.
12. Hold staff meetings on perceptual domain, senior marking, and reports from district committees.
13. Meet with nurse/social worker regarding students with problems.
14. Meet weekly with Dietician/Hd Custodian/Off. Mgr.
15. Notify Personnel Department of potential staff openings for next year.

16. Post all positions of vacancies on the staff.
17. Interview to fill staff positions on the staff.

APRIL TASKS IN SCHOOL/COMMUNITY RELATIONS

1. Publish monthly newsletter.
2. Provide information for press releases.
3. Attend community organization meetings.
4. Attend monthly PTA meeting.
5. Attend school planning committee meeting.

6. Meet with Chapter I/Article 3 Advisory committees. 2-04
7. Meet with vocational advisory committee representatives. 2-04
8. Write position paper on Leaving the Word PUBLIC in Public Education.
9. Invite a speaker from the community for the monthly

assembly.
10. Verify students and staff are participating in the community and school spring clean up.

11. Verify which students and staff members are participating in the Easter Seal Walk-A-Thon.
12. Plan for and celebrate National Teacher Week.
13. Coordinate and visit eighth grade classes of public and non-public schools to recruit prospective students.
14. Make a slide/tape/video presentation of programs within the high school.
15. Publicize Board of Education millage issue.

16. Verify food basket collection for needy families.
17. Verify monthly speaker for a school-wide assembly.
18. Verify and publicize student field trips for Business, Industry, and Education Day.
19. Honor non-instructional staff at school.
20. Meet with Parent Curriculum Review Committee.

21. Publish honor rolls for students.
22. Mail mid-marking period failure notices to parents of students.

APRIL TASKS IN BUSINESS/BUILDING MGT.

1. Attend Board of Education meetings.
2. Attend principals' meeting at central office.
3. Supervise transportion, custodial, secretarial, and cafeteria programs.
4. Prepare weekly calendars for the month (distribute each Friday).
5. Monitor field trip arrangements.

6. Inform staff of new material and equipment received.
7. Control budget and internal accounts.
8. Review all planning, control, and evaluation tools.
9. Supervise cumulative records for health, testing, behavior, etc.
10. Supervise staff certification, transcripts, evaluations,

observations, commendations, etc.

11. Prepare local, state, federal reports for: _____.
12. Interpret law and school policy.
13. Maintain adequate supply of materials.
14. Supervise selection of supplies/equipment/materials.
15. Order/invoice/inventory/control supplies/materials.

16. Supervise lunchrooms and noon hours.
17. Supervise student traffic on site.
18. Monitor school master and time schedules regular year.
19. Monitor sports and recognition programs.
20. Monitor community programs and facility use.

21. Implement fire/civil defense/inclement weather drills.
22. Check with custodial staff on building safety.
23. Inspect site/building monthly for maintenance and
    cleanliness.
24. Develop secretarial staff to meet needs of program.
25. Review heating/utilities costs for year.

26. Follow up suggestions made by staff.
27. Inspect equipment safety/boiler room/HVAC/labs.
28. Evaluate all grievances from each section of staff.
29. Inspect kitchen weekly.
30. Check safety and protection lighting.

31. Verify building and special room security provisions.
32. Check for vandalism.
33. Meet weekly with Dietician/Hd Custodian/Off. Mgr.
34. Verify room equipment is in proper repair.
35. Check athletic facilities and equipment at least semi-
    monthly.

36. Monitor vehicle registration procedures.

- UNIT NINETEEN -
May Work in the Form of Task Lists

PRINCIPAL'S MAY TASKS IN INSTRUCTION

1. Prepare position paper on Don Stewart's work on student evaluation.
2. Review fifth marking period's reports for "trends" by teachers.
3. Initiate development of form to collect information for end-of-year.
4. Construct field trip schedule.
5. Meet with BCC for fall semester preparation.

6. Finalize study groups' reports.
7. Make all faculty aware of retention policies.
8. Initiate evaluation of special instructional presentation modes.
9. Initiate evaluation of pilot programs.
10. Evaluate productivity of master schedule for current year.

11. Monitor senior progress - BEGIN TO CALL PARENTS OF DOUBTFUL GRADS.
12. Prepare revised graduation list for June - VERIFIED BY GUIDANCE DEPARTMENT.
13. Finalize commencement program.
14. Finalize preparation for Honors Assembly.
15. Appoint student leadership forum planning committee for next year.

16. Prepare for staff recognition program.
17. Monitor team learning program.
18. Finalize orders for all equipment and supplies for next year.
19. Meet with curriculum review groups.
20. Meet with department representatives.

21. Prepare review of journal articles.
22. Assign report of Foreign Language Department at staff

meetings.

23. Assign showcase to Foreign Language Department.
24. Finalize observation of teachers.
25. Assign Practical Arts Department to review journals for staff.

26. Distribute teacher assignments and load for next year
    for teacher assessment of program with first DTLF.
27. Present new teaching method at faculty meeting.
28. Prepare second DTLF for fall semester.
29. Finalize plans for summer school offerings and
    registration.
30. Write curriculum newsletter.   .   .   2-06

31. Monitor satellite programs.
32. Meet with directors of special and satellite programs.
33. Meet with Faculty Advisory Committee on summer
    school plans, activity program, and building com-
    mittee reports.
34. Meet with curriculum review committees.
35. Monitor special programs.

36. Emphasize microteaching clinic at inservice program.
37. Post honor rolls.
38. Meet with conference, planning period study groups on
    STAMP, and utilizing the facility better next year.
39. Distribute form to collect Survival, Literacy, Com-
    petence Vocabulary data.   .   .   2-07
40. Conduct educational assembly program.

41. Continue to work on fall master schedule.
42. Serve on district-wide committees.
43. Review activity program in relation to instructional
    program.
44. Monitor adolescent suicide prevention program.
45. Review "programs" for slow learners, middle group,
    and talented.

PRINCIPAL'S MAY TASKS WITH STUDENTS

1. Attend student activities as listed on yearly calendar.
2. Meet with Policy, Activities, and Curriculum Advisory Committees.
3. Meet with all student presidents of activitiy groups.
4. Read information from entrance and exit interviews of students.
5. Attend (when appropriate) all case conferences--or delegate.   2-05

6. Meet with student committee to update the student handbook.
7. Students continue to complete entrance/exit question- naires.   2-05
8. Orient new students and staff.
9. Verify student working permits.
10. Monitor substance abuse program.

11. Handle due process proceedings for student discipline.
12. Generate positive morale.
13. Verify athletic/activity eligibility of students.
14. Monitor student discipline program.
15. Attend student class organization meetings.

16. Send graduate survey forms to printer.
17. Attend spring sports banquet.
18. Finalize commencement activities.
19. Monitor senior activities.
20. Verify honors graduates.

21. Collect cards for Problem Census III.
22. Evaluate responses to Problem Census Survey III.
23. Present to staff the data from Problem Census III.
24. Meet with counselors about kids with problems.
25. Verify plans for summer drivers training program, 4th session.

26. Meet with new students.
27. Post choices for Students of the Month.
28. Review attendance policy with students.

29. Monitor new student credentials.
30. Verify student credit standing of seniors in difficulty.

31. Conclude spring driver training program.
32. Have student body evaluate faculty.
33. Finalize senior class ranking.
34. Finalize senior prom committee work.

PRINCIPAL'S MAY TASKS WITH STAFF

1. Assign extra-curricular activities for next year.
2. Compile tentative teaching assignments.
3. Assist with teacher transfers.
4. Make recommendations for promotions.
5. Plan end of year party.

6. Do problem census and FFA for the year.   1-01
7. Meet with counselors regarding exceptional kids'
    performance.
8. Interview to fill vacancies on the staff.
9. Select Teacher and Staff Member of the Month.
10. Recognize and support excellence.

11. Meet weekly with Dietician/Hd Custodian/Off. Mgr.
12. Meet with Quality of Work Life Committee.
13. Meet with spring coaches.
14. Hold staff meetings on team learning, Problem Census
    III, district committee reports.
15. Post all known vacancies on the staff.

16. Meet with nurse and social worker for students with
    problems.
17. Notify personnel department of potential vacancies for
    next year.

MAY TASKS IN SCHOOL/COMMUNITY RELATIONS

1. Publish monthly newsletter.

2. Provide information for press releases.
3. Attend community organization meetings.
4. Attend monthly PTA meeting.
5. Attend school planning committee meeting.

6. Meet with Chapter I/Article 3 advisory committees. .
     2-04
7. Meet with vocational advisory committee reps.   2-04
8. Write position paper on "Building Links with Business
   and Industry."
9. Invite a speaker from the community for the monthly
   assembly.
10. Verify plans for staff and student participation in the
    American Red Cross Blood Drive.
11. Invite members of American Bar Association to school
    for Law Day (May 1st).
12. Organize assembly for Alumni Recognition Day
    (night).
13. Plan for and celebrate National Secretaries' Day/
    Week.
14. Send mid-marking period failure reports to parents.
15. Plan, publicize, and attend the honors program.

16. Plan, publicize, and attend an athletic awards program.
17. Promote Ethnic Festival Day.
18. Recognize and thank community volunteers and sup-
    port people.
19. Recruit community members and business persons for
    Project Graduation.
20. Encourage seniors to join the WDIV (TV Channel 4)[1]
    and get others to pledge not to drink on prom night.

21. Write a congratulatory letter to class valedictorian, top
    ten, salutatorian, and appointments to armed forces
    academies.
22. Verify and publicize seniors who became registered
voters.
23. Publicize and celebrate Michigan Week.
24. Invite church leaders into building for summer
    program review.
25. Recruit chaperones for the prom.
    [1] = a major, local TV station (Detroit, MI area)

MAY TASKS IN BUSINESS/BUILDING MGT.

1. Supervise transportion, custodial, secretarial, and cafeteria programs.
2. Prepare weekly calendars for the month (distribute each Friday).
3. Monitor field trip arrangements.
4. Inform staff of new material and equipment received.
5. Control budget and internal accounts.

6. Supervise cumulative records for health, testing, behavior.
7. Supervise staff certification, transcripts, evaluations, observations, commendations, etc.
8. Prepare local, state, federal reports for: _____.
9. Interpret law and school policy.
10. Maintain adequate supply of materials.

11. Supervise selection of supplies/equipment/materials.
12. Order/invoice/inventory/control supplies/materials.
13. Supervise lunchrooms and noon hours.
14. Supervise student traffic on site.
15. Monitor school master and time schedules.

16. Monitor sports and recognition programs.
17. Monitor community programs and facility use.
18. Implement fire/civil defense/inclement weather drills.
19. Check with custodial staff on building safety.   1-03
20. Inspect site/building for needs in maintenance and cleanliness.

21. Develop secretarial staff to meet needs of program.
22. Monitor policy initiation with impact statements.
23. Follow up suggestions made by staff.
24. Inspect equipment safety/boiler room/HVAC/labs.
      1-03
25. Evaluate all grievances from each section of staff.

26. Inspect kitchen weekly.

27. Check safety and protection lighting.
28. Verify building and special room security provisions.. 1-03
29. Check building and site for vandalism.
30. Attend principals' meeting at central office.

31. Verify room equipment is in proper repair.   1-03
32. Check athletic facilities and equipment at least semi-monthly.
33. Monitor vehicle registration procedures.
34. Act on all budget requests.
35. Organize orders for annual supplies, materials and equipment.

36. Estimate funds needed for library enrichment.
37. Develop summer recess work schedule.
38. Review needs for grounds keeper.
39. Meet with teacher aides to see what they need for next year.
40. Attend Board of Education meeting.

41. Review all planning, control, and evaluation tools.
42. Verify with City Clerk regarding voting machine use for building elections and use by the precinct personnel.
43. Meet weekly with Dietician/Hd Custodian/Off. Mgr.

- UNIT TWENTY -
June Work in the Form of Task Lists

PRINCIPAL'S JUNE TASKS IN INSTRUCTION

1. Prepare position paper on Epstein's brain growth patterns for faculty to use with incoming freshmen this fall.
2. Monitor homework policy implementation.
3. Distribute Problem Census material for staff, student input.
4. Meet with BCC on teacher evaluation and staffing program individualization.
5. Prepare final report on sixth marking period/compare

with first five marking periods for final report to superintendent.

6. Distribute closing-out school blanks for staff.
7. Collect Year-End Reports from each staff member.
8. Review teacher observation form with faculty for possible corrections.   .   .   .   1-03
9. Update field trip procedure and card file.
10. Meet with curriculum review groups.

11. Meet with department representatives on staffing.
12. Review journal articles.
13. Present report of Practical Arts Dept at staff meeting.
14. Assign showcase to Practical Arts Department.
15. Review Survival, Literacy, Competency Vocabulary program.   2-07

16. Construct field trip schedule for month.
17. Report to faculty on all student marks given to date.
18. Hold commencement program.
19. Prepare book inventory.
20. Post both honor rolls.

21. Emphasize Don Stewart's work in faculty meeting.
22. Work with librarian for inventory of library resources.
23. Send books for rebinding.
24. Publish student achievement reports.
25. Supervise the closing of school. (see form in Exhibits)

26. Evaluate teacher-led workshops.
27. Evaluate all in-services.
28. Develop instructional goals for next year to review with faculty.
29. Implement summer school programs.
30. Write applications for grant program continuance and initiation.

31. Collect textbook evaluation forms.
32. Prepare annual report for the Board of Education.
33. Plan a VACATION.
34. Write curriculum newsletters.
35. Initiate summer school.

36. Meet with study groups.
37. Monitor satellite program culmination.
38. Meet with directors of special and satellite programs.
39. Assign journal review to librarians.
40. Request achievement/ability study composite information.

41. Construct field trip schedule for next school year.
42. Monitor special programs.
43. Meet with special program directors.
44. Meet with Faculty Advisory Committee on end of year procedures, activity program, and building committee reports.
45. Initiate summer school driver training program.

46. Present new teaching method at faculty meeting.
47. Conduct educational assembly program.
48. "Finalize" fall master schedule.
49. Serve on district-wide committees.
50. Review activity program in relation to instructional program.

51. Monitor adolescent suicide prevention program.2-06
52. Review "programs" for slow learners, middle group, and talented.

PRINCIPAL'S JUNE TASKS WITH STUDENTS

1. Pull files for summer school enrollees.
2. Prepare survey for student activities wanted for next year.
3. Select orientation team for fall semester.
4. Students complete entrance/exit questionnaires. 2-05
5. Discuss incoming class - generally - with counselors.

6. Collect and discuss student discipline summary with assistants.
7. Attend student activities as listed on yearly calendar.
8. Meet with Policy, Activities, and Curriculum Advisory

Committees.
9. Meet with all student presidents of activitiy groups.
10. Read information from entrance and exit interviews of students.

11. Attend (when appropriate) all case conferences.2-05
12. Verify student working permits.
13. Monitor substance abuse program.
14. Handle due process proceedings for student discipline.
15. Generate positive morale.

16. Verify eligibility for activities/athletics.
17. Monitor student discipline program.
18. Attend student organization meetings.
19. Compile staff evaluations by students.
20. Prepare closing school ceremony and say good-bye to student body.

21. Invite all available incoming students to attend classes for the program, "High School for a Day."
22. Mail final report cards with inclusion of their honor rolls.
23. Orient all new students and staff.
24. Attend and oversee commencement program.
25. Prepare for the "care and feeding" of dignitaries for commencement.

26. Oversee student record care for all students.
27. Write college and job recommendations.
28. Guide new student government's first meeting.
29. Verify accuracy of student attendance records.
30. Evaluate student morale.

31. Recognition of exceptional student behavior.
32. Meet with students to plan next year's substance abuse program.
33. Verify the start of the summer drivers training program.
34. Prepare for and attend spring sports banquet.
35. Post Students of the Month.

36. Plan Yearbook/Camera dance for the fall.

37. Attend Prom.
38. Distribute graduate survey forms with a response date of July 30.
39. Meet with all new students.
40. Monitor new students' credentials.

PRINCIPAL'S JUNE TASKS WITH STAFF

1. Meet with Quality of Work Life Committee.
2. Hold staff meetings on microteaching clinics, end of year procedures, district committee reports.
3. Select next year's BCC.
4. Select next year's department representatives.
5. Meet weekly with Dietician/Hd Custodian/Off. Mgr.

6. Plan inservice programs by reviewing evaluations and year-end reports.
7. Finalize teaching/coaching/activity assignments.
8. Meet with custodial staff to review summer plans.
9. Collect summer addresses of staff from Year-end Report.
10. Prepare staff activity duty calendar and teacher load.

11. Develop a list of housing contacts for new faculty and staff.
12. Review faculty handbook based upon Year-End report suggestions.
13. Verify certification for fall semester.
14. Check credentials to assure teachers are certifiable for next year's class schedule.
15. Interview to fill positions on the staff.

16. Recruit new teacher aides and paraprofessionals.
17. Verify certification and regional accrediting records.
18. Plan orientation for next fall.   .   .   3-10
19. Select Teacher of the Month and Staff Member of the Month.
20. Recognize and support excellence.

21. Meet with fall coaches to verify safety of all equipment

on hand.
22. Check with needs for staff for next fall.
23. Determine faculty who will be available for interviewing candidates during summer recess.
24. Evaluate spring coaches.
25. Post notice of all vacancies on the staff.

26. Notify personnel department of known needs.
27. Meet with nurse / social worker on students with problems and program for their care over the summer

JUNE TASKS IN SCHOOL/COMMUNITY RELATIONS

1. Publish monthly newsletter.
2. Provide information for press releases.
3. Attend community organization meetings.
4. Attend monthly PTA meeting.
5. Attend school planning committee meeting.

6. Meet with Chapter I/Article 3 Advisory comms. 2-04
7. Meet with vocational advisory committee reps. 2-04
8. Write position paper on "School-community Relations" during vacation.
9. Publicize the school's alumni association.
10. Get nominations for speakers from the community for next year's assembly program.

11. Receive report from the local school's public/ community relations committee.
12. Compile a directory of key contacts in the news media.
13. Evaluate total public relations program for the year.
14. Write thank you letters to millage election workers.
15. Publicize the rise in students' scores on standardized achievement tests.

16. Publish honor rolls and attendance awards.
17. Write thank you letters to prom night chaperones.
18. Honor retiring staff members.
19. Publish summer school and registration information.

20. Publicize summer recreational and scholastic programs.

JUNE TASKS IN BUSINESS/BUILDING MGT.

1. Review all groups' accounting books.
2. Verify and compare price of ordered items.
3. Determine text/rebinding costs.
4. Review and evaluate repairs on facility and equipment.
5. Order new curriculum material.

6. Order staff printing needs.
7. Inventory office supplies.
8. Order additional student supplies.
9. Review accounting procedures in building.
10. Examine for care and storage of dangerous chemicals.

11. Meet with Athletic Director to arrange for the giving of athletes' physicals for fall sports.
12. Take final inventory of building supplies/order.
13. Monitor field trip program changes by Transportation Dept.
14. Review all planning, control, and evaluation tools.2-05
15. Attend principals' meetings in central office.

16. Control budget and internal accounts.
17. Prepare monthly calendars for next year's program to mail to staff for consideration this next month.
18. Monitor transportion, custodial, secretarial, and cafeteria programs.
19. Prepare weekly calendars for the month (distribute each Friday)
20. Monitor field trip arrangements.

21. Inform staff of new material and equipment received.
22. Attend Board of Education Meeting.
23. Review needs for grounds keeper.
24. Supervise cumulative records for health, testing, behavior.
25. Supervise staff certification, transcripts, evaluations, observations, commendations, etc.

26. Prepare local, state, federal reports for: _____.
27. Interpret law and school policy.
28. Maintain adequate supply of materials.
29. Supervise selection of supplies/equipment/materials.
30. Order/invoice/inventory/control supplies/materials.

31. Supervise lunchrooms and noon hours.
32. Supervise student traffic on site.
33. Monitor school master and time schedules summer.
34. Monitor sports and recognition programs.
35. Monitor community programs and facility use.

36. Verify fire/civil defense/inclement weather drills have been held to meet state and local laws and guidelines.
37. Check with custodial staff on building safety.   1-03
38. Inspect site/building for needs in maintenance and cleanliness.
39. Develop secretarial staff to meet needs of program.
40. Follow up suggestions made by staff.

41. Inspect equipment safety/boiler room/HVAC/labs.
42. Evaluate all grievances from each section of staff.
43. Inspect kitchen weekly.
44. Check safety and protection lighting.
45. Verify building and special room security provisions.

46. Check for vandalism in building and on site.
47. Verify room equipment is in proper repair.
48. Check athletic facilities and equipment at least semi-monthly.
49. Monitor vehicle registration procedures.
50. Act on all budget requests.

51. Organize orders for annual supplies, materials and equipment.
52. Estimate funds needed for library enrichment.
53. Develop summer recess work schedule.
54. Monitor policy implementation with impact statements.
55. Meet weekly with Dietician/Hd Custodian/Off. Mgr.

Some summary grids or charts are provided so that the entire year can be posted more easily. The recommended tasks are NOT carved in stone nor will any of the following data. It behooves the principal to use the following to design his/her package for the year.

	Bldg. Curr. Comm.	Dept. Heads (Reps.)
July	Set goals for instruction Curriculum Review	all discussions are made in the context of 3 levels
Aug.	Review Achievement/ Ability Study from prior year	Role in total program Facilities and Material
Sept.	Studies in Progress AND Blue Cards for suicide prevention	Text evaluation / 4 Domain Grid / Start-up concerns
Oct.	Research in field and trends	Student Marking / Team Learning / 4 Domain Grid
Nov.	Student marking / Emergent Curriculum	Spring sem. offer-ings. Faculty Hdbk.
Dec. pact	Spring semester prep. Field trips	SLC Vocabulary 4 domain grid work
Jan.	SLC Vocabulary impact Internal/external testing program	Fog/Smog/Flesch work New courses? 4 domain grid work
Feb.	Mat'l. acquisition in levels continued	Community & Advisory committees' reports
Mar.	Resources in both the community & univer-sities	Budget review for submission - Summer workshops
Apr.	Budget review / Field	Fall sem. offerings

	trips' purposes	Faculty handbook
May	Fall semester prep.	Year-end preparation Individualized Progs.
June	Teacher evaluation /	Staffing for next year's program

Inservice staff mtgs.   Conference Pd. Planning

	Inservice staff mtgs.	Conference Pd. Planning
July		These teams can work in several phases of the program in the
Aug.	Bloom's Taxonomy Cognitive	building. The following lists can be the ones to choose
Sept.	Learning Styles	and there are several others.
Oct.	Flanders/Grant/ Hennings	5 Curriculum areas
Nov.	Allen's material – microteaching schools	Roles of public schools
Dec.	Leslie Hart's – David Begg's materials	Student contacts – marking – Maslow – Hart – discipline –
Jan.	Krathwohl's Taxonomy Affective	Learning styles – Epstein
Feb.	Simpson's Taxonomy Psychomotor	Teaching methods – and there are 39
Mar.	Moore's Taxonomy Perception	Individualization Resource gathering
Apr.	Team Learning	Observations/ evaluations
May	Microteaching clinic	Accountability STAMP

	put into operation	Facilities improved
June	Stewart's material on effectiveness	Many of the other items discussed here

Regular staff mtgs.   Faculty Advisory Council[1]

	Regular staff mtgs.	Faculty Advisory Council
July		Building Handbooks Student activities
Aug.	Maslow's Hierarchy	Standard operating procedures/Activities
Sept.	Substance Abuse Prog. Bloom – Cognition Explain ALL programs Rev. observation/Eval	Bite and Gripe Bkfst. Activity Program Bldg. comm. reports
Oct.	Student marking – Honor rolls/Studies in progress/District committee reports	Progressive honor roll/Learning Styles Bldg. comm. reports
Nov.	Flanders/Grant and Hennings/Stewart's material on marking Students present PCI data/Senior marking practices/Dist. committee reports	List of teaching methods/Activiey program/Bldg. comm. reports
Dec.	Allen's Microteaching Emergent curriculum Dist. comm. reports	Budget for this/next year/Activiey program Bldg. comm. reports
Jan.	Hart's Proster Theory SLC Vocabulary Dist. comm. reports	Program as scheduled Activity program Bldg. comm. reports
Feb.	Simon's Participation Hypothesis/Affective	Resources for staff Activity program

437

	Domain/Students presents PCII data Dist. comm. reports	Bldg. comm. reports
Mar.	Psychomotor Domain Morale booster time!! Dist. comm. reports	Professional library Activity program Bldg. comm. reports
Apr.	Perceptual Domain Senior marking prac- Dist. comm. reports	Graduate work in summer/Activity program Bldg. comm. reports
May	Team Learning Students present PC III data/District committee reports	Summer school plans Activity program Bldg. comm. reports
June	Microteaching Clinic End of yr. procedures Dist. comm. reports	End of year procedures/Activities Bldg. comm. reports

Departmental Assignments for Faculty

	Journals' Rev.[1] by Depts --Handout at staff mtg.	Staff Mtg. Dept. Report[2]	Display Case Ex- hibits
Sept.	English	Library	Library
Oct.	Science	English	English
Nov.	Math	Science	Science
Dec.	Soc. Sci.	Math.	Mathematics
Jan.	Physical and athletics	Social studies	Social Studies
Feb.	Fine Arts	Phys. Ed. & sports	Phys. Ed. and sports

438

Mar.	Guidance	Fine Arts	Fine Arts
Apr.	Foreign	Guidance	Guidance
May	Practical Arts	For. Lang.	For. Language
June	Library	Practical Arts and	Practical Arts Drivers Ed.

[1]for the following journals. Put the list in here that the high subscribes to for its professional library. They might be from the following selected journals for high school staffs.

Clearing House
The Instructor
Phi Delta Kappan
Learning
Educational Leadership
High School Journal
Learning Styles Network
Departmental journals
Theory Into Practice
Professional Association journals from NEA/AFT
School Review
Fastbacks from P. D. K.
Journal of Res. & Dev't

[2]emphasis on SPICS/ 5-M's/Planning/Stu-Community Relations/ Honor Students/ Courses offered, and Things in the works

Journals referenced are the material for the administration to review monthly. They may be from the list below:

The Bulletin
St. Assoc. of Principals
Executive Educator
Rev. of Educ'l. Research
The Administrator
Amer.Sch.Bd.Journal
Educ'l Admin. Abstracts
Educ'l Admin. Quarterly
PCM (computer journal - general)

In the table on the next page, the meeting topics with the Head custodian, Office Manager, and Dietician are high-lighted as suggestions to fit into the principal's year. The second column is the listing of suggested position papers' topics. They are marked as columns A and B, respectively.

	A[1]	B
July	Summer schedules	Individualized Programming
Aug.	School readiness	Learning Styles
Sept.	Start-up frustra-tions	Study Groups' Relationship
Oct.	Safety for fall and winter	How to talk to reporters Allen's Microteaching
Nov.	Holiday schedules and staffing	Leslie Hart's Proster Theory/Student concentra-tion length
Dec.	Intrastaff coop.	Affective Domain Use Community and Interviews
Jan.	Schedule changes for 2nd sem.	Psychomotor Domain Uses of Cable T. V.
Feb.	Policy Manual re-view	Perception Domain The Use of Issue Papers
Mar.	Budget review present & next year's	Personnel-Prog. evaluation Negativism in the community
Apr.	Scheduling Pro-cess and team's involvement	Microteaching Clinicians PUBLIC in Public Educa-tion
May	Staff handbook changes	Don Stewart's Marking Program Building links with business and industry
June	Schedules for fall semester	Herman Epstein's Findings School-Community Relations

[1] The topics which can be listed for each month's meeting with these staff heads might include some or all of the following:

Exceptionalities, Attendance/Memberships, Staff Concerns, Glitches-Gnomes-Gremlins, Material-Resources, School Conflicts, Programming, Problem Census results and an item called FOR THE GOOD OF THE ORDER.

- UNIT 21 -
End of Year Preparation

The second most important set of tasks the effective principal has to perform is the proper closing of the school year. If the orientation was and has been conducted properly, the closing procedures will go much more routinely and easily. Be that as it may, the principal must now get all things put into line for the next year. As such s/he will have to collect the appropriate information and material from the current year's operation so it will be assistive when next year is launched. A good orientation will be the backbone of a good closing. If both the opening and closing are done well, next year will be even better than the current one -- the goal of all good principals.

There were several sets of material that were distributed in September. Collecting it can be routine. Hopefully, the Tickler Bucket information is at hand after having all reminders and material placed in May's bucket. If this was not done, go to the files and retrieve the pertinent information from separate folders or from both the August and September buckets so the closing can be done properly.

To compile information for a summation of the year's activities, the principal should have made notes from lesson plans, papers that were presented, classroom observations, and committees. Here is a form to follow to collect information. The lines are not drawn on which to supply the answers as an effort to save space. The items about which information is needed are written for the

441

department members to follow to provide valuable and descriptive facts. When compiled from each department, the year-end report will come together rather nicely.

================================

FORM A - D E P A R T M E N T S

DEPARTMENT_____ DATE:__/__/__.

1. List the names of the students recognized throughout the school year as being EXCEPTIONAL by the department's faculty.

2. State the goals of the department and discuss what occured when they were exceeded by the advanced students.

3. Explain the new techniques of instruction employed in the department.

4. Itemize the community resources (material and personnel) used by the teachers in the department this year.

5. What do teachers feel are the strengths of the department?

6. What do teachers feel are the weaknesses of the department?

7. List recommendations on the attached recommendation form so that the department may continue to become better and improve upon the strengths identified above.

8. List below what departmental faculty members feel are means to inhibit and discontinue the weaknesses stated above.

9. List the specific studies completed by the department.

10. List and identify the use of all resources needed to do an improved job in the department next year. (Separate those already ordered and approved and others on the Unmet Needs List).

11. In an attempt to strengthen the administration and management of the operation, please identify what policies, practices, procedures, and/or planning influenced the department (both positively and negatively) for this past year.

12. Examine the "finalized" master schedule. Be specific specific in writing those complications and problems the department still perceives are built in for next year for departmental faculty.

13. Based upon the names already listed as enrollees for the summer school program, what implications do they have for the department?

= =

FORM B - I N D I V I D U A L T E A C H E R

NAME: _____

As a (full)(part) time teacher here this year, . . .I

1. introduced the following new techniques, methodologies, and practices in instruction:

2. used these major visual aids (names of films, filmstrips, diskettes, recordings, tapes, videos, etc.):

3. made use of these resources (people, places, things) (A) from my community of residence and (B) from the school's community:

4. tried out these varied home assignment projects:

5. helped to identify these exceptional children (names of the students and their special abilities) so they could receive further attention, as noted:

6. had serious disciplinary problems as follows (name of the student, nature of the problem, and the resolution):

7. feel my disciplinary problems probably arose because:

8. can look back and recall these teaching activities with pride:

9. attended case conferences for the following students:

10. feel I can strengthen my units by making the following changes with the material and equipment already requested for next year:

11. feel I can further strengthen my teaching with the following assistance from the (A) administration and (B) fellow teachers next year:

12. served on the following committees in the building:

13. served on the following committees in the district:

14. served on the following committees in the teachers' association:

15. took part in the following community activities:

16. took part in the following school activities, (A) for pay and (B) without pay:

17. volunteered for the following activity program sponsorship for next year:

18. was assigned to these following activity program components:

19. made these suggestions for improving procedures in school operations (other than the classroom):

20. would make the following changes in the administrative routine to strength instruction if I were in administration:

21. contributed the following material to professional magazines and bulletins: (Attach a copy whether or not it was accepted.)

22. engaged in the following research projects (A) for graduate courses, (B) purely for improvement of the school:

23. read these professional resources and used the information in my classroom instruction: The reference is (not) in the professional library of the school. Be specific in the reference:

24. attended these professional clinics, conferences, conventions, meetings, etc.:

25. completed the following graduate courses this year (where and what, # hours of work completed and professor's name):

26. completed the following degree (or will have by the end of the summer session):

27. now meet the regional accreditation standards to teach:

28. visited the following classrooms, schools, colleges, industries, businesses, and agencies to strengthen classroom teaching or assist others to improve upon their skills:

29. used _____ as an observational dyad:

30. completed the following microteaching clinics this past year:

31. took classes on the following field trips:

32. will be involved in the following professional activities this summer:

33. would suggest the following additions (changes?) to the faculty handbook for next year:

34. would suggest the following topics to be discussed within the student Curriculum, Activities, and Policy committees next year:

35. feel next year's program can be improved in the area of student-staff relations by:

36. feel the Faculty Advisory Committee can be strengthened by:

37. feel the Principal's Community Advisory Committee can be improved by:

38. feel the staff meetings can be improved, generally, by the following:

39. have listed the textbooks (and other printed sources) I used. Each shows its own readability level as prescribed in the Faculty Handbook. I used the noted formula: SMOG/FOG.

40. would like to add the following to this information so the principal can use it to improve upon the school's goal to make the school a true House of Intellect:

41. know you can count on me for the following next year:

Staff Curriculum Study Group _____
Student Study Committee (Sponsor) _____
Student teacher for direction ___ 1st sem. ____ 2nd sem.
Activity Club Sponsor for _____
Coach of the following sport(s) _____
Faculty Membership on the Athletic Council _____

_____ ____
_____ ____
_____ ____
_____ ____
_____ ____

Here is a checklist of things for teachers to turn into the office. Each school will add different items to this list. The list here is for the routine issuance at orientation.

1. Report Cards (Mark-sensed, or whatever), date, time and location

2. Attendance Reports for the year, semester, and marking period

3. Student Profile Sheets for the Guidance Department summary

4. Field Trip Summary Reports verified as turned-in

5. Conference Attendance Follow-up Sheet for application in teaching

6. Homeroom Teacher Cumulative folders for each student

7. Activity Sponsor Cumulative folders for each participant

8. Inventory Verification Card *

9. Financial records for classes, activities, and others

10. Examination copies verified with Office Manager as being on file

11. Summer Address

12. Library check-out of professional material and class room sets

13. Resource Center - Card of A.V. equipment checked out

14. Cap, Hood, and Gown from Commencement

15. Room secured for the summer

16. Questionnaires

17. Departmental Questionnaire from Department Rep.

18. Inventory Card -- may list the following (or something similar)

Scissors	Stapler	Keys for Bldg.	Dispensers
Textbook	Handbook	Grade Books	Attendance
Inventory List			Books

THE PRINCIPAL MAY WISH TO ADD TO THIS AS NECESSARY.

= =

The closing of the year is important. All students and staff members ought to feel good about the year just ended. The best way to do this is to be available, be responsive, and be helpful with each question of the many which are bound to come about. The object is to encourage all concerned to want to come back.

The expectations on the principal's time by the central cadre will cause some concern on the part of the building administration. However, with the proper preparation, the principal can be ready to meet the challenge. There is no reason to hide in a closet to get the required work done. *It is vital to conclude the year properly with the staff.* The principal may well have to work before the school opens and long after the students and teachers leave the building. There is no reason to have to take a "grief" case home -- especially at this time of the year. There is another day! Time must be used well and with some sort of plan. Plan your work, and work your plan.

EXHIBITS

Some Additional Assistance

Material for reference when using this text

- THREE TIME CLASSROOM OBSERVATION FORM -

```
Date:__ /__ /___Teacher:_____Subject:_____
Observer:_____ Topic presented:_____
Times: in ___:___ out___:___ Gr. level_____
Years' experience _____ in bldg._____
Observation #s__1_            ____
            current,   total while in bldg.
College Major:_____ Minors: _____ /_____
```

I. PRE-OBSERVATION CONFERENCE TOPICS:
A. Definitions of words to be used in observation
   and summary.
B. Objectives to be covered by the teacher.
C. Expectations to be observed -- from last obser-
   vation.
D. Role of Observer in the class (front and rear
   of the room)
E. Teacher input for the observer to take note of
   in observation
F. Checklist for skills to be taught.
G. Formation of needs groups
H. Teacher Preparation/Preplanning/Organization of
   lesson
I. Theories of Learning to be emphasized
J. Principles of Teaching to be used
K. Child Growth and Development exceptions for
   awareness
L. Sociology of the classroom
II. INITIAL OBSERVATION INFORMATION

A. STUDENT ENTRANCE TO ROOM:

1. Teacher's Reactions		2. Students' Reactions	
pleasant	_____	eager	_____
positive	_____	positive	_____
encouraging	_____	pleasant	_____
friendly	_____	orderly	_____
indifferent	_____	tardinesses	_____
negative	_____	negative	_____
punctual	_____	sullen	_____

Comments:_____

_____
_____
_____
_____
_____
_____
_____
_____
_____
_____
_____
_____
_____
_____
_____
_____
_____

B. VARIABLES
1. CONTROLLED: 2. UNCONTROLLED:

Safe Environment_____ Temp. _____
Day: M   T   W   T   F Air Movement_____
Weather _____Drafts in room_____
Nearest Holiday_____Glare in room_____
Interruptions_____Adjusted Furniture_____
Membership # _____Seat Arrangement_____
Attendance # _____Student Work shown_____
Date w/in Unit _____Grouping practices_____
Period of the Day _____Lighting _____
Unsafe Situations_____Visible Resources_____
Intercom Usage_____Orderliness of rm_____
Marking Period # _____Lighting w/ A.V. _____
Clrm. Eq't. Working_____Overall tone _____
Lesson Plans_____

_____
_____
_____
_____
_____
_____
_____

Comments on Variables: _____

_____
_____
_____
_____
_____
_____
_____
_____
_____
_____
_____

- Second CLASSROOM OBSERVATION COVER, 19___/____ -

Date:__ /__ /___Teacher:_____Subject:_____
Observer:_____ Topic presented:_____
Times: in ___:___ out___:___ Gr. level_____
Years' experience _____ in bldg._____
Observation #s__2_   ____
              current,   total while in bldg.
College Major:_____ Minors: _____ /_____

I. <u>PRE-OBSERVATION CONFERENCE TOPICS</u>:
A. Definitions of words to be used in observation
    and summary.
B. Objectives to be covered by the teacher.
C. Expectations to be observed -- from last obser-
    vation.
D. Role of Observer in the class (front and rear
    of the room)
E. Teacher input for the observer to take note of
    in observation
F. Checklist for skills to be taught.
G. Formation of needs groups
H. Teacher Preparation/Preplanning/Organization of
    lesson
I. Theories of Learning to be emphasized
J. Principles of Teaching to be used
K. Child Growth and Development exceptions for
    awareness
L. Sociology of the classroom

452

II. <u>INITIAL OBSERVATION INFORMATION</u>
     second visit
A. STUDENT ENTRANCE TO ROOM:
   1. Teacher's Reactions   2. Students' Reactions
      pleasant _____   eager _____
      positive _____   positive _____
      encouraging_____   pleasant _____
      friendly _____   orderly _____
      indifferent_____   tardinesses _____
      negative _____   negative _____
      punctual _____   sullen _____

Comments:_____
_____
_____
_____
_____
_____
_____
_____
_____
_____
_____
_____
_____
_____
_____
_____
_____

B. VARIABLES - second visit
1. CONTROLLED: 2. UNCONTROLLED:

Safe Environment_____ Temp. _____
Day: M   T   W   T   F Air Movement_____
Weather _____Drafts in room_____
Nearest Holiday_____Glare in room_____
Interruptions_____Adjusted Furniture_____
Membership # _____Seat Arrangement_____
Attendance # _____Student Work shown_____
Date w/in Unit _____Grouping practices_____

Period of the Day _____ Lighting _____
Unsafe Situations_____ Visible Resources_____
Intercom Usage_____ Orderliness of rm_____
Marking Period # _____ Lighting w/ A.V. _____
Clrm. Eq't. Working____ Overall tone _____
Lesson Plans_____

Comments on Variables: _____
_____
_____
_____
_____
_____
_____
_____
_____
_____
_____
_____

- third CLASSROOM OBSERVATION COVER, 19____- ____

Date:__ /__ /___Teacher:_____Subject:_____
Observer:_____ Topic presented:_____
Times: in ___:___ out___:___ Gr. level_____
Years' experience _____ in bldg._____
Observation #s__3_   ____
                current, total while in bldg.
College Major:_____ Minors: _____ /_____

I. PRE-OBSERVATION CONFERENCE TOPICS:
A. Definitions of words to be used in observation
   and summary.
B. Objectives to be covered by the teacher.
C. Expectations to be observed -- from last obser-
   vation.
D. Role of Observer in the class (front and rear
   of the room)
E. Teacher input for the observer to take note of
   in observation
F. Checklist for skills to be taught.
G. Formation of needs groups
H. Teacher Preparation/Preplanning/Organization of

lesson
I. Theories of Learning to be emphasized
J. Principles of Teaching to be used
K. Child Growth and Development exceptions for
      awareness
L. Sociology of the classroom

II. <u>INITIAL OBSERVATION INFORMATION</u>
        third visit
A. STUDENT ENTRANCE TO ROOM:
    1. Teacher's Reactions   2. Students' Reactions
          pleasant _____   eager   _____
          positive _____   positive   _____
          encouraging_____   pleasant   _____
          friendly _____   orderly   _____
          indifferent_____   tardinesses   _____
          negative _____   negative   _____
          punctual _____   sullen   _____

Comments:_____
_____
_____
_____
_____
_____
_____
_____
_____
_____
_____
_____
_____
_____
_____
_____

B. VARIABLES - third visit
1. CONTROLLED: 2. UNCONTROLLED:

Safe Environment_____ Temp. _____
Day: M   T   W   T   F Air Movement_____

455

Weather _____ Drafts in room_____
Nearest Holiday_____ Glare in room_____
Interruptions_____Adjusted Furniture_____
Membership # _____Seat Arrangement_____
Attendance # _____Student Work shown_____
Date w/in Unit _____Grouping practices_____
Period of the Day _____Lighting _____
Unsafe Situations_____Visible Resources_____
Intercom Usage_____Orderliness of rm_____
Marking Period # _____Lighting w/ A.V. _____
Clrm. Eq't. Working_____Overall tone _____
Lesson Plans_____

Comments on Variables: _____

_____
_____
_____
_____
_____
_____
_____
_____
_____
_____
_____

III. <u>CLASSROOM OBSERVATION OF ALL THREE LESSONS</u>:

A. CLASS INITIATION:

1. organized _____   2. goal oriented _____
3. motivational _____   4. creative _____

	Very Good	Good	Re-sour-ces	Needs Help
5. Implements at Correct Level	____	____	____	____
6. Lesson at Current Level	____	____	____	____
7. Material is Available	____	____	____	____
8. Establishes Appropriate				
Frames of Reference	____	____	____	____
Use of analogy	____	____	____	____
discussion	____	____	____	____
examples	____	____	____	____
questioning	____	____	____	____

456

	Very Good	Good	Re-sour-ces	Needs Help
role-playing	____	____	____	____
demonstration	___	____	____	____
illustration	____	____	____	____
lecture	____	____	____	____
reading	____	____	____	____
prob. solving	___	____	____	____

9. Checks for Understanding

Oral Signals	____	____	____	____
Silent Signals	____	____	____	____
Written Signals	____	____	____	____
Pre-Cueing	____	____	____	____

10. Anticipatory Set ____ ____ ____ ____

11. Objectives Presented ____ ____ ____ ____

12. Focuses Attention on Unit ____ ____ ____ ____

13. Relates to Previous Work ____ ____ ____ ____

14. Skills - Auditory use ____ ____ ____ ____
- Tactile use ____ ____ ____ ____
- Visual use ____ ____ ____ ____
- Kinesthetic ____ ____ ____ ____
- Olfactory ____ ____ ____ ____

15. Solicited Participation ____ ____ ____ ____

16. Uses Examples ____ ____ ____ ____

Comments:_____

_____
_____

B. LESSON DEVELOPMENT:
Elements of an effective lesson:

1. Modeling
Boardwork Illustrations ____ ____ ____ ____

457

	Very Good	Good	Re-sour-ces	Needs Help
Demonstrations	____	____	____	____
Visual Uses	____	____	____	____
Uses of Examples	____	____	____	____
2. Checks for Understanding	____	____	____	____
3. Guided Practice				
Worksheet / Workbook	____	____	____	____
Textbook	____	____	____	____
Boardwork	____	____	____	____
A. V. Material	____	____	____	____
4. Planned Repetition (objs.)	____	____	____	____
5. Student Participation				
Completes Communication	____	____	____	____
Controls Participation	____	____	____	____
Uses Non-verbal Cues	____	____	____	____
Reinforcement	____	____	____	____
Recognizes Attending Behavior	____	____	____	____
6. Feedback	____	____	____	____
7. Reinforcement	____	____	____	____
8. Reteaching	____	____	____	____
9. Independent Practice	____	____	____	____
10. Transitions Used Well	____	____	____	____
Orderly	____	____	____	____
Time Efficient	____	____	____	____
Organized/Planned	____	____	____	____

C. TEACHING STRATEGIES / METHODS USED

	Very Good	Good	Re-sour-ces	Needs Help
1. Lecture	____	____	____	____
2. Variety of Activities	____	____	____	____

	Very Good	Good	Re-sour-ces	Needs Help
3. Discussion	___	___	___	___
4. Questioning	___	___	___	___
5. Lecture	___	___	___	___
6. Demonstration	___	___	___	___
7. Role Playing	___	___	___	___
8. Individualization	___	___	___	___
9. Problem Solving	___	___	___	___
10. Independent Research	___	___	___	___
11. Concept Attainment	___	___	___	___
12. Discovery	___	___	___	___
13. EGRUL	___	___	___	___
14. Experience Centered	___	___	___	___
15. Gaming/Simulation	___	___	___	___
16. Guided Discovery	___	___	___	___
17. Intuitive. . .	___	___	___	___
18. Inquiry. . .	___	___	___	___
19. RULEG . . .	___	___	___	___
20. Socratic. . .	___	___	___	___
21. Deductive. . .	___	___	___	___
22. Inductive. . .	___	___	___	___

459

	Very Good	Good	Re-sour-ces	Needs Help
23. Computer Assisted. .	___	___	___	___

D. PROFESSIONAL COMPETENCE:

	Very Good	Good	Re-sour-ces	Needs Help
1. Use of Pacing. . .	___	___	___	___
2. Pronunciation. . .	___	___	___	___
3. Appropriate Vocabulary	___	___	___	___
4. Correct Grammar. .	___	___	___	___
5. Time on Task Used. .	___	___	___	___
6. Motivation of Students	___	___	___	___
7. Non-verbal Interactions	___	___	___	___
8. Gestures Used . .	___	___	___	___
9. Proxemics Used. .	___	___	___	___
10. Student Rapport-Teacher	___	___	___	___
11. Student Rapport-Students	___	___	___	___
12. Writing Skills Emphasis	___	___	___	___
13. Use of Illustrations.	___	___	___	___

E. GENERAL FLOW OF LESSON:

	Very Good	Good	Re-sour-ces	Needs Help
1. Lesson at Correct Level	___	___	___	___
2. Concepts at Grade Level				
By Epstein's Work	___	___	___	___
By Piaget's Work	___	___	___	___
By McCarthy's Work	___	___	___	___
By Thorndike's Work	___	___	___	___

	Very Good	Good	Re-sour-ces	Needs Help
3. Prerequisites Mastered	___	___	___	___
4. Diagnostic/Prescriptive Teaching	___	___	___	___
5. Materials Utilized				
Appropriate	___	___	___	___
Correct Level	___	___	___	___
Available and Accessible	___	___	___	___
6. Effective "Grouping"				
Whole Group	___	___	___	___
Needs Groups	___	___	___	___
Peer Teaching	___	___	___	___
Cooperative Learning	___	___	___	___
7. Achieves Student Participation				
Completes Communication	___	___	___	___
Controls Participation	___	___	___	___
Uses Non-verbal Cues	___	___	___	___
Recognizes Attending Behavior.	___	___	___	___
Redirects When Appropriate.	___	___	___	___
Reinforces Appropriately	___	___	___	___
Uses Planned Repetition	___	___	___	___
8. Attends to Learning Element				
Physical	___	___	___	___
Emotional	___	___	___	___
Environmental	___	___	___	___
Physiological	___	___	___	___
Sociological	___	___	___	___
9. Uses Questioning Well				
Convergent Questions	___	___	___	___
Divergent Questions	___	___	___	___
Fluency of Questions	___	___	___	___
High Order Questions	___	___	___	___

461

	Very Good	Good	Resources	Needs Help
Probing Questions	___	___	___	___
10. Lecture Skills	___	___	___	___
11. Demonstrations	___	___	___	___
12. Role Playing Used	___	___	___	___
13. Individualization	___	___	___	___
14. Problem Solving	___	___	___	___
15. Independent Research	___	___	___	___
16. Motivation				
Feeling Tone	___	___	___	___
Level of Concern	___	___	___	___
Interest in Students	___	___	___	___
Success orientation	___	___	___	___
Knowledge of Results	___	___	___	___
Extrinsic/Intrinsic	___	___	___	___
17. Nonverbal Interactions				
Controlling Participation	___	___	___	___
Obtaining Attending Beh.	___	___	___	___
Emphasizing	___	___	___	___
Illustrating	___	___	___	___
Role Playing/Pantomime	___	___	___	___
Direct Wielding	___	___	___	___
Indirect Wielding	___	___	___	___
Instrumental Wielding	___	___	___	___
Soliciting Movements	___	___	___	___
Structuring Movements	___	___	___	___
Reacting Movements	___	___	___	___
Responding Movements	___	___	___	___
Anticipates Student Lack of Comprehension	___	___	___	___

462

Comments:_____

_____
_____
_____

F. CLOSURE/BRIDGING:

	Very Good	Good	Re-sour-ces	Needs Help
1. Orderliness	___	___	___	___
2. Time Efficiency	___	___	___	___
3. Organized Summary	___	___	___	___
4. Linking	___	___	___	___
5. Assignments - One to One	___	___	___	___
6. Homework Assignments				
Individualized	___	___	___	___
Student Understands Work	___	___	___	___

Comments:_____

_____
_____
_____

G. EVALUATION:

	Very Good	Good	Re-sour-ces	Needs Help
1. Observational Skills	___	___	___	___
2. Participation Skills	___	___	___	___
3. Structure of Quizzes	___	___	___	___
4. Test Items--Statements	___	___	___	___
5. Verbal Skills in Eval.	___	___	___	___
6. Formative/Summative	___	___	___	___
7. Diagnostic	___	___	___	___

463

	Very Good	Good	Resources	Needs Help
8. Individualized/Class	____	____	____	____
9. Pre-test/Post-testing	____	____	____	____
10. Item Analysis Results Used	____	____	____	____
11. Biserial Coefficient Used?	____	____	____	____
12. Standard Deviation Used?	____	____	____	____
13. Correlations	____	____	____	____
14. Standard Errors Used?	____	____	____	____
15. Mastery Learning Marking	____	____	____	____
16. Relates Work to Objectives	____	____	____	____
17. Previous Tests Used for Planning	____	____	____	____

Comments on Evaluation: _____

_____
_____
_____

H. MATERIALS - RESOURCES USED:

	Very Good	Good	Resources	Needs Help
1. Textbooks	____	____	____	____
2. Workbooks	____	____	____	____
3. Handouts	____	____	____	____
4. Chalkboard	____	____	____	____
5. Tackboard	____	____	____	____
6. Audio-Visual Aids	____	____	____	____

464

	Very Good	Good	Re-sour-ces	Needs Help
7. Laboratory Equipment	___	___	___	___
8. Persons _____	___	___	___	___
9. Worksheets prepared	___	___	___	___
10. Overhead Projector	___	___	___	___
11. Films - Proper Use	___	___	___	___
12. Mock-ups Used	___	___	___	___
13. Models Used	___	___	___	___
14. Realia Used for Unit	___	___	___	___
15. Pictures Used in Lesson	___	___	___	___
16. Computers Used in Room	___	___	___	___
17. Bulletin Boards Proper	___	___	___	___
18. Charts and Graphs	___	___	___	___
19. Learning Kits (___)	___	___	___	___
20. Listening Centers	___	___	___	___

Comments:_____
_____
_____

I. DISCIPLINE METHODOLOGY:

1. Warnings Used	___	___	___	___
2. Immediacy	___	___	___	___
3. Consistency	___	___	___	___

465

	Very Good	Good	Re- sour- ces	Needs Help
4. Effectiveness	___	___	___	___
5. Positiveness	___	___	___	___
6. Non-Selective	___	___	___	___
7. Fairness in Implementation	___	___	___	___
8. Rules Displayed in Room?	___	___	___	___
9. Student Awareness	___	___	___	___
10. Use Positive Reinforcement	___	___	___	___
11. Use of Distinctions	___	___	___	___
12. Frequency w/One Child	___	___	___	___

Comments:_____

_____

_____

IV. <u>USE OF BACKGROUND INFORMATION IN CLASSROOM</u>

A. USE OF TAXONOMIES:

1. BLOOM'S
COGNITIVE
_____Knowledge
_____Comprehension
_____Application
_____Analysis
_____Synthesis
_____Evaluation

2. KRATHWOHL'S
AFFECTIVE
_____Receiving
_____Responding
_____Valueing
_____Organization
_____Characterized
    by a Value or
    Value Concept

3. SIMPSON'S
PSYCHOMOTOR
_____Perception
_____Set

4. MOORE'S
PERCEPTUAL
_____Sensation
___Figure Perception

_____Guided Response   ___Symbol Perception
_____Mechanism   __Perception-Meaning
_____Complex Overt   ____Perceptive-
     Response   Performance
_____Adaptation
_____Origination

Comments:_____
_____
_____
_____

B. USE OF MASLOW'S HIERARCHY OF HUMAN NEEDS:

Assuming nothing about the first three levels
having been cared for before school enrollment,
how is this teacher working with the students'
SELF-ESTEEM in this classroom?

Comments:_____
_____
_____
_____

C. APPLICATION OF EPSTEIN'S WORK ON BRAIN GROWTH:
    #4 - 10-12 years of age_____
    #5 - 14-16 years of age_____

Therefore, types of material presented_____
_____
_____
_____

D. USE OF SURVIVAL/LITERACY/COMPETENCY VOCABULARY:

Comments:_____
_____
_____
_____

V. POST – CONFERENCE TOPICS FOR DISCUSSION

A. STRENGTHS OF THE LESSON AS PRESENTED:

1. Followed intent of plans

2. Lesson coor. w/Curr. guides

3. Teacher movement grid is attached

4. Rapport with class based upon sociology of the day

Comments:_____
_____
_____
_____
_____
_____
_____
_____
_____
_____
_____

Flander's Grids are Attached

B. GRID COMMENTARY
FLANDERS' VERBAL

1. Accepts Feelings of Students
2. Encourages or Praises
3. Accepts/Uses Ideas of Students
4. Asks Questions

5. Lectures
6. Gives Directions
7. Criticizes/Justifies Authority
8. Student Talk - Responses
9. Student Talk - Initiatory
10. Silence and Confusion

GALLOWAY'S NON-VERBAL

2.	Congruent	to	Incongruent
3.	Implement	to	Perfunctory
4.	Personal	to	Impersonal
5.	Responsive	to	Unresponsive
6.	Involvement	to	Dismissal
7.	Firm	to	Harsh
8.	Receptive	to	Inattentive
9.	Receptive	to	Inattentive
10.	Comfort	to	Distress

Comments:_____
_____
_____
_____

5. SETTING
    a. Decor of room _____ 2. Uses of Color ____
    b. Efficient use of furniture _____
    c. Easy student access to material for inde-
    pendent, creative activities _____
    d. Safety features attended to _____
    e. Use of space:
        vertical _____
    and   floor space _____
    f. Student work displayed _____

Comments:_____
_____
_____
_____

469

6. VOICE

      a. Tone _____   b. Rate _____   c. Loudness _____

      d. Pitch ___   e. Pausings __f. Attitude_____

Comments:_____

_____

_____

_____

C. FLANDERS SUMMARY FOR 1st OBSERVATION:

Initiatory:
1. Extended indirect influence # _____ (f) _____ %
2. Extended direct influence # _____ (f) _____ %
3. Indirect responses to student comments-
   # _____ (f) _____ %
4. Direct responses to student comments
   # _____ (f) _____ %

5. Noninterrupted student talk # _____ (f) _____ %
6. Statements to stimulate talk# _____ (f) _____ %
7. Silence and / or confusion # _____ (f) _____ %
8. Emphasis on subject content # _____ (f) _____ %

Comments:_____
_____
_____

Developmental:
1. Extended indirect influence# _____ (f) _____ %
   2. Extended direct influence
      # _____ (f) _____ %
   3. Indirect responses to student comments-
      # _____ (f) _____ %
   4. Direct responses to student comments
      # _____ (f) _____ %
   5. Noninterrupted student talk
      # _____ (f) _____ %
   6. Statements to stimulate talk
      # _____ (f) _____ %
   7. Silence and/or confusion
      # _____ (f) _____ %
   8. Emphasis on subject content
      # _____ (f) _____ %
Comments:_____
_____
_____

Summary/Closure:
   1. Extended indirect influence
      # _____ (f) _____ %
   2. Extended direct influence
      # _____ (f) _____ %
   3. Indirect responses to student comments-

471

$$\#\ \rule{2cm}{0.4pt}\ (f)\ \rule{2cm}{0.4pt}\ \%$$

4. Direct responses to student comments- -

$$\#\ \rule{2cm}{0.4pt}\ (f)\ \rule{2cm}{0.4pt}\ \%$$

5. Noninterrupted student talk

$$\#\ \rule{2cm}{0.4pt}\ (f)\ \rule{2cm}{0.4pt}\ \%$$

6. Statements to stimulate talk

$$\#\ \rule{2cm}{0.4pt}\ (f)\ \rule{2cm}{0.4pt}\ \%$$

7. Silence and/or confusion

$$\#\ \rule{2cm}{0.4pt}\ (f)\ \rule{2cm}{0.4pt}\ \%$$

8. Emphasis on subject content

$$\#\ \rule{2cm}{0.4pt}\ (f)\ \rule{2cm}{0.4pt}\ \%$$

Comments: _____

_____

_____

D. ASSISTANCE REQUIRED: **FIRST OBSERVATION:**

_____ _____ ____ date

1. Human Resources _____

_____

_____

_____

2. Material Resources _____

_____

_____

_____

3. Goals for Improvement before next obser-vation:

_____

_____

_____

E. SECOND OBSERVATION SCHEDULED:

1. Date ____ / ____ / _____   Period: _____

_____   _____
Teacher's Signature   Observer's Signature

472

F. TEACHER COMMENTARY:

Comments:_____
_____
_____
_____
_____
_____
_____
_____

G. FLANDERS SUMMARIES FOR 2nd OBSERVATION

Initiatory:
1. Extended indirect influence # _____ (f) _____ %
2. Extended direct influence # _____ (f) _____ %
3. Indirect responses to student comments-
                              # _____ (f) _____ %
4. Direct responses to student comments
                              # _____ (f) _____ %
5. Noninterrupted student talk # _____ (f) _____ %
6. Statements to stimulate talk# _____ (f) _____ %
7. Silence and / or confusion # _____ (f) _____ %
8. Emphasis on subject content # _____ (f) _____ %

Comments:_____
_____
_____

Developmental:
1. Extended indirect influence #_____ (f) _____ %
2. Extended direct influence #_____ (f) _____ %
3. Indirect responses to student comments-
                              #_____ (f) _____ %
4. Direct responses to student comments
                              #_____ (f) _____ %
5. Noninterrupted student talk #_____ (f) _____ %
6. Statements to stimulate talk#_____ (f) _____ %
7. Silence and/or confusion   #_____ (f) _____ %
8. Emphasis on subject content #_____ (f) _____ %
Comments:_____
_____
_____

Summary/Closure:

473

1. Extended indirect influence # _____ (f) _____ %
2. Extended direct influence # _____ (f) _____ %
3. Indirect responses to student comments-
                             # _____ (f) _____ %
4. Direct responses to student comments- -
                             # _____ (f) _____ %
5. Noninterrupted student talk # _____ (f) _____ %
6. Statements to stimulate talk# _____ (f) _____ %
7. Silence and/or confusion   # _____ (f) _____ %
8. Emphasis on subject content # _____ (f) _____ %
Comments:_____
_____
_____
_____

H. ASSISTANCE REQUIRED: SECOND OBSERVATION
_____ _____ ____ date
    1. Human Resources _____
_____
_____
_____

    2. Material Resources _____
_____
_____
_____

    3. Goals for Improvement before next obser-
vation:
_____
_____
_____

I. THIRD OBSERVATION SCHEDULED:
    1. Date ____ / ____ / _____   Period: _____

_____   _____
Teacher's Signature   Observer's Signature

J. TEACHER COMMENTARY:

Comments:_____
_____
_____

474

_____
_____
_____
_____
_____

K. FLANDERS GRID SUMMARIES FOR 3rd OBSERVATION

Initiatory:

1. Extended indirect influence # _____ (f) _____ %
2. Extended direct influence # _____ (f) _____ %
3. Indirect responses to student comments-
                             # _____ (f) _____ %
4. Direct responses to student comments
                             # _____ (f) _____ %
5. Noninterrupted student talk # _____ (f) _____ %
6. Statements to stimulate talk# _____ (f) _____ %
7. Silence and / or confusion # _____ (f) _____ %
8. Emphasis on subject content # _____ (f) _____ %

Comments:_____
_____
_____

Developmental:

1. Extended indirect influence # _____ (f) _____ %
2. Extended direct influence
                             # _____ (f) _____ %
3. Indirect responses to student comments-
                             # _____ (f) _____ %
4. Direct responses to student comments
                             # _____ (f) _____ %
5. Noninterrupted student talk
                             # _____ (f) _____ %
6. Statements to stimulate talk
                             # _____ (f) _____ %
7. Silence and/or confusion
                             # _____ (f) _____ %
8. Emphasis on subject content
                             # _____ (f) _____ %

Comments:_____
_____
_____

475

Summary/Closure:
1. Extended indirect influence
                          # _____ (f) _____ %
2. Extended direct influence   # _____ (f) _____ %
3. Indirect responses to student comments-
                          # _____ (f) _____ %
4. Direct responses to student comments- -
                          # _____ (f) _____ %
5. Noninterrupted student talk # _____ (f) _____ %
6. Statements to stimulate talk
                          # _____ (f) _____ %
7. Silence and/or confusion   # _____ (f) _____ %
8. Emphasis on subject content # _____ (f) _____ %
Comments:_____

_____
_____

L. Assistance Required: 3rd OBSERVATION
_____ _____ ____ date
    1. Human Resources _____

_____
_____
_____

    2. Material Resources _____

_____
_____
_____

    3. Goals for Improvement before next obser-
vation:

_____
_____
_____

        M. FOURTH OBSERVATION SCHEDULED:
    1. Date ____ / ____ / _____   Period: _____

_____   _____
Teacher's Signature   Observer's Signature

            N. TEACHER COMMENTARY:

476

Comments:_____

_____
_____
_____
_____
_____
_____

Reason for the process:	1	2	3	4	5	6	7	8	9	10	TOTAL X's
1	WW										
2	WW	WW									
3	WW	WW	WW								
4	WW	WW	WW	WW							
5	WW	WW	WW	WW	WW						
6	WW	WW	WW	WW	WW	WW					
7	WW	WW	WW	WW	WW	WW	WW				
8	WW	WW	WW	WW	WW	WW	WW	WW			
9	WW	WW	WW	WW	WW	WW	WW	WW	WW		
10	WW	WW	WW	WW	WW	WW	WW	WW	WW	WW	

	1	2	3	4	5	6	7	8	9	10
Vert'l spaces										
Horiz'l X's										
Total										
Rank Order										

To complete the above grid, follow the simple directions on the next page.

478

1. List each project twice, once on a horizontal line AND on the vertical line.
2. Evaluate each horizontally listed item against each vertically listed item.
3. If the horizontal item is <u>more</u> important, put an X in the cell where they meet.
4. If the horizontal item is less important, leave the box blank or place a O in it.
5. Add blank spaces, (O) under each column and enter the total in the row marked "Vert'l Spaces."
6. Add the X's <u>across</u>. The row's total is placed on the row marked "Horiz'l X's" in the same order as they are now shown vertically.
7. Add the rows of "O's" to the row of "X's" and place the sum on the row marked "TOTAL"
8. The highest sum is the #1 priority and the lowest number equals the last priority.
9. In case of a tie, redo the two comparisons.

When you rank, if a tie is found, number them both the same and continue by skipping the count. Example:
1   2   3   3   5   is what you would have if the third and fourth items ranked the same. Do not rank them with half decimals.

DIRECTIONS TO USE FOR THE TEXTBOOK EVALUATION FORM

Title _____Author(s)_____

                                            and

Copyright date __ /__ /___   _____

edition # ____ printing #____   ISBN #_____

Background of the authors: Use the reverse side of this form to record information about each of the authors.

1. Study the entire form to visualize the scope.

2. Use one form for each book to be evaluated.

3. Departments can make numerical rating changes *within an area* set aside by Roman numerals or capital letters only before beginning.

4. Under no circumstances are the *total* values assigned to an area set aside by Roman numerals or capital letters to be changed.

5. The remarks sections are to be used for comments relative to the immediately covered materials.

6. The area of general comments is to be used for comments concerning the entire book.

7. Bear in mind that the work will be culminated when recommendations are forwarded to the superintendent. The Board must approve or disapprove his/her recommendation in time to reserve the right amount of money as a line-item in the budget for ordering new books, around March 1. Therefore, it is a good idea to work on the adoption on a calendar year basis rather than on the normal school fiscal year. The report -- and pilot can be done by the March date easily. Plus, the work in the summer is much more productive than the usual afterschool hours assigned for such tasks.

8. Once any textbook adoption has been made by the Board, the book shall remain in use for five years.

PROCEDURE TO FOLLOW TO ADOPT A NEW TEXTBOOK

1. Basically, the school authorities must publish, after BOE approval, the philosophy of the system. Textbook evaluators should choose only those texts which promote the philosophy of the system.

2. The teaching staff shall be carefully screened by the administration for inclusion on a study team. The membership will be based on:

    a. experience in field of study
    b. proved teaching competence
    c. judgment
    d. resourcefulness
    e. willingness to work
    f. ability to take criticism
    g. principles of teaching use
    h. theories of learning use
    i. use in child growth and
    j. subject matter competence development

3. All members shall be given a copy of the district's philosophy.

4. The Central Office shall contact book publishers' representatives regarding the dates, places and times of committee meetings. The name of the chairperson, the philosophy of the system, the type of book being sought through evaluation and a copy of the rating sheet being employed, will also be mailed to the representatives. Lastly, the letter will make a request for copies of the text (series) and the supplementary material that is desired to complement the text.

5. A date shall be arranged for a meeting with the representative once the books and material are ready for delivery.

6. Members may change the rating sheet as they gain more insight in the study of textbooks with the limitations already given.

7. Committees shall recommend in only one subject area unless blocktime or core classes are to be included.

8. Ample time, yet with reasonable time limits, shall be given to the committee:

      a. for a subject - 24 weeks is recommended.
      b. for a series -- 48 weeks is recommended.

9. A meeting shall be held with each book company's representative. A close screening of needed reference materials shall be done prior to a meeting with the representative. A full set of recommended software materials needed to use the texts fully shall be supplied by the publisher before the study is finalized.

10. Recommendations shall be forwarded to the superintendent's office no later than February 1 of the year in which the the result of the study is to be initiated. Staff shall realize they are making a recommendation and in no way dictating to the superintendent or the Board.

TEXTBOOK EVALUATION FORM

To: Superintendent   Date: ___/___/____

From: Principal, _____

I. *BACKGROUND*:

  A. Name of textbook:_____

  B. Author(s):_____

  C. Date of Publication:_____, Revision:_____

  D. Name/Address of Publisher: _____

     _____

     _____

     _____

  E. Edition: _____, Printing # _____

  F. Dates book was under consideration:

     ___/___/____ to ___/___/____.

  G. Is book being used in the district?_____

     In the area?_____, where _____

  H. List of school districts using the book
     at this time:

DISTRICT   CONTACT PERSON

DISTRICT	CONTACT PERSON
_____	_____
_____	_____
_____	_____
_____	_____
_____	_____
_____	_____

II. *AUTHOR:*

	POINTS	
	This bk.	MAX.
A. Are viewpoints supported by recent research? . .	_____	30
B. Are the approaches to pre-sentation commensurate with the district philoso-phy?		20
C. Experiences as a classroom teacher . . .		10
D. Remarks_____		
_____		
_____		
_____ Total=	_____	60

483

III. *PHYSICAL ASPECTS*:

A. Durable Covers? . .	_____	10
B. Is size suitable for student handling?	_____	10
C. Construction – does the book lie open easily?. . .	_____	5
D. Type dark and distinct?. .	_____	5
suitable to the subject. matter?. . . .	_____	5
cause a glare on the paper?	_____	5
E. Illustrations-Appealing? .	_____	10
Functional? . . .	_____	10
F. Remarks_____		

_____ Total =_____ | 60

IV. *CONTENT*

A. Material:

1. Does it help to meet the objectives? . . .	_____	75
2. Is information accurate and timely? . . .	_____	40
3. Is content appealing and interesting? . .	_____	55
4. Does it aid in applying to experiences outside the classroom? . . .	_____	30
5. Is it appropriate for. geographical area?. .	_____	20
B. Remarks_____		

_____ Total = _____ | 220

C. Organization:

1. Major teaching points highlighted?. . .	_____	10
2. Satisfactory order of topics. . . .	_____	10
3. Chapters/Lessons easy to follow. . . .	_____	30
4. Provision for re-teach-		

484

ing/cumuulative practice
on specific skills.   .   60
5. Is there provision for
continity and sequence
in skill or concept   .
development?.   .   .   40
6. Table of Contents/Index
make location of material
easy for pupils/teachers?   20
7. Is there current re-
search referenced?   .   20
8. Are references given to
more material?.   .   .   20
D. Remarks_____

_____
_____
_____ Total = _____ _210_

E. Methods
1. Teaching proceeds from
the simple to more complex
concepts?.   .   .   .   30
2. Are skills taught in
relation to needs?.   .   50
3. Are provisions made for
self-evaluation by pupils?._____   20
4. Are skill development
references made for pupils
to follow?   .   .   .   20
5. Are provisions made for
individuals?.   .   .   40
6. Is there good balance
of oral/written/kinesthetic
activities? .   .   .   20
7. Is there purposeful
drill work in text?.   .   10
8. Is sufficient emphasis
placed on critical thought?_____   20
F. Remarks_____

_____
_____
_____Total = _____   _210_

G. Vocabulary and readability
    1. Is vocabulary.   .
    appropriate for subject? _____ | 50
    2. Can directions for les-
    sons be easily read and .
    understood? .   .   . _____ | 50
    3. Are the concepts within
    the range of the pupil's
    comprehension?   .   . _____ | 50
    4. Are new words explained/
    used frequently?. .   . _____ | 50

H. Remarks_____

_____

_____

_____Total = _____ | 200

I. Supplementary Aids
    1. Do the teacher aids
    contain carefully prepared
    suggestions and procedures
    that will be helpful to
    teachers   regardless of
    teaching experience?   . _____ | 30
    2. Are there outside ref-
    erences for teachers and
    given in the unit?.   . _____ | 5
    3. Is it necessary to have
    a workbook or manual to .
    supplement the text?   . _____ | 5

J. Remarks_____

_____

_____

_____Total = _____ | 40

V. *PROFESSIONAL COMPETENCIES COVERED*

A. Cognitive Domain referenced material?
    1. Knowledge.   .   . | 5
    2. Comprehension   .   . _____ | 5
    3. Application.   .   . | 10
    4. Analysis.   .   . _____ | 10
    5. Synthesis.   .   . | 15
    6. Evaluation.   .   . | 15

Remarks:_____
_____Total =_____ |__60__

B. Affective Domain referenced material?
    1. Receiving 2. Responding_____ | 5+ 5
    3. Valuing 4. Organization_____ | 10+10
       5. Characterization
       by Value/Value Concept_____ | 10
Remarks:_____
              Total = _____ |__40__

C. Perceptual Domain referenced material?
    1. Sensation.   .   . _____ | 5
    2. Fig. Perception.   . _____ | 5
    3. Symbol Perception. . _____ | 10
    4. Perception by meaning _____ | 10
    5. Perceptive Performance _____ | 15
Remarks: _____
              Total =_____ |_45__

D. Psychomotor Domain referenced material
    1. Perception.   .   . | 5
    2. Set.   .   .   . | 5
    3. Guided Response.   . _____ | 5
    4. Mechanism.   .   . _____ | 10
    5. Complex Overt Response | 10
    6. Adaptation.   .   . | 10
    7. Origination.   .   . | 15
Remarks: _____
              Total =_____ |__70__

E. Research Oriented?
    1. Piaget levels
        a. Sensorimotor. . | 5
        b. Preoperational | 5
        c. Intuitive.   . | 10
        d. Concrete Operation _____ | 10
        e. Formal Operational _____ | 15
    Remarks: _____
              Total = _____ |_45__

```
   2. Epstein's Levels of Brain Growth
       a. represented by grade
          level in series?                        25
       b. represented by
          grade level in book? _____         10
       # 4 (10-12) year olds
       # 5 (14-16) year olds
Remarks:_____
                         Total = _____        35
   3. Mc Carthy's 4Mat System
   a. Innovative .    .      .                     10
   b. Analytic.        .      . _____         10
   c. "Common Sense" Learners _____           10
   d. Dynamic Learners                             10
Remarks: _____
                         Total = _____        40
   4. Leslie Hart's Proster Theory
   a. Unity      .      .      .                     5
   b. Availability   .      . _____             5
   c. Foundation     .      . _____             5
   d. Connection     .      . _____             5
   e. Rutting  .      .      .                       5
   f. Change         .      . _____             5
   g. Threat   .      .      .                       5
   h. Search         .      . _____             5
   i. Mode     .      .      .                       5
   j. Totality .      .      . _____            5
Remarks:_____
                         Total =  _____       50

   5. Gregorc's Learning Styles
   a. Concrete Random.        .                     10
   b. Concrete Seq'l .        . _____          10
   c. Abstract Random.        .                     10
   d. Abstract Seq'l .        .                     10
Remarks: _____
                         Total = _____         40
```

Grand Total for all scores =   1,425

GENERAL COMMENT: Realizing each textbook area
meets specific needs, please list any comment not
mentioned above and discuss it on the reverse
side.

S U M M A R Y   S H E E T

To: Board of Education
Thru:_____, Principal
_____, Supt.
From:_____ faculty at_____
Date: ___ / ___ / _____

Book needing replacement   Book recommended

TITLE _____ TITLE _____
       Prime   Prime
Ed.__ Author_____   Ed.__ Author_____

Copyright Date ____   Copyright Date _____
Net Price $ ___.___   Net Price $ ____.___

new on hand _____   # to replace_____
Used_____   Cost $ _____.____
Need reconditioning_____

RATING OF BOOK CONSIDERED

                 points
II. Author _____ (60) II. Author   _____

III. Physical_____ (60) III. Phys. Aspect._____

IV. Material _____ (220) IV. Material   _____

C. Organ.   _____ (210) C. Organ.   _____

E. Methods   _____ (210) E. Methods   _____

G. Vocabulary   G. Vocabulary
  Readability_____ (200)   Readability _____

I. Supplemental___ (40) I. Supplemental _____

V. Information_____ (425) V. Prof'l Info. _____

TOTALS.   _____ (1425)   _____

489

REASONS TO DISCONTINUE   REASONS TO ADOPT

_____/_____

_____/_____

_____/_____

_____/_____

_____/_____

_____/_____

_____/_____

_____/_____

_____/_____

_____/_____

_____/_____

_____/_____

_____/_____

_____/_____

_____/_____

_____/_____

_____/_____

_____/_____

_____/_____

_____/_____

AREA	VOLUNTEERS	AIDES
Tutorial Work	Used outside of the instructional arena and in the area of personal development and image enhancement (Maslow)	Used primarily with instructional specifics for short-term measurable objectives. (Bloom)
Enrichment Work	Assist the regular teacher in the process of conducting a field trip within the community during the day.	Help to determine, in advance, the best location for a curricular field trip and help during the day.
Small Groups	Can work with individuals in all areas in the building for any task.	Can work with small groups in and out of the classroom.
Library Assist-	Do any type of clerical work in the library and assist in the location of material when the students enter to get reading books.	Work with teachers in the development of a professional list of publications needed for improvement of the instructional program.
Non-instructional Work in the Classroom	Great assistance in the classroom for taking attendance, cleaning boards, sorting material, recording marks of papers which have been graded by another and readied for recording by the volunteer.	Collect and make available all material for the objectives of the day or/ and unit and in general do work to assist the teacher for direct instruction.
School	Assist in recording	Usually do work that

Office Work	attendance or other "whatever" tasks that can be done if there is some help to catch-up.	needs to be complete on a routine and day by day basis for consistency in performance.
Special Projects	Tests individual students new to school, or building	Test students for make-up or advanced credit standing.
Research for classes	Work based on skill orientation of the volunteer.	Work based on skill orientation of the aide.
Computer Assistance	Can run copies of programs for individual or group work.	Design programs to satisfy objectives in instructional work.
Activity program both in co- and extra-curricular	Direct, skill orientation work with individual students while the teacher works with others.	Can perform work to relieve regular sponsor of needed time for the class.
Classroom special Assistance	Can work in lab setting where no special training is needed and the work is directed by the teacher in the classroom.	Can work in labs where chemicals and other substances or tools used can be used can be done with training and consistency on a daily basis
Industrial Educ.	Can work in tool cribs, in material labs for check-out and control. Can work in safety and goggle control.	Can assist in actual instructional procedures. Can do work in processes and procedures of learning.

Typing Classes	Can do all paper correction and recording. Can monitor make-up work by individuals. Work with specific skill development.	Completes statistics for the teacher and helps design work to eliminate errors. Works to assure that all equipment is in good repair.
Art Classes	Same as above plus supply orientation room orderliness. Works with outside contacts for display or housing of finished projects of students	Does work in specific skill development with individual or small groups. Displays work in the building for students.
Music Classes	Sit with students in practice sessions on instruments. Prepares concert facilities for performances. Constructs special platforms for practices or performances	Assists students in preparation for auditions for advancing. Does work with ensemble groups File and serve as librarian for the papers.
Extended School Day	Work to develop special recreational skills. Supervise play. Make home contacts for behavioral concerns	Can assist in tutorial work by the students. Supervise schoolwork. Contact parents for special assistance.

493

WHAT IS A PUBLIC HIGH SCHOOL?

A school is where everyone must learn to learn
        -- from teachers who care and really discern.
A school is spelling C. A. T. and cyphering 2 plus 4
        -- is logrithms, equations, and a whole lot more.
A school is learning how to read and reading to learn
        -- is training to do work for money to earn.
A school is a slate, a scope, a shop, a lab
        -- a place to mope, cope, and learn not to blab.
A school is learning to type 60 words a minute or more
        -- and finding your requirements are a bore.
A school is tears and cheers
        -- is filled with love and fears.
A school is complex and simple
        -- is a 250 pound tackle and a cheerleader's dimple.
A school is headed by adults -- run by kids
        -- is kindergarten games and seniors on the skids.
A school is a place which observes all the right codes
        -- and students come in all types and modes.
A school is a house of intellect for all to use
        -- yet some come there just to abuse.
A school is where custodialship of the masses is done
        -- and the custodian's work is never fun.
A school is a place to flirt, to like, to love, and to fail.
        -- to find out what it's like to be a female or male.
A school is a social place with lots of grace
        -- a series of individuals, groups, cliques, and others
          to face.
A school is a place for the kids, all who can get there
        -- not a place for the adults -- they have but a share.
A school is an inspiration for the masses in a common as-
        sault
        -- a beginning, a start, a push, and a place with fault.
A school is activities, sports, classes, and committees for
        plying
        -- is leadership, followership, voting, and trying.
A school is for learning to succeed and prevent jail
        -- to help, tutor, attack and assail.
A school is where everyone must be safe from harm
        -- whether the person is troubled or living a charm.
A school is a place which harbors many secrets

494

-- and if worked at, will not harbor any regrets.
A school is shop, physics, forensics, rhetoric, and plays
  -- where 8% of a student's life means many, many
    days.
A school is where a student learns about seeing, hearing,
    feeling
  -- growing up and becoming appealing.
A school is where a student can be one in a crowd or a
    crowd of one
  -- dependent upon how s/he wants to have her/his
    fun.
A school is selection, placement, instruction, and all that
  -- socialization, health, and fitness and where you
    sit to chat.
A school is headed by a principal with many principles and
    notions
  -- by a staff dedicated to student welfare and emo-
    tions.
A school is a fun place to be in your youth
  -- learning about behavior and all that couth.
A school is a building, a culture, and people who care
  -- is a place of trust and others who share.
A school is a place offering challenge, excitement, and
    learning
  -- it is taking tests by kids while stomachs are a
    churning.
A school is a place for public relations when at its best
  -- so blow off steam and get it off your chest.
A school is a place where one can calm the nerves
  -- and that is one of a thousand roles it serves.
A school is the future of yours and mine
  -- a place that opens doors through which we can
    climb.
A school is whatever you want it to be or make it become
  -- even if you are leading or playing the bum.
A school is an American dream for the student massess
  -- as they attend countless and endless classes.

BUT, MOSTLY. . . .
A school is ANYTHING YOU WANT IT TO BE....
COME VISIT, OBSERVE AND YOU WILL SEE!!

- LISTS FOR THAT "QUICK FIX" -

The lists that follow are referenced as a "quick fix" and this may be a little misleading to you. The intent is to have a place in this book where you can turn to find the 5 M's, the Five Roles of the Public Schools, or just about any other thing used in this material. There are times when you wish to send out that quick memo and want to call the faculty's attention to something like the list of Allen's Microteaching terms, for example. Rather than to have to look for the term Microteaching or the author Allen in other sources, the lists for such topics are here in compact form for the harried principal.

EIGHT STEPS TO ACCOMPLISH ACCOUNTABILITY IN IN-
STRUCTION: (1)

1. State Philosophical Goals
2. Develop Operational Goals
3. Complete a Needs Determination
4. Structure Concept Grids
5. Write Performance Objectives
6. Select Delivery Systems
7. Finalize an Evaluation
8. Recommend and Disseminate

5 M's of Management:
                    (2)

Men
Minutes
Material
Money
Minutes

4 Parts to an Objec-
            tive: (3)

Givens
Expectations
Time Line
Proficiency

5 Roles of Pub Schs:
                    (4)

Selection
Socialization
Instruction
Custodialship
Placement

5 Roles of Prin-
            cipalship: (5)

Students
Instruction
Bus./Bldg. Mgt.
Staff
Comm./Sch. Relations

496

Microteaching Skills: (6)

Reward - Punishment
Stimulation Variation
Complete Communication
Attending Behavior
Higher-Order Questions
Divergent Questions
Probing Questions
Planned Repetition
Providing Feedback
Establish Frames of Reference
Nonverbal Cues
Closure
Silence   Illustrating
Reinforcement
Pausing
Pre-cueing Lecturing
Using Examples
Set Induction

5 Partners in Accountability (10)

S tudents
T eachers
A dministrators
M anagement
P ublic

Course Development Flow: (12)

Objectives Rationale Based
Learning Activities Developed
Methodology Designed
Pilot of course completed
C. R. T. Developed
Evaluation completed
Approval Given

6 Subj. Matter Curr. Areas: (7)

1. Basic Skills
2. Career Ed.
3. Hard Sciences
4. Soft Sciences
5. Phys./Mental Health
6. Arts/Humanities

Barbe's 3 Keys to Learning (8)

Sensation/
Perception/ Memory

4 Curves for Human Development: (9)

Social - Emotional
Physical - Intellec-
          tual

Bloom's Taxonomy Cognitive:
(simple to complex) (11)

1. Knowledge
2. Comprehension
3. Application
4. Analysis
5. Synthesis
6. Evaluation

Krathwohl's Taxonomy Affective: (13)

Receiving
Responding
Valuing
Organization
Characterization by
 Value or Value
 Concept

Simpson's Taxonomy (Psychomotor):
(14)
1. Perception
2. Set
3. Guided Response
4. Mechanism
5. Complex Overt Response
6. Adaptation
7. Origination

Moore's Taxonomy (Perception):
(16)
1. Sensation
2. Figures
3. Symbols
4. Perception of Meaning
5. Perceptive Performance

4 Essentials for Teachers:
(18)
Child Growth and Development
Subject Matter Content
Theories of Learning
Principles of Teaching

5 Curr. Orientations
(20)
Dev't. of Cognitive Processes
Personal Relevance
Academic Rationalism
Curriculum as Technology
Soc. Adaptation/Reconstruction

4 Parts of McCarthy's Profile
(22)
AC = Abstract Concepts
AE = Active Experimentation
CE = Concrete Experiences
RO = Reflective Observation

Epstein's Brain Growth Spurts
(15)
3 - 10 months
2 - 4 years
6 - 8 years
10 - 12 years
14 - 16 years

8 Rungs of Citizen Involvement
(17)
1. Manipulation
2. Placation
3. Therapy
4. Partnership
5. Informing
6. Delegated Power
7. Consultation
8. Control

Eisner's 3 Curricula
(19)
Null
Implicit
Explicit

8 Agenda Headings
(21)
Proper Heading
Membership + Guests
Announcements
Discussion Topics +
    Leaders named
Action Motions
Update Items
Handouts Enclosed
Date of Next Meeting

4 Gregorc Styles
(24)
Concrete Random
Concrete Sequential

4 Bases of Observation
(23)

M aterials / M ethods
O rganization
S taff Ability
T raining

5 Levels of Maslow's Human Needs Hierarchy:
(25)

Physiological Need
Safety and Security
Belonging
Self Esteem
Self Actualization

4 Basic Parts of Grant's Nonverbal Cues:
(27)

Conducting:
Controlling Participation
Obtaining Attending Behavior
Acting:
    Emphasing
    Illustrating
    Role-Playing
Wielding:
    Direct
    Indirect
    Instrumental
Moves:
    Structuring
    Soliciting
    Responding
    Reacting

Abstract Random
Abstract Sequential

Madeline Hunter Program (26)

S elect Objectives
T each Objectives
U se principles of teaching
M onitor learning
I nformation (give)
R espond
A ctivities (plan specific)
Q uestions (ask)

External Barriers to Listening
(28)

Noise Distraction
Speaker's Voice Quality
Room Temperature

Herbart's 5 Steps in Teaching
(29)

Preparation
Presentation
Assumption
Generalization
Application

VARIABLES IN THE CLASSROOM:
(30)

Controlled	Noncontrolled
Temperature	Day of the Week
Air Movement in room	Weather outside

499

Drafts in the room   Nearest Holiday
Glare in the room   Interruptions
Adjustments to Furniture   Class Membership
Seating Arrangements   Attendance
Student Work Displayed   Date within the Unit
Grouping Practices Practiced Period of the Day
Lighting in the room
Orderliness of the room
Visible Resources
Overall Tone of the Lesson

Characteristics of Formal and Informal Groups

(31)	(32)
Each person interacts w/ each other	
	Participants don't interact
Group develops own structure	
	Group has structure developed
Group selects own leaders	
	Leader is appointed
Voluntary formulation -- purpose	
	Volunteered membership
No official hierarchal structure	
	Becomes part of the structure

Forces Acting on Admins.:

(33)	Comm. Appoint-ment Outline (34)
Fed./St. Regs and Rules	Membership groups
Evolving Legal Intracies	Responsibility
Collective Negotiations	Determined
Political Changes (laws)	Function Listed
	Duties Enumerated
	Dates Set

Dates in Educ. History:

1635 - First Secondary School
1647 - Old Deluder Satan Act
1751 - Franklin's Academy
1791 - 10th Amendment Passed
1821 - 1st Public H.S.-Boston
1874 - Kalamazoo - Free H. S.

500

1884 - Manual Tr'g. School-Baltimore, Maryland
1893 - Comm. of Ten Recommendations Prepared
1910 - 1st J.H. Berkeley, CA
1917 - Smith-Hughes Act = H.S given program money
1918 - Cardinal Principles of Secondary Education
1937 - George-Deen Act = money for vocation-
           al education
1947 - School Lunch Act
1949 - Nat'l Citizen's Commission for the Pub-
           lic Schools formed
1951 - Ford Fndt. started
1954 - Segregation Illegal
1956 - 1st Nat'l Merit Scholarships awarded

Accreditation Regions/States: H.S.

New England Association
        Maine, New Hampshire,
        Vermont, Connecticut,
        Rhode Island, Massachusetts
Middle States Association
        New York, Pennsylvania,
        New Jersey, Deleware,
        Maryland
Southern Association
        Kentucky, Virginia, Tennessee,
        N.+S.Carolina, Florida, Georgia,
        Alabama, Mississippi, Louisi-
        ana, Texas
North Central Association
        Michigan, Indiana, Illinois,
        Wisconsin, West Virginia,
        Ohio, Minnesota, Iowa, Missouri,
        Nebraska, N.+S. Dakota, Arkansas,
        Oklahoma, New Mexico, Arizona,
        Kansas, Montana, Colorado
Northwest Association
        Wyoming, Washington, Idaho,
        Oregon, Utah, Alaska, Nevada,
        California, Hawaii
Western Association

<u>Determinations for schools to make?</u>
                (35)
Who should be educated?
What knowledge, skills, and values should be
        taught in the schools?
What social, political, and economic views should
        be expressed in the schools?
Which ones should be censored or ignored?
Are public schools better than private ones?
Who should pay for schooling?
How do we assess the quality of schools?
How should schools address such social problems as
        racism, sexism, drug abuse, alienation,
        crime, prejudice, and illiteracy?
What role should teachers have in schools and in
        society?
How should teachers be prepared?
Who should control the schools?
What expectations should a society have for its
        schools?
Do schools, and teachers, have a responsibility to
        maintain stability in society, or to try to
        make changes in that society?

<u>Ralph Tyler's Four Questions for Curriculum</u>
                (36)   (<u>Considerations</u>

1. What educational purposes should the school
seek to attain?

2. What educational experiences can be provided
that are likely to attain these purposes?

3. How can these educational experiences be effectively organized?

4. How can we determine whether these purposes are
being attained?

502

SOURCES FOR THE ABOVE MATERIAL

1. Designed by Monroe, MI Central Administrators.

2. First heard reference by Dr. R. Alec Mackenzie at The Seminar on Relevence in Univ. S. Alabama.

3. Designed by Monroe, MI Central Administrators.

4. Listed by Dr. John R. Porter when St. Supt. MI

5. Structured by Dr. Gene E. Megiveron

6. As separated-out from material by Dr. Dwight Allen's Invitational Workshop at U. Mass.

7. Prioritized by two communities in surveys 1974-81

8. From Barbe, Walter B. and Swassing, Raymond H. *Teaching Through Modality Strengths.* Columbus, OH: Zaner-Bloser, Inc., 1979, p. 1.

9. Referenced from notes in lecture at MSNC.

10. Designed by Monroe, MI Central Administrators.

11. Bloom, Benjamin S. *Taxonomy of Cognitive Domain. Hdbk I.* NY: David McKay, 1956.

12. From work by Dr. Jerry Blanchard, in Waterford School District, Pontiac, MI

13. Krathwohl, David R., Benjamin S. Bloom, Bertram Masia. *Taxonomy of Educational Objectives. Hdbk II.* NY: David McKay, Inc., 1964.

14. Simpson, Elizabeth J. *The Classification of Educational Objectives, Psychomotor Domain.* Wash., D.C.: Vo. Tech. Ed. Grant Contract No. OE 5-85-104, 1966.

15. Epstein, Herman T., "Stages in Human Brain Development," *Developmental Brain Research.* 30 (1986)

503

114-119.

16. Moore, Maxine R. *A Proposed Taxonomy of the Perceptual Domain and Some Suggested Applications.* Princeton, NJ: Educational Testing Service, 1967.

17. Arnstein's Ladder from Porter, John W. chrm. *The Adolescent, Other Citizens, and Their Schools.* NY: McGraw-Hill Book Co., 1975.

18. From Lecture Notes by Dr. Robert Fontonet, Prof. of Education, Univ. Southwestern LA

19. Eisner, Elliot. *The Educational Imagination: On the Design and Evaluation of School Programs.* NY: Macmillan Publishing Co., Inc., 1979, pp. 74-92.

20. _____. pp. 50-73

21. Designed by author in work as consultant in management.

22. Mc Carthy, Bernice. *The 4Mat System.* Arlington Hgts., IL: Excel, Inc., 1980.

23. Designed by Monroe, MI Central Administrators.

24. Gregorc, Anthony. "Style as a Symptom: A Phenomenological Perspective." *Theory Into Practice.* XXIII, (Winter, 1984) 51-55.

25. Sergiovanni, Thomas J. and Fred D. Carver. *The New School Executive: A Theory of Administration,* 2nd ed., NY: Harper & Row, Publishers, 1980.

26. From Notes taken at a presentation re: ITIP

27. Grant, Barbara and Dorothy Hennings. *The Teacher Moves.* NY: Teacher's College Press, 1977.

28. Provided by Terry G. Semones, Monroe, MI.

29. Marks, James R., Emery Stoops, and Joyce King-Stoops. *Handbook of Educational Supervision*. Boston: Allyn and Bacon, 1971,502.

30. Designed by author for observation formwork.

31. Morphet, Edgar L., Roe L. Johns, and Theodore L. Reller. *Educational Organization and Administration: Concepts, Practices, and Issues*: Englewood Cliffs, New Jersey, 4th ed., 1982, pp. 102-103.

32. _____.,

33. _____.,

34. Designed by author in work as a consultant to management.

35. Besag, Frank and Jack L. Nelson. *The Foundations of Education: Stasis and Change.* NY: Random House, 1984.

36. Eisner, Elliot. *The Educational Imagination: On the Design and Evaluation of School Programs.* NY: Macmillan Publishing Co., Inc., 1979, p. 9.

Draw these two lines and link them with any of a dozen on
this list to get a perspective of any one hour period in the
principal's day. There may be more or less some hours,
but during the day, the principal will see many reps. of the
groups on this list. This list is generic for ALL high schools
so any added at the bottom can be considered a bonus for
the locale in which the high school is located for the
reader.

Here is a start:

COOKS

ACTIVITY CLUBS
ADMINISTRATIVE COUNCIL
ADMINISTRATIVE TEAM IN
AUDITOR
ATTORNEY (IES?)
BOARD OF ED. MEMBERS
BOOKKEEPER
BUILDING
ADVISORY COMMITTEES
ARBITRATION HEARINGS
ATHLETES
ATHLETIC BOOSTERS
ATTORNEY
BAKERS
BAND PARENTS
BLDG. ADVISORY
BLDG. CURR. COMM.
BUS DRIVERS
BUSINESS CLUBS
CAFETERIA MGR.
CASE CONFERENCES
C.C.C.= CENTRAL CURR
        COUNCIL
CENTRAL STAFF
CHEERLEADERS
CLASS PRESIDENTS

COUNSELORS
CUSTODIAL FRMN.
DEPT. CHAIRMEN
DIR. SEC. EDUC.
DISTRICT-WIDE ADMINS.
FACT FINDERS
FAC'Y ADV'Y COMM.
FATERNAL GROUPS
GRIEVANCES
HUMAN RESOURCE MANAGER
JUVENILE COURT
LEGISLATIVE BODIES
LEGISLATORS
LIBRARIANS
LITTLE LEAGUERS
M.A.D.D.
MAINTENANCE CREWS
MEDIA REPS
MEDIATORS
MINISTERIAL SOCIETY
NAACP
N /St. A.S.S.P.
OMBUDSMAN
OTHER SCHOOLS' TEAMS
OTHERS' COACHES
OUT-OF-DIST. STUDENTS